Easy Wedding Shopping Guide

Everything you need to select and purchase
all your service providers, accessories, jewelry, invitations,
and much more!

Concise and Easy to Use

BY
ELIZABETH & ALEX LLUCH
Professional Wedding Consultants

Written by
Elizabeth & Alex Lluch; Professional Wedding Consultants

Published by Wedding Solutions Publishing, Inc.
© Copyright 2000

Contributing Photographers:

Jon Barber
Barber Photography
34085 Pacific Coast Highway #117
Dana Point, CA 92629
Tel: (949) 493-5840
www.barberphotography.com

Karen French
Karen French Photography
8351 Elmcrest
Huntington Beach, CA 92646
Tel: (800) 734-6219
www. karenfrenchphotography.com

Carolyn Marie
Carolyn Marie Photography
9849 Dauntless Street
San Diego, CA 92126
Tel: (858) 695-6852

Photos Credits:
Front Cover: Jon Barber
Back Cover: Karen French (top), Carolyn Marie (2nd photo),
Jon Barber (3rd photo), Karen French (bottom)

Cover design by: Amy Allen Graphics, San Diego, CA

Printed in Korea
ISBN 1-887169-19-9
1st. Edition

CONTENTS

*I*NTRODUCTION

ear Bride and Groom,

Congratulations on your engagement! You must be looking forward to what will be the happiest day of your life -- your wedding! Planning your wedding can be fun and exciting. But it can also be very stressful. That is why Wedding Solutions, a professional wedding planning company, created the *Easy Wedding Shopping Guide*.

The *Easy Wedding Shopping Guide* contains all the information you will need to plan and budget your wedding. Also included is a comprehensive guide for selecting service providers, purchasing accessories, jewelry, invitations, and much more!

The *Easy Wedding Shopping Guide* begins with a very detailed wedding planning checklist containing everything you need to do or consider when planning your wedding and the best time frame in which to accomplish each activity. The wedding planning checklist is followed by a comprehensive and detailed budget checklist, listing all the expenses that are typically incurred in a wedding.

The budget checklist is followed by a detailed description of each category in the budget including: Options, Things To Consider, Questions To Ask, Things To Beware Of, Tips To Save Money, and Price Ranges. Our clients find this format to be both informative and easy to use, and we know you will too!

As a unique feature of this book, we have also included hundreds of some of the most beautiful and unique wedding accessories, jewelry, decorations, and invitations. These products are from some of the most popular wedding manufacturers in the United States. This selection will greatly help you in choosing the perfect products for your wedding. You can purchase these items at your local bridal boutique or, for your convenience, you may simply purchase them on line from the comfort of your own home at www.yourbridalsuperstore.com.

We are confident that you will enjoy planning your wedding with the help of *Easy Wedding Shopping Guide*. So come join the many couples who have used this book to plan a stress-free wedding. Also, if you know other options, things to consider, tips to save money, new products, or anything else that you would like to see included in this book, please write to us at: Wedding Solutions Publishing, Inc.; 6347 Caminito Tenedor; San Diego, CA 92120.

Sincerely,

Elizabeth H. Lluch

WEDDING PLANNING CHECKLIST

The following Wedding Planning Checklist itemizes everything you need to do or consider when planning your wedding, and the best time frame in which to accomplish each activity.

Many of the items are explained in more detail within the book. This will help you find the information you need, when you need it.

This checklist assumes that you have nine months or more to plan your wedding. If your wedding is in less than nine months, just start at the beginning of the list and try to catch up as quickly as you can!

Nine Months and Earlier

- Announce your engagement.

- Select a date for your wedding.

- Hire a professional wedding consultant.

- Determine the type of wedding you want: location, formality, time of day, number of guests, etc.

- Determine budget and how expenses will be shared.

- Develop a record-keeping system for payments made.

- Consolidate all guest lists: bride's, groom's, bride's family, groom's family, and organize as follows:
  1) those who must be invited
  2) those who should be invited
  3) those who would be nice to invite

- Decide if you want to include children among guests.

- Select and reserve ceremony site.

- Select and reserve your officiant.

- Select and reserve reception site.

- Select and order your bridal gown and headpiece.

- Determine your color scheme.

- Send engagement notice with a photograph to your local newspaper.

- Buy a calendar and note all important activities: showers, luncheons, parties, get-togethers, etc.

- If ceremony or reception is at home, arrange for home or garden improvements as needed.

- Order passport, visa or birth certificate, if needed for your honeymoon or marriage license.

NINE MONTHS AND EARLIER (Cont.)

- Select and book photographer.

- Select maid of honor, best man, bridesmaids and ushers (approx. one usher per 50 guests).

SIX TO NINE MONTHS BEFORE THE WEDDING

- Select flower girl and ring bearer.

- Select and book reception musicians or DJ.

- Schedule fittings and delivery dates for yourself, attendants, flower girl and ring bearer.

- Select and book videographer.

- Select and book florist.

FOUR TO SIX MONTHS BEFORE WEDDING

- Start shopping for each other's wedding gifts.

- Reserve rental items needed for ceremony & reception.

- Finalize guest list.

- Select and order wedding invitations, announcements and other stationery such as thank-you notes, wedding programs, and seating cards.

- Address invitations or hire a calligrapher.

- Set date, time and location for your rehearsal dinner.

- Arrange accommodations for out-of- town guests.

- Start planning your honeymoon.

- Select and book all miscellaneous services, i.e. gift attendant, valet parking, etc.

- Register for gifts.

Four to Six Months Before Wedding (Cont.)

- Purchase shoes & accessories.

- Begin to break-in your shoes.

Two to Four Months Before Wedding

- Select bakery and order wedding cake.

- Order party favors.

- Select and order room decorations.

- Purchase honeymoon attire & luggage.

- Select and book transportation for wedding day.

- Check blood test and marriage license requirements.

- Shop for wedding rings and engrave them.

- Consider having your teeth cleaned or bleached.

- Consider writing a will and/or prenuptial agreement.

- Plan activities for your out-of-town guests both before and after the wedding.

- Purchase gifts for wedding attendants.

Six to Eight Weeks Before Wedding

- Mail invitations. Include accommodation choices and a map to assist guests in finding the ceremony and reception sites.

- Maintain a record of RSVPs and all gifts received. Send thank-you notes upon receipt of gifts.

- Determine hair style and makeup.

SIX TO EIGHT WEEKS BEFORE WEDDING (Cont.)

- Schedule to have your hair, makeup and nails done the day of the wedding.

- Finalize shopping for wedding day accessories such as toasting glasses, ring pillow, guest book, etc.

- Set up an area or a table in your home to display gifts as you receive them.

- Check with your local newspapers for wedding announcement requirements.

- Have your formal wedding portrait taken.

- Send wedding announcement & photograph to your local newspapers.

- Change name & address on drivers license, social security card, insurance policies, subscriptions, bank accounts, memberships, etc.

- Select and reserve wedding attire for groom, ushers, father of the bride and ring bearer.

- Select a guest book attendant. Decide where and when to have guests sign in.

- Mail invitations to rehearsal dinner.

- Get blood test and health certificate.

- Obtain marriage license.

- Plan a luncheon or dinner with your bridesmaids. Give them their gifts at that time or at the rehearsal dinner.

- Find "something old, something new, something borrowed, something blue, and a six pence (or shiny penny) for your shoe."

- Finalize your menu, beverage and alcohol order.

TWO TO SIX WEEKS BEFORE WEDDING

- Confirm ceremony details with your officiant.

- Arrange final fitting of bridesmaids' dresses.

TWO TO SIX WEEKS BEFORE WEDDING (Cont.)

- Have final fitting of your gown and headpiece.

- Finalize rehearsal dinner plans; arrange seating and write names on place cards, if desired.

- Make final floral selections.

- Make a detailed timeline for your wedding party.

- Make a detailed timeline for your service providers.

- Confirm details with all service providers, including attire. Give them a copy of your wedding timeline.

- Start packing for your honeymoon.

- Finalize addressing and stamping announcements.

- Decide if you want to form a receiving line. If so, determine when and where to form the line.

- Contact guests who haven't responded.

- Pick up rings and check for fit.

- Meet with photographer and confirm special photos you want.

- Meet with videographer and confirm special events or people you want videotaped.

- Meet with musicians and confirm music to be played during special events such as first dance.

- Continue writing thank-you notes as gifts arrive.

- Remind bridesmaids and ushers of when and where to pick up their wedding attire.

- Purchase the lipstick, nail polish and any other accessories you want your bridesmaids to wear.

- Determine ceremony seating for special guests. Give a list to the ushers.

TWO TO SIX WEEKS BEFORE WEDDING (Cont.)

- Plan reception room layout and seating with your reception site manager or caterer. Write names on place cards for arranged seating.

THE LAST WEEK

- Pick up wedding attire and make sure everything fits.

- Do final guest count and notify your caterer or reception site manager.

- Gather everything you will need for the rehearsal and wedding day as listed in the *Wedding Party Responsibility Cards*.

- Arrange for someone to drive the getaway car.

- Review the schedule of events and last minute arrangements with your service providers.

- Confirm all honeymoon reservations and accommodations. Pick up tickets and travelers checks.

- Finish packing your suitcases for the honeymoon.

- Familiarize yourself with guests' names. It will help during the receiving line and reception.

- Have the Post Office hold your mail while you are away on your honeymoon.

THE REHEARSAL DAY

- Review list of things to bring to the rehearsal as listed in the *Wedding Party Responsibility Cards*.

- Put suitcases in getaway car.

- Give your bridesmaids the lipstick, nail polish and accessories you want them to wear for the wedding.

- Give best man the officiant's fee and any other checks for service providers. Instruct him to deliver these checks the day of the wedding.

THE REHEARSAL DAY (Cont.)

- Arrange for someone to bring accessories such as flower basket, ring pillow, guest book & pen, toasting glasses, cake cutting knife and napkins to the ceremony and reception.

- Arrange for someone to mail announcements the day after the wedding.

- Arrange for someone to return rental items such as tuxedos, slip and cake pillars after the wedding.

- Provide each member of your wedding party with a detailed schedule of events for the wedding day.

- Review ceremony seating with ushers.

THE WEDDING DAY

- Review list of things to bring to the ceremony as listed in the *Wedding Party Responsibility Cards*.

- Give the groom's ring to the maid of honor. Give the bride's ring to the best man.

- Simply follow your detailed schedule of events.

- Relax and enjoy your wedding!

BUDGET ANALYSIS

This comprehensive Budget Analysis has been designed to provide you with all the expenses that can be incurred in any size wedding, including such hidden costs as taxes, gratuities and other "items" that can easily add up to thousands of dollars in a wedding. After you have completed this budget, you will have a much better idea of what your wedding will cost. You can then prioritize and allocate your expenses accordingly.

This budget is divided into fifteen categories: Ceremony, Wedding Attire, Photography, Videography, Stationery, Reception, Music, Bakery, Flowers, Decorations, Transportation, Rental Items, Gifts, Parties, and Miscellaneous.

At the beginning of each category is the percentage of your total wedding budget that is typically spent in that category, based on national averages. Multiply your intended wedding budget by this percentage and write that amount in the "typical" space provided.

To determine the total cost of your wedding, estimate the amount of money you will spend on each item in the budget analysis and write that amount in the "Budget" column after each item. Items printed in italics are traditionally paid for by the groom or his family.

Add all the "Budget" amounts within each category and write the total amount in the "Budget Subtotal" space at the end of each category. Then add all the "Subtotal" figures to come up with your final wedding budget. The "Actual" column is for you to input your actual expenses as you purchase items or hire your service providers. The "Deposit" and "Balance Due" columns are to help you keep track of all deposits paid out and the balance due for each item. Writing down the actual expenses will help you stay within your budget.

For example, if your total wedding budget is $10,000, write this amount at the top of page 18. To figure your typical ceremony expenses, multiply $10,000 x .05 (5%) = $500.00. Write this amount on the "Typical" line in the "Ceremony" category to serve as a guide for all your ceremony expenses.

If you find, after adding up all your "Budget Subtotals," that the total amount is more than what you had in mind to spend, simply decide which items are more important to you and adjust your expenses accordingly.

Wedding Budget Checklist

CEREMONY

- ☐ Ceremony Site Fee
- ☐ *Officiant's Fee*
- ☐ *Officiant's Gratuity*
- ☐ Guest Book, Pen
- ☐ Penholder
- ☐ Ring Bearer Pillow
- ☐ Flower Girl Basket

WEDDING ATTIRE

- ☐ Bridal Gown
- ☐ Alterations
- ☐ Headpiece & Veil
- ☐ Gloves
- ☐ Jewelry
- ☐ Stockings
- ☐ Garter
- ☐ Shoes
- ☐ Hairdresser
- ☐ Makeup Artist
- ☐ Manicure/Pedicure
- ☐ *Groom's Formal Wear*

PHOTOGRAPHY

- ☐ Bride & Groom's Album
- ☐ Parents' Album
- ☐ Extra Prints
- ☐ Proofs/Previews
- ☐ Negatives
- ☐ Engagement Photograph
- ☐ Formal Bridal Portrait

VIDEOGRAPHY

- ☐ Main Video
- ☐ Titles
- ☐ Extra Hours
- ☐ Photo Montage
- ☐ Extra Copies

STATIONERY

- ☐ Invitations
- ☐ Response Cards
- ☐ Reception Cards
- ☐ Ceremony Cards
- ☐ Pew Cards
- ☐ Seating/Place Cards
- ☐ Rain Cards/Maps
- ☐ Ceremony Programs
- ☐ Announcements
- ☐ Thank-You Notes
- ☐ Stamps
- ☐ Calligraphy
- ☐ Napkins/ Matchbooks

RECEPTION

- ☐ Reception Site Fee
- ☐ Hors D' Oeuvres
- ☐ Main Meal/Caterer
- ☐ Liquor/ Beverages
- ☐ Bartending Fee
- ☐ Bar Set-up Fee
- ☐ Corkage Fee

RECEPTION (Cont.)

- ☐ Fee to Pour Coffee
- ☐ Service Providers' Meals
- ☐ Gratuity
- ☐ Party Favors
- ☐ Disposable Cameras
- ☐ Rose Petals/Rice
- ☐ Gift Attendant
- ☐ Parking Fee
- ☐ Valet Services

MUSIC

- ☐ Ceremony Music
- ☐ Reception Music

BAKERY

- ☐ Wedding Cake
- ☐ *Groom's Cake*
- ☐ Cake Delivery
- ☐ Set-up Fee
- ☐ Cake-Cutting Fee
- ☐ Cake Top
- ☐ Cake Knife/Toast Glasses

Items in italics are traditionally paid for by the groom or his family

WEDDING BUDGET CHECKLIST (CONT).

FLOWERS

Bouquets

- [ ] *Bride's*
- [ ] Tossing
- [ ] Maid of Honor's
- [ ] Bridesmaids'

Floral Hairpiece

- [ ] Maid of Honor
- [ ] Bridesmaids'
- [ ] Flower Girl's

Corsages

- [ ] *Bride's Going Away*
- [ ] *Other Family Members'*

Boutonnieres
- [ ] *Groom's*
- [ ] *Ushers*
- [ ] *Other Family's*

Ceremony Site

- [ ] Main Altar
- [ ] Alter Candelabra
- [ ] Aisle Pews

Reception Site (Cont.)

- [ ] Reception Site
- [ ] Head Table
- [ ] Guest Tables
- [ ] Buffet Table
- [ ] Punch Table

FLOWERS (Cont.)

Reception Site (Cont.)

- [ ] Cake Table
- [ ] Cake
- [ ] Cake Knife
- [ ] Toasting Glasses
- [ ] Floral Delivery & Setup

DECORATIONS

- [ ] Table Centerpieces
- [ ] Balloons

TRANSPORTATION

- [ ] Transportation

RENTAL ITEMS

- [ ] Bridal Slip
- [ ] Ceremony Accessories
- [ ] Tent/Canopy
- [ ] Dance Floor
- [ ] Tables/Chairs
- [ ] Linen/Tableware
- [ ] Heaters
- [ ] Lanterns

GIFTS

- [ ] *Bride's Gift*
- [ ] Groom's Gift
- [ ] Bridesmaids' Gifts
- [ ] *Ushers' Gifts*

PARTIES

- [ ] Bridesmaids' Luncheon
- [ ] *Rehearsal Dinner*

MISCELLANEOUS

- [ ] Newspaper Announ.
- [ ] *Marriage License*
- [ ] *Prenuptial Agreement*
- [ ] Bridal Gown/Bouquet
- [ ] Preservation
- [ ] Wedding Consultant
- [ ] Wedding Software
- [ ] Taxes

*Items in italics are traditionally paid for by the groom or his family

Budget Analysis

	BUDGET	ACTUAL	DEPOSIT	BAL. DUE
Your Total Wedding Budget	$	$		
CEREMONY (Typical = 5% of Budget)				
Ceremony Site Fee	$	$	$	$
Officiant's Fee	$	$	$	$
Officiant's Gratuity	$	$	$	$
Guest Book, Pen, Penholder	$	$	$	$
Ring Bearer Pillow	$	$	$	$
Flower Girl Basket	$	$	$	$
Subtotal 1	$	$	$	$
WEDDING ATTIRE (Typical = 10% of Budget)				
Bridal Gown	$	$	$	$
Alterations	$	$	$	$
Headpiece & Veil	$	$	$	$
Gloves	$	$	$	$
Jewelry	$	$	$	$
Stockings	$	$	$	$
Garter	$	$	$	$
Shoes	$	$	$	$
Hairdresser	$	$	$	$
Makeup Artist	$	$	$	$
Manicure/Pedicure	$	$	$	$
Groom's Formal Wear	$	$	$	$
Subtotal 2	$	$	$	$

* Items in italics are traditionally paid for by the groom or his family

	BUDGET	ACTUAL	DEPOSIT	BAL. DUE
PHOTOGRAPHY (Typical = 9% of Budget)				
Bride & Groom's Album	$	$	$	$
Parents' Album	$	$	$	$
Extra Prints	$	$	$	$
Proofs/Previews	$	$	$	$
Negatives	$	$	$	$
Engagement Photograph	$	$	$	$
Formal Bridal Portrait	$	$	$	$
Subtotal 3	$	$	$	$
VIDEOGRAPHY (Typical = 5% of Budget)				
Main Video	$	$	$	$
Titles	$	$	$	$
Extra Hours	$	$	$	$
Photo Montage	$	$	$	$
Extra Copies	$	$	$	$
Subtotal 4	$	$	$	$
STATIONERY (Typical = 4% of Budget)				
Invitations	$	$	$	$
Response Cards	$	$	$	$
Reception Cards	$	$	$	$
Ceremony Cards	$	$	$	$
Pew Cards	$	$	$	$
Seating/Place Cards	$	$	$	$
Rain Cards/Maps	$	$	$	$
Ceremony Programs	$	$	$	$
Announcements	$	$	$	$
Thank-You Notes	$	$	$	$
Stamps	$	$	$	$
Calligraphy	$	$	$	$

*Items in italics are traditionally paid for by the groom or his family

	BUDGET	ACTUAL	DEPOSIT	BAL. DUE
STATIONERY (CONT.)				
Napkins and Matchbooks	$	$	$	$
Subtotal 5	$	$	$	$
RECEPTION (Typical = 35% of Budget)				
Reception Site Fee	$	$	$	$
Hors D' Oeuvres	$	$	$	$
Main Meal/Caterer	$	$	$	$
Liquor/ Beverages	$	$	$	$
Bartending/Bar Set-up Fee	$	$	$	$
Corkage Fee	$	$	$	$
Fee To Pour Coffee	$	$	$	$
Service Providers' Meals	$	$	$	$
Gratuity	$	$	$	$
Party Favors/Disposable Cameras	$	$	$	$
Rose Petals/Rice	$	$	$	$
Gift Attendant	$	$	$	$
Parking Fee/Valet Services	$	$	$	$
Subtotal 6	$	$	$	$
MUSIC (Typical = 5% of Budget)				
Ceremony Music	$	$	$	$
Reception Music	$	$	$	$
Subtotal 7	$	$	$	$
BAKERY (Typical = 2% of Budget)				
Wedding Cake	$	$	$	$
Groom's Cake	$	$	$	$
Cake Delivery & Set-up Fee	$	$	$	$
Cake-Cutting Fee	$	$	$	$

Items in italics are traditionally paid for by the groom or his family

	BUDGET	ACTUAL	DEPOSIT	BAL. DUE
BAKERY (CONT.)				
Cake Top, Cake Knife, Toasting Glasses	$	$	$	$
Subtotal 8	$	$	$	$
FLOWERS (Typical = 6% of Budget)				
BOUQUETS				
Bride's	$	$	$	$
Tossing	$	$	$	$
Maid of Honor's	$	$	$	$
Bridesmaids'	$	$	$	$
FLORAL HAIRPIECES				
Maid of Honor/ Bridesmaids'	$	$	$	$
Flower Girl's	$	$	$	$
CORSAGES				
Bride's Going Away	$	$	$	$
Other Family Members'	$	$	$	$
BOUTONNIERES				
Groom's	$	$	$	$
Ushers and Other Family's	$	$	$	$
CEREMONY SITE FLOWERS				
Main Altar	$	$	$	$
Alter Candelabra	$	$	$	$
Aisle Pews	$	$	$	$
RECEPTION SITE FLOWERS				
Reception Site	$	$	$	$
Head Table	$	$	$	$
Guest Tables	$	$	$	$
Buffet Table	$	$	$	$

*Items in italics are traditionally paid for by the groom or his family

	BUDGET	ACTUAL	DEPOSIT	BAL. DUE
RECEPTION SITE FLOWERS (CONT.)				
Punch Table	$	$	$	$
Cake Table	$	$	$	$
Cake	$	$	$	$
Cake Knife	$	$	$	$
Toasting Glasses	$	$	$	$
Floral Delivery & Setup	$	$	$	$
Subtotal 9	$	$	$	$
DECORATIONS (Typical = 3% of Budget)				
Table Centerpieces	$	$	$	$
Balloons	$	$	$	$
Subtotal 10	$	$	$	$
TRANSPORTATION (Typical = 2% of Budget)				
Transportation	$	$	$	$
Subtotal 11	$	$	$	$
RENTAL ITEMS (Typical = 3% of Budget)				
Bridal Slip	$	$	$	$
Ceremony Accessories	$	$	$	$
Tent/Canopy	$	$	$	$
Dance Floor	$	$	$	$
Tables/Chairs	$	$	$	$
Linen/Tableware	$	$	$	$
Heaters, Lanterns, Other	$	$	$	$
Subtotal 12	$	$	$	$

*Items in italics are traditionally paid for by the groom or his family

	BUDGET	ACTUAL	DEPOSIT	BAL. DUE
GIFTS (Typical = 3% of Budget)				
Bride's/Groom's *Gift*	$	$	$	$
Bridesmaids'/ *Ushers' Gifts*	$	$	$	$
Subtotal 13	$	$	$	$
PARTIES (Typical = 4% of Budget)				
Bridesmaids' Luncheon	$	$	$	$
Rehearsal Dinner	$	$	$	$
Subtotal 14	$	$	$	$
MISCELLANEOUS (Typical = 4% of Budget)				
Newspaper Announcements	$	$	$	$
Marriage License	$	$	$	$
Prenuptial Agreement	$	$	$	$
Bridal Gown/Bouquet Preservation	$	$	$	$
Wedding Consultant	$	$	$	$
Wedding Planning Software	$	$	$	$
Taxes	$	$	$	$
Subtotal 15	$	$	$	$
GRAND TOTAL (Add subtotals 1-15 for all four columns)	$	$	$	$

*Items in italics are traditionally paid for by the groom or his family

Vendor Payment Tracking Chart

	Business Name & Phone No.	Contract Date & Total Cost	Deposit & Date	Next Pay. & Date	Final Pay. & Date
Wedding Consultant					
Ceremony Site					
Officiant					
Reception Site					
Caterer					
Liquor Services					
Wedding Gown					
Tuxedo Rental					
Photographer					
Videographer					
Stationer					
Calligrapher					
Music (Ceremony)					
Music (Reception)					
Florist					
Bakery					
Decorations					
Ice Sculpture					
Party Favors					
Balloonist					
Transportation					
Rental & Supplies					
Gift Suppliers					
Valet Services					
Gift Attendant					
Rehearsal Dinner					

*C*EREMONY

*C*EREMONY SITE FEE

The ceremony site fee is the fee to rent a facility for your wedding. In churches, cathedrals, chapels, temples, or synagogues, this fee may include the organist, wedding coordinator, custodian, changing rooms for the bridal party, and miscellaneous items such as kneeling cushions, aisle runner, and candelabra. Be sure to ask what the site fee includes prior to booking a facility. Throughout this book, the word church will be used to refer to the site where the ceremony will take place.

Options: Churches, cathedrals, chapels, temples, synagogues, private homes, gardens, hotels, clubs, halls, parks, museums, yachts, wineries, beaches, and hot air balloons.

Things To Consider: Your selection of a ceremony site will be influenced by the formality of your wedding, the season of the year, the number of guests expected and your religious affiliation. Make sure you ask about restrictions or guidelines regarding photography, videography, music, decorations, candles, and rice or rose petal-tossing. Consider issues such as proximity of the ceremony site to the reception site, parking availability, handicapped accessibility, and time constraints.

Tips To Save Money: Have your ceremony at the same facility as your reception to save a second rental fee. Set a realistic guest list and stick to it. Hire an experienced wedding consultant. At a church or temple, ask if there is another wedding that day and share the cost of floral decorations with that bride. Membership in a church, temple or club can reduce rental fees. At a garden wedding, have guests stand and omit the cost of renting chairs.

Price Range: $100 - $800

*O*FFICIANT'S FEE

The officiant's fee is the fee paid to whomever performs your wedding ceremony.

Options: Priest, Clergyman, Minister, Pastor, Chaplain, Rabbi, Judge, or Justice of the Peace.

Discuss with your officiant the readings you would like incorporated into your ceremony. Some popular readings are:

Beatitudes	Corinthians 13:1-13	Ecclesiastes 3:1-9
Ephesians 3:14-19; 5:1-2	Genesis 1:26-28	Genesis 2:4-9, 15-24
Hosea 2:19-21	Isaiah 61:10I	John 4:7-16
John 15:9-12, 17:22-24	Mark 10:6-9	Proverbs 31:10-31
Romans 12:1-2, 9-18	Ruth 1:16-17	Tobit 8:56-58

Things To Consider: Some officiants may not accept a fee, depending on your relationship with him/her. If a fee is refused, send a donation to the officiant's church or synagogue.

Price Range: $50 - $500

OFFICIANT'S GRATUITY

The officiant's gratuity is a discretionary amount of money given to the officiant.

Things To Consider: This amount should depend on your relationship with the officiant and the amount of time he/she has spent with you prior to the ceremony. The groom puts this fee in a sealed envelope and gives it to his best man or wedding consultant, who gives it to the officiant either before or immediately after the ceremony.

Price Range: $25 - $250

GUEST BOOK / PEN / PENHOLDER

The guest book is a formal register where your guests sign-in as they arrive at the ceremony or reception. It serves as a memento of who attended your wedding. This book is often placed outside the ceremony or reception site, along with an elegant pen and penholder. A guest book attendant is responsible for inviting all guests to sign-in. A younger sibling or close friend who is not part of the wedding party may be well-suited for this position.

Options: There are many styles of guest books, pens and penholders to choose from. Some books have space for your guests to write a short note to the bride and groom.

Things To Consider: Make sure you have more than one pen in case one runs out of ink. If you are planning a large ceremony (over 300 guests), consider having more than one book and pen so that your guests don't have to wait in line to sign-in.

Price Range: $10 -$75

RING BEARER PILLOW

The ring bearer, usually a boy between the ages of four and eight, carries the bride and groom's rings or mock rings on a pillow. He follows the maid of honor and precedes the flower girl or bride in the processional.

Options: These pillows come in many styles and colors. You can find them at most gift shops and bridal boutiques.

Things To Consider: If the ring bearer is very young (less than 7 years), place mock rings on the pillow in place of the real rings to prevent losing them. If mock rings are used, instruct your ring bearer to put the pillow upside down during the recessional so your guests don't see the mock rings.

Tips To Save Money: Make your own ring bearer pillow by taking a small white pillow and attaching a pretty ribbon to it to hold the rings.

Price Range: $5 - $35

FLOWER GIRL BASKET

The flower girl, usually between the ages of four and eight, carries a basket filled with flowers, rose or paper rose petals to strew as she walks down the aisle. She follows the ring bearer or maid of honor and precedes the bride during the processional.

Options: Flower girl baskets come in many styles and colors. You can find them at most florists, gift shops, and bridal boutiques.

Things To Consider: Discuss any restrictions regarding rose petal, flower, or paper-tossing with your ceremony site. Select a basket which complements your guest book and ring bearer pillow. If the flower girl is very young (less than 7 years), consider giving her a small bouquet instead of a flower basket.

Tips To Save Money: Ask your florist if you can borrow a basket and attach a pretty white bow to it.

Price Range: $5 - $35

Questions To Ask Ceremony Site

- What is the name of the ceremony site?

- What is the address of the ceremony site?

- What is the name & phone number of my contact person?

- What dates & times are available?

- Do vows need to be approved?

- What is the ceremony site fee?

- What is the payment policy?

- What is the cancellation policy?

- Does the facility have liability insurance?

- What are the minimum & maximum number of guests allowed?

- What is the denomination, if any, of the facility?

- What restrictions are there with regards to denomination?

- Is an officiant available? At what cost?

- Are outside officiants allowed?

- Are any musical instruments available for our use?

- If so, what is the fee?

- What music restrictions are there, if any?

- What photography restrictions are there, if any?

QUESTIONS To Ask CEREMONY Site (CONT.)

- What videography restrictions are there, if any?

- Are there are any restrictions for rice or rose petal-tossing?

- Are candlelight ceremonies allowed?

- What floral decorations are available/allowed?

- When is my rehearsal to be   scheduled?

- Is there handicap accessibility and parking?

- How many parking spaces are available for my wedding party?

- Where are they located?

- How many parking spaces are available for my guests?

- What rental items are necessary?

WEDDING ATTIRE

BRIDAL GOWN

Bridal gowns come in a wide variety of styles, materials, colors, lengths and prices. You should order your gown at least four to six months before your wedding if your gown has to be ordered and then fitted.

Options: Different gown styles can help create a shorter, taller, heavier, or thinner look. Here are some tips:

♦ **A short, heavy figure:** To look taller and slimmer, avoid knit fabrics. Use the princess or A-line style. Chiffon is the best fabric choice because it produces a floating effect and camouflages weight.

♦ **A short, thin figure:** A shirtwaist or natural waist style with bouffant skirt will produce a taller, more rounded figure. Chiffon, velvet, lace and Schiffli net are probably the best fabric choices.

♦ **A tall, heavy figure:** Princess or A-line are the best styles for slimming the figure; satin, chiffon and lace fabrics are recommended.

♦ **A tall, thin figure:** Tiers or flounces will help reduce the impression of height. A shirtwaist or natural waist style with a full skirt are ideal choices. Satin and lace are the best fabrics.

The guidelines below will help you select the most appropriate gown for your wedding:

Informal wedding: Street-length gown or suit
Corsage or small bouquet
No veil or train

Semi-formal wedding: Floor-length gown
Chapel train
Finger-tip veil
Small bouquet

Formal daytime wedding:	Floor-length gown Chapel or sweep train Fingertip veil or hat Gloves Medium-sized bouquet
Formal evening wedding:	Same as formal daytime except longer veil
Very formal wedding:	Floor-length gown Cathedral train Full-length veil Elaborate headpiece Long sleeves or long arm-covering gloves Cascading bouquet

Things To Consider: In selecting your bridal gown, keep in mind the time of year and formality of your wedding. It is a good idea to look at bridal magazines to compare the various styles and colors. If you see a gown you like, call boutiques in your area to see if they carry that line. Always try on the gown before ordering it.

When ordering a gown, make sure you order the correct size. If you are between sizes, order the larger one. You can always have your gown tailored down to fit, but it is not always possible to have it enlarged or to lose enough weight to fit into it! Don't forget to ask when your gown will arrive, and be sure to get this in writing. The gown should arrive at least six weeks before the wedding so you can have it tailored and select the appropriate accessories to complement it.

Beware: Some bridal boutiques have the practice of ordering gowns a size larger than needed. This requires more alterations which may mean extra charges. Ask for all alteration pricing in advance. Tailoring is a great source of income for boutiques. Also, gowns often fail to arrive on time, creating unnecessary stress for you. Have the store manager state, in writing, when the gown will arrive. And be sure to check the reputation of the boutique before buying.

Tips To Save Money: Consider renting a gown or buying one secondhand. Renting a gown usually costs about forty to sixty percent of its retail price. Consider this practical option if you are not planning to preserve the gown. The disadvantage of renting, however, is that your options are more limited. Also, a rented gown usually does not fit as well as a custom tailored gown.

Ask about discontinued styles and gowns. Watch for clearances and sales, or buy your gown "off the rack."

Restore or refurbish a family heirloom gown. If you have a friend, sister, or other family member who is planning a wedding, consider purchasing a gown that you could both wear. Change the veil and headpiece to personalize it.

Price Range: $300 - $3,000

ALTERATIONS

Alterations may be necessary in order to make your gown fit perfectly and conform smoothly to your body.

Things To Consider: Alterations usually require several fittings. Allow four to six weeks for alterations to be completed. However, do not alter your gown months before the wedding. Your weight may fluctuate during the final weeks of planning and the gown might not fit properly. Alterations are usually not included in the cost of the gown.

You may also want to consider making some modifications to your gown such as shortening or lengthening the train, customizing the sleeves, beading and so forth. Ask your bridal boutique what they charge for the modifications you are considering.

Tips To Save Money: Consider hiring an independent tailor. Their fees are usually lower than bridal boutiques.

Price Range: $50 - $150

HEADPIECE & VEIL

The headpiece is the part of the bride's outfit to which the veil is attached.

Options for Headpieces: Banana Clip, Bow, Garden Hat, Headband, Juliet Cap, Mantilla, Pillbox, Pouf, Snood, Tiara.

Options for Veils: Ballet, Bird Cage, Blusher, Cathedral Length, Chapel Length, Fingertip, Flyaway.

Things To Consider: The headpiece should complement but not overshadow your gown. In addition to the headpiece, you might want a veil. Veils come in different styles and lengths.

Select a length which complements the length of your train. Consider the total look you're trying to achieve with your gown, headpiece, veil, and hairstyle.

Tips To Save Money: Some boutiques offer a free headpiece or veil with the purchase of a gown. Make sure you ask for this before purchasing your gown.

Price Range: $60 - $250

$\mathscr{G}$LOVES

Gloves add a nice touch with either short-sleeved, three-quarter length, or sleeveless gowns.

Options: Gloves come in various styles and lengths. Depending on the length of your sleeves, select gloves that reach above your elbow, just below your elbow, halfway between your wrist and elbow, or only to your wrist. Fingerless mitts are another option that you may want to consider.

Things To Consider: You may want to consider fingerless mitts which allow the groom to place the wedding ring on your ring finger without having to remove your glove. You should not wear gloves if your gown has long sleeves, or if you're planning a small, at-home wedding.

Price Range: $5 - $30

$\mathscr{J}$EWELRY

You will need to decide what jewelry to wear on your wedding day.

Options: Select pieces of jewelry that can be classified as "something old, something new, something borrowed, or something blue."

Things To Consider: Brides look best with just a few pieces of jewelry -- perhaps a string of pearls and earrings with a simple bracelet. Purchase complementary jewelry for your bridesmaids, to match the colors of their dresses. This will give your bridal party a coordinated look.

Price Range: $60 - $1,000

$\mathscr{S}$TOCKINGS

Stockings should be selected with care, especially if the groom will be removing a garter from your leg at the reception.

Things To Consider: Consider having your maid of honor carry an extra pair, just in case you get a run.

Price Range: $5 - $15

GARTER

It is customary for the bride to wear a garter just above or below the knee on her wedding day. After the bouquet tossing ceremony, the groom takes the garter off the bride's leg. All the single men gather on the dance floor. The groom then tosses the garter to them over his back. According to age-old tradition, whoever catches the garter is the next to be married!

Things To Consider: You will need to choose the proper music for this event. A popular and fun song to play during the garter removal ceremony is *The Stripper,* by David Rose.

Price Range: $5 - $15

SHOES

Things To Consider: Make sure you select comfortable shoes that complement your gown; and don't forget to break them in well before your wedding day. Tight shoes can make you miserable and ruin your wedding day!

Price Range: $25 -$100

HAIRDRESSER

Many brides prefer to have their hair professionally arranged with their headpiece the day of the wedding rather than trying to do it themselves.

Things To Consider: Consider having your professional hairdresser experiment with your hair and headpiece before your wedding day so that there are no surprises. On your wedding day, you can go to the salon or have the stylist meet you at your home or dressing site. Consider having him/her arrange your mother's and your bridesmaids' hair for a consistent look.

Tips To Save Money: Negotiate having your hair arranged free of charge or at a discount in exchange for bringing your mother, your fiancé's mother and your wedding party to the salon.

Price Range: $20 - $75 per person

MAKEUP ARTIST

Many brides prefer to have their makeup professionally applied on their wedding day rather than trying to do it themselves.

Things To Consider: It's smart to go for a trial run before the day of the wedding so that there are no surprises. You can either go to the salon or have the makeup artist meet you at your home or dressing site. Consider having him/her apply makeup for your mother, your fiancé's mother and your bridesmaids for a consistent look. In selecting a makeup artist, make sure he/she has been trained in makeup for photography. It is very important to wear the proper amount of makeup for photographs.

Tips To Save Money: Try to negotiate having your makeup applied free of charge or at a discount in exchange for bringing your mother, your fiancé's mother and your wedding party to the salon.

Price Range: $15 - $75 per person

MANICURE / PEDICURE

As a final touch, it's nice to have a professional manicure and/or pedicure the day of your wedding.

Things To Consider: Don't forget to bring the appropriate color nail polish with you for your appointment. You can either go to the salon or have the manicurist meet you at your home or dressing site. Consider having him/her give your mother, your fiancé's mother and your bridesmaids a manicure in the same color for a consistent look.

Tips To Save Money: Try to negotiate getting a manicure or pedicure free of charge or at a discount in exchange for bringing your mother, your fiancé's mother and your wedding party to the salon.

Price Range: $10 - $30 per person

GROOM'S FORMAL WEAR

The groom should select his formal wear based on the formality of the wedding. For a semi-formal or formal wedding, the groom will need a tuxedo. A tuxedo is the formal jacket worn by men on special or formal occasions. The most popular colors are black, white, and gray.

Options: Use the following guidelines to select customary attire for the groom:

Informal wedding:
Business suit
White dress shirt and tie

Semi-formal daytime:
Formal suit
White dress shirt
Cummerbund or vest
Four-in-hand or bow tie

Semi-formal evening:
Formal suit or dinner jacket
Matching trousers
White shirt
Cummerbund or vest
Black bow tie
Cufflinks and studs

Formal daytime:
Cutaway or stroller jacket
Waistcoat
Striped trousers
White wing-collared shirt
Striped tie
Studs and cufflinks

Formal evening:
Black dinner jacket
Matching trousers
Waistcoat
White tuxedo shirt
Bow tie
Cummerbund or vest
Cufflinks

Very formal daytime:	Cutaway coat
	Wing-collared shirt
	Ascot
	Striped trousers
	Cufflinks
	Gloves
Very formal evening:	Black tailcoat
	Matching striped trousers
	Bow tie
	White wing-collared shirt
	Waistcoat
	Patent leather shoes
	Studs and cufflinks
	Gloves

Things To Consider: In selecting your formal wear, keep in mind the formality of your wedding, the time of day, and the bride's gown. Consider darker colors for a fall or winter wedding and lighter colors for a spring or summer wedding. When selecting a place to rent your tuxedo, check the reputation of the shop. Make sure they have a wide variety of makes and styles to choose from.

Reserve tuxedos for yourself and your ushers several weeks before the wedding to insure a wide selection and to allow enough time for alterations. Plan to pick up the tuxedos a few days before the wedding to allow time for last minute alterations in case they don't fit properly. Out-of-town men in your wedding party can be sized at any tuxedo shop. They can send their measurements to you or directly to the shop where you are going to rent your tuxedos.

Ask about the store's return policy and be sure you delegate to the appropriate person (usually your best man) the responsibility of returning all tuxedos within the time allotted. Ushers customarily pay for their own tuxedos.

Tips To Save Money: Try to negotiate getting your tuxedo for free or at a discount in exchange for having your father, your fiancé's father and ushers rent their tuxedos at that shop.

Price Range: $60 - $120

Questions To Ask Bridal Boutique

- What is the name of the bridal boutique?

- What is the address of the bridal boutique?

- What is the name & phone number of my contact person?

- What are your hours of operation? Are appointments needed?

- Do you offer any discounts or giveaways?

- What major bridal gown lines do you carry?

- Do you carry outfits for the mother of the bride?

- Do you carry bridesmaids gowns and/or tuxedos?

- Do you carry outfits for the flower girl and ring bearer?

- What is the cost of the desired bridal gown?

- What is the cost of the desired headpiece?

- Do you offer in-house alterations? If so, what are your fees?

- Do you carry bridal shoes? What is their price range?

- Do you dye shoes to match outfits?

- Do you rent bridal slips? If so, what is the rental fee?

- What is the estimated delivery date of my gown?

- What is your payment policy/cancellation policy?

$\mathcal{P}$HOTOGRAPHY

$\mathcal{B}$RIDE & GROOM'S ALBUM

The bride and groom's photo album is the best way to preserve your special day. Chances are you and your fiancé will look at the photos many times during your lifetime. Therefore, hiring a good photographer is one of the most important tasks in planning your wedding.

Options: There are a large variety of wedding albums. They vary in size, color, material, construction and price. Find one that you like and will feel proud of showing to your friends and family. Some of the most popular manufacturers of wedding albums are Art Leather, Leather Craftsman and Renaissance.

Make sure you review the differences between these albums before selecting one. You will also need to select the finish process of your photos. Ask your photographer to show you samples of various finishes. Some of the most popular finishes are glossy, luster, semi-matte, pebble finish, spray texture and oil.

Things To Consider: Make sure you hire a photographer who specializes in weddings. Your photographer should be experienced in wedding procedures and familiar with your ceremony and reception sites. This will allow him/her to anticipate your next move and be in the proper place at the right time to capture all the special moments. Personal rapport is extremely important. The photographer may be an expert, but if you don't feel comfortable or at ease with him or her, your photography will reflect this. Comfort and compatibility with your photographer can make or break your wedding day and your photographs!

Look at his/her work. See if the photographer captured the excitement and emotion of the bridal couple. Also, remember that the wedding album should unfold like a story book -- the story of your wedding. Be sure to discuss with your photographer the photos you want so that there is no misunderstanding. A good wedding photographer should have a list of suggested poses to choose from.
Look at albums ready to be delivered, or proofs of weddings recently photographed. Look at the photographer's preferred style. Some photographers are known for formal poses, while others specialize in more candid, creative shots. Some can do both.

When asked to provide references, many photographers will give you the names of people they know are happy with their work. Some may even give you names from weddings they performed several years ago. This may not indicate the photographer's current ability or reputation. So when asking for references, be sure to ask for recent weddings the photographer has performed. This will give you a good idea of his/her current work. Be sure to ask if the photographer was prompt, cordial, properly dressed and whether he/she performed his/her duties as expected.

When comparing prices, consider the number, size and finish of the photographs and the type of album the photographer will use. Ask how many proofs you will get to choose your photos from. The more proofs, the better the selection you will have. Some photographers do not work with proofs. Rather, they simply supply you with a finished album after the wedding. Doing this may reduce the cost of your album but will also reduce your selection of photographs.

Beware: Make sure the photographer you interview is the one who will photograph your wedding. There are many companies with more than one photographer. Often these companies use the work of the best photographer to sell their packages and then send a less experienced photographer to the wedding. Don't get caught in this trap! Be sure you meet with the photographer who will shoot your wedding. This way you can get an idea of his/her style and personality.

Also, some churches do not allow photographs to be shot during the ceremony. Make sure your photographer understands the rules and regulations of your church before planning the ceremony shots.

Tips To Save Money: Consider hiring a professional photographer for the formal shots of your ceremony only. You can then place disposable cameras on each table at the reception and let your guests take candid shots. This can save you a considerable amount of money in photography.

You can also lower the price of your album by paying for the photographs and then putting them into the album yourself. This is a very time-consuming task, so your photographer may reduce the price of his/her package if you opt to do this. To really economize, select a photographer who charges a flat fee to shoot the wedding and will allow you to purchase the film.

Compare at least 3 photographers for quality, value and price. Photographers who shoot weddings "on the side" are usually less expensive than professional wedding photographers.

Select a few 8" x 10"s for your album and more 4" x 5"s, and choose a moderately priced album. Ask for specials and package deals.

Price Range: $400 - $3000

PARENTS' ALBUM

The parents' album is a smaller version of the bride and groom's album. It usually contains about twenty 5" x 7" photographs. Photos should be carefully selected for each individual family. If given as a gift, the album can be personalized with the bride and groom's names and date of their wedding on the front cover.

Tips To Save Money: Try to negotiate at least one free parents' album with the purchase of the bride and groom's album.

Price Range: $60 - $300

EXTRA PRINTS

Extra prints are photographs ordered in addition to the main album or parents' albums. These are usually purchased as gifts for the bridal party, close friends and family members.

Things To Consider: It is important to discuss the cost of extra prints with your photographer since prices vary considerably. Some photographers offer the main album at great bargains to get the job, but then charge a fortune on extra prints. Think how many extra prints you would like to order and figure this into your budget before selecting a photographer.

Tips To Save Money: Ask your photographer to sell you the negatives. It's always less expensive to have the negatives developed into prints yourself than to order them from a professional photographer.

If you can wait, consider not ordering any reprints during the first few years after the wedding. A few years later, contact the photographer and ask if he/she will sell you the negatives. Most photographers will be glad to sell them at a bargain price. You can then make as many prints as you wish for a fraction of the cost.

Price Range: (5" x 7") = $3 - $15; (8" x 10") = $10 - $25; (11" x 14") = $25 - $75

$\mathscr{P}$ROOFS / PREVIEWS

Proofs/previews are the preliminary prints from which the bride and groom select photographs for their album and for their parents' albums. They are normally 5" x 5" in size.

Things To Consider: When selecting a package, ask how many proofs the photographer will take. The more proofs, the wider the selection you will have to choose from. For a wide selection, the photographer must take at least 2 to 3 times the number of prints that will go into your album.

Ask the photographer how soon after the wedding you will get your proofs. Request this in writing. The proofs should be ready by the time you get back from your honeymoon. Also request to see your proofs before you make the final payment.

Tips To Save Money: Ask your photographer to use your proofs as part of your album package to save developing costs.

Price Range: $100 - $600

$\mathscr{N}$EGATIVES

Negatives come in different sizes depending on the type of film and equipment used. The most popular camera for weddings is the medium format camera. When a medium format camera is used, the size of the negatives is 2 1/4" x 2 1/4." When a 35 mm camera is used, the negatives are only 1" x 1 1/2." The larger the negative, the higher the quality of the photograph, especially when enlarged. Don't let a photographer convince you that there is no difference in quality between a 35 mm camera and a medium format camera.

Things To Consider: Most photographers will not sell you the negatives since they hope to make a profit on selling extra prints after the wedding. Ask the photographers you interview how long they keep the negatives. A professional photographer should keep the negatives at least five years. Make sure you get this in writing.

Tips To Save Money: Purchasing the negatives will save you a lot of money when duplicating prints for family and friends. But don't spend money on purchasing negatives unless you are planning to make a lot of reprints. If you can wait, consider not buying the negatives right away. Contact the photographer a few years later and ask if he/she will sell you the negatives. Most photographers will be glad to sell them at a bargain price.

Price Range: $100 - $800

*E*NGAGEMENT PHOTOGRAPH

The engagement photograph is sent to your local newspapers, along with information announcing your engagement to the public. This announcement is usually made by the bride's parents or her immediate family.

Things To Consider: The photograph (usually in black and white) was traditionally of the bride alone, but today is usually of the engaged couple.

Tips To Save Money: Look at engagement photographs in your local newspaper. Then have a friend or family member take a photograph of you and your fiancé in a pose similar to the ones you have seen.

Price Range: $35 - $75

*F*ORMAL BRIDAL PORTRAIT

If you intend to announce your marriage in the newspaper the day after your wedding, you will need to have a formal bridal portrait taken several weeks before the wedding. This is a photograph of the bride taken before the wedding in the photographer's studio. This photograph, along with an announcement, must be sent to your local newspapers as soon as possible.

Things To Consider: Some fine bridal salons provide an attractive background where the bride may arrange to have her formal bridal photograph taken after the final fitting of her gown. This will save you the hassle of bringing your gown and headpiece to the photographer's studio and dressing up once again.

Tips To Save Money: If you don't mind announcing your marriage several weeks after the wedding, consider having your formal portrait taken the day of your wedding. This will save you the studio costs, the hassle of getting dressed for the photo, and the photograph will be more natural since the bridal bouquet will be the one you carry down the aisle. Also, brides are always most beautiful on their wedding day!

Price Range: $50 - $150

Questions To Ask Photographer

- What is the name and phone number of the photographer?

- What is the address of the photographer?

- How many years of experience do you have as a photographer?

- What percentage of your business is dedicated to weddings?

- Approximately how many weddings have you photographed?

- Are you the person who will photograph my wedding?

- Will you bring an assistant with you to my wedding?

- How do you typically dress for weddings?

- Do you have a professional studio?

- What type of equipment do you use?

- Do you bring backup equipment with you to weddings?

- Do you visit the ceremony and reception sites prior to the wedding?

- Do you have liability insurance?

- Are you skilled in diffused lighting & soft focus?

- Can you take studio portraits?

- Can you retouch negatives?

- Can negatives be purchased? If so, what is the cost?

QUESTIONS TO ASK PHOTOGRAPHER (CONT.)

- What is the cost of the package I am interested in?

- What is your payment policy?

- What is your cancellation policy?

- Do you offer a money-back guarantee?

- Do you use proofs?

- How many proofs will I get?

- When will I get my proofs?

- When will I get my album?

- What is the cost of an engagement portrait? Formal bridal portrait?

- What is the cost of a parent album?

- What is the cost of a 5" x 7" reprint?

- What is the cost of an 8" x 10" reprint?

- What is the cost of an 11" x 14" reprint?

- What is the cost per additional hour of shooting at the wedding?

VIDEOGRAPHY

MAIN VIDEO

Next to your photo album, videography is the best way to preserve your wedding memories. Unlike photographs, videography captures the mood of the wedding day in motion and sound. You have the option of selecting one, two, or three cameras. The more cameras used, the more action captured and the more expensive. An experienced videographer, however, can do a good job with just one camera.

Options: There are various types of video cameras available. Commercial cameras are the best. These are used for television and special events. The next best cameras are Super VHS followed by Super 8 mm. Compare videographer's equipment when comparing their packages and prices. And don't forget to ask if your videographer has a wireless microphone. It will come in handy during the ceremony when you want to capture all the words at a distance without the need for a long cable.

Things To Consider: Look at previous weddings the videographer has videotaped. Notice the color and brightness of the screen, as well as the quality of the sound. This will indicate the quality of his/her equipment. Notice the picture -- is it smooth or jerky? This will indicate the videographer's level of skill. Notice any special effects such as titles, dissolve, and multiple screens.

Make sure you hire someone who specializes in weddings. Just like your photographer, your videographer should be experienced in wedding procedures and, ideally, should be familiar with the layout of your ceremony and reception sites. This will allow him/her to anticipate your next move and be in the proper place at the right time to capture all the special moments. Remember to ask your videographer to interview your wedding party, close friends and family members, asking them to make a wish or toast to both of you as a married couple, or to tell any "wild" stories they may want to share for the record. This personalizes your video and is a onderful memento. Consider both personality and professionalism when hiring your videographer.

Find out what is included in each package you are considering: hours of coverage, titling, in-camera editing or post-editing. If you will be getting married in a church, find out the church's policies regarding videography. Some churches do not allow a videographer to be close to the ceremony.

To preserve your wedding video for many years to come, store it in a cool, dark place.

Beware: As in photography, there are many companies with more than one videographer. These companies often use the work of the best videographer to sell their packages and then send a less experienced videographer to the wedding. Again, don't get caught in this trap! Be sure to interview the videographer who will shoot your wedding so you can get a good idea of his/her style and personality. Ask to see his/her own work.

Tips To Save Money: Compare videographers' quality, value and price. There is a wide range, and the most expensive is not necessarily the best. One camera is the most cost effective and may be all you need. Consider hiring a company that offers both videography and photography. You may save overall.

Ask a family member or close friend to videotape your wedding. However, realize that without professional equipment and expertise the final product may not be quite the same.

Price Range: $350 - $2,000

TITLES

Titles and subtitles can be edited into your video before or after the filming. Titles are important since twenty years from now you might not remember the exact time of your wedding or the names of your wedding party members. Some videographers charge more for titling. Make sure you discuss this with your videographer and get in writing exactly what titles will be included.

Options: Titles may include the date, time and location of the wedding, the bride and groom's names, and names of special family members and/or the wedding party. Titles may also include special thanks to those who helped with the wedding. You can send these people a copy of your video after the wedding. This is a very appropriate and inexpensive gift!

Tips To Save Money: Consider borrowing a camera with a character generator from a friend and doing the titling yourself.

Price Range: $40 - $75

EXTRA HOURS

Find out how much your videographer would charge to stay longer than contracted for in your original package. Don't forget to get this in writing.

Tips To Save Money: Avoid paying extra hours beyond what's included in your selected package. You can do this by calculating the number of hours you think you'll need and negotiating that into your package price. Consider taping the ceremony only.

Price Range: $35 - $60/hour

PHOTO MONTAGE

A photo montage is a series of photographs set to music on video. The number of photographs depends on the length of the song and the amount of time allotted for each photograph. A typical song usually allows for approximately 40 to 50 photographs. Photo montages are a great way to display and reproduce your photographs. Copies of this video can be made for considerably less than the cost of reproducing photographs.

Options: Photo montages can include photos of you and your fiancé growing up, the rehearsal, the wedding day, the honeymoon, or any combination thereof.

Things To Consider: Send copies of your photo montage video to close friends and family members as mementos of your wedding.

Tips To Save Money: Consider making a photo montage yourself. This is very easily done with any video camera, a tripod, and a good stereo. The secret is in holding the camera very still and having the proper lighting while videotaping the photographs.

Price Range: $50 - $100

EXTRA COPIES

A professional videographer can reproduce your video much better than you can. Ask your videographer how much he/she charges. You'll certainly want to give your parents a copy!

Tips To Save Money: Borrow a VCR from a friend and make copies yourself.

Price Range: $5 - $35

Questions To Ask Videographer

- What is the name & phone number of the videographer?

- What is the address of the videographer?

- How many years of experience do you have as a videographer?

- Approximately how many weddings have you videotaped?

- Are you the person who will videotape my wedding?

- Will you bring an assistant with you to my wedding?

- What type of equipment do you use?

- Do you have a wireless microphone?

- What format do you use (VHS, Super VHS, 8mm)?

- Do you bring backup equipment with you?

- Do you visit the ceremony and reception sites before the wedding?

- Do you edit the tape after the event? Who keeps the raw footage?

- When will I receive the final product?

- Cost of the desired package: What does it include?

- Can you make a photo montage? If so, what is your price?

- What is your payment policy? What is your cancellation policy?

- Do you offer a money-back guarantee?

*S*TATIONERY

*I*NVITATIONS

Begin creating your guest list as soon as possible. Ask your parents and the groom's parents for a list of the people they would like to invite. You and your fiancé should make your own list. Make certain that all names are spelled correctly and that all addresses are current. Determine if you wish to include children; if so, add their names to your list. All children over the age of 16 should receive their own invitation.

Order your invitations at least 4 months before the wedding. Allow an additional month for engraved invitations. Invitations are traditionally issued by the bride's parents; but if the groom's parents are assuming some of the wedding expenses, the invitations should be in their names also. Mail all invitations at the same time, 6 - 8 weeks before the wedding.

Options: There are three types of invitations: traditional/formal, contemporary, and informal. The traditional/formal wedding invitation is white, soft cream, or ivory with raised black lettering. The printing is done on the top page of a double sheet of thick quality paper; the inside is left blank. The contemporary invitation is typically an individualized presentation that makes a statement about the bride and groom. Informal invitations are often printed on the front of a single, heavyweight card and may be handwritten or preprinted.

There are three types of printing: engraved, thermography, and offset printing. Engraving is the most expensive, traditional and formal type of printing. It also takes the longest to complete. In engraved printing, stationery is pressed onto a copper plate, which makes the letters rise slightly from the page. Thermography is a process that fuses powder and ink to create a raised letter. This takes less time than engraving and is less expensive because copper plates do not have to be engraved. Offset printing, the least expensive, is the quickest to produce and offers a variety of styles and colors. It is also the least formal.

Things To Consider: If all your guests are to be invited to both the ceremony and the reception, a combined invitation may be sent without separate enclosure cards. Order one invitation for each married or cohabiting couple that you plan to invite. The officiant and his/her spouse as well as your attendants should receive an invitation.

Order approximately 20% more stationery than your actual count. Allow a minimum of two weeks to address and mail the invitations, longer if using a calligrapher or if your guest list is very large. You may also want to consider ordering invitations to the rehearsal dinner, as these should be in the same style as the wedding invitation. For samples of wording etiquette, invitation wording and verses, reception, response, thank you, and ceremony program verses, military etiquette and much more, see the invitation order forms at the back of the book.

Tips To Save Money: Thermography looks like engraving and is one-third the cost. Choose paper stock that is reasonable and yet achieves your overall look. Select invitations that can be mailed using just one stamp. Order at least 25 extra invitations, just in case you add people to your list or you make a mistake. To reorder this small number of invitations later would cost nearly three times the amount you'll spend up front.

Price Range: $.69 - $2.00 each (for orders of 100 invitations or more)

RESPONSE CARDS

Response cards are enclosed with the invitation to determine the number of people who will be attending your wedding. They are the smallest card size accepted by the postal service and should be printed in the same style as the invitation. An invitation to only the wedding ceremony does not usually include a request for a reply. However, response cards should be used when it is necessary to have an exact head count for special seating arrangements. Response cards are widely accepted today. If included, these cards should be easy for your guests to understand and use. Include a self-addressed and stamped return envelope to make it easy for your guests to return the response cards.

Things To Consider: You should not include a line that reads "number of persons" on your response cards because only those whose names appear on the inner and outer envelopes are invited. Each couple, each single person, and all children over the age of 16 should receive their own invitation. Indicate on the inner envelope if they may bring an escort or guest. The omitting of children's names from the inner envelope infers that the children are not invited.

Price Range: $.40 - $.80 each (for orders of 100 cards or more)

RECEPTION CARDS

If the guest list for the ceremony is larger than that for the reception, a separate card with the date, time and location for the reception should be enclosed with the ceremony invitation for those guests also invited to the reception. Reception cards should be placed in front of the invitation, facing the back flap and the person inserting them. They should be printed on the same quality paper and in the same style as the invitation itself.

Things To Consider: You may also include a reception card in all your invitations if the reception is to be held at a different site than the ceremony.

Tips To Save Money: If all people invited to the ceremony are also invited to the reception, include the reception information on the invitation and eliminate the reception card. This will save printing and postage costs.

Price Range: $.35 - $.70 each (for orders of 100 cards or more)

*C*EREMONY CARDS

If the guest list for the reception is larger than the guest list for the ceremony, a special insertion card with the date, time, and location for the ceremony should be enclosed with the reception invitation for those guests also invited to the ceremony.

Ceremony cards should be placed in front of the invitation, facing the back flap and the person inserting them. They should be printed on the same quality paper and in the same style as the invitation itself.

Price Range: $.35 - $.60 each (for orders of 100 cards, or more)

*P*EW CARDS

Pew cards may be used to let special guests and family members know they are to be seated in the reserved section on either the bride's side or the groom's side. These are most typically seen in large, formal ceremonies. Guests should take this card to the ceremony and show it to the ushers, who should then escort them to their seats.

Options: Pew cards may indicate a specific pew number if specific seats are assigned, or may read "Within the Ribbon" if certain pews are reserved but no specific seat is assigned.

Things To Consider: Pew cards may be inserted along with the invitation, or may be sent separately after the RSVPs have been returned. It is often easier to send them after you have received all RSVPs so you know how many reserved pews will be needed.

Tips To Save Money: Include the pew card with the invitation to special guests and just say "Within the Ribbon." After you have received all your RSVPs, you will know how many pews need to be reserved This will save you the cost of mailing the pew cards separately.

Price Range: $.20 - $.60 each (for orders of 100 cards or more)

SEATING / PLACE CARDS

Seating/place cards are used to let guests know where they should be seated at the reception and are a good way of putting people together so they feel most comfortable. Place cards should be laid out alphabetically on a table at the entrance to the reception. Each card should correspond to a table -- either by number, color, or other identifying factor. Each table should be marked accordingly.

Options: Select a traditional or contemporary design for your place cards, depending on the style of your wedding.

Regardless of the design, place cards must contain the same information: the bride and groom's names on the first line; the date on the second line; the third line is left blank for you to write in the guest's name; and the fourth line is for the table number, color, or other identifying factor.

Price Range: $.20 - $.60 each (for orders of 100 cards, or more)

RAIN CARDS

These cards are enclosed when guests are invited to an outdoor ceremony and/or reception, informing them of an alternate location in case of bad weather. As with other enclosures, rain cards should be placed in front of the invitation, facing the back flap and the person inserting them. They should be printed on the same quality paper and in the same style as the invitation itself.

Price Range: $.20 - $.30 each (for orders of 100 cards, or more)

MAPS

Maps to the ceremony and/or reception are becoming frequent inserts in wedding invitations. They need to be drawn and printed in the same style as the invitation and are usually on a small, heavier card. If they are not printed in the same style or on the same type of paper as the invitation, they should be mailed separately.

Options: Maps should include both written and visual instructions, keeping in mind the fact that guests may be coming from different locations.

Things To Consider: Order extra maps to hand out at the ceremony if the reception is at a different location.

Tips To Save Money: If you are comfortable with computers, you can purchase software that allows you to draw your own maps. Print a map to both the ceremony and reception on the same sheet of paper, perhaps one on each side. This will save you the cost of mailing two maps. Or have your ushers hand out maps to the reception after the ceremony.

Price Range: $.20 - $.40 each (for orders of 100 cards, or more)

CEREMONY PROGRAMS

Ceremony programs are printed documents showing the sequence of events during the ceremony. These programs add a personal touch to your wedding and are a convenient way of letting guests know who your attendants, officiant, and ceremony musicians are.

Options: Ceremony programs can be handed out to guests by the ushers, or they can be placed at the back of the church for guests to take as they enter.

Price Range: $.36 - $1.75 each (for orders of 100 programs, or more)

ANNOUNCEMENTS

Announcements are not obligatory but serve a useful purpose. They may be sent to friends who are not invited to the wedding because the number of guests must be limited, or because they live too far away. They may also be sent to acquaintances who, while not particularly close to the family, might still wish to know of the marriage.

Announcements are also appropriate for friends and acquaintances who are not expected to attend and for whom you do not want to give an obligation of sending a gift. They should include the day, month, year, city, and state where the ceremony took place.

Things To Consider: Announcements should never be sent to anyone who has received an invitation to the ceremony or the reception. They are printed on the same paper and in the same style as the invitations. They should be addressed before the wedding and mailed the day of or the day after the ceremony.

Price Range: $.35 - $1.00 each (for orders of 100 announcements, or more)

THANK-YOU NOTES

Regardless of whether the bride has thanked the donor in person or not, she must write a thank-you note for every gift received.

Things To Consider: Order thank-you notes along with your other stationery at least four months before your wedding. You should order some with your maiden initials for thank-you notes sent before the ceremony, and the rest with your married initials for notes sent after the wedding and for future use. Send thank-you notes within two weeks of receiving a gift that arrives before the wedding, and within two months after the honeymoon for gifts received on or after your wedding day. Be sure to mention the gift you received in the body of the note and let the person know how much you like it and what you plan to do with it.

Price Range: $.20 - $.55 (for orders of 100 cards, or more)

STAMPS

Don't forget to budget stamps for response cards as well as for invitations!

Things To Consider: Don't order stamps until you have had the post office weigh your completed invitation. It may exceed the size and weight for one stamp. Order commemorative stamps that fit the occasion.

Price Range: $.34 - $1.00 each

CALLIGRAPHY

Calligraphy is a form of elegant handwriting often used to address invitations for formal occasions. Traditional wedding invitations should be addressed in black or blue fountain pen.

Options: You may address the invitations yourself, hire a professional calligrapher, or have your invitations addressed using calligraphy by computer. Make sure you use the same method or person to address both the inner and outer envelopes.

Tips To Save Money: You may want to consider taking a short course to learn the art of calligraphy so that you can address your own invitations. If you have a computer with a laser printer, you can address the invitations yourself using one of many beautiful calligraphy fonts.

Price Range: $.30 - $3.00 each (for orders of 100 or more cards/envelopes)

GUIDELINES FOR ADDRESSING INVITATIONS

We recommend that you start addressing your envelopes at least three months before your wedding, and preferably four months if you are using calligraphy or if your guest list is above 200.

You may want to ask your maid of honor or bridesmaids to help you with this time-consuming task, as this is traditionally part of their responsibilities. Organize a luncheon or late afternoon get-together with hors d'oeuvres and make a party out of it! If you are working with a wedding consultant, she can also help you address invitations.

There are typically two envelopes that need to be addressed for wedding invitations: an inner envelope and an outer envelope. The inner envelope is placed unsealed inside the outer envelope, with the flap away from the person inserting it.

The invitation and all enclosures are placed inside the inner envelope facing the back flap. The inner envelope contains the name (or names) of the person (or people) who are invited to the ceremony and/or reception. The address is not included on the inner envelope.

The outer envelope contains the name (or names) and address of the person (or people) to whom the inner envelope belongs

NAPKINS AND MATCHBOOKS

Napkins and matchbooks may also be ordered from your stationer. These are placed around the reception room as decorative items and mementos of the event.

Things To Consider: Napkins and matchbooks can be printed in your wedding colors or white with gold or silver lettering. Include both of your names and the wedding date. You may consider including a phrase or thought, or a small graphic design above your names.

Price Range: $.5 - $1.60 each (for orders of 100 napkins and matchbooks, or more)

Questions To Ask Stationer

- What is the name & phone number of the stationery provider?

- What is the address of the stationery provider?

- How many years of experience do you have?

- What lines of stationery do you carry?

- What types of printing process do you offer?

- How soon in advance does the order have to be placed?

- What is the turn around time?

- What is the cost of the desired invitation? Announcement?

- What is the cost of the desired response card? Reception card?

- What is the cost of the desired thank-you note?

- What is the cost of the desired party favors? cards?, Pew Cards?

- What is the cost of the desired wedding program?

- What is the cost of addressing the envelopes in calligraphy?

- What is your payment policy?

- What is your cancellation policy?

*R*ECEPTION

*R*ECEPTION SITE FEE

The reception is a party where all your guests come together to celebrate your new life as a married couple. It should reflect and complement the formality of your ceremony. The selection of a reception site will depend on its availability, price, proximity to the ceremony site, and the number of people it will accommodate.

There are two basic types of reception sites. The first type charges a per person fee which includes the facility, food, tables, silverware, china, and so forth. Examples: hotels, restaurants and catered yachts. The second type charges a room rental fee and you are responsible for providing the food, beverages, linens, and possibly tables and chairs. Examples: clubs, halls, parks, museums, and private homes.

The advantage of the first type is that most everything is done for you. The disadvantage, however, is that your choices of food, china, and linen are limited. Usually you are not permitted to bring in an outside caterer and must select from a predetermined menu.

Options: Private homes, gardens, hotels, clubs, restaurants, halls, parks, museums, yachts, and wineries are some of the more popular choices for receptions.

Things To Consider: When comparing the cost of different locations, consider the rental fee, food, beverages, parking, gratuity, set-up charges and the cost of rental equipment needed such as tables, chairs, canopies, and so forth. If you are planning an outdoor reception, be sure to have a backup site in case of rain.

Beware: Some hotels are known for double booking. A bride may reserve the largest or most elegant room in a hotel for her reception, only to find out later that the hotel took the liberty to book a more profitable event in the room she had reserved and moved her reception over to a smaller or less elegant room.

Also be careful of hotels that book events too close together. You don't want your guests to wait outside while your room is being set up for the reception. And you don't want to be "forced out" before you are ready to leave because the hotel needs to arrange the room for the next reception. Get your rental hours and the name of your room in writing.

Tips To Save Money: Since the cost of the reception is approximately 35% of the total cost of your wedding, you can save the most money by limiting your guest list. If you hire a wedding consultant, she may be able to cut your cake and save you the cake-cutting fee. Check this out with your facility or caterer. Reception sites that charge a room rental fee may waive this fee if you meet minimum requirements on food and beverages consumed. But try to negotiate this before you book the facility.

Price Range: $300 - $1,000

HORS D' OEUVRES

At receptions where a full meal is to be served, hors d' oeuvres may be offered to guests during the first hour of the reception. However, at a tea or cocktail reception, hors d' oeuvres will be the "main course."

Options: There are many options for hors d' oeuvres, depending on the formality of your reception and the type of food to be served at the meal. Popular items are foods that can easily be picked up and eaten with one hand. Hors d' oeuvres may be set out on tables "buffet style" for guests to help themselves, or they may be passed around on trays by waiters and waitresses.
Things To Consider: When selecting hors d' oeuvres for your reception, consider whether heating or refrigeration will be available and choose your food accordingly. When planning your menu, consider the time of day. You should select lighter hors d' oeuvres for a midday reception and heavier hors d' oeuvres for an evening reception.

Tips To Save Money: Tray pass hors d' oeuvres during cocktail hour and serve a lighter meal. Avoid serving hors d' oeuvres that are labor intensive or that require expensive ingredients. Compare two or three caterers; there is a wide price range between caterers for the same food. Compare the total cost of catering (main entrée plus hors d' oeuvres) when selecting a caterer. Consider serving hors d' oeuvres "buffet style." Your guests will eat less this way than if waiters and waitresses are constantly serving them hors d' oeuvres.

Price Range: $1 - $10/person

MAIN MEAL / CATERER

If your reception is going to be in a hotel, restaurant or other facility that provides food, you will need to select a meal to serve your guests. Most of these facilities will have a predetermined menu from which to select your meal. If your reception is going to be in a facility that does not provide food, you will need to hire an outside caterer. The caterer will be responsible for preparing, cooking, decorating and serving the food.

The caterer will also be responsible for beverages and for cleaning up after the event. Before signing a contract, make sure you understand all the services the caterer will provide. Your contract should state the amount and type of food and beverages that will be served, the way in which they will be served, the number of servers who will be available, the cost per item or person,

Options: Food can be served either buffet style or as a sit-down meal. It should be chosen according to the time of day, year, and formality of the wedding. Although there are many main dishes to choose from, chicken and beef are the most popular selections for a large event. Ask your facility manager or caterer for their specialty. If you have a special type of food you would like to serve at your reception, select a facility or caterer who specializes in preparing it.

Things To Consider: When hiring a caterer, check to see if the location for your reception provides refrigeration and cooking equipment. If not, make sure your caterer is fully self supported with portable refrigeration and heating equipment. A competent caterer will prepare much of the food in his/her own kitchen and should provide an adequate staff of cooks, servers, and bartenders. Ask for references and look at photos from previous parties so you know how the food will be presented; or better yet, visit an event they are catering.

Beware: Avoid mayonnaise, cream sauces, or custard fillings if food must go unrefrigerated for any length of time.

Tips To Save Money: Give only 85 to 95 percent of your final guest count to your caterer or facility manager, depending on how certain you are that all of your guests who have responded will come. Chances are that several, if not many, of your guests will not show up. If they do, your caterer should have enough food for all of them. This is especially true with buffet style receptions, in which case the facility or caterer will charge extra for each additional guest. However, if you give a complete count of your guests to your caterer and some of them don't show up, you will still have to pay for their plates. If offering a buffet meal, have the catering staff serve the food onto guests' plates rather than allowing guests to serve themselves. This will help to regulate the amount of food consumed.

Select food that is not too time-consuming to prepare, or food that does not have expensive ingredients. Also, consider a brunch or early afternoon wedding so the reception will fall between meals, allowing you to serve hors d' oeuvres instead of a full meal. Or tray pass hors d' oeuvres during cocktail hour and choose a lighter meal.

Price Range: $10 - $60/person

$\mathscr{L}$IQUOR / BEVERAGES

Prices for liquor and beverages vary greatly, depending on the amount and brand of alcohol served. Traditionally, at least champagne or punch should be served to toast the couple.

Options: White and red wines, scotch, vodka, gin, rum, and beer are the most popular alcoholic beverages. Sodas and fruit punch are popular nonalcoholic beverages served at receptions. And of course, don't forget coffee or tea. There are a number of options and variations for serving alcoholic beverages: a full open bar where you pay for your guests to drink as much as they wish; an open bar for the first hour, followed by a cash bar where guests pay for their own drinks; cash bar only; beer and wine only; nonalcoholic beverages only; or any combination thereof.

Things To Consider: If you plan to serve alcoholic beverages at a reception site that does not provide liquor, make sure your caterer has a license to serve alcohol and that your reception site allows alcoholic beverages. If you plan to order your own alcohol, do so three or four weeks before the event. If you plan to have a no-host or "cash" bar, consider notifying your guests so they know to bring cash with them. A simple line that says "No-Host Bar" on the reception card should suffice.

In selecting the type of alcohol to serve, consider the age and preference of your guests, the type of food that will be served, and the time of day your guests will be drinking.

On the average, you should allow 1 drink per person per hour at the reception. A bottle of champagne will usually serve six glasses. Never serve liquor without some type of food. Use the following guide to plan your beverage needs:

Beverages	**Amount based on 100 guests**
Bourbon	3 Fifths
Gin	3 Fifths
Rum	2 Fifths
Scotch	4 Quarts
Vodka	5 Quarts
White Wine	2 Cases
Red Wine	1 Case
Champagne	3 Cases
Other	2 Cases each: Club Soda, Seltzer Water, Tonic Water, Ginger Ale, Cola, Beer

If you are hosting an open bar at a hotel or restaurant, ask the catering manager how they charge for liquor: by consumption or by number of bottles opened. Get this in writing before the event and then ask for a full consumption report after the event.

Beware: In today's society, it is not uncommon for the hosts of a party to be held legally responsible for the conduct and safety of their guests. Keep this in mind when planning the quantity and type of beverages to serve. Also, be sure to remind your bartenders not to serve alcohol to minors.

Tips To Save Money: To keep beverage costs down, serve punch, wine, or nonalcoholic drinks only. If your caterer allows it, consider buying liquor from a wholesaler who will let you return unopened bottles. Also, avoid salty foods such as potato chips, pretzels or ham. These foods will make your guests thirstier so they will tend to drink more.

Host alcoholic beverages for the first hour, then go to a cash bar. Or host beer, wine, and soft drinks only and have mixed drinks available on a cash basis. The bartending fee is often waived if you meet the minimum requirements on beverages consumed. For the toast, tray pass champagne only to those guests who want it, not to everyone. Many people will make a toast with whatever they are currently drinking. Consider serving sparkling cider in place of champagne.

Omit waiters and waitresses. Instead, have an open bar in which your guests have to get their own drinks. People tend to drink almost twice as much if there are waiters and waitresses constantly asking them if they would like another drink and then bringing drinks to them.

Price Range: $8 - $25/person

*B*ARTENDING / BAR SET-UP FEE

Some reception sites and caterers charge an extra fee for bartending and for setting up the bar.

Tips To Save Money: The bartending fee could be and often is waived if you meet a minimum requirement on beverages consumed. Try to negotiate this with your caterer prior to hiring him/her.

Price Range: $50 - $375

CORKAGE FEE

Many reception sites and caterers make money by marking up the food and alcohol they sell. You may wish to provide your own alcohol for several reasons. First, it is more cost effective. Second, you may want to serve an exotic wine or champagne that the reception site or caterer does not offer. In either case, and if your reception site or caterer allows it, be prepared to pay a corkage fee. This is the fee for each bottle brought into the reception and opened by a member of their staff.

Things To Consider: You need to consider whether the expenses saved after paying the corkage fee justify the hassle and liability of bringing in your own alcohol.

Price Range: $5 - $20/bottle

FEE TO POUR COFFEE

In addition to the corkage and cake-cutting fees, some facilities also charge extra to pour coffee with the wedding cake.

Things To Consider: Again, when comparing the cost of various reception sites, don't forget to add up all the extra miscellaneous costs, such as the fee for pouring coffee.

Price Range: $0.25 - $0.75/person

SERVICE PROVIDERS' MEALS

Things To Consider: It is considered a courtesy to feed your photographer, videographer, and any other "service provider" at the reception. Check options and prices with your caterer or reception site manager. Make sure you allocate a place for your service providers to eat. You may want them to eat with your guests, or you may prefer setting a place outside the main room for them to eat. Your service providers may be more comfortable with the latter.

Tips To Save Money: You don't need to feed your service providers the same meal as your guests. You can order sandwiches or another less expensive meal for them. If the meal is a buffet, there should be enough food left after all your guests have been served for your service providers to eat. Tell them they are welcome to eat after all your guests have been served. Be sure to discuss this with your catering manager.

Price Range: $7 - $25/person

GRATUITY

It is customary to pay a gratuity fee to your caterer. The average gratuity is 15% to 18% of your food and beverage bill.

Tips To Save Money: Gratuities can range from 15% to 25%. Ask about these costs up front and select your caterer or reception site accordingly.

Price Range: 15% - 18%

PARTY FAVORS

Party favors are little gift items given to your guests as mementos of your wedding. They add a very special touch to your wedding and can become keepsakes for your guests.

Options: White matchboxes engraved with the couple's names and wedding date; cocktail napkins marked in the same way; individually wrapped and marked chocolates, almonds, or fine candy are all popular party favors. Wine or champagne bottles marked with the bride and groom's names and wedding date on a personalized label are also very popular. These come in different sizes and can be purchased by the case.

If you can afford it, you may also consider porcelain or ceramic party favors. These can be custom-fired with your name and wedding date on them. A new idea that's gaining in popularity among environmentally conscientious couples is to present each guest with a tiny shoot of an endangered tree to be planted in honor of the bride and groom.

Things To Consider: Personalized favors need to be ordered several weeks in advance.

Price Range: $1 - $8/person

DISPOSABLE CAMERAS

A great way to inexpensively obtain many candid photographs of your wedding day is to place a disposable 35 mm camera loaded with film on each table at your reception, and to have your guests take shots of the event! Disposable cameras come pre-loaded with film. Your guests can leave the cameras at their table or drop them in a basket or other labeled container near the entrance to the reception site. Arrange for someone to collect the cameras after the event. Tell your DJ, musician, or wedding coordinator to encourage your guests to take photographs with the disposables. You will end up with many beautiful, memorable and candid photographs of your reception.

Things To Consider: Disposable cameras are sold with and without flash. Disposable cameras with flash are more expensive but necessary if your reception is going to be held indoors or in the evening. If you are planning a large reception, consider buying cameras with only 12 exposures. Otherwise, you may end up with too many photographs. For example, if 200 guests attend your reception and you seat 8 guests per table, you will need to purchase 25 cameras. If each camera has 36 exposures, you will end up with 825 photographs. If the cameras have only 12 exposures, you will end up with 300 photographs, which is a more reasonable quantity!

Tips To Save Money: Instead of developing these photographs into print and then placing them into a big album, have your videographer transfer the negatives directly onto video set to your favorite music. You can then reproduce this "photo montage" and send it as a gift to your friends and family members. You can later decide which of these photographs you want to develop into print.

Price Range: $4 - $13/camera

ROSE PETALS / RICE

Rose petals or rice are traditionally tossed over the bride and groom as they leave the church after the ceremony or when they leave the reception. These are usually handed out to guests in little sachet bags while the bride and groom are changing into their going away clothes. This tradition was initiated in the Middle Ages whereby a handful of wheat was thrown over the bridal couple as a symbol of fertility. Rose petals are used to symbolize happiness, beauty, and prosperity.

Options: Rose petals, rice, or confetti is often used. However, an environmentally correct alternative is to use grass or flower seeds, which do not need to be "cleaned up" if tossed over a grassy area. These come wrapped in attractive, recycled packages with the couple's names and wedding date printed on the front.

Things To Consider: Rose petals can stain carpets; rice can sting faces, harm birds and make stairs dangerously slippery; confetti is messy and hard to clean. Clubs and hotels seldom permit the use of any of these. Ask about their policy.

Price Range: $.35 - $1/person

*G*IFT ATTENDANT

The gift attendant is responsible for watching over your gifts during the reception so that no one walks away with them. This is necessary only if your reception is held in a public area such as a hotel or outside garden where other people may be walking by. It is not proper to have a friend or family member take on this duty as he/she would not enjoy the reception. The gift attendant should also be responsible for transporting your gifts from the reception to your car or bridal suite.

Tips To Save Money: Hire a young boy or girl from your neighborhood to watch over your gifts at the reception.

Price Range: $20 - $80

*P*ARKING FEE / VALET SERVICES

Many reception sites such as hotels, restaurants, etc. charge for parking. It is customary, although not necessary, for the host of the wedding to pay this charge. At a large home reception, you should consider hiring a professional, qualified valet service if parking could be a problem. If so, make sure the valet service is fully insured.

Things To Consider: When comparing the cost of reception sites, don't forget to add the cost of parking to the total price.

Tips To Save Money: To save money, let your guests pay their own parking fees.

Price Range: $1.50 - $9/car

Questions To Ask Reception Site

- What is the name of the reception site?

- What is the address of the reception site?

- What is the name & phone number of my contact person?

- What dates & times are available?

- What is the maximum number of guests for a seated reception?

- What is the maximum number of guests for a cocktail reception?

- What is the reception site fee?

- What is the price range for a seated lunch?

- What is the price range for a buffet lunch?

- What is the price range for a seated dinner?

- What is the price range for a buffet dinner?

- What is the corkage fee?

- What is the cake-cutting fee?

- What is the ratio of servers to guests?

- How much time will be allotted for my reception?

- What music restrictions are there, if any?

- What alcohol restrictions are there, if any?

QUESTIONS To Ask RECEPTION Site (cont.)

- Are there any restrictions for rice or rose petal-tossing?

- What room and table decorations are available?

- Is a changing room available?

- Is there handicap accessibility?

- Is a dance floor included in the site fee?

- Are tables, chairs, and linens included in the site fee?

- Are outside caterers allowed?

- Are kitchen facilities available for outside caterers?

- Does the facility have full liability insurance?

- What "perks" or giveaways are offered?

- How many parking spaces are available for my wedding party?

- How many parking spaces are available for my guests?

- What is the cost for parking, if any?

- What is the cost for sleeping rooms, if available?

- What is the payment policy?

- What is the cancellation policy?

- Are credit cards accepted?

Questions To Ask Caterer

- What is the name of the caterer?

- What is the address of the caterer?

- What is the name & phone number of my contact person?

- How many years have you been in business?

- What percentage of your business is dedicated to wedding receptions?

- Do you have liability insurance? Are you licensed to serve alcohol?

- When is the final head-count needed?

- What is your ratio of servers to guests?

- How do your servers dress for wedding receptions?

- What is your price range for a seated lunch/ buffet lunch?

- What is your price range for a seated/buffet dinner?

- How much gratuity is expected?

- What is your labor fee per employee?

- What is your cake-cutting fee?

- What is your bartending fee?

- What is your fee to cleanup after the reception?

- What is your payment/cancellation policy?

- Do you accept credit cards?

*M*USIC

*C*EREMONY MUSIC

Ceremony music is the music played during the ceremony; i.e., prelude, processional, ceremony, recessional, and postlude. Prelude music is played 15 to 30 minutes before the ceremony begins and while guests are being seated. Processional music is played as the wedding party enters the ceremony site. Ceremony music is played during the ceremony. Recessional music is played as the wedding party leaves the ceremony site. Postlude music is played while guests leave the ceremony site.

Options: The most traditional musical instrument for wedding ceremonies is the organ. But guitars, pianos, flutes, harps and violins are also popular today.

Popular selections for a Christian wedding:

> *Trumpet Voluntary* by Purcell
> *The Bridal Chorus* by Wagner
> *Wedding March* by Mendelssohn
> *Postlude in G Major* by Handel
> *Canon in D Major* by Pachelbel
> *Adagio in A Minor* by Bach

Popular selections for a Jewish wedding:

> *Erev Shel Shoshanim*
> *Erev Ba*
> *Hana' Ava Babanot*

Things To Consider: Music may or may not be included as part of the ceremony site fee. Be sure to check with your ceremony site about restrictions pertaining to music and the availability of musical instruments for your use. Discuss the selection of ceremony music with your officiant and musicians. Make sure the musicians know how to play the selections you request.

When selecting ceremony music, keep in mind the formality of your wedding, your religious affiliation, and the length of the ceremony. Also consider the location and time of day. If the ceremony is outside where there may be other noises such as traffic, wind, or people's voices, or if a large number of guests will be attending your ceremony, consider having the music, your officiant, and your vows amplified. Make sure there are electrical outlets close to where the instruments will be set up.

Tips To Save Money: Hire student musicians from your local university or high school. Ask a friend to sing or play at your ceremony; they will be honored. If you're planning to hire a band for your reception, consider hiring a scaled-down version of the same band to play at your ceremony, such as a trio of flute, guitar, and vocals. This could enable you to negotiate a "package" price. If you're planning to hire a DJ for your reception, consider hiring him/her to play pre-recorded music at your ceremony.

Price Range: $50 - $400

RECEPTION MUSIC

Music is a major part of your reception, and should be planned carefully. Music helps create the atmosphere of your wedding. Special songs will make your reception unique. When you select music for your reception, keep in mind the age and musical preference of your guests, your budget, and any restrictions that the reception site may have. Bands and musicians are typically more expensive than DJ's.

Options: There are many options for reception music: you can hire a DJ, a band, an orchestra, or any combination of one or more instruments and vocalists.

Things To Consider: Consider hiring an entertainment agency that can help you choose a reliable DJ or band that will play the type of music you want. Whoever you choose should have experience performing at wedding receptions.

If you want your musician to act as a master of ceremonies, make sure he/she has a complete timeline for your reception so he/she knows when to announce the various events such as the toasts, first dance, and cutting of the cake. Consider watching your musicians perform at another event before booking their services.

If you need a large variety of music to satisfy all your guests, consider hiring a DJ. A professional DJ can play any type of music and may even offer a light show. Make sure you give him/her a list of the songs you want played at your reception and a timeline for playing each one. Make sure there are electrical outlets at the reception site close to where the musicians will be performing.

Tips To Save Money: You will probably get a better price if you hire a band or DJ directly than if you hire them through an entertainment agency. Check the music department of local colleges and universities for names of student musicians and DJs. You may be able to hire a student for a fraction of the price of a professional musician or DJ. A DJ is typically less expensive than a "live" musician, saving $200 - $1,000. Some facilities have contracts with certain DJ's, and you may be able to save money by hiring one of them.

Price Range: $300 -$3,000

*Q*UESTIONS TO *A*SK FOR *C*EREMONY *M*USIC

- What is the name of the musician or band?

- What is your address?

- What is the name & phone number of my contact person?

- How many years of professional experience do you have?

- What percentage of your business is dedicated to weddings?

- Are you the person who will perform at my wedding?

- What instrument(s) do you play?

- What type of music do you specialize in?

- What are your hourly fees?

- What is the cost of a soloist?

- What is the cost of a duet?

- What is the cost of a trio?

- What is the cost of a quartet?

- How would you dress for my wedding?

- Do you have liability insurance?

- Do you have a cordless microphone?

- What is your payment/cancellation policy?

Questions to Ask for Reception Music

- What is the name of the musician? Band? DJ?

- What is your address?

- What is the name & phone number of my contact person?

- How many years of professional experience do you have?

- What percentage of your business is dedicated to wedding receptions?

- How many people are in your band?

- What type of music do you specialize in?

- What type of sound system do you have?

- Can you act as a master of ceremonies? How do you dress?

- Can you provide a light show?

- Do you have a cordless microphone?

- How many breaks do you take? How long are they?

- Do you play recorded music during breaks?

- Do you have liability insurance?

- What are your fees for a 4-hour reception?

- What is your cost for each additional hour?

- What is your payment/cancellation policy?

EDDING CAKE

Wedding cakes may be ordered from a caterer or from a bakery. Some hotels and restaurants may also be able to provide a wedding cake. However, you will probably be better off ordering your cake from a bakery that specializes in wedding cakes. Ask to see photographs of other wedding cakes your baker has created, and by all means, ask for a tasting!

Options: When ordering your cake, you will have to decide not only on a flavor, but also on a size, shape and color. Size is determined by the number of guests. You can choose from one large tier to two, three, or more smaller tiers. The cake can be round, square or heart-shaped. The most common flavors are chocolate, carrot, lemon, rum, and "white" cakes. You can be creative by adding a filling to your cake, such as custard, strawberry, or chocolate. You may also want to consider having tiers of different flavors.

Things To Consider: Price, workmanship, quality, and taste vary considerably from baker to baker. In addition to flavor, size, and cost, consider decoration and spoilage (sugar keeps longer than cream frostings). The cake should be beautifully displayed on its own table decorated with flowers or greenery. Make sure the baker, caterer, or reception site manager can provide you with a pretty cake-cutting knife. If not, you will need to purchase or rent one.
When determining the size of the cake, don't forget that you'll be saving the top tier for your first anniversary. This top tier should be removed before the cake is cut, wrapped in several layers of plastic wrap or put inside a plastic container, and kept frozen until your anniversary.

Tips To Save Money: Some bakers have set-up and delivery fees, some don't. Check for individuals who bake from their home. They are usually more reasonable, but you should check with your local health department before hiring one of these at-home bakers. Also, some caterers have contracts with bakeries and can pass on savings to you.

Some bakeries require a deposit on columns and plates. Other bakeries use disposable columns and plates, saving you the rental fee and the hassle of returning these items.

Price Range: $1 - $8/piece

G ROOM'S CAKE

The groom's cake is an old southern tradition whereby this cake is cut up and distributed to guests in little white boxes engraved with the bride and groom's names. Today the groom's cake, if offered, is cut and served along with the wedding cake.

Options: Usually a chocolate cake decorated with fruit.

Tips To Save Money: Because of its cost and the labor involved in cutting and distributing the cake, very few people offer this delightful custom any more.

Price Range: $0.75 - $1.50/piece

C AKE DELIVERY & SET-UP FEE

This is the fee charged by bakers to deliver and set up your wedding cake at the reception site. It usually includes a deposit on the cake pillars and plate which will be refunded upon their return to the baker.

Tips To Save Money: Have a friend or family member get a quick lesson on how to set up your cake. Have them pick it up and set it up the day of your wedding, then have the florist decorate the cake and/or cake table with flowers and greenery.

Price Range: $20 - $50

C AKE-CUTTING FEE

Most reception sites and caterers charge a fee for each slice of cake they cut if the cake is brought in from an outside bakery. This fee will probably shock you. It is simply their way of enticing you to order the cake through them. And unfortunately, many sites and caterers will not allow a member of your party to cut the cake.

Tips To Save Money: Many hotels and restaurants include a dessert in the cost of their meal packages. If you forego this dessert and substitute your cake as the dessert, they may be willing to waive the cake-cutting fee. Be sure to ask them.

Price Range: $.75 - 1.75/person

CAKE TOP

The bride's cake is often topped and surrounded with fresh flowers, but traditional cake tops are also very popular.

Options: Bells, love birds, a bridal couple or replica of two wedding rings are popular choices for cake tops and can be saved as mementos of your wedding day.

Beware: Some porcelain and other heavier cake tops need to be anchored down into the cake. If you're planning to use a cake top other than flowers, be sure to discuss this with your baker.

Tips To Save Money: Borrow a cake top from a friend or a family member as "something borrowed," an age-old wedding tradition

Price Range: $25 - $150

CAKE KNIFE / TOASTING GLASSES

Your cake knife and toasting glasses should compliment your overall setting; these items will bring you happy memories of your wedding day every time you use them. The cake knife is used to cut the cake at the reception. The bride usually cuts the first two slices of the wedding cake with the groom's hand placed over hers. The groom feeds the bride first, then the bride feeds the groom. This tradition makes beautiful wedding photographs.

You will need toasting glasses to toast each other after you cut the cake. They are usually decorated with ribbons or flowers and kept near the cake. This tradition also makes beautiful wedding photographs.

Things To Consider: Consider having your initials and wedding date engraved on your wedding knife as a memento. Consider purchasing crystal or silver toasting glasses as a keepsake of your wedding. Have your florist decorate your knife and toasting glasses with flowers or ribbons.

Tips To Save Money: Borrow your cake knife or toasting glasses from a friend or family member as "something borrowed," an age-old wedding tradition. Use the reception facility's glasses and knife, and decorate them with flowers or ribbon.

Price Range: $15 - $120/knife; $30 - $80/toasting glasses

Questions To Ask Bakery

- What is the name of the bakery?

- What is the address of the bakery?

- What is the name & phone number of my contact person?

- How many years have you been making wedding cakes?

- What are your wedding cake specialties?

- Do you offer free tasting of your wedding cakes?

- Do you freeze your wedding cakes?

- How far in advance should I order my cake?

- Can you make a groom's cake?

- Do you lend, rent or sell cake knives?

- What is the cost per serving of my desired cake?

- What is your cake pillar and plate rental fee, if any?

- Is this fee refundable upon the return of these items?

- When must these items be returned?

- What is your cake delivery and set-up fee?

- What is your payment policy?

- What is your cancellation policy?

$\mathcal{F}$LOWERS

$\mathcal{B}$RIDE'S BOUQUET

The bridal bouquet is one of the most important elements of the bride's attire and deserves special attention. Start by selecting the color and shape of the bouquet. The bridal bouquet should be carried low enough so that all the intricate details of your gown are visible.

Options: There are many colors, scents, sizes, shapes and styles of bouquets to choose from. Popular styles are the cascade, cluster, contemporary and hand-tied garden bouquets. The traditional bridal bouquet is made of white flowers. Stephanotis, gardenias, white roses, orchids and lilies of the valley are popular choices for an all-white bouquet.

If you prefer a colorful bouquet, you may want to consider using roses, tulips, stock, peonies, freesia, and gerbera, which come in a wide variety of colors. Using scented flowers in your bouquet will evoke memories of your wedding day whenever you smell them in the future. Popular fragrant flowers for bouquets are gardenias, freesia, stephanotis, bouvardia, and narcissus. Select flowers that are in season to assure availability.

Things To Consider: Your flowers should complement the season, your gown, your color scheme, your attendants' attire, and the style and formality of your wedding. If you have a favorite flower, build your bouquet around it and include it in all your arrangements. Some flowers carry centuries of symbolism. Consider stephanotis -- tradition regards it as the bridal good-luck flower! Pimpernel signifies change; white flowers radiate innocence; forget-me-nots indicate true love; and ivy stands for friendship, fidelity, and matrimony -- the three essentials for a happy marriage.

No flower, however, has as much symbolism for brides as the orange blossom, having at least 700 years of nuptial history. Its unusual ability to simultaneously bear flowers and produce fruit symbolizes the fusion of beauty, personality, and fertility.

Whatever flowers you select, final arrangements should be made well in advance of your wedding date to insure availability. Confirm your final order and delivery time a few days before the wedding. Have the flowers delivered before the photographer arrives so that you can include them in your pre-ceremony photos. n determining the size of your bouquet, consider your gown and your overall stature. Carry a smaller bouquet if you're petite or if your gown is fairly ornate. A long, cascading bouquet complements a fairly simple gown or a tall or larger bride. Arm bouquets look best when resting naturally in the crook of your arm.

For a natural, fresh-picked look, have your florist put together a cluster of flowers tied together with a ribbon. For a Victorian appeal, carry a nosegay or a basket filled with flowers. Or carry a Bible or other family heirloom decorated with just a few flowers. For a contemporary look, you may want to consider carrying an arrangement of calla lilies or other long-stemmed flower over your arm. For a dramatic statement, carry a single stem of your favorite flower!

Beware: If your bouquet includes delicate flowers that will not withstand hours of heat or a lack of water, make sure your florist uses a bouquet holder to keep them fresh. If you want to carry fresh-cut stems without a bouquet holder, make sure the flowers you select are hardy enough to go without water for the duration of your ceremony and reception.

Tips To Save Money: The cost of some flowers may be significantly higher during their off-season. So try to select flowers which are in bloom and plentiful at the time of your wedding. Avoid exotic, out-of-season flowers. Allow your florist to emphasize your colors using more reasonable, seasonal flowers to achieve your total look. If you have a favorite flower that is costly or out of season, consider using silk for that one flower.

Avoid scheduling your wedding on holidays such as Valentine's Day and Mother's Day when the price of flowers is higher. Because every attendant will carry or wear flowers, consider keeping the size of your wedding party down to accommodate your floral budget.

Price Range: - $60 - $500

TOSSING BOUQUET

If you want to preserve your bridal bouquet, consider having your florist make a smaller, less expensive bouquet specifically for tossing. This will be the bouquet you toss to your single, female friends toward the end of the reception. Tradition has it that the woman who catches the bouquet is the next to be married. Have your florist include a few sprigs of fresh ivy in the tossing bouquet to symbolize friendship and fidelity.

Tips To Save Money: Use the floral cake top or guest book table "tickler bouquet" as the tossing bouquet. Or omit the tossing bouquet altogether and simply toss your bridal bouquet.

Price Range: $10 - $30

*M*AID OF HONOR'S BOUQUET

The maid of honor's bouquet can be somewhat larger or of a different color than the rest of the bridesmaids' bouquets. This will help to set her apart from the others.

Price Range: $25 - $75

*B*RIDESMAIDS' BOUQUETS

The bridesmaids' bouquets should complement the bridal bouquet but are generally smaller in size. The size and color should coordinate with the bridesmaids' dresses and the overall style of the wedding. Bridesmaids' bouquets are usually identical.

Options: To personalize your bridesmaids' bouquets, insert a different flower in each of their bouquets to make a statement. For example, if one of your bridesmaids has been sad, give her a lily of the valley to symbolize the return of happiness. To tell a friend that you admire her, insert yellow jasmine. A pansy will let your friend know that you are thinking of her.

Things To Consider: Choose a bouquet style (cascade, cluster, contemporary, hand-tied) that compliments the formality of your wedding and the height of your attendants. If your bridesmaids will be wearing floral print dresses, select flowers that complement the floral print.

Tips To Save Money: Have your attendants carry a single stemmed rose, lily or other suitable flower for an elegant look that also saves money.

Price Range: $15 - $60

*M*AID OF HONOR / BRIDESMAIDS' HAIRPIECE

For a garden-look, have your maid of honor and bridesmaids wear garlands of flowers in their hair. If so, provide your maid of honor with a slightly different color or variety of flower to set her apart from the others.

Options: You may consider using artificial flowers for the hairpieces as long as they are in keeping with the flowers carried by members of the bridal party. Since it is not always easy to find good artificial blooms, other types of hairpieces may be more satisfactory, durable, and attractive.

Things To Consider: Flowers used for the hairpiece must be a sturdy and long-lived variety

Price Range: $8 - $25

FLOWER GIRL'S HAIRPIECE

Flower girls often wear a wreath of flowers as a hairpiece.

Options: This is another place where artificial flowers may be used, but they must be in keeping with the flowers carried by members of the bridal party. Since it is not always easy to find good artificial blooms, other types of hairpieces may be more satisfactory, durable, and attractive.

Things To Consider: If the flowers used for the hairpiece are not a sturdy and long-lived variety, a ribbon, bow, or hat might be a safer choice.

Price Range: $8 - $25

BRIDE'S GOING AWAY CORSAGE

You may want to consider wearing a corsage on your going-away outfit. This makes for pretty photos as you and your new husband leave the reception for your honeymoon. Have your florist create a corsage which echoes the beauty of your bouquet.

Beware: Put a protective shield under lilies when using them as a corsage, as their anthers will easily stain fabric. Be careful when using Alstroemeria as a corsage, as its sap can be harmful if it enters the human bloodstream.

Tips To Save Money: Ask your florist if he/she can design your bridal bouquet in such a way that the center flowers may be removed and worn as a corsage. Or omit this corsage altogether.

Price Range: $10 - $25

OTHER FAMILY MEMBERS' CORSAGES

The groom is responsible for providing flowers for his mother, the bride's mother, and the grandmothers. The officiant, if female, may also be given a corsage to reflect her important role in the ceremony. The corsages don't have to be identical, but they should be coordinated with the color of their dresses.

Options: The groom may order flowers that can be pinned to a pocketbook or worn around a wrist. He should ask which style the women prefer, and if a particular color is needed to coordinate with their dresses. Gardenias, camellias, white orchids, or cymbidium orchids are excellent choices for corsages, as they go well with any outfit.

Things To Consider: The groom may also want to consider ordering corsages for other close family members, such as sisters and aunts. This will add a little to your floral expenses, but will make these female family members feel more included in your wedding and will let guests know that they are related to the bride and groom. Many women do not like to wear corsages, so the groom should check with the people involved before ordering the flowers.

Beware: Put a protective shield under lilies when using them as corsages, as their anthers will easily stain fabric. Be careful when using Alstroemeria as corsages, as its sap can be harmful if it enters the human bloodstream.

Tips To Save Money: Ask your florist to recommend reasonable flowers for corsages. Dendrobium orchids are reasonable and make lovely corsages.

Price Range: $10 - $25

GROOM'S BOUTONNIERE

The groom wears his boutonniere on the left lapel, nearest to his heart.

Options: Boutonnieres are generally a single blossom such as a rosebud, stephanotis, freesia or a miniature carnation. If a rosebud is used for the wedding party, have the groom wear two rosebuds, or add a sprig of baby's breath to differentiate him from the groomsmen.

Things To Consider: Consider using a small cluster of flowers instead of a single bloom for the groom's boutonniere.

Beware: Be careful when using Alstroemeria as a boutonniere, as its sap can be harmful if it enters the human bloodstream.

Tips To Save Money: Use mini-carnations rather than roses.

Price Range: $4 - $10

*U*SHERS AND OTHER FAMILY MEMBERS' BOUTONNIERES

The groom gives each man in his wedding party a boutonniere to wear on his left lapel. The officiant, if male, may also be given a boutonniere to reflect his important role in the ceremony. The ring bearer may or may not wear a boutonniere, depending on his outfit. A boutonniere is more appropriate on a tuxedo than on knickers and knee socks.

Options: Generally, a single blossom such as a rosebud, freesia, or miniature carnation is used as a boutonniere.

Things To Consider: The groom should also consider ordering boutonnieres for other close family members such as fathers, grandfathers, and brothers. This will add a little to your floral expenses, but will make these male family members feel more included in your wedding and will let guests know that they are related to the bride and groom.

Beware: Be careful when using Alstroemeria as boutonnieres, as its sap can be harmful if it enters the human bloodstream.

Tips To Save Money: Use mini-carnations rather than roses.

Price Range: $3 - $7

*M*AIN ALTAR

The purpose of flowers at the main altar is to direct the guests' visual attention toward the front of the church or synagogue and to the bridal couple. Therefore, they must be seen by guests seated in the back. The flowers for the ceremony site can be as elaborate or as simple as you wish. Your officiant's advice, or that of the altar guild or florist, can be most helpful in choosing flowers for the altar and chancel.

Options: If your ceremony is outside, decorate the arch, gazebo, or other structure serving as the altar with flowers or greenery. In a Jewish ceremony, vows are said under a Chuppah, which is placed at the altar and covered with greens and fresh flowers.

Things To Consider: In choosing floral accents, consider the decor of your ceremony site. Some churches and synagogues are ornate enough and don't need extra flowers. Too many arrangements would get lost in the architectural splendor. Select a few dramatic showpieces that will complement the existing decor. Be sure to ask if there are any restrictions on flowers at the church or synagogue. Remember, decorations should be determined by the size and style of the building, the formality of the wedding, the preferences of the bride, the cost, and the regulations of the particular site.

Tips To Save Money: Decorate the ceremony site with greenery only. Candlelight and greenery are elegant in and of themselves. Use greenery and flowers from your garden. Have your ceremony outside in a beautiful garden or by the water, surrounded by nature's own splendor.

Price Range: $50 - $1,000

ALTAR CANDELABRA

In a candlelight ceremony, the candelabra may be decorated with flowers or greens for a dramatic effect.

Options: Ivy may be twined around the candelabra, or flowers may be strung to them.

Price Range: $25 - $50

AISLE PEWS

Flowers, candles or ribbons are often used to mark the aisle pews and add color.

Options: A cluster of flowers, a cascade of greens, or a cascade of flowers and ribbons are all popular choices. Candles with adorning greenery add an elegant touch.

Things To Consider: Use hardy flowers that can tolerate being handled as pew ornaments. Gardenias and camellias, for example, are too sensitive to last long.

Beware: Avoid using Allium in your aisle pew decorations as they have an odor of onions.

Tips To Save Money: It is not necessary to decorate all of the aisle pews, or any at all. To save money, decorate only the reserved family pews. Or decorate every second or third pew.

Price Range: $5 - $40

RECEPTION SITE

Flowers add beauty, fragrance, and color to your reception. Flowers for the reception, like everything else, should fit your style and color scheme. Flowers can help transform a stark reception hall into a warm, inviting and colorful room.

Things To Consider: Consider renting indoor plants or small trees to give your reception a garden-like atmosphere. Decorate them with twinkle lights to achieve a magical effect.

Tips To Save Money: You can save money by taking flowers from the ceremony to the reception site for decorations. However, you must coordinate this move carefully to avoid having your guests arrive at an undecorated reception room. Use greenery rather than flowers to fill large areas. Trees and garlands of ivy can give a dramatic impact for little money. Use greenery and flowers from your garden. Have your reception outside in a beautiful garden or by the water, surrounded by nature's own beauty.

Price Range: $300 - $1,500

HEAD TABLE

The head table is where the wedding party will sit during the reception. This important table should be decorated with a larger or more dramatic centerpiece than the guest tables.

Things To Consider: Consider using a different color or style of arrangement to set the head table apart from the other tables.

Beware: Avoid using highly fragrant flowers, such as narcissus, on tables where food is being served or eaten, as their fragrance may conflict with other aromas.

Tips To Save Money: Decorate the head table with the bridal and attendants' bouquets.

Price Range: $50 - $300

GUEST TABLES

At a reception where guests are seated, a small flower arrangement may be placed on each table.

Things To Consider: The arrangements should complement the table linens and the size of the table, and should be kept low enough so as not to hinder conversation among guests seated across from each other.

Beware: Avoid using highly fragrant flowers, like Narcissus, on tables where food is being served or eaten, as their fragrance may conflict with other aromas.

Tips To Save Money: To keep the cost down and for less formal receptions, use small potted flowering plants placed in white baskets, or consider using dried or silk arrangements that you can make yourself and give later as gifts. Or place a wreath of greenery entwined with colored ribbon in the center of each table. Use a different colored ribbon at each table and assign your guests to tables by ribbon color instead of number.

Price Range: $10 - $60

BUFFET TABLE

If buffet tables are used, have some type of floral arrangement on the tables to add color and beauty to your display of food.

Options: Whole fruits and bunches of berries offer a variety of design possibilities. Figs add a festive touch. Pineapples are a sign of hospitality. Vegetables offer an endless array of options to decorate with. Herbs are yet another option in decorating. A mixture of rosemary and mint combined with scented geraniums makes a very unique table decoration.

Things To Consider: Depending on the size of the table, place one or two arrangements at each side.

Beware: Avoid placing certain flowers, such as carnations, snapdragons, or the star of Bethlehem, next to buffet displays of fruits or vegetables, as they are extremely sensitive to the gasses emitted by these foods.

Price Range: $50 - $300

PUNCH TABLE

Put an assortment of greens or a small arrangement of flowers at the punch table. See "Buffet Table."

Price Range: $10 - $50

CAKE TABLE

The wedding cake is often the central location at the reception. Decorate the cake table with flowers.

Tips To Save Money: Have your bridesmaids place their bouquets on the cake table during the reception, or decorate the cake top only and surround the base with greenery and a few loose flowers.

Price Range: $15 - $25

CAKE

Flowers are a beautiful addition to a wedding cake and are commonly seen spilling out between the cake tiers.

Things To Consider: Use only nonpoisonous flowers, and have your florist – not the caterer – design the floral decorations for your cake. A florist will be able to blend the cake decorations into your overall floral theme.

Price Range: $20 - $60

CAKE KNIFE

Decorate your cake knife with a white satin ribbon and/or flowers.

Things To Consider: Consider engraving the cake knife with your names and wedding date.

Price Range: $5 - $20

TOASTING GLASSES

Tie small flowers with white ribbons on the stems of your champagne glasses. These wedding accessories deserve a special floral touch since they will most likely be included in your special photographs.

Things To Consider: Consider engraving your toasting glasses with your names and wedding date.

Price Range: $10 - $30

𝓕LORAL DELIVERY & SET-UP

Most florists charge a fee to deliver flowers to the ceremony and reception sites and to arrange them on site.

Things To Consider: Make sure your florist knows where your sites are and what time to arrive for set-up.

Price Range: $25 - $100

Questions To Ask Florist

- What is the name of the florist?

- What is the address of the florist?

- What is the name & phone number of my contact person?

- How many years of professional floral experience do you have?

- What percentage of your business is dedicated to weddings?

- Do you have access to out-of-season flowers?

- Will you visit my wedding sites to make floral recommendations?

- Can you preserve my bridal bouquet?

- Do you rent vases and candleholders?

- Can you provide silk flowers?

- What is your cost of a bridal bouquet made of a dozen white roses?

- What is your cost of a boutonniere made of a single white rose?

- What is your cost of a corsage made with two gardenias?

- Do you have liability insurance? fee? Do you accept credit cards?

- What are your delivery/set-up fees?

- What are your business hours?

- What is your payment/cancellation policy?

*D*ECORATIONS

*T*ABLE CENTERPIECES

Each of the tables at your reception, including the head table, should be decorated with a centerpiece.

Options: Candles, mirrors and flowers are popular choices for table centerpieces. However, the options are endless. Just be creative! An arrangement of shells, for example, makes a very nice centerpiece for a seaside reception. Votive candles set on top of a mirror make a romantic centerpiece for an evening reception.

A wreath of greenery woven with colored ribbon makes a delightful centerpiece. Use a different color ribbon at each table and have your guests seated according to ribbon color!

Things To Consider: Select a table centerpiece which complements your colors and/or setting. The centerpiece for the head table should be larger or more elaborate than for the other tables. Make sure that your centerpiece is kept low enough so as not to hinder conversation among guests seated across from each other. Consider using a centerpiece that your guests can take home as a memento of your wedding.

Tips To Save Money: Make your own table centerpieces using materials that are not expensive.

Price Range: $5 - $30 each

*B*ALLOONS

Balloons are often used to decorate a reception site. A popular idea is to release balloons at the church or reception. This adds a festive, exciting, and memorable touch to your wedding. Balloons can be used to create an arch backdrop for the wedding cake or inexpensive centerpieces for the tables.

Things To Consider: Color coordinate your balloons to match your wedding color scheme. Choose colors from your bouquet or your bridesmaids' dresses. Balloons should be delivered and set-up well in advance – at least before the photographer shows up.

If you are planning to release balloons at the church or reception, check with your city. Releasing balloons in some cities might be illegal. Also make sure there are no wires where balloons can get entangled. If they do, you could be held responsible for damages or cleanup expenses.

Tips To Save Money: Balloons are less expensive than fresh flowers and can be used as a substitute for flowers to decorate the reception site.

Price Range: $75 - $500

TRANSPORTATION

TRANSPORTATION

It is customary for the bride and her father to ride to the ceremony site together on the wedding day. You may also include some or all members of your wedding party. Normally a procession to the church begins with the bride's mother and several of the bride's attendants in the first vehicle. If desired, you can provide a second vehicle for the rest of the attendants. The bride and her father will go in the last vehicle. This vehicle will also be used to transport the bride and groom to the reception site after the ceremony.

Options: There are various options for transportation. The most popular choice is a limousine since it is big and open and can accommodate several people as well as your bridal gown. You can also choose to rent a car that symbolizes your personality as a couple.

There are luxury cars such as Mercedes Benz, sports cars such as a Ferraris, and vintage vehicles such as 1950's Thunderbirds or 1930's Cadillacs. If your ceremony and reception sites are fairly close together, and if weather permits, you might want to consider a more romantic form of transportation, such as a horse-drawn carriage.

Things to Consider: In some areas of the country, limousines are booked on a 3-hour minimum basis.

Beware: Make sure the company you choose is fully licensed and has liability insurance. Do not pay the full amount until after the event.

Tips To Save Money: Consider hiring only one large limousine. This limousine can transport you, your parents and your attendants to the ceremony, and then you and your new husband from the ceremony to the reception.

Price Range: $35 - $100/hour

QUESTIONS TO ASK TRANSPORTATION

- What is the name of the transportation service?

- What is the address of the transportation service?

- What is the name & phone number of my contact person?

- How many years have you been in business?

- How many vehicles do you have available?

- Can you provide a back-up vehicle in case of an emergency?

- What types of vehicles are available?

- What are the various sizes of vehicles available?

- How old are the vehicles?

- How many drivers are available?

- Can you show me photos of your drivers?

- How do your drivers dress for weddings?

- Do you have liability insurance?

- What is the minimum amount of time required to rent a vehicle?

- What is the cost per hour? Two hours? Three hours?

- How much gratuity is expected?

- What is your payment/cancellation policy?

RENTAL ITEMS

BRIDAL SLIP RENTAL

The bridal slip is an undergarment which gives the bridal gown its proper shape.

Things To Consider: Be sure to wear the same slip you'll be wearing on your wedding day during your fittings. Many bridal salons rent slips. Schedule an appointment to pick up your slip one week before the wedding; otherwise, you run the risk of not having one available on your wedding day. If rented, the slip will have to be returned shortly after the wedding. Arrange for someone to do this for you within the allotted time.

Tips To Save Money: Rent a slip rather than purchasing one; chances are you will never use it again.

Price Range: $15 - $45

CEREMONY ACCESSORIES

Ceremony rental accessories are additional items needed for the ceremony but not included in the ceremony site fee.

Options: Ceremony rental accessories may include the following items:

Aisle Runner: A thin rug made of plastic, paper or cloth extending the length of the aisle. It is rolled out after the mothers are seated, just prior to the processional. Plastic or paper doesn't work well on grass; but if you must use one of these types of runners, make sure the grass is clipped short.

Kneeling Cushion: A small cushion or pillow placed in front of the altar where the bride and groom kneel for their wedding blessing.

Arch (Christian):   A white lattice or brass arch where the bride and groom exchange their vows, often decorated with flowers and greenery.

Chuppah (Jewish):   A canopy under which a Jewish ceremony is performed, symbolizing . cohabitation and consummation.

You may also need to consider renting audio equipment, aisle stanchions, candelabra, candles, candlelighters, chairs, heaters, a gift table, a guest book stand, and a canopy.

Things To Consider: If you plan to rent any accessories for your ceremony, make sure the rental supplier has been in business for a reasonable period of time and has a good reputation. Reserve the items you need well in advance. Find out the company's payment, reservation and cancellation policies.

Some companies allow you to reserve emergency items such as heaters or canopies without having to pay for them unless needed, in which case you would need to call the rental company a day or two in advance to request the items. If someone else requests the items you have reserved, the company should give you the right of first refusal.

Tips To Save Money: When considering a ceremony outside of a church, figure the cost of rental items. Negotiate a package deal, if possible, by renting items for both the ceremony and the reception from the same supplier. Consider renting these items from your florist so you only have to pay one delivery fee.

Price Range: $100 - $400

*T*ENT / CANOPY

A large tent or canopy may be required for receptions held outdoors to protect you and your guests from the sun or rain. Usually rented through party rental suppliers, tents and canopies can be expensive due to the labor involved in delivery and set-up.

Options: Tents and canopies come in different sizes and colors. Depending on the shape of your reception area, you may need to rent several smaller canopies rather than one large one. Contact several party rental suppliers to discuss the options.

Things To Consider: Consider this cost when making a decision between an outdoor and an indoor reception. In cooler weather, heaters may also be necessary.

Tips To Save Money: Shop early and compare prices with several party rental suppliers.

Price Range: $300 - $3,000

*D*ANCE FLOOR

A dance floor will be provided by most hotels and clubs. However, if your reception site does not have a dance floor, you may need to rent one through your caterer or a party rental supplier.

Things To Consider: When comparing prices of dance floors, include the delivery and set-up fees.

Price Range: $100 - $300

*T*ABLES / CHAIRS

You will have to provide tables and chairs for your guests if your reception site or caterer doesn't provide them as part of their package. For a full meal, you will have to provide tables and seating for all guests. For a cocktail reception, you only need to provide tables and chairs for approximately 30 to 50 percent of your guests. Ask your caterer or reception site manager for advice.

Options: There are various types of tables and chairs to choose from. The most common chairs for wedding receptions are white wooden or plastic chairs. The most common tables for receptions are round tables that seat 8 guests. The most common head table arrangement is several rectangular tables placed end-to-end to seat your entire wedding party on one side, facing your guests. Contact various party rental suppliers to find out what types of chairs and tables they carry as well as their price ranges.

Things To Consider: When comparing prices of renting tables and chairs, include the cost of delivery and set-up.

Tips To Save Money: Attempt to negotiate free delivery and set-up with party rental suppliers in exchange for giving them your business.

Price Range: $3 - $8/person

LINEN / TABLEWARE

You will also need to provide linens and tableware for your reception if your reception site or caterer doesn't provide them as part of their package.

Options: For a sit-down reception where the meal is served by waiters and waitresses, tables are usually set with a cloth (usually white, but may be color coordinated with the wedding), a centerpiece, and complete place settings. At a less formal buffet reception where guests serve themselves, tables are covered with a cloth but place settings are not mandatory. The necessary plates and silverware may be located at the buffet table, next to the food.

Things To Consider: Linens and tableware depend on the formality of your reception. When comparing prices of linens and tableware, include the cost of delivery and set-up.

Price Range: $3 -$20/person

HEATERS

You may need to rent heaters if your reception will be held outdoors and if the temperature may drop below sixty-five degrees.

Options: There are electric and gas heaters, both of which come in different sizes. Gas heaters are more popular since they do not have unsightly and unsafe electric cords.

Price Range: $25 - $50

LANTERNS

Lanterns are often used at evening receptions.

Options: Many choices are available, from fire lanterns to electric ones.

Things To Consider: Consider the formality of the reception and choose the proper lighting to complement your decorations.

Price Range: $6 - $40/lamp

OTHER RENTAL ITEMS (TRASH CANS, GIFT TABLE, ETC.)

If your reception site or caterer doesn't provide them, you will need to purchase, rent or borrow other miscellaneous items for your reception, such as trash cans, a gift table, trash bags, and so on.

QUESTIONS TO ASK RENTAL SUPPLIER

- What is the name of the party rental supplier?

- What is the address of the party rental supplier?

- What is the name & phone number of my contact person?

- How many years have you been in business?

- What are your hours of operation?

- Do you have liability insurance?

- What is the cost per item needed?

- What is the cost of pickup and delivery?

- What is the cost of setting up the items rented?

- When would the items be delivered?

- When would the items be picked up after the event

- What is your payment policy?

- What is your cancellation policy?

$\mathscr{G}$IFTS

$\mathscr{B}$RIDE'S GIFT

The bride's gift is traditionally given by the groom to the bride. It is typically a personal gift such as a piece of jewelry.

Options: A string of pearls, a watch, pearl earrings, or a gold chain with a heart-shaped charm holding photos of the two of you.

Things To Consider: This gift is not necessary and should be given only if budget allows.

Tips To Save Money: Consider omitting this gift. A pretty card from the groom proclaiming his eternal love for the bride is a very special yet inexpensive gift.

Price Range: $50 - $500

$\mathscr{G}$ROOM'S GIFT

The groom's gift is traditionally given by the bride to the groom.

Options: A nice watch, an elegant pen set, or a dramatic photo of the bride framed in silver or crystal.

Things To Consider: This gift is not necessary and should be given only if budget allows.

Tips To Save Money: Consider omitting this gift. A pretty card from the bride proclaiming her eternal love for the groom is a very special yet inexpensive gift.

Price Range: $50 - $5

Bridesmaids' Gifts

Bridesmaids' gifts are given by the bride to her bridesmaids and maid of honor as a permanent keepsake of the wedding. The best gifts are those that can be used both during and after the wedding, such as jewelry.

Options: For bridesmaids' gifts, consider items of jewelry that can be worn during the wedding to give your wedding party a coordinated and elegant look. Choose the collection that most fits your style, then select the type and color of stone to match the color of your flowers and/or bridesmaids dresses. We believe this is the perfect bridesmaids' gift!

Things To Consider: Bridesmaids' gifts are usually presented at the bridesmaids' luncheon, if there is one, or at the rehearsal dinner. The gift to the maid of honor may be similar to the bridesmaids' gifts but should be a bit more expensive.

Tips To Save Money: Ask your photographer to take, at no extra charge, professional portraits of each bridesmaid and her escort for use as bridesmaids' gifts. Select a beautiful background that will remind your bridesmaids of the occasion, such as your cake table. Put the photo in a pretty frame. This makes a very special yet inexpensive gift for your attendants.

Price Range: $25 - $100/gift

Ushers' Gifts

Ushers' gifts are given by the groom to his ushers as a permanent keepsake of the wedding.

Options: For ushers' gifts, consider fancy pen sets, wallets, leather belts, silver frames, watches, and desk clocks.

Things To Consider: The groom should deliver his gifts to the ushers at the bachelor party or at the rehearsal dinner. The gift to the best man may be similar to the ushers' gifts but should be a bit more expensive.

Tips To Save Money: Negotiate with your photographer to take, at no extra charge, professional portraits of each usher and his escort for use as ushers' gifts. Select a beautiful background that will remind your ushers of the occasion, such as your cake table.

Price Range: $25 - $100/gift

YOUR BRIDAL SUPERSTORE

proudly presents

THE

Hortense B. Hewitt Co.

COLLECTION

The Hortense B. Hewitt Collection offers low prices, beautiful selection and great quality. This, coupled with the unparalleled customer service of Your Bridal Superstore, makes it easy and convenient to order all your wedding accessories and gifts from this beautiful collection.

*We also invite you to visit our on-line store at **www.YourBridalSuperstore.com**, featuring the most extensive collection of accessories, invitations, jewelry, gifts, favors and much more!*

YOUR BRIDAL
SUPERSTORE
...everything but the groom℠

www.YourBridalSuperstore.com

A Pearl Heart Candle.
#37300 ~ $32.95
Pearl Heart Tapers.
#37310 ~ $32.95

B Silver-Finish Unity
Candle Holder. 12½" long.
#23800 ~ $27.95

C Western Candle.
#37700 ~ $32.95
Western Tapers.
#37710 ~ $32.95

D Brass-Finish Unity
Candle Holder. 12½" long.
#23700 ~ $27.95

E Iridescent Pearl Candle.
#37400 ~ $32.95
Iridescent Pearl Tapers.
#37410 ~ $32.95

▼ **E, F**

A, B ▶

*Hand-carved candles add a
beautiful touch to the wedding ceremony.
Single 9" candle or pair of 11¾" tapers.*

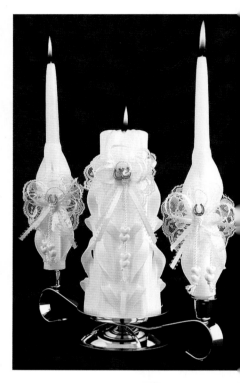

C, D ▶

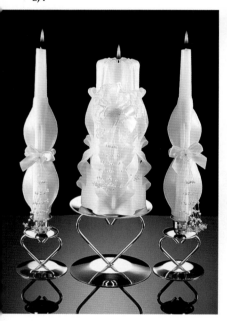

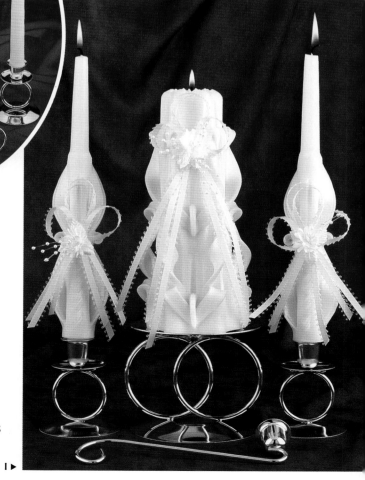

G, H ▶

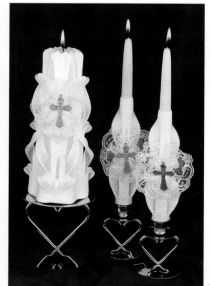

F Heart Candle Holder Set.
#38100 ~ $31.95

G Unity Candles. Available in white
only. Set of 3 candles. 8" tall.
#20901 ~ $26.95

H Brass-Finish Candle Holders.
Single holder has a single ring. 3¼"
tall. Large holder is enhanced by
double rings. 4" tall. Candle snuffer
is included. 7" long.
#23405 ~ $31.95

I Ivory Candle. – #37600 ~ $32.95
Ivory Tapers. – #37610 ~ $32.95

J Cross Candle. – #37200 ~ $32.95
Cross Tapers. – #37210 ~ $32.95

◀ **J**

I ▶

A White floating candles to establish an atmosphere of splendor. Perfectly sized glass bowls magnify the luster of the lighted candles. Glass bowl measures 4" with a 3" opening. Carnation candle.
Carnation candle – **#52010** ~ **$2.95**
Heart candle – **#52020** ~ **$2.95**
Glass bowl – **#52000** ~ **$6.95**

B White scalloped-edge bride and groom luminaries project familiar motifs of love and marriage. 6" x 11".
Package of 12.
#52500 ~ **$10.95**

C Tea Lights. Package of 6.
3/4" tall.
#52600 ~ **$2.50**

▼ B, C

D Wedding Cake Candle. 5" tall. 5" diameter.
#32700 ~ $14.95

▼ D

Candles are hand-poured in the U.S.A.

E ▶

F

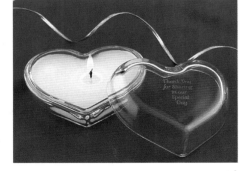

E White Lovebirds Candle. 4" tall. 8" long. – **#33800**
~ **$27.95**
F Fancy Organza Pearl Candle. 9" tall. – **#27901**
~ **$27.95**
G Lace-covered Candle. Trimmed with a satin rose and pearls. 9" tall.
#31100 ~ $27.95

▲ I

H Ivory Lace-covered Candle. Trimmed with a spiral of pearls and painted heart. 9" tall. – **#38203** ~ **$30.95**

I Heart candle enclosed in glass heart has two-fold use. Enjoy the candle, then make use of the glass, heart-shaped trinket box. An expression of thanks embellishes the lid. Gift boxed. 4" x 2". – **#53000** ~ **$12.95**

G ▶

◀ H

Hortense B. Hewitt Co.

A ▶

A A truly charming square pillow trimmed with a multi-loop chiffon bow. 9" x 9".
#80301 ~ **$29.50**

B Elegance in Brocade. A gathered band of satin accented with iridescent flowers and beads sets this pillow apart with its distinctive style. 10" x 10".
#83901 ~ **$31.50**

B ▶

Love...
Never Fails

C Lace-skirted candle gives extra magic to moonlight glow. 9" high.
#27901 ~ **$32.95**

D Satin heart pillow is decorated with swirl-patterned organza and the glimmer of faux pearls.
14" x 13". – **#27701** ~ **$52.95**

E Coordinating tie-ons with fancy beaded flower. – **#28101** ~ **$11.95**

F Pen base enhanced with organza and ribbon comes with sleek silver pen standing 8" high.
#28025 ~ **$25.50**

G Garter with swirled organza, pearl and ribbon embellishments.
#27801 ~ **$17.50**

▲ **C, D, E, F, G**

H Bride's Purse. Rich floral brocade is edged with pearls. 4½" tall. 5½" diameter.
White – **#82301** ~ **$37.95**
Ivory – **#82303** ~ **$37.95**

◀ **H**

Rich, Lacy Presentations

◄ **A, B**

Organza ribbon-striped trim is the crisp flourish making this set stand out as innovative and fresh.

A Garter – **#79901** ~ **$7.95**

B Heart Pillow. 10" x 10". **#79801** ~ **$23.95**

C ►

C Square ivory pillow with iridescent pearl trim has a tailored look with classical appeal. 13" x 13". **#82403** ~ **$24.95**

D Square Pillow. 13" x 13". **#80401** ~ **$22.95**

E Garter – **#80501** ~ **$7.50**

◄ **D, E**

▼ **F**

F Romantic white treasure chest ring holder has lacy, pearlized edgings. 4" x 4½" x 3". **#20800** ~ **$24.95**

G Opulent ivory ring-bearer treasure chest is encrusted with decorative faux jewel detailing. Provides magnificent presentation of the cherished ring. Measures 4" x 4½" x 3". **#20803** ~ **$24.95**

G ►

A Bouquet of Lovely Frills and Flourishes

◄ B, C

A►

A Contemporary garter of organza artistry has a lovely decorative pearl detail. – #27801 ~ $17.50

B Ribbon-striped garter exudes fun and flare as well as beauty. – #79901 ~ $7.95

C Wide 2" eyelet lace makes a garter to complement springtime innocence. – #86301 ~ $16.95

D Charming chiffon garter features strings of pearls and a dainty blue flower. – #72201 ~ $8.95

E Filigree, scalloped-edge heart motif lace garter. #84501 ~ $17.95

F "One to Keep and One to Throw" Garter Set. Our most popular deluxe garter for the bride to keep and a less expensive garter for the traditional throw. White Set – #85901 ~ $13.95 Blue Set – #85907~ $13.95

G Dangling Pearls Garter (shown on model's leg). Laceless simplicity with elegant pearl highlights. #27501 ~ $11.95

H A garter with the popular iridescent look. The detail of triple flower buds add appeal. #80501 ~ $7.50

I A delicate garter featuring frothy puffs of chiffon. – #87101 ~ $9.50

◄ D

◄ E

F ▼

G►

◄ H, I

▲ **A**

Garters Galore

A Dainty Schiffli
Garter.
White – #70601 ~ $4.70
Ivory – #70603 ~ $4.70
Blue – #70607 ~ $4.70
Blue/Ivory Lace
#70600 ~ $4.70

FULL FIGURE SIZE
White – #40601 ~ $5.70
Ivory – #40603 ~ $5.70
Blue – #40607 ~ $5.70

B Lots-of-Marabou
Garter.
White – #47501 ~ $8.50
Ivory – #47503 ~ $8.50
Blue – #47507 ~ $8.50

C Garter with Multi-loop
Bow and Frosted Flower.
White – #30101 ~ $8.50
Blue – #30107 ~ $8.50

D "One to Keep and One
to Throw" Garter Set.
Cupid charm on the
garter.
White – #40401 ~ $9.30
Ivory – #40403 ~ $9.30
Blue – #40400 ~ $9.30

E Schiffli Garter with
Single-Loop Bow.
White – #41801 ~ $5.95
Ivory – #41803 ~ $5.95
Blue – #41807 ~ $5.95

B ▶

▼ **C**

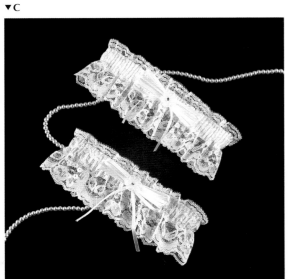

D ▶

E ▶

Tie-Ons: Additions of Frill & Style

Tie-ons are a clever way of using your creativity to add a personal touch to the wedding or party festivities. A small Velcro dot attaches the tie-on securely to knives & servers, toasting glasses, cake tops, favors, etc. Packaged in poly bags. Sold in pairs.

A Floral Spray. – #10401   ~ $13.95

B Fancy Beaded Flower. – #28101   ~ $11.95

C Pearl Hearts. – #19201   ~ $12.95

D White Western Hat & Rope. – #29101~ $11.95

E Bride & Groom Bow Set. – #14160   ~ $5.95

F Ivory Flowers and Pearls. – #19003   ~ $11.95

G Chiffon Bow. – #10501   ~ $13.95

H Ivory Western Hat with Rope. – #29103 ~ $11.95

I Ivory Fan with Cupid. – #29003 ~ $13.95

J Dangling Pearl Star. – #10301   ~ $14.95

K White Accent Bows. – #14179   ~ $3.50

L Silver Bows. – #14091   ~ $4.80

M Ivory Accent Bows. – #14157   ~ $3.50

N Gold Bows. – #14092   ~ $4.80

O Iridescent Rosebud. Can be used with either white or ivory weddings. – #28800   ~ $13.95

P White Flowers and Pearls. – #19001 ~ $11.95

Q Ivory Double Ring. – #10203   ~ $11.95

See picture to the left for sugesstions on how Tie-Ons can be used to decorate your accessories.

www.YourBridalSuperstore.com

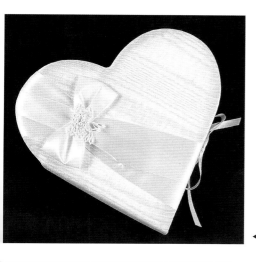

A Heart-Shaped Guest Book. Features white brocade and satin beaded bow. Pen included. Space to record 396 guests. 11" x 10".
#50601 ~ **$40.95**

◄ A

B ►

B Guest Book. All occasion book with a swivel mounted pen. Space for 912 guest entries. 6 3/4" x 10".
White/Gold Imprint – **#20123** ~ **$22.95**   Burgundy – **#40124** ~ **$22.95**
White/Silver Imprint – **#20122** ~ **$22.95**   Blue – **#40125** ~ **$22.95**

◄ **C, D**

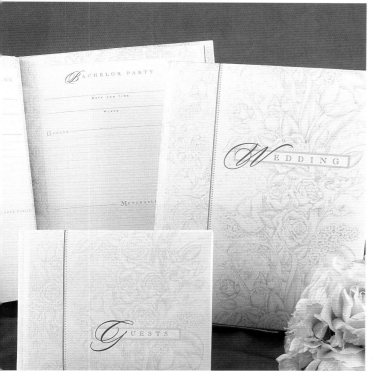

◄ **E, F**

C Tightbound Album. A registry for 300 guests and gifts is included. 9" x 11 1/4".
#30701 ~ **$30.50**

A soft, subtle hint of roses overlays the pearlized cover highlighted with delicate accents of gold. This album ensemble will allow the romance of the occasion to come alive again in years to come.

D Guest Book. Records the signatures of 1,000 guests. 7 1/2" x 5 1/2".
#30702 ~ **$14.95**

E. Our Wedding Memories. Pink flowers enhance this tightbound album. Space for noting 274 guest and 201 gifts. Sections to record all the important details of the wedding. 8" x 10".
#40100 ~ **$18.50**

F Our Wedding Memories. Pearl foil-stamped tightbound album. Space for recording 224 guests and 155 gifts. 8" x 10".
#40102 ~ **$18.50**

G Our Wedding Memories. White tightbound album with embossed wedding bell design. Space for noting 274 guests, 201 gifts. 8 7/8" x 11 1/4".
#58501 ~ **$30.50**

◄ **G**

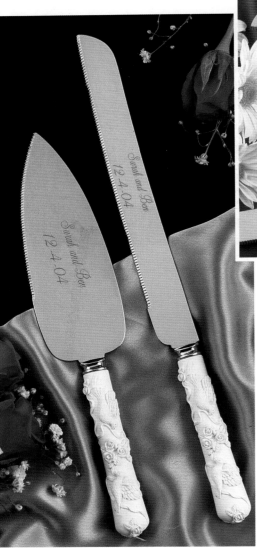

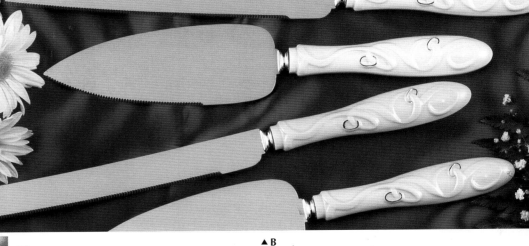

◀ **A**

A White Doves Knife and Server.
Set – #22900   ~ **$36.95**

B Porcelain Double Rings. Available
in white and ivory.
White Set – #45800   ~ **$41.95**
Ivory Set – #40800   ~ **$41.95**

C Gold-Handle Knife and Server.
Set – #40503   ~ **$33.95**

▲ **B**

*For an additional charge most knives and
servers can be personalized with names and date.*

*Date is indicated numerically:
month - day of month - year.*

C ▶

D Mother-of-Pearl Knife and Server.
Set – #20068   ~ **$16.95**

E Silver-plated Knife and Server
Set – #20014   ~ **$32.95**

▼ **D, E**

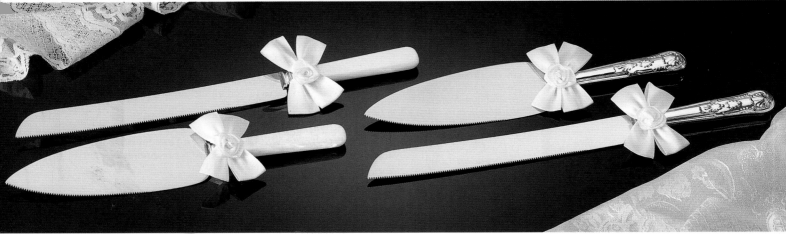

◄ A, B, C　　　　　　　　　　▲ D

A Flute and Mother-of-Pearl
Server Set.
#20074 ~ $27.95

B Champagne and Mother-of-Pearl
Server Set.
#20072 ~ $21.95

C Flute and Silver Server Set.
#20084 ~ $35.50

D All-Occasion Ensemble. Our
acrylic-handle server and clear
toasting flutes can be used for
any event. 6 oz.
#20050 ~ $23.50

E Silver Pistol-Handle Knife and
Server Set.
#23900 ~ $39.95

F Deluxe Sculpted Acrylic-Handle
Knife and Server Set.
#45100 ~ $36.95

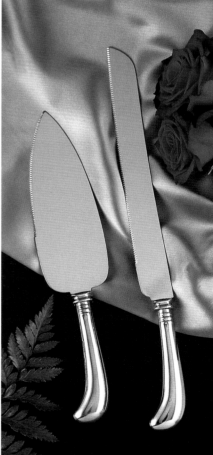

▼ F　　　　　　　　　　　E ▶

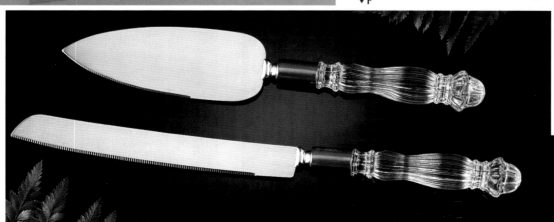

A Joined Silver-plated Heart Goblets. Celebrate unity! The sleek toasting set creates a oneness when placed together. Separately each boasts an appealing oblique silhouette. Not recommended for engraving. 7 7/8" tall. 4 oz.
#20670 ~ $39.95

B Toasting Flutes. Our popular hearts and candles design is featured on these clear flutes. 8" tall. 6 oz.
#29301 ~ $20.95

C Elegant Crystal Toasting Set. Frosted petals accent this 24% lead crystal set. 6" tall. 6 oz.
#33700 ~ $49.95

D Little Kids Flute Set. Engraved with "This Day I Will Marry My Friend" 8" tall. 6 oz.
#34600 ~ $20.95

E Toasting Glass Set. Toast your loved ones with our elegant stemware. Each 4 1/2" tall, 5 oz. glass is tastefully accented. Gift Boxed.
#20058 ~ $12.95

F Brass and Silver Flute Set. The unique simplicity of brass and silver. Not recommended for engraving. 8 3/4" tall. 5 oz.
#20700 ~ $32.95

Note: Bows are available with stemware pictured with bows. Otherwise bows are not included. See our large selection of tie-ons and bows on page 112.

B ▶

◀ A

▼ C

◀ D

▲ E

F ▶

Simply Elegant

◄ A

A Gold-Rimmed 24% Lead Crystal Flutes. 6 oz. 8" tall.
#35018 ~ **$46.95**

B Heart & Tux Set. Heart and flowers for the woman and
tux for the man. 8" tall. 6 oz.
Bride & Groom – **#22611** ~ **$22.50**
Maid of Honor & Best Man – **#22612** ~ **$22.50**
Bridesmaid & Groomsman – **#22641** ~ **$22.50**
Bridesmaid & Usher – **#22640** ~ **$22.50**

▼ B

Bride - Groom
Maid of Honor - Best Man
Bridesmaid - Groomsman
Bridesmaid - Usher

▲ C

C Toasting Flutes. Accented with frosted petals for a truly elegant look. 24%
lead crystal. 8 1/4" tall. 6 oz.
#33710 ~ **$47.95**

D Pewter Heart Flutes. Distinctive
pewter heart is bordered by gold
embellishments. 7 1/2" tall. 6 oz.
#23885 ~ **$38.95**

E Iridescent Flutes. Unique
manufacturing process creates the
luminous rainbow colors.
8 3/4" tall. 7 oz.
#35200 ~ **$53.95**

D ►

◄ E

*For an additional charge most glassware
can be personalized with names and date.
Date is indicated numerically:
month - day of month - year.*

A Panorama of Pens

A A large, luminous oval pearl forms the center of the sheer chiffon bow. Available with white pen.
#87301   ~ **$24.95**

B Fancy Beaded Flower Pen Base. A simple satin bow and silver pen complete the design.
#28025   ~ **$25.50**

C Gold and Silver Heart Pens.
Silver – **#58125**   ~ **$19.95**
Gold – **#58118**   ~ **$19.95**

A, B ▶

C ▶

◀ D

D White Plastic Heart and Pen. With Lace Heart Appliqué
#21001   ~ **$7.95**

◀ E

E Chiffon Ruffled Heart Pen Base.
#21075   ~ **$14.95**

F ▶

F Western Pen. Lucky horseshoe on a Lucite base is a complement to the Western-theme wedding. Available with white, gold or silver pens.
White – **#31901**   ~ **$13.95**
Gold – **#31918**   ~ **$13.95**
Silver – **#31925**   ~ **$13.95**

G Round Lead Crystal Base Pen Holder. Available with white, gold or silver pens.
White – **#31701**   ~ **$13.50**
Gold – **#31718**   ~ **$13.50**
Silver – **#31725**   ~ **$13.50**

G ▼

Organizing Memories with Care and Flare

◄ A, B

◄ C

Matching wedding album and guest book with satiny patterned covers, each has the handsome touch of a swatch of textured thick paper with embossed flower.

A Wedding Album is 9" x 11¼". There are places to chronicle highlights of courtship, family information, honeymoon and more plus pages for listings of gifts and 324 guest entries.
#21601   ~ $30.50

B Guest Book is 7½" x 5¾" and has space for recording 1848 signatures.
#21602   ~ $14.95

C Victorian Marriage Certificate. 11" x 14".
#39700   ~ $9.95

D ►

E, F ►

◄ G

D Wedding Memories Video Case.
#39100   ~ $6.95

E Moiré Finish Guest Book has gold foil lettering and decorative line border. The 8¾" x 6" book has room for 1,300 signatures.
#21702   ~ $15.50

F "Our Wedding" Photo Album (6¼" x 6½") will display one hundred 4" x 6" photos on plastic-covered pages.
#21700   ~ $5.95

G Gold-finish engravable hearts give a decorative label and historic finish to any keepsake book. Order plain or engraved. If engraving is wanted, make sure to specify first names and date. Adhesive back attaches the heart to the book. Sold separately. 2½" x 2½"
Gold plain – **#22318   ~ $2.50**
Gold engraved – **#22319   ~ $6.50**

Hortense B. Hewitt Co.

Enhancements for the Wedding Cake

Personalize your wedding cake with mix & match cake tops and figurines. Items are sold separately.

▼ A

A Bride and Groom Ivory with gold accents. 7 1/4" tall. **#32203** ~ $29.95

B Bride and Groom 8 1/2" tall. **#13301** ~ $29.95

◄ B

▼ C, D, E, F

C Black Groom. 5" tall. – **#12302** ~ **$6.70**

D Black Bride. 5" tall. – **#12202** ~ **$6.70**

E White Groom. 5" tall. – **#12301** ~ **$6.70**

F White Bride. 5" tall. – **#12201** ~ **$6.70**

Variations may occur in the hair and tuxedo colors.

▲ G, H, I

G Black Bride and Groom. 5 1/4" tall. – **#29932** ~ **$14.95**

H White Bride and Groom. 5 1/4" tall. – **#29931** ~ **$14.95**

I Porcelain Doves. 3 1/2" tall. **#14163** ~ **$6.70**

▲ J

J Bears in a Swing tops a cake with delightful fun. A great momento for remembering the celebration. 5" tall. **#13200** ~ **$10.95**

◄ K

▼ L, M

K Choose from frilly white or ivory versions of cake top with versatile mirror platform and blown glass arch. Full height is 8 3/4", base is 2 1/2" tall, circle diameter 4".
White – **#17301** ~ **$47.95**
Ivory – **#17303** ~ **$47.95**

L Pig Bride and Groom. 3 1/2" tall. – **#12400** ~ **$9.95**

M Cow Bride and Groom. 3 1/2" tall. – **#12450** ~ **$9.95**

The Purity of Glass

A Butterfly Cake Top.
8" tall.
#43901 ~ $59.95

B Glass Double Heart
and Doves Cake Top.
6" tall.
White – **#32001** ~ $33.95
Ivory – **#32003** ~ $33.95

▼B

C ▶

C Glass Heart with Gold Cross and
Double Rings Cake Top. 7" tall.
#44301 ~ $55.95

D Glass Heart with Gold-trimmed
Hummingbirds. 8" tall.
#44001 ~ $55.95

E Glass Heart with Bride and Groom.
8" tall.
#42001 ~ $55.95

▼E

A ▶

D ▶

Cake Tops Distinguished by Glass-Blown Artistry

*The specialized skills of glass-blowing artisans create
the defining characteristics for each of these cake tops.
Handcrafted in the U.S.A.*

Baskets for the Flower Girls

◄B

A ►

A A brocade-bowl, corded-handle basket provides an exquisite receptical for any type of flower arrangement. Basket height measurement with handle is 8 ½". Flowers shown in the basket are not included. – #84701   ~ $39.95

B An arrangement of ruffled chiffon defines the beauty of a flower girl basket made with a flat wicker base (9 ½" tall). Packaged in poly bag. #84801   ~ $28.50

C Battenburg Lace Flower Basket. 8 ½" tall. Packaged in poly bag.
White – #48901 ~$22.50
Ivory – #48903 ~$22.50

D Chiffon Trim Flower Basket. Satin lined. The basket is appropriate for more formal and sumptuous wedding ceremonies. Flowers not included. 8 ½" tall. #81801   ~$37.95

◄ C

D ►

E Flat Wicker and Lace Flower Basket. Designed to suit the coy manner of every adorable flower girl. Flowers are not included. 9 ½" tall. Packaged in poly bag. #80701   ~ $16.95

F Satin Flower Girl Basket. Flowers are not included. 8 ½" tall.
White – #86401   ~ $25.95
Ivory – #86403   ~ $25.95

E, F ►

A Teddy Bears. Personalize with embroidered name on the back of the Teddy Bear's T-shirt. Please specify name. Available in Century typestyle only.
Ringbearer Bear(blank) – #20141   ~$17.50
Ringbearer Bear (light blue embroidered name) – #20241   ~$27.50
Flowergirl Bear (blank) – #20140   ~$17.50
Flowergirl Bear (pink embroidered name) – #20240   ~$27.50

B Flower Girl and Ringbearer T-shirt and Caps. High quality materials are highlighted by boldly embroidered titles of honor. Youth sizes.
Flower Girl Cap (white, pink embroidered wording) – #10630   ~$11.95
Flower Girl Shirt (white, pink embroidered wording)
Size 6-8 – #10530   ~$16.95   Size 10-12 – #10531   ~$16.95
Ringbearer Cap (white, blue embroidered wording) – #10620   ~$11.95
Ringbearer Shirt (white, blue embroidered wording)
Size 6-8 – #10520   ~$16.95   Size 10-12 – #10521   ~$16.95

Novel Gift Ideas

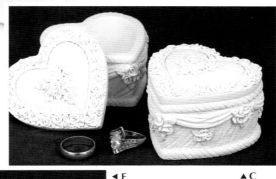

◄ E   ▲ C

◄ D

Glass-encased Candles. Vanilla-scented candle is inside a 5 1/2" tall glass apothecary jar. Gift boxed.

C Resin Heart Box. The softness of flounces, delicate detail and tiny blossoms are captured forever in long-lasting resin. The 2 1/2" x 2 1/2" lidded container is a wonderful trinket box. – #55300   ~$5.95

D A friendship verse marks this candle gift as just right for extending appreciation. – #55800   ~$16.50

E Horse-and-carriage gift is functional and decorative. The romantic resin creation has lidded carriage to be used as a container for jewelry or other tiny treasures. White finish has iridescent glow with pink and green flowers. Measures 5"long, 2"high. – #55410   ~$5.95

F Silver Imprinted Wishing Well. 12" x 26" x 13". Packaged in poly bag, kit form. – #23851   ~$27.95

White Textured Runner. Made of tear-resistant
stic. 36" x 100' long with pull cord.– #23733   ~$19.95

Fabric Aisle Runner. Delicate lace design made of durable
/on 36" x 100' long, with pull cord to help unroll.
hite – #29709   ~$44.95

◄ F

▼

H ►

A Colored Tissue Bells. The most vibrant colors on the market. Colored bells are available in five sizes: 5", 7", 9", 12" and 15". Available in: 01 white, 02 black, 03 ivory, 04 red, 06 pink, 07 light blue, 08 emerald green, 09 lavender, 10 burgundy, 13 peach, 16 royal blue, 23 teal, 27 hot pink, 28 coral, 33 purple, 35 dusty rose, 37 fuchsia, 40 hunter green, 47 navy.

5" Bells -	#21388	~$1.20
7" Bells -	#21188	~$1.60
9" Bells -	#21488	~$1.99
12" Bells -	#21288	~$2.90
15" Bells -	#21588	~$3.95

B Newlyweds On Board Sign 5"x 5" #23843 ~$2.99

C Crepe Paper Streamers. More vibrant colors. Our big roll crepe paper streamers are available in those hard-to-find colors. 2" x 500'. 01 white, 02 black, 03 ivory, 04 red, 06 pink, 07 light blue, 08 emerald green, 09 lavender, 10 burgundy, 11 mauve, 13 peach, 16 royal blue, 23 teal, 33 purple, 35 dusty rose, 37 fuchsia, 40 hunter green. #20788 ~$4.50

D Pompoms. Decorate the honeymoon car or use in a number of other ideas.
Available in: 01 white, 02 black, 03 ivory, 04 red, 06 pink, 08 green, 09 lavender, 10 burgundy, 13 peach, 16 royal blue, 17 yellow, 23 teal, 33 purple, 35 dusty rose, 37 fuchsia, 40 hunter green, 42 red & white, 47 navy.
Package of 25. - #22788 ~$3.90
Also available in iridescent - #22724 ~$9.50

E Double-Heart Just-Married Sign. This sign is for the front or back of the car. It holds 35 pompoms and attaches with wire to the car. Available with black printing only. Solid white on opposite side. Pompoms not included. 31" x 17".
#20100 ~$1.90

F Just-Married Single-Heart Sign. Black imprint. Solid white on opposite side. Pompoms not included. 24" x 24". #20101 ~$1.90

G Metallic Pompoms. 02 black, 04 red, 06 pink, 08 emerald, 10 burgundy, 16 royal blue, 18 gold, 23 teal, 25 silver, 27 hot pink, 33 purple, 37 fuchsia, 40 hunter green. #42788 ~$8.95

When placing your order, please give item number, color name and color number.

YOUR BRIDAL SUPERSTORE

proudly presents

THE

Kerenza

COLLECTION™

*It is with great pleasure that we introduce the luxury and elegance of The Kerenza Collection,
the newest and most sophisticated line of bridal accessories and unique gifts.*

These items will radiate romance and enhance your wedding day.

They will surely become heirlooms for generations to come.

We also invite you to visit our on-line store at **www.YourBridalSuperstore.com**, *featuring the most
extensive collection of accessories, invitations, jewelry, gifts, favors and much more!*

YOUR BRIDAL
SUPERSTORE

...everything but the groom℠

www.YourBridalSuperstore.com

Pillows

SILVER ACCENTS ▶
A whisper of silver tulle.

10601 ~ $47.95
Silver Ring Pillow – White satin 8"
square pillow with silver tulle, chiffon
bow and frosted heart

10701 ~ $17.95
Garter – White satin with silver tulle,
chiffon bow and frosted heart

20550 ~ $59.95
Silver-plated Stemmed Flutes, stand
9¾" tall, hold 6½ ounces

32825 ~ $99.95
Silver-plated Serving Set – 11" server,
13½" knife

◀ PRINCESS PILLOW
Regal and romantic pearls.

10801 ~ $49.95
Princess Pillow – White satin
6" x 4" ring pillow with pearl
trim and chiffon bow sits atop
12½" square satin pillow

SATIN SHIMMER ▶
An opulent pattern.

10901 ~ $33.95
White Jacquard Pillow –
7" x 4" white satin ring
pillow with chiffon bow

PEARL SET ▶
Elegance from every angle.

14001 ~ $47.95
Heart-Shaped Satin Ring
Pillow – White 9" heart-
shaped satin pillow with
4" chiffon pearl edge and
chiffon bow

14101 ~ $21.95
Garter – White chiffon
with pearl edge and
white chiffon bow

PEARL PILLOW ▲
Surrounded with beauty.

13001 ~ $47.95
Rectangle Pillow – 7" x 4"
white satin pillow with 4"
chiffon pearl edge accented
with chiffon pearl flower

SHIMMERING WHITE COLLECTION

A hint of white shimmer.

11701 ~ $43.95
White Ring Pillow – White satin 8"
square pillow with white chiffon bow

11801 ~ $13.95
White Chiffon Garter

11901 ~ $9.95
White Chiffon Flower Girl Garter

12101 ~ $53.95
White Flower Girl Basket – 8" tall
with white chiffon trim (flowers not included)

32801 ~ $31.95
Unity Candle – 9" white candle with
white chiffon bow

32901 ~ $21.95
Set of Tapers – 12" white tapers with white
satin and chiffon accent bows with pearls

21800 ~ $97.95
Frosted Stem Crystal Flutes – Crystal flutes
with etched, frosted stems stand 9" tall and
hold 6 ounces

12001 ~ $15.95
White Accent Bow Set – White chiffon and
satin bows with pearls

32825 ~ $99.95
Silver-plated serving set with handsomely
sculpted handles, 11" server, 13½" knife

Kerenza – page 127

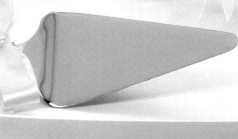

PILLOWS
CANDLES
KNIFE
GLASSES
GARTERS
BASKETS
BOWS

*Pillows, Baskets, Garters & Bows
are also available in:*

Lilac Mist   *Petal Pink*

Ice Blue   *Ecru*

PILLOWS
CANDLES
GARTERS

IRIDESCENT LACE ▲
Subtle sparkle.

35901   ~ $41.95
Iridescent Lace Pillow – White 8"
square ring pillow with iridescent
lace overlay, accented with tassels,
cord and pearl appliqué

PURE WHITE ▲
Satin Glistens.

14301   ~ $57.95
White Jacquard Pillow – White 8" square
satin ring pillow with tassels and cord,
accented with white satin bow and faux pearl

14401   ~ $17.95
Garter – White satin with chiffon bow and
faux pearl

33001   ~ $35.95
Unity Candle – White 9" candle with satin
and chiffon bow and faux pearl in center

33101   ~ $27.95
Set of Tapers – White 12" taper candles
with satin and chiffon bows and faux
pearl in center

14201   ~ $17.95
Accent Bow Set – White satin and chiffon
bows with faux pearl in center

39325   ~ $15.95
Silver-tone Taper Stands – 3¼" tall taper
stands hold standard taper candles

BROCADE ACCENTS ▲
The beauty of brocade.

34301   ~ $27.95
White Brocade Pillow – White 8½" square
brocade pillow with cord and satin bow accent

34303   ~ $27.95
Ecru Brocade Pillow – Ecru 8½" square
brocade pillow with cord and satin bow accent

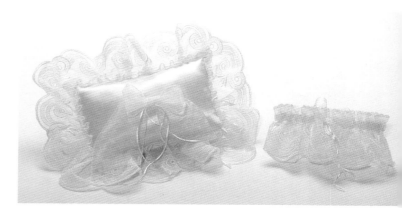

SWIRLED ORGANZA ▲
A swirl of romance.

16701   ~ $43.95
White Swirl Pillow – 9" x 5" white satin
rectangle ring pillow featuring 2" swirl-
patterned organza and white chiffon bow

16801   ~ $21.95
Garter – White swirl-patterned organza
with white chiffon bow

SATIN FLOWER COLLECTION

A floral fantasy.

16101 ~ $43.95
Satin Flower Pillow – White satin 8" pillow with 1½" chiffon trim, satin and pearl flower and strand of pearls

16201 ~ $21.95
Garter – White chiffon with satin and pearl flower

16301 ~ $69.95
Flower Girl Basket – 8" tall with white satin flower accent and pearl trim (flowers not included)

16501 ~ $43.95
Bridal Purse – White satin with satin and pearl flower accent, trimmed with white pearl cord, 8¾" x 9¾"

10201 ~ $39.95
Unity Candle – 9" white candle with satin and pearl flower

18210 ~ $27.95
Set of Tapers – 12" white tapers with white chiffon accent bows with pearl

33791 ~ $119.95
Crystal Flute Set – Elegant flutes with frosted glass and accented with white satin and pearl flower stand 10¾" tall and hold 6½ ounces each

16401 ~ $27.95
Accent Bow Set – White satin and pearl flowers

PILLOWS
CANDLES
GLASSES
GARTER
BASKET
BOWS

PILLOWS
CANDLES
KNIFE
GLASSES
GARTER
BASKET

GLIMMERING SATIN COLLECTION
White satin & the impeccable pearl.

16901   ~ $37.95
White Ring Pillow – White satin 8" square pillow with white chiffon bow and faux pearl

14401   ~ $17.95
Garter – White satin and chiffon bow with faux pearl

12101   ~ $53.95
White Flower Girl Basket – 8" tall with white chiffon trim (flowers not included)

17901   ~ $27.95
Bridal Purse – White satin 5" x 9" clutch purse trimmed with pearl accents and faux pearl

33001   ~ $35.95
Unity Candle – 9" white candle with satin and chiffon bow and faux pearl

33101   ~ $27.95
Set of Tapers – 12" white tapers with satin and chiffon bows with faux pearls

32326   ~ $73.95
Silver Beaded Serving Set – Features white satin and chiffon bows with faux pearls, 10" server, 12" knife

33792   ~ $109.95
Crystal Flute Set – Elegant flutes with frosted glass and accented with white satin and chiffon bows with faux pearls stand 10¾" tall and hold 6½ ounces eac

14201   ~ $17.95
Accent Bow Set – White satin and chiffon bows with faux pearls

All above items are also available in:

Ecru

PILLOWS
GARTERS
CANDLES

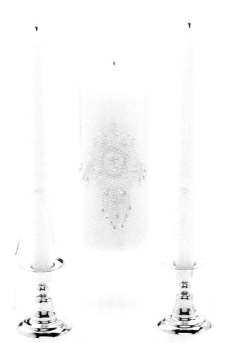

PEARL TRIM ▲

Pearl perfects it.

18001   ~ $43.95
Heart-Shaped Jacquard Ring Pillow –
White 10" heart-shaped jacquard pillow
with pearl and sequin appliqué

18101   ~ $17.95
Garter – White satin with pearl appliqué

18200   ~ $39.95
Unity Candle – 9" white candle with
pearl and sequin appliqué

18210   ~ $27.95
Tapers – 12" white tapers with white
chiffon accent bows with pearls

39325   ~ $15.95
Silver-tone Taper Stands – 3¼" tall
taper stands hold standard taper candles

SATIN HEART PILLOW ▲

Sweet white satin.

17101   ~ $67.95
Heart-Shaped Satin Ring Pillow – White
12" heart-shaped satin pillow with 2"
swirl-patterned organza and white satin
bow with faux pearl

16801   ~ $21.95
Garter – White swirl-patterned organza
with white chiffon bow

PASTEL SAGE ▶

A hint of sage.

19382   ~ $43.95
Sage Ring Pillow – White satin
8" square pillow with sage tulle
and faux pearl

19482   ~ $17.95
Garter – White satin with pastel
sage tulle and faux pearl

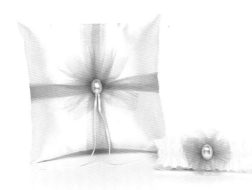

ICE BLUE ▼

A hint of ice blue.

19307   ~ $43.95
Blue Ring Pillow – White satin
8" square pillow with blue tulle
and faux pearl

19407   ~ $17.95
Garter – White satin with pastel
blue tulle and faux pearl

◀ PETAL PINK

A hint of petal pink.

19306   ~ $43.95
Pink Ring Pillow – White satin
8" square pillow with pink tulle
and faux pearl

19406   ~ $17.95
Garter – White satin with pastel
pink tulle and faux pearl

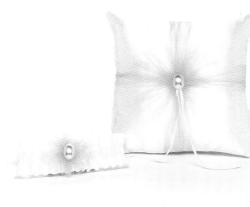

Pillow
Purse
Album
Guest book
Garter
Bows

ECRU SPLENDOR COLLECTION
Magnificent moiré

18703 ~ $49.95
Moiré Heart Pillow – Ecru moiré 13" heart-shaped pillow with chiffon ruffle and chiffon blossom and pearls accent

18803 ~ $13.95
Garter – Ecru chiffon with chiffon blossom and pearls

26603 ~ $35.95
Bridal Purse – Ecru satin 8¾" x 9½" purse with chiffon blossom and pearls accent and cord handle

57803 ~ $59.95
Ecru Moiré Wedding Album - Tied with ecru chiffon ribbon. Includes 52 pages for recording wedding memories, and registry for 240 guests and 224 gifts, 11¼" x 11¼"

57703 ~ $47.95
Ecru Moiré Guest Book – Tied with ecru chiffon ribbon. Holds signatures of 600 guests. 7¼" x 7¼"

18903 ~ $17.95
Accent Bow Set – Ecru chiffon blossoms with pearls

WHITE ROSEBUD SET ▲

The radiance of a rose.

19501 ~ $53.95
Lace Ring Pillow – White satin 8" square pillow with elegant lace edging, satin gather and white chiffon rose and pearls

19601 ~ $21.95
Garter – White lace with chiffon rose and pearls

19701 ~ $17.95
Accent Bow Set – White chiffon roses and pearls

32328 ~ $73.95
Silver Beaded Serving Set – Accented with white chiffon roses and pearls, 10" server, 12" knife

PETAL PILLOW ▶

A trail of petals.

23101 ~ $75.95
Rose Petal Pillow – 7" x 4" white satin pillow trimmed with 1½" white chiffon and delicate pink rose petals. Center accented with white chiffon bow.

LACE ACCENT ▶

A trace of delicate lace.

25801 ~ $19.95
Handkerchief – White with delicate lace trim

SOMETHING BLUE KEEPSAKE

A tradition of blue.

25701 ~ $7.95
Something Blue Keepsake Pin – Periwinkle chiffon and satin accented with pearls on a silver pin. Simply pin inside the hem of a wedding dress.

PETAL PILLOW ▲

A trail of petals.

23201 ~ $75.95
Hydrangea Petal Pillow – 7" x 4" white satin pillow trimmed with 1½" white chiffon and delicate lavender hydrangea petals. Center accented with chiffon bow.

SATIN ACCENTS

A trace of satin.

16601 ~ $31.95
Bridal Purse – Ecru satin purse with satin cord handle, 8¾" x 9¼"

16603 ~ $31.95
Bridal Purse – White satin purse with satin cord handle, 8¾" x 9¼"

SATIN ACCENTS

A trace of satin.

17903 ~ $27.95
Bridal Purse – Ecru satin clutch purse with pearl accents and faux pearl, 5" x 9"

17901 ~ $27.95
Bridal Purse – White satin clutch purse with pearl accents and faux pearl, 5" x 9"

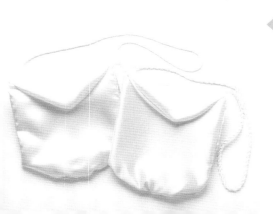

PILLOW
CANDLE
KNIFE
GLASSES
GARTER

ECRU AND GOLD ELEGANCE
Exquisitely rich.

25303 ~ $53.95
Ecru Jacquard Pillow – Ecru 9"
square satin pillow with elegant
cord edging and a tassel accent

25403 ~ $17.95
Ecru Garter – Ecru satin with
chiffon bow

35603 ~ $11.95
Love Candle – 2" x 2" square
ivory candle with "Love"
inscribed on all sides

32518 ~ $39.95
Gold Serving Set – Gold-plated
handles with stainless steel
blades, 10" server, 12" knife

31400 ~ $99.95
Gold Rim Toasting Flutes – 24k
gold accents at stem and rim,
stand 11" tall, hold 5½ ounces

SILVER-PLATED FLUTES ▲

Silver elegance.

20350 ~ $49.95
Traditional long-stemmed flutes
stand 9½" tall and hold 7¼ ounces

HEART-SHAPED GOBLET ▲

A toast from the heart.

20660 ~ $57.95

The unique two-piece silver-plated wedding goblet
stands 5¾" tall and each piece holds 5 ounces

SILVER STEM FLUTES ▲

Shimmering silver.

20550 ~ $59.95
Stunning long-stemmed flutes with silver-plated
stems stand 9¾" tall and hold 6½ ounces

SILVER AND GOLD FLUTES ▲

Gleaming silver, glimmering gold

20500 ~ $59.95
Silver-plated flutes featuring stems with gold
band accents are 9" tall and hold 7 ounces

All toasting glasses can be personalized for an additional charge. See order form for details.

◀ **CRYSTAL FLUTES**

The glamour of frosted glass.

33790 ~ $95.95
Elegant long-stemmed flutes
with frosted glass where
stem meets bowl are 10¾"
tall and hold 6½ ounces

◀ **FROSTED STEM
CRYSTAL FLUTES**

Crystal that is clearly unique.

21800 ~ $97.95
Stylish crystal flutes
featuring a unique frosted
ribbed design stand 9" tall
and hold 6 ounces

◀ **GOLD SWIRL FLUTES**

Inspire eloquence with gold.

31318 ~ $39.95
Gold swirls encircle the bowls of
classic, long-stemmed toasting
flutes that stand 10" tall and
hold 6¾ ounces

◀ **GOLD RIM GLASSES**

A new twist.

31518 ~ $55.95
Gold accentuates the rims
of these 9" tall toasting
glasses featuring stems of
entwined crystal. Each flute
holds 5 ounces

◀ **TALL CRYSTAL
FLUTES**

For sophisticated toasts.

21900 ~ $55.95
Chic crystal flutes with
circular accents between
stem and bowl stand 10¼"
tall and hold 5½ ounces

◀ **REMEMBRANCE
FLUTES**

Splendidly golden.

31400 ~ $99.95
Gorgeous crystal toasting
flutes have 24k gold
accents at the stem and rim.
The flutes stand 11" tall and
hold 5½ ounces each

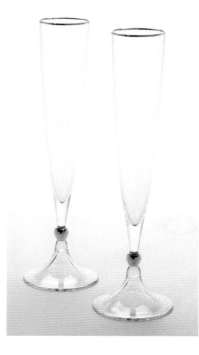

All toasting glasses can be personalized for an additional charge. See order form for details.

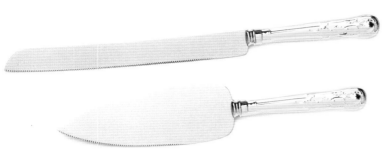

GOLD SERVING SET ▲
Scintillating gold.

32518 ~ $39.95
Gold-plated handles with stainless steel blades, 10" server, 12" knife

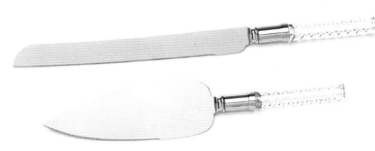

CRYSTAL-HANDLED SERVING SET ▲
Peerless in craft.

32400 ~ $63.95
Crystal-handled serving set with stainless steel blades, 10" server, 12" knife

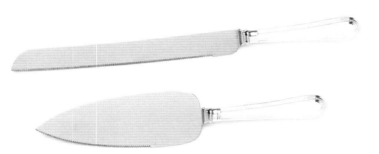

SILVER BEADED SERVING SET ▲
Lustrous silver.

32325 ~ $59.95
Elegant silver-plated handles are edged in fine beading, 10" server, 12" knife

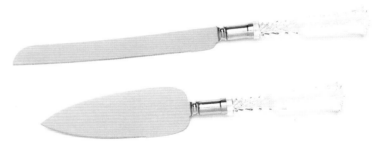

CRYSTAL SERVING SET ▲
Crystal at its best.

32500 ~ $91.95
Handles are made of 24% lead crystal, 10½" server, 12½" knife

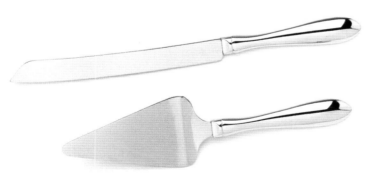

SILVER-PLATED SERVING SET ▲
Simply silver.

32825 ~ $99.95
Silver-plated with handsomely sculpted handles, 11" server, 13½" knife

SILVER & GOLD SERVING SET ▶
Silver & a touch of gold.

32600 ~ $37.95
Elegant silver-plated handles feature gold accents, 10½" server, 12½" knife

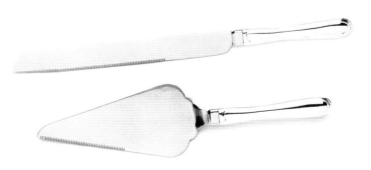

All Serving Sets can be personalized for an additional charge. See order form for details.

CAKE TOPS
CANDLES

◄ **ROMANTIC COUPLE CAKE TOP**

In light of romance.

90700 ~ $49.95
The 5" tall figurine is made from ecru resin and features veil of netting

▲ **PORCELAIN COUPLE CAKE TOP**

Passion in porcelain.

12703 ~ $33.95
The ecru glazed cake top stands 7½" tall and the base measures 3¾" x 4¾"

◄ **SCULPTED ROSE UNITY CANDLE**

A couple of roses.

35300 ~ $55.95
White unity candle with two long-stemmed roses sculpted on the front. 12½" tall, 3" diameter

CALLA LILY UNITY CANDLE ►

Shimmering lilies.

35400 ~ $51.95
White unity candle with sculpted iridescent calla lilies. 11" tall, 3" diameter

WHITE UNITY CANDLE ►

Luminous white.

33001 ~ $35.95
White 9" candle with satin and faux pearl bow accent

ECRU UNITY CANDLE ►

Luminous ecru.

17200 ~ $35.95
Ecru 9" candle with chiffon and faux pearl bow accent

◄ **LOVE CANDLE**

Light of love.

35603 ~ $11.95
2" x 2" square ivory candle with "Love" inscribed on all sides

RELIGIOUS UNITY CANDLE ►

A traditional flame.

35500 ~ $43.95
White candle features inscription: "And Two Become One" in silver. 10" tall, 3" diameter

GLASS CYLINDER AND FLOATING DAISY CANDLE ►

The glow of a daisy.

37010 ~ $17.95
3½" x 9" glass cylinder holds 2½" white and yellow daisy candle (included)

CANDLES
PEN HOLDERS
ALBUMS

SILVER FILIGREE CANDLE ▲ STAND SET
A radiant silver.

35925 ~ $11.95
Silver-tone Unity Candle Base – 2" pillar stand holds up to 3" diameter candle

39325 ~ $15.95
Silver-tone Taper Stands – 3¼" tall taper stands hold standard taper candles

Sculpted Rose Unity Candle (Item # 35300) sold separately on page 14. Pearl tapers (Item # 39500) sold on this page.

GOLD FILIGREE CANDLE ▲ STAND SET
A golden brilliance.

35918 ~ $11.95
Gold-tone Unity Candle Base – 2" pillar stand holds up to 3" diameter candle

39318 ~ $15.95
Gold-tone Taper Stands – 3¼" tall taper stands hold standard taper candles

Calla Lily Unity Candle sold separately on page 14. Pearl tapers (Item # 39500) sold on this page.

PEARLIZED UNITY CANDLE ▲ AND CANDLE STAND SET
A luminous pearl.

39400 ~ $23.95
Unity Candle – Pearlized unity candle sculpted with striped pattern. 9" tall, 3" diameter

39500 ~ $15.95
Set of Pearl Tapers – 12" pearlized tapers

35800 ~ $17.95
White Resin Unity Candle Base – 3" decorative pillar stand holds up to 3" diameter candle

35810 ~ $21.95
White Resin Taper Stands – 2" tall taper stands hold standard taper candles

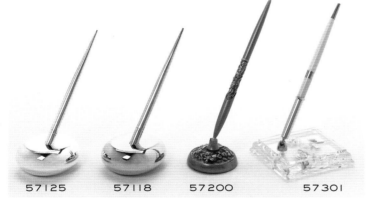

57125   57118   57200   57301

SILVER PLATED PEN
Sleek silver.

57125 ~ $35.95
Heavyweight rounded base and pen. Base measures 2¾" x 3" x 1¼". Base and pen together stand 5½" tall

GOLD PLATED PEN
Shiny gold.

57118 ~ $35.95
Heavyweight rounded base and pen. Base measures 2¾" x 3" x 1¼". Base and pen together stand 5½" tall

PEWTER PEN SET
Precious metal.

57200 ~ $35.95
Genuine pewter with sculpted cherubs. Base measures 2" x 2¼" x 1¼". Base and pen together stand 8½" tall

FLOWERED PEN SET
Elegant etching.

57301 ~ $25.95
Lucite base etched in flowers measures 3¼" x 3¾" x ¾". Base and white and gold-tone pen together stand 8" tall

WHITE AND ECRU SATIN ALBUMS
Surrounded with satin.

56101 WHITE ~ $51.95

56103 ECRU ~ $51.95
Wedding Albums – Wrapped in white or ecru satin with matching chiffon ribbon. Include 52 embossed pages for recording wedding memories, and registry for 240 guests and 224 gifts, 11¼" x 9"

56201 WHITE ~ $35.95

56203 ECRU ~ $35.95
Guest Books – Wrapped in white or ecru satin with matching chiffon ribbon. Hold signatures of 600 guests, 7½" x 5¾"

Albums
Thank You Notes

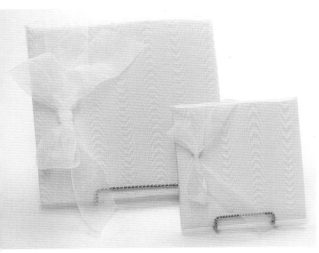

WHITE MOIRÉ SET ▲

Enwrapped in white moiré.

57801 ~ **$59.95**
White Moiré Wedding Album – Tied with matching chiffon ribbon. Includes 52 pages for recording wedding memories, and registry for 240 guests and 224 gifts, 11¼" x 11¼"

57701 ~ **$47.95**
White Moiré Guest Book – Tied with matching chiffon ribbon. Holds signatures of 600 guests, 7¼" x 7¼"

ECRU MOIRÉ SET ▲

Enwrapped in ecru moiré.

57803 ~ **$59.95**
Ecru Moiré Wedding Album – Tied with matching chiffon ribbon. Includes 52 pages for recording wedding memories, and registry for 240 guests and 224 gifts, 11¼" x 11¼"

57703 ~ **$47.95**
Ecru Moiré Guest Book – Tied with matching chiffon ribbon. Holds signatures of 600 guests, 7¼" x 7¼"

HANDMADE BOTANICAL ▲
PAPER ALBUMS

Naturally lovely.

57600 ~ **$47.95**
Botanical Paper Scrapbook – Includes 24 blank pages for recording wedding memories, 11¼" x 11¼"

57401 ~ **$59.95**
Botanical Paper Wedding Album – Includes 52 pages for recording wedding memories, and registry for 240 guests and 224 gifts, 11¼" x 11¼"

57402 ~ **$47.95**
Botanical Paper Guest Book – Holds signatures of 600 guests, 7¼" x 7¼"

HANDMADE PETAL ▲
PAPER ALBUMS

A whisper of flowers.

58200 ~ **$47.95**
Petal Paper Scrapbook – Includes 24 blank pages for recording wedding memories, 11¼" x 11¼"

57501 ~ **$59.95**
Petal Paper Wedding Album – Includes 52 pages for recording wedding memories, and registry for 240 guests and 224 gifts, 11¼" x 11¼"

57502 ~ **$47.95**
Petal Paper Guest Book – Holds signatures of 600 guests, 7¼" x 7¼"

One-of-a-kind, handcrafted paper is used in creating these albums, books and thank you notes, making each item truly exceptional.

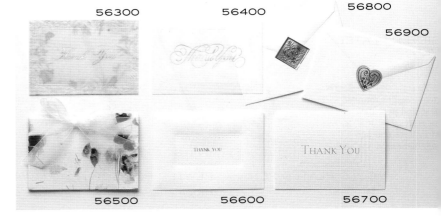

56300   56400   56800
56900
56500   56600   56700

THANK YOU NOTES & SEALS ▲

Beautifully sincere.

(Notes are 4⁷/₈" x 3¹/₂" folded and include envelopes)

56300 ~ **$11.95**
Translucent white paper with floral pattern inside, embossed border and gold foil "Thank You" (25 per box)

56400 ~ **$11.95**
Translucent white paper with embossed filigree border and gold foil "Thank You" (25 per box)

56500 ~ **$27.95**
Handmade petal paper wrap with translucent white insert and chiffon ribbon (25 per box)

56600 ~ **$9.95**
White paper with embossed border, inner frame of embossed dots and gold foil "Thank You" (25 per box)

56700 ~ **$9.95**
Crisp white triple panel with silver foil "Thank You" (25 per box)

56800 ~ **$7.95**
A flourish design is embossed on a gold square seal (25 per sheet)

56900 ~ **$7.95**
An intricate gold design is embossed on a silver heart seal (25 per sheet)

FAVOURS
CAKE BOXES
CANDY WRAP

72302   72300   72301   72306

HEART-SHAPED FAVOUR BOXES

72302   ~ $5.95
White 3½" x 4" favour boxes are prepunched with heart-shaped holes for threading the included 7" precut white chiffon ribbon (12 per package)

BOW FAVOUR BOXES

72300   ~ $3.95
White 2¾" x 1½" x 2" favour boxes with bow-shaped closures (12 per package)

HEART-HANDLED FAVOUR BOXES

72301   ~ $3.95
White 3½" x 2¼" x 1¼" favour boxes with heart-shaped handles (contents not included) (12 per package)

TREASURE CHEST FAVOUR BOXES

72306   ~ $5.95
White 2¾" x 2⅛" x 1¾" treasure chest-shaped boxes with moiré finish (contents not included) (12 per package)

FLORAL CAKE BOXES

72305   ~ $5.95
White 3½" x 3½" x 3" boxes with pastel floral pattern (contents not included) (12 per package)

SILVER & GOLD GLITTER FAVOUR BAGS ▲

72325 (Silver)   ~ $31.95

72318 (Gold)   ~ $31.95
The 4" x 5" favour bags feature white netting with silver glitter swirls or ecru netting with gold glitter. Ribbon is attached for tying closed (contents not included)   (12 per package)

WHITE & ECRU CONE FAVOUR BOXES ▲

72501 (White)   ~ $17.95

72503 (Ecru)   ~ $17.95
White or ecru 6¼" cone boxes with filigree pattern and flower-shaped handle. 12" matching chiffon ribbon included (12 per package)

◀ SILVER & GOLD FOIL FAVOUR BOXES

72304 (Silver)   ~ $7.95

72303 (Gold)   ~ $7.95
White Favour boxes with silver or gold foil border, 2½" x 2½" x 1", and pretied silver or gold cords (contents not included) (12 per package)

GOLD & SILVER ▶ CANDY BAR WRAPPERS

64718 (Gold)   ~ $7.95
64725 (Silver) ~ $7.95
The 5¼" x 5½" wrappers are preprinted with verse as shown in black ink. (chocolate bars not included) (12 per package)

◀ SHEER WRAP FAVOUR BOXES

72307   ~ $9.95
White 2¼" x 1¾" x 2" favour boxes wrapped in translucent overlay with filigree pattern and white chiffon ribbon. Overlay is prepunched with holes for inserting the ribbon (12 per package)

WHITE CANDY BAR ▶ WRAPPERS

64701   ~ $7.95
The 5¼" x 5½" wrappers are preprinted with "Thank You" verse as shown in black ink. (chocolate bars not included) (12 per package)

◀ SHEER HEART FAVOUR ENVELOPES

72308   ~ $5.95
Translucent white paper with pearlescent design. Envelope has heart-shaped closures and folds to 2⅞" square (contents not included) (12 per package)

ACCESSORIES GIFTS

WEDDING DAY EMERGENCY KIT ▶

72601 ~ $23.95
The 6½" x 5" white satin bag includes a sewing kit with mini scissors, needle and thread, aspirin, antiseptic pads, smelling salts and more

WEDDING CAMERA ▲

72600 ~ $15.95
Disposable wedding camera with flash has 27 exposures. Packaged in white box with pearlized flourish design. Includes matching table tent with instructions

◀ SILVER BASKET

72425 ~ $6.95
Sturdy silver basket measures 3" x 3" x 4" with 1¾" deep basket (contents not included)

SILVER & GOLD ▶ TUSSIE MUSSIES

72725 ~ $21.95
Silver Tussie Mussie is 6¾" long with a 1¾" wide opening (flowers not included)

72818 ~ $25.95
Gold Tussie Mussie is 6" long with a 2" wide opening (flowers not included)

FLOWER GIRL ▶ NECKLACE

58400 ~ $31.95
Italian sterling silver 18" necklace with ½" guardian angel charm

◀ RING BEARER AND FLOWER GIRL BOXES

58700 (Ring Bearer) ~ $21.95
58600 (Flower Girl) ~ $21.95
Clear Lucite box holds a mat to display 3½" x 5" photograph. "World's Greatest Ring Bearer" is printed in red and "World's Sweetest Flowergirl" is printed in pink. Boxes measure 7⅝" x 5⅝" and are 2" deep

CHILDREN'S MUGS ▶

59001 (Ring Bearer) ~ $11.95
59002 (Flower Girl) ~ $11.95
Children's mugs are engraved with "Ringbearer" or "Flowergirl." Each 2¾" mug holds 3½ ounces

SILVER PHOTO ▲ FRAME ALBUM

60700 ~ $27.95
A silver frame forms the cover of an album that holds 100 4" x 6" photographs (ideal for engraving)

BRIDESMAID ▲ PHOTO MAT

60900 ~ $9.95
Ecru 10" x 8" mat printed in taupe ink with "Bridesmaid / Best of Friends"

BRIDESMAID & MAID OF HONOR ▲ CARDS

61000 (BRIDESMAID) ~ $5.95
61100 (MAID OF HONOR) ~ $2.50
Appreciation cards feature a floral border and verse as shown. Bridesmaid cards are sold in packs of three; maid of honor cards are sold individually. Envelopes are included

◀ PICTURE FRAMES

63100 ~ $5.95
Solid brass picture frame measures 2" x 3"

63000 ~ $5.95
Silver-plated picture frame measures 2" x 3"

◀ CHERRY WOOD AND PEWTER BOX

58900 ~ $57.95
Wooden box is 7¼" x 5½" x 2". A pewter plaque is accented with flowers and "Friendship Comes From The Heart." (ideal for engraving)

◀ HEART COMPACT

61600 ~ $15.95
Heart-shaped silver- and gold-plated mirror compact (ideal for engraving)

SILVER ROSE ▶ KEEPSAKE BOX

61500 ~ $13.95
Silver-tone 3" x 3" x 1½" box is decorated with a sculpted rose (ideal for engraving)

◀ COMPACT CALCULATOR

62800 ~ $29.95
3½" x 2" silver-plated calculator features embossed stripes and oval with solar-powered calculator inside (cover of calculator ideal for engraving)

BRIDESMAID CANDLE ▶

60500 ~ $15.95
Clear glass box holds a vanilla-scented candle. The lid features "To my Bridesmaid...and special friend" preprinted in gold.

◀ MAKEUP BRUSHES

62900 ~ $41.95
Six-piece silver-plated cosmetic brush set with black satin carrying pouch

BRIDESMAID ▶ BOOKMARKS

62600 ~ $19.95
Bookmarks are accented with pastel flowers, "With Love & Thanks" and verse shown printed in gold ink and 7" precut white chiffon ribbon (package of six)

GIFTS

MEN'S JEWELRY BOX ▶

63300   ~ $27.95
Sturdy wooden box with four
velvet-lined compartments.
Gold-tone plate on lid is
included for engraving.

◀ **GROOMSMAN PEN
WITH CASE**

63200   ~ $29.95
Black and gold-tone pen
with solid cherry wood case.
Gold-tone plate is included
for engraving.

SHAVING KIT ▲

63500   ~ $17.95
Silver-plated shaving kit holds
razor in a 3" x 2½" mirrored
case (ideal for engraving)

◀ **BEST MAN AND
GROOMSMAN MUGS**

64400 (BEST MAN) ~ $45.95
64300 (GROOMSMAN) ~ $45.95
Wide-bowled, 20-ounce glass
mug with pewter plaque engraved
with "World's Greatest" in Latin

STAINLESS STEEL ▶
FLASK

63900   ~ $35.95
Stainless steel pocket flask
with gold-tone plate is 4½"
tall and holds 6 ounces
(ideal for engraving)

CIGAR TRIMMER ▲

63800   ~ $9.95
Silver-plated 4" cigar trimmer
(ideal for engraving)

CIGAR CASE ▲

63600   ~ $27.95
Silver-plated 7" cigar case
(ideal for engraving)

A selection of gifts (item numbers 63300, 63200, 63500, 63800, 63600, 63900) can be personalized for an additional charge. See order form for details.

YOUR BRIDAL SUPERSTORE

proudly presents

THE

Lillian Rose™

COLLECTION

The Lillian Rose Collection includes beautifully crafted wedding accessories, gifts and keepsakes to make your wedding day truly unforgettable. From traditional and classic styles to fun new products that celebrate a new beginning, Lillian Rose has it all.

*We also invite you to visit our on-line store at **www.YourBridalSuperstore.com**, featuring the most extensive collection of accessories, invitations, jewelry, gifts, favors and much more.*

YOUR BRIDAL SUPERSTORE

...everything but the groom℠

www.YourBridalSuperstore.com

FA125 Set of 24 - 3.5" Gold Bell & Boxes $46.00
✿ Bell sold separately on page 147

FA125 B Set of 144 - 3.5" Gold Bell & Boxes $226.95

FA700 B Set of 4 - 2.5" Bell Place Card Holders $20.45

FA125

WEDDING DAY

FA700 B

FR925

FA700 B

FA900 B

FR925 Set of Six 3.25" Frames $24.45

FA700 B Set of Four 2.5" Bell Place Card Holders $20.45

FA900 B Set of Six 2" Butterfly Place Card Holders $25.45

FA500 BX

FS542

FA900 V

FA500 BX Set of Six 3.5" Boxes of Potpourri $24.45

FS542 Box of 48 Kazoos $23.45

FA900 V Set of Six 2.75" Vase Place Card Holders $16.95

FA700 FR

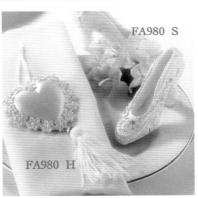
FA980 S

FA980 H

FA700 N

FA700 FR Set of Six 2" Silver Frames $14.45

FA980 H Set of Six 2.5" Heart Ornaments $20.45

FA980 S Set of Six 3.5" Shoes $24.45

FA700 N Set of Four 2.5" Silver Frame Napkin Holders $19.45

FA900 T

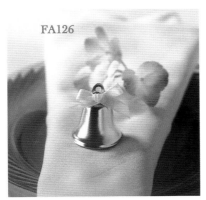
FA126

FA500 FB

FA900 T Set of Six 4" Topiary Favors $34.45

FA126 Box of 12 1.5" Bells W/Bows **Gold, Silver** $6.95

FA500 FB Set of Six 9" Bags of Potpourri $21.95

FA925 C Set of Six 3"
Chests $27.95

FA540 Set of 24 3" Place
Cards $7.45

FA925 T Set of Six 2.5"
Teacups $20.45

FA150 CH Set of 24
2.75" Churches $16.95

FA925 S Set of Six 4"
Slippers $27.95

FR920 SW Set of Six 3"
Satin White Frames
$16.45

FA925 CC Set of Six
2.5" Coaches $46.00

FA925 N Set of Six 2"
Napkin Rings $22.45

FR920 P Set of Six 3"
Painted Frames $16.95

FA925 SH Set of Six
2.75" Shells $34.95

FA542 Set of 24 Seed
Favor Packets $43.95

FA925 SW Set of Six
2.5" Swans $25.45

FA925 B Set of Six
3.5" Baskets $26.45

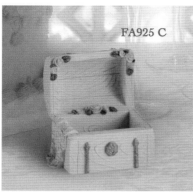

FA925 C

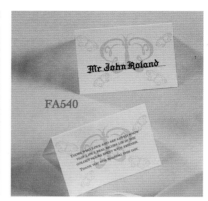

FA540

FA925 T

FA150 CH

FA925 S

FR920 SW

FA925 CC

FR920 P

FA925 N

FA925 SH

FA542

FA925 SW

FA925 B

C50 PP

C50 B

C50 GR

C50 C

C50 Box of Four 2" Floating Candles $7.45

B – Blue   **C** – Clear   **GR** – Green   **PP** – Purple   **Y** – Yellow

C50 Y

C60 G

C60 W

C60 Box of Six 2" Floating Candles $6.95
C60G   Gold Pearl
C60W   White Pearl

GB305
GB304

G310

GB300

SP100

PEN710

FB140

SP135

Candle follower & base is a 2 piece resin set. The candle is not included. Candle available on page 174.

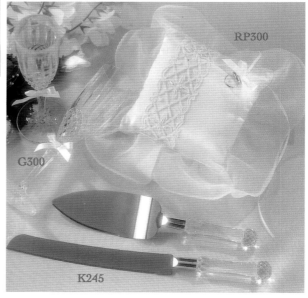

RP300

G300

K245

FB140 12" Basket **White, Ivory** $33.95

G310 10" Crystal Toasting Flutes $48.45

GB300 8.5" Guest Book $23.95

GB304 10" Heart Book $45.95

GB305 10" Heart Book W/Pen $47.45

PEN710 2.5" Crystal Base Pen $32.45

SP100 8.5" Easel $8.45

SP135 3" Candle Base & Follower $13.45

* All items this page are available in white only, unless otherwise specified.

RP300 5.5" Ring Pillow $25.45

G300 8" Crystal Toasting Glasses $36.95

K245 12.5" Knife & Server Set $19.45

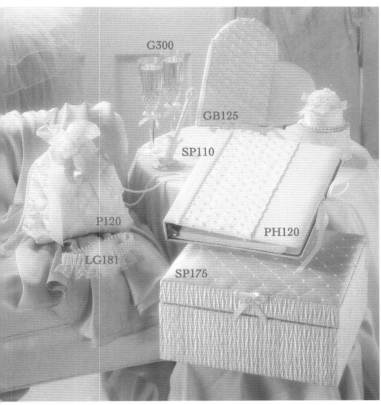

G300 8.5" Crystal Toasting Glasses $36.45

GB125 10" Heart Book W/Pen $45.95

SP110 6" Pen Set $11.45

P120 10" Bridal Purse $17.95

PH120 11.5" Photo Album $61.45

LG181 Tossing Garter **White, Ivory, Blue** $7.45

SP175 13" Covered Box $35.45

SP160 8" x 10" Frame $23.95

SP150 5" x 7" Frame $11.95

SP140 3.5" x 5" Frame $8.45

SP100 8.5" Easel $8.45

GB120 8.5" Guest Book $24.95

SP110 6" Pen Set $11.45

* All items this page are available in white only, unless otherwise specified.

SPC140 9" Pillar Candle $32.45

SPC100 10" Tapers $11.95

GB127 11.5" Fan Book W/Pen $52.95

SP130 4" Pillar Holder $16.95

SP120 Pair of 3.5" Taper Holders $14.45

SP170 6" Cake Box $17.95

RP120 5.5" Ring Pillow $27.45

C184 11" Carved Candle $25.45

GB180 8.5" Guest Book $23.95

SP120 Pair of 3.5" Taper Holders $14.45

SP130 4" Pillar Holder $16.95

A510 9.5" Easel **Brass, Pewter** $15.00

SP110 6" Pen Set $11.45

TIE180 Pair of 4" Tie-Ons $10.95

G180 8.5" Glasses $23.95

K185 12" Knife & Server Set $25.95

LG180 Keepsake Garter $11.95

LG181 Tossing Garter $7.45

RP180 5.5" Ring Pillow $28.95

* All items this page available in white only,
unless otherwise specified.

www.YourBridalSuperstore.com

GB185 10" Heart Book W/Pen $43.95

PH180 11.5" Photo Album $54.95

GB180 8.5" Guest Book $23.95

FB180 12" Flower Basket $34.45

PEN180 Plume Pen Set $25.45

* All items this page available in white only.

GB284 10" Heart Guest Book $50.95

GB285 10" Heart Book W/Pen $52.95

PH280 11.5" Photo Album $64.95

WJ280 11" Wedding Journal $43.95

PEN280 Plume Pen Set $25.45

GB287 11.5" Fan Book W/Pen $56.95

GB280 8.5" Guest Book $33.95

G281 8.5" Toasting Glasses $23.45

K286 12.5" Knife & Server Set $25.95

RP285 8" Ring Pillow $43.45

LG280 Keepsake Garter $18.00

LG153 Tossing Garter $9.45

LG282 Garter Set $26.45

* All items this page available in white and ivory.

LG280

LG288
Queen Size

P285

P280

FB280

LG281

LG283

LG280 Keepsake Garter $18.00

LG288 Queen Size Garter $18.95

P285 8" Bridal Purse $32.45

FB280 12" Basket $22.95

P280 15" Money Bag $41.45

LG281 Keepsake Garter $19.45

LG283 Keepsake Garter $32.45

* All items available in white and ivory unless
otherwise specified.

C280

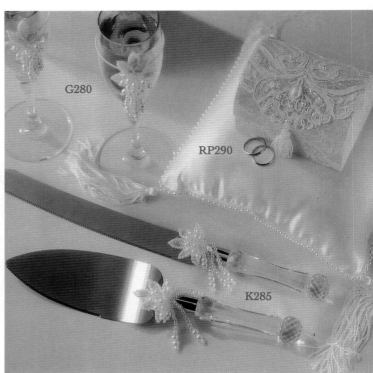

G280

RP290

K285

C287

Unity Set
WSET282

TIE280

C280 10" Tapers $28.95

G280 8.5" Glasses $33.95

RP290 8" Ring Pillow W/Box $41.45

K285 12.5" Knife & Server Set $33.95

WSET282 3 Piece Unity Candle Set **White** $42.95

C287 9" Pillar Candle $28.95

TIE280 4" Tie-Ons $10.95

✤ All items available in white and ivory unless otherwise specified.

A510 9.5" Easel **Brass, Pewter** $15.00

GB170 8.5" Guest Book $32.45

FB170 12" Flower Basket $27.95

RP175 5.5" Ring Pillow $44.45

PEN170 Plume Pen Set $28.95

LG170 Chiffon Pearl Keepsake Garter $14.45

* All items this page available in white and ivory,
unless otherwise specified.

A510 9.5" Easel **Brass, Pewter** $15.00

C171 10" Tealight Candle $29.95

GB170 8.5" Guest Book $32.45

PEN170 Plume Pen Set $28.95

G171 4.25" Champagne Glasses $29.95

GB175 10" Heart Book W/ Pen $45.45

FB170 12" Flower Basket $27.95

G170 8.5" Toasting Glasses $40.95

BX923 6.5" Trinket Box **Painted** $20.45

C176 9" Pillar Candle $25.95

PEN170 Plume Pen Set $28.95

LG153 Satin Tossing Garter $9.45

K175 12" Knife & Server Set $33.45

* All items this page available in white and ivory, unless otherwise specified.

PH130

GB134
GB135

GB130

PEN130

PH130 11.5" Photo Album $64.95	**PEN130** Plume Pen Set $24.00
GB134 10" Heart Guest Book $49.95	**GB130** 8.5" Guest Book $31.45
GB135 10" Heart Book W/Pen $51.95	* All items this page available in white only.

G130 8.5" Toasting Glasses $28.95

K135 12" Knife & Server Set $34.45

C136 9" Satin Rose Unity Candle $25.45

G650 8.5" Engraved Glasses $19.45

SP130 4" Pillar Holder $16.95

SP120 Pair of 3.5" Taper Holders $14.45

TIE130 4" Tie-Ons $9.95

RP131 11" Heart Ring Pillow $21.95

LG154 Keepsake Garter **White, Ivory** $10.95

P130 15" Money Bag $30.45

GB130 8.5" Guest Book $31.45

LG131 Keepsake Garter $13.95

FB135 9" Flower Basket $26.45

* All items this page available in white only, unless otherwise specified.

CA391 3" Porcelain Taper Holder $9.45

A390 5.25" Porcelain Bell $11.95

C456 9" Pillar Candle $27.95

TIE450 4" Tie-Ons As Shown $12.00

FR381 5" x 7" Frame $23.95

G450 8.5" Toasting Glasses As Shown $29.95

K455 12" Knife & Server Set As Shown $33.45

* All items available in white and ivory, unless otherwise specified.

RP450 11" Ring Pillow $24.45

LG453 Keepsake Garter $23.45

GB457 11.5" Guest Book W/Pen $57.45

GB456 11.5" Fan Guestbook - Not Shown $51.45

CT920 9.5" Gazebo Caketop $40.95

G920 8.5" Toasting Glasses $33.45

FR921 5" x 7" Frame W/Certificate $19.95

FR920 Set of Six 3" Frames $16.95

BX920 5" Trinket Box $23.95

BX921 2.5" Trinket Box $10.95

A920 4.5" Figurine $13.45

✻ All items this page available in white and painted only, unless otherwise specified.

CT920   9.5" Gazebo Caketop $40.95

GB452   10.5" Guest Book W/Pen   **White, Ivory** $33.45

GB454   10" Heart Book   **White, Ivory** $50.95

GB455   10" Heart Book W/Pen   **White, Ivory** $52.95

G920   8.5" Toasting Glasses $33.45

PEN920   3.5" Pen Set   **Painted** $20.45

K925   12" Knife & Server Set   **Painted** $24.45

° All items this page available in white and painted only, unless otherwise specified.

GB150 8.5" Guest Book $28.45

G150 8.5" Toasting Glasses $32.95

LG150 Keepsake Garter **White** $23.95

K155 12" Knife & Server Set $23.95

PEN150 Plume Pen Set $25.45

GB154 10" Heart Guest Book $44.95

GB155 10" Heart Book W/Pen $45.45

GB156 11.5" Fan Guest Book $39.45

GB157 11.5" Fan Book W/Pen $47.45

RP150 5.5" Ring Pillow $29.45

PEN150 Plume Pen Set $25.45

GB150 8.5" Guest Book $28.45

C154 11" Carved Candle $25.45

G150 8.5" Toasting Glasses $32.95

❀ All items this page available in white and ivory only, unless otherwise specified.

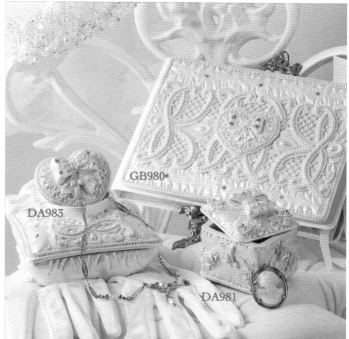

CA985 6.5" Votive Holder $13.45

CA986 5" Votive Holder $11.95

CA987 3" Votive Holder $10.95

DA984 13.5" Vanity Tray $21.00

DA986 4.5" Decanter $20.45

CT980 7.25" Caketop $27.95

G650 8.5" Engraved Glasses With the words "Bride" and "Groom" $19.45

TM981 8.25" Tussy Mussy $22.95

RP980 8" Ring Pillow $38.95

F980 3.5" Figurine $6.00

F981 4.25" Figurine $11.45

DA981 2.75" Trinket Box $9.95

DA983 4.5" Trinket Box $18.00

GB980 8.5" Guest Book $36.95

C910 12" Pillar Candle As Shown $24.00

C911 10" Pillar Candle As Shown $20.45

C912 6" Column Candle As Shown $18.00

C913 5.75" Column Candle As Shown $18.00

C914 5" Column Candle As Shown $12.00

* All items this page available in white only.

GB980 8.5" Guest Book $36.95

CT981 7.25" Caketop $32.45

G980 8.5" Toasting Flutes $36.95

PEN980 4" Pen Set $20.45

K985 12" Knife & Server Set $25.45

GB805 10" Heart Guest Book W/Pen $50.95
* inside pages and liner may change with reprinting.

P805 8" Bridal Purse $35.95

RP805 8" Ring Pillow $44.95

FB800 12" Flower Basket $21.00

LG805 Victorian Garter $11.45

* All items this page available in white only.

WJ800 11" Wedding Journal $43.95

PH800 11.5" Photo Album $64.95

GB800 8.5" Guest Book $33.95

C808 12" Pillar Candle $31.45
(Please Specify Verse **A** or **L**)

G800 10" Toasting Glasses $41.45

P800 15" Money Purse $37.95

CT800 10" Bell Caketop $36.95

* All items this page available in white and ivory.

Verses Available For **C808**
A: And The Two Shall Become As One
L: Love Is Patient, Love Is Kind. Love Does Not Delight In Evil, But Rejoices With The Truth. It Always Protects, Always Trusts, Always Hopes, Always Perseveres. Love Never Fails.

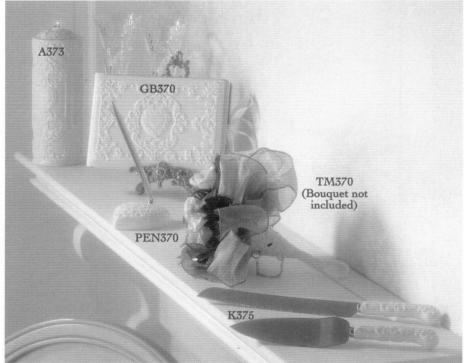

CT430 8" Caketop **White, Ivory** $34.45

RP430 8" Ring Pillow **White, Ivory** $32.45

FB430 12" Flower Basket **White, Ivory** $21.45

P430 15" Money Bag **White, Ivory** $29.45

G200 8.25" Toasting Glasses $25.45

SB260 12.25" Scrap Book **White** $31.45

GB260 8.5" Guest Book **White** $19.45

K215 12.5" Knife & Server Set $35.95

A373 9" Pillar Oil Lamp $33.45

GB370 8.5" Guest Book $36.95

PEN370 3.5" Pen Set $23.45

TM370 5.5" Tussy Mussy $15.95

K375 12.5" Knife & Server Set $31.45

✿ All items above available in white and ivory.

www.YourBridalSuperstore.com

F920 H

F900 A

G626
(glass not
included)

F920 A

F910 A

F920 4.75" Figurine (A) African-American, (C) Caucasian, (H) Hispanic $9.45

G626 10.5" Breaking Bag $27.95

F900 7" Figurine (A) African-American, (C) Caucasian $25.45

F910 4.75" Figurine (A) African-American, (C) Caucasian, (H) Hispanic $9.45

F920 4.75" Figurine (A) African-American, (C) Caucasian, (H) Hispanic $9.45

RP680 8" Ring Pillow $37.95

GB682 10.5" Guest Book W/Pen $28.95

C686 9" Pillar Candle $27.95

G680 8.75" Glasses $28.95

LG680 Keepsake Garter $16.45

* All items this page available in white only, unless otherwise specified.
* Ankhs may be silver according to availability.

FR750 5" x 7" Frame **Gold, Silver** $19.45

K385 12.5" Knife & Server Set **White, Ivory** $25.45

C701 10" Tealight Candle **25th, 50th** $27.95

PEN380 3.5" Pen Set **White, Ivory** $23.45

GB380 8.5" Guest Book **White, Ivory** $35.95

FA900 T Set of Six 4" Topiary Favors **White** $34.45

A505 8" Silver Tray $21.95

* White Porcelain has Silver Rings and Ivory has Gold Rings.

FR750 5" x 7" Frame **Gold, Silver** $19.45

PH380 4" x 6" Photo Album **White, Ivory** $24.45

PH500 4" X 6" Photo Album **Gold, Silver** $21.00

DA752 4.5" Candle Jar **Gold, Silver** $19.45

DA750 1.5" Clock **Gold, Silver** $25.45

FR380 3" x 5" Frame **White, Ivory** $16.95

A380 8.25" Porcelain Cross **White, Ivory** $10.95

C701 10" Tealight Candle **25th, 50th** $27.95

CT700 8" Caketop **25th, 50th** $36.95

CT705 10" Caketop **25th, 50th** $46.00

° White Porcelain has Silver Rings and Ivory has Gold Rings.

SPC140

SPC150

SPC120

SPC130

SPC110

SPC100

SPC100 10" Tapers $11.95

SPC110 4" Ball Candle $19.45

SPC120 5" Heart Candle $18.00

SPC130 5" Heart Cake Candle $23.95

SPC140 9" Pillar Candle $32.45

SPC150 6.5" Split Heart Candle $33.45

* All items this page available in white only.

www.YourBridalSuperstore.com

SPC150

C40   9" Plain Pillar Candle $18.95

SP135   3" Candle Base & Follower
White $13.45

FB140   12" Basket $33.95

C756   9" Pillar W/Verse $18.00
(Available In Verse **AC** or **IB**)
(See page 174 for these verses)

C456   9" Country Floral Pillar
Candle $27.95

FR381   5" x 7" Porcelain Frame
$23.95

TIE450   Pair of 4" Floral Tie-Ons
As Shown $12.00

C136   9" Satin Rose Pillar Candle
White $25.45

TIE130   Pair of 4" Satin Rose Tie-
Ons **White** $9.95

C826   9" Butterfly Pillar Candle
White $24.45

C820   10" Butterfly Tapers **White**
$14.45

C287   9" Sequin & Pearl Pillar
Candle $28.95

TIE280   Pair of 4" Sequin Pearl
Tie-Ons $10.95

❋ All items on this page available in
white and ivory, unless otherwise
specified

C606 9" Angel Pillar W/Verse $23.45
(Available In Verses **1, 4** or **6**, See Below)

C807 9" Pillar W/Verse $22.95
(Available In Verses **1, 4** or **6**, See Below)

C808 12" Lace Pillar W/Verse $31.45
(Available In Verse **A** or **L**, See Page 167 for these verses)

C136 9" Satin Rose Pillar Candle **White** $25.45

C178 12" Invitation Pillar $31.45

C756 9" Pillar W/Verse $18.00
(Available In Verse **AC** or **IB**)

C40 9" Plain Pillar Candle $18.95

C286 9" Invitation Pillar $26.45

Verses Available for **C756**:
AC: A Cord of Three Is Not Easily Broken. Faith. Hope. Love.
IB: Irish Marriage Blessing

* All items this page available in white and ivory, unless otherwise specified.

C801 10" Tealight Candle $27.95

C501 10" Invitation Tealight Candle $31.45

C191 10" Tealight Candle $27.95

C631 10" Tealight Candle $27.95

C171 10" Tealight Candle $29.95

C133 10" Double Wick W/Verse $24.95
(Please Specify Verse **1, 4** or **6**)

C803 10" Double Wick Candle $24.95

* All items this page available in white and ivory, unless otherwise specified.

Verses Available:
1 – Faith, Hope And Love Abide; But The Greatest Of These Is Love.   (1Corinthians 13;13)

4 – This Day I Will Marry My Friend, The One I Laugh With, Live For, Dream With, Love.

6 – Just As Two Flames Unite And Blend Into One, So Shall Our Lives Unite, And Blend To Ascend Higher.

TIE600

C604

C184

C284

C194

C634

C154

TIE600   3" Tie-Ons $13.45

C604   11" Carved Candle $24.45

C194   11" Carved Candle $22.95

C184   11" Carved Candle   **White** $25.45

C634   11" Carved Candle $24.00

C284   11" Carved Candle $27.45

C154   11" Carved Candle $25.45

www.YourBridalSuperstore.com

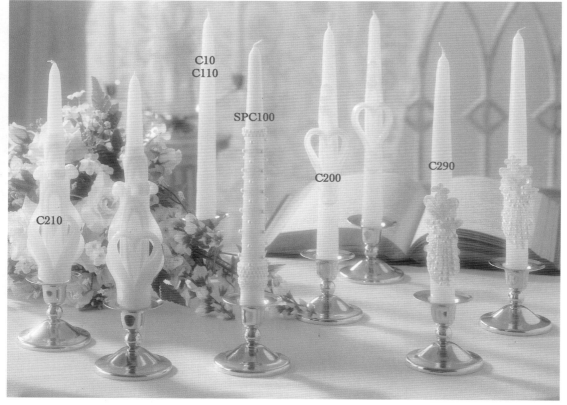

C826 9" Pillar $24.45

C820 10" Tapers $14.45

C280 10" Tapers **White, Ivory** $28.95

* All items available in white only, unless otherwise specified.

C210 10" Tapers $14.45

C10 Dozen 12" Plain Tapers $19.45

C110 Pair 10" Plain Tapers $3.95

SPC100 10" Tapers **White** $14.45

C200 10" Tapers $13.45

C290 10" Tapers $15.00

* All items this page available in white and ivory, unless otherwise specified.

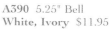

BX390 5" Trinket Box **White, Ivory** $18.95

CA390 5.75" Candle Holder **White, Ivory** $31.95

CA391 3.25" Single Taper Holder **White, Ivory** $9.95

A390 5.25" Bell **White, Ivory** $11.95

B50 2" Single Taper Holder **Gold, Silver** $7.45

CA920 12" 3 in 1 Unity Stand As Shown $28.95

B200 13" 3 in 1 Unity Stand **Gold, Silver** $21.45

SP135 3" Candle Base & Follower **White** $13.45

B210 3.5" Single Taper Holder **Gold, Silver** $7.45

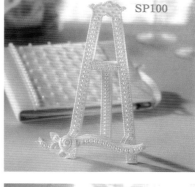

DA982 5" Single Taper Holder **White** $10.95

CA981 4" Candle Holder **White** $11.45

CA980 3" Candle Holder **White** $9.00

B100 2" Reversible Candle Holder **Gold, Silver** $7.45

SP100 8.5" Easel **White** $8.45

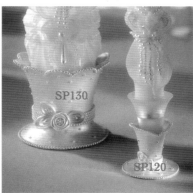

A710 4.50" Single Taper Holder $7.45

A740 5" Crystal Candle Base $32.45

SP130 4" Candle Holder **White** $16.95

SP120 Pair of 3" Taper Holders **White** $14.45

B225 4.5" Centerpiece Holder **Gold, Silver** $16.95

CR131 1" Taper Ring $5.45

C40 9" Pillar Candle $18.95

CR130 3" Candle Ring $16.45

CR450 3.25" Candle Ring (As Shown) $9.95

www.YourBridalSuperstore.com

CR451 1.5" Taper Ring (As Shown) $4.95

C456 9" Pillar Candle $27.95

* All items this page available in white and ivory, unless otherwise specified.

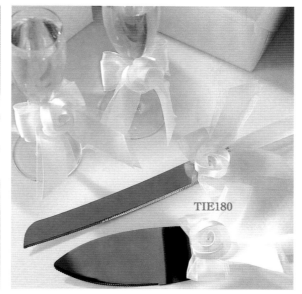

C136 9" Pillar Candle **White** $25.45

TIE130 Pair of 4" Tie-Ons **White** $9.95

TIE180 Pair of 4" Tie-Ons **White** $10.95

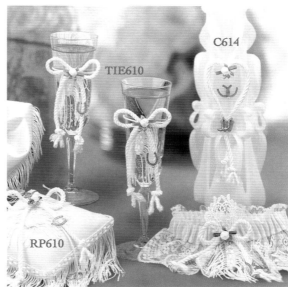

TIE450 Pair of 4" Tie- Ons As Shown $12.00

RP610 5" x 5" Ring Pillow $25.45

TIE610 Pair of 3" tie-Ons $8.45

C614 11" Western Candle $25.45

TIE600 Pair of 3" Tie-Ons $13.45

C604 11"Angel Candle $24.45

C287 9" Sequin & Pearl Pillar $28.95

TIE280 Pair of 4" Tie-Ons $10.95

* All items this page available in white and ivory, unless otherwise specified.

G505 5.25" Split Heart Goblets $48.45

G510 8.5" Split Heart Flutes $45.95

G500 3" Split Heart Cups $38.95

K500 12" Knife & Server Set $19.45

G800 10" Victorian Lace Flutes **White, Ivory** $41.45

* All items this page available in silver only,
unless otherwise specified.

G450 8.5" Toasting Glasses $29.95

K455 12.5" Knife & Server Set $33.45

LG300 Keepsake Garter **White, Ivory** $13.45

G310 10" Crystal Toasting Glasses $48.45

G130 8.5" Toasting Glasses **White** $28.95

K135 12" Knife & Server Set **White** $34.95

G281 8.5" Toasting Glasses **White, Ivory** $23.45

K286 12.5" Knife & Server Set **White, Ivory** $25.95

LG550 Keepsake Garter **White, Ivory** $9.45

K755 13.5" Knife & Server Set **Gold, Silver** $35.95

G280 8.5" Toasting Glasses **White, Ivory** $33.95

K285 12.5" Knife & Server Set **White, Ivory** $33.95

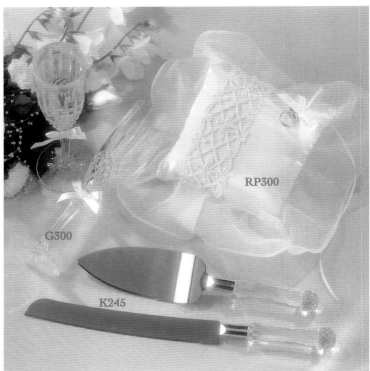

G920 8.5" Toasting Flutes **White, Painted** $33.45

K925 12.5" Knife & Server Set **Painted** $24.45

G830 8.5" Toasting Glasses $23.95

* All items this page available in white only,
unless otherwise specified.

G300 8" Crystal Toasting Glasses $36.95

K245 12.5" Knife & Server Set $19.45

RP300 5.5" Ring Pillow $25.45

K985 12" Knife & Server Set $25.45

G980 8.5" Toasting Flutes $36.95

CT180

CT185

CT205

CT132

CT135

CT180 9" Dove Heart Caketop $41.45

CT185 9" Double Ring Caketop $45.95

CT205 10" Etched Crystal Caketop $52.95

CT132 11" Figurine Caketop $47.45

CT135 10" Glass Heart Caketop $45.45

*All items on this page are available in white only.

CT360 10" Cupid Caketop $36.95

CT430 8" Dove Caketop $34.45

CT800 10" Bell Caketop $36.95

CT980 7.25" Couple Caketop **White** $27.95

CT610 12" Western Caketop $40.45

CT617 12" Western Cupid Caketop $44.95

LG610 Tossing Garter $9.95

LG616 Keepsake Garter $13.45

CT280 10" Couple Caketop $37.95

* All items on this page are available in white and ivory, unless otherwise specified.

CT285 10" Swan Caketop **White, Ivory** $33.95

CT910 10" Couple Caketop **African-American, Caucasian, Hispanic** $38.95

CT830 10" Butterfly Caketop **White** $35.45

CT350 10" Porcelain Rose Caketop **White, Ivory** $35.95

RC900 F

RC900 B

RC900 F 8.25" Fountain
Caketop $20.45

RC900 B 6" Basket Caketop
Box $20.45

RC900 SH

RC900 C

RC900 C 6.5" Cross Caketop
Box $20.45

RC900 SH 6.75" Seashell
Caketop $19.45

CT920 9.5" Gazebo Caketop
White, Painted $40.95

RC900 H 5.5" Heart Caketop
Box $26.45

* All items this page
available in white only,
unless otherwise specified.

CT920

RC900 H

RC900 LC
RC900 SC
RC900 MC Musical
RC900 MC Musical
RC900 SC
RC900 LC

RC900 LC *7" Large Keepsake Box Tier* $28.95

RC900 MC *4" Musical Cake Tier* $25.45

RC900 SC *4" Small Keepsake Box Tier* $13.45

° All items this page available in white only.

F371 N *7.5" Bride & Groom* **Natural** $21.45

F372 *8.5" Bride & Groom* $24.45

F371 P *7.5" Bride & Groom* **Painted** $23.95

F370 *6" Bride & Groom* $25.45

CT980 *7.25" Caketop* **White** $27.95

G650 *8.5" Engraved Toasting Glasses* **White** $19.45

RP980 *8" Ring Pillow* **White** $38.95

F980 *3.5" Figurine* $6.00

F981 *4.25" Figurine* $11.45

CT981 *7.25" Fairytale Caketop* $32.45

CT910 10" Caketop (A) African-American, (C) Caucasian, (H) Hispanic $38.95

F900 7" Figurine (A) African-American, (C) Caucasian $25.45

F910 4.75" Figurine (A) African-American, (C) Caucasian, (H) Hispanic $9.45

F920 4.75" Figurine (A) African-American, (C) Caucasian, (H) Hispanic $9.45

Lillian Rose

BX920
3 Tier Cake Box Set
Shown together on
next page.

BX920 5" Trinket Box **White, Painted**
$23.95

KS510 Set of 6 Cake Charms **Silver** $35.45

LG481 Daisy Garter **White** $8.45

KS510
Set of 6

LG481

BX920 5" Trinket Box **(W) White, (P) Painted** $23.95

BX921 2.5" Trinket Box **(W) White, (P) Painted** $10.95

A920 4.5" Figurine **(W) White, (P) Painted** $13.45

BX922 2.75" Trinket Box **Painted** $11.45

BX923 6.5" Trinket Box **Painted** $20.45

CA700 6.75" Votive Holder $18.00

CA710 8.25" Candle Holder $21.95

MB285 15.5" Cake Card Box **White** $249.95

CA720 12.5" Candle Holder $24.45

CA740 6.5" Candle Holder $34.95

MB200 14" Card Chest Box **White** $157.95

MB280 12" Card Box **White, Ivory** $233.45

FA900 V Set of Six 2.75" Vase Card Holders $16.95

MB130 29.5" Card Box **White** $157.95

CA730 11.25" Candle Holder $25.45

RP800

LG802

LG285

RP110

LG804

KS100 BI

KS100 SP

LG286

KS100 HT

LG185

LG801

LG280

RP800 11" Ring Pillow **White, Ivory** $22.95

RP110 8" Ring Pillow **White, Ivory** $21.45

LG185 Something Blue Garter **White, Ivory, Blue** $9.45

LG280 Keepsake Garter **White, Ivory** $18.00

LG285 Keepsake Garter **White, Ivory** $16.95

LG286 Keepsake Garter **White, Ivory** $11.95

LG801 Tossing Garter **White, Ivory, Blue** $8.45

LG802 Garter Set **White, Ivory** $18.00

LG804 Garter W/Pence **White, Ivory** $15.95

KS100 BI 1.5" Bible $8.45

KS100 HT 1" Blue Heart $6.00

KS100 SP Six Pence $6.00

LG130

LG920

Keepsake
Garter

LG362
Garter
Set

LG150

Tossing
Garter

LG805

LG174

LG153

LG130 Keepsake Garter **White** $22.95

LG362 Garter Set $25.45

LG174 Keepsake Garter $15.95

LG920 Keepsake Garter $13.45

LG150 Keepsake Garter **White** $23.95

LG805 Keepsake Garter $11.45

LG153 Tossing Garter $9.45

*All items on this page available in white and ivory, unless otherwise specified.

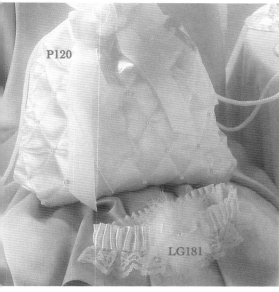

P120

LG181

LG283

P120 10" Bridal Purse
White $17.95

LG181 Tossing Garter $7.45

LG283 Keepsake Garter
$32.45

LG170

LG281

LG170 Keepsake Garter
$14.45

LG281 Keepsake Garter
$19.45

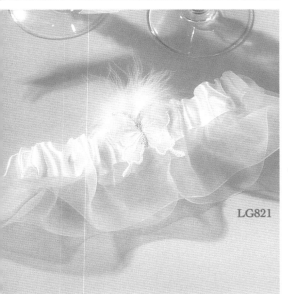

LG821

LG453

LG821 Tossing Garter
White $12.00

LG453 Keepsake Garter
$23.45

° All items on this page available in white and ivory, unless otherwise specified.

HA100 10" Hankie **White** $14.45

HA150 Hankie and Garter Set **White** $23.95

PENCE P Six Pence W/Pouch **White** $12.00

HA280 Hankie & Garter Set **White** $21.45

HA170 Hankie & Garter Set **White** $32.45

FA541 Set of Six 8" Book Marks **See Below** $7.45

Book Mark Choices: **B** – Brides Maid,
   D – Daughter, **FR** – Friend, **FA** – Father,
   M – Mother, **MH** – Maid Of Honor,
   S – Sister, **SF** - Stepfather

HA540 10" Embroidered Hankie $21.00

Hankie Choices: **B** – Brides Maid, **D** – Daughter, **FR** – Friend, **SF** – Stepfather, **M** – Mother,

FA – Father, **S** – Sister, **MH** – Maid Of Honor

GB120 8.5" Guest Book $24.95

SP100 8.5" Easel $8.45

SP160 8" x 10" Frame $23.95

SP150 5" x 7" Frame $11.95

SP140 3.5" x 5" Frame $8.45

SP110 6" Pen Set $11.45

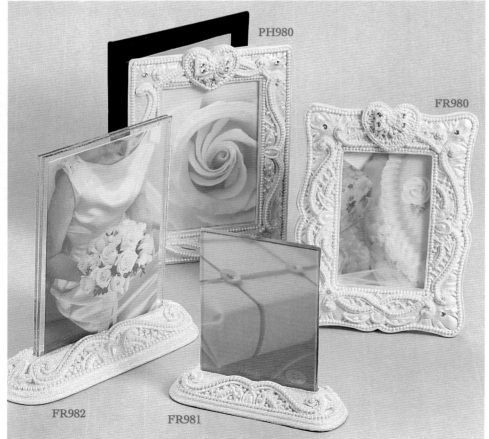

FR982 4" x 6" Photo Stand $10.95

PH980 4" x 6" Photo Album $23.95

FR981 3.5" x 5" Photo Stand $9.45

FR980 3" x 5" Frame $12.00

° All items on this page as shown.

FR502 5" x 7" Silver Frame $16.95

FR501 3" x 5" Silver Frame $12.00

FR503 8" x 10" Silver Frame $27.95

FR500 4" x 5" Silver Frame $18.95

VCR500 8" Silver Video Box $20.45

° All items on this page as shown.

MC5X7 5" x 7" Marriage Certificate $4.95

MC8X10 8" x 10" Marriage Certificate $6.00

* Marriage certificates available in white and ivory.

K500 12" Silver Knife & Server Set $19.45

MC750 9.5" Silver Certificate Holder $24.95

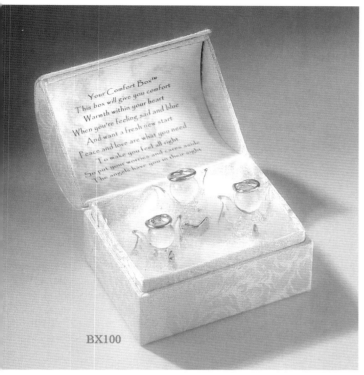

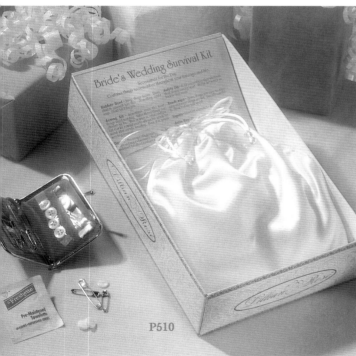

BX100 4" x 3" Comfort Box **White** $25.45

P510 8" Survival Kit **White** $25.45

CAP280 Bride's Cap **White** $19.45

P505 8" Embroidered Kit **White** $36.95

(Kit Accessories May Vary Due To Availability)

FS549 WP

SH540 BR

FS550

FS549 WP Set of Six Temporary Tattoos **Wedding Party** $32.45

SH540 BR X-Large T-Shirt **Bride** $21.45

FS550 Box of 24 Clappers $18.00

CAP540 BR

FS547 BR
FS547 GR
FS547 WP

FS541 GR
FS541 BR

CAP540 BR Wedding Cap **Bride** $18.00

FS547 Wedding Cozy **(BR) Bride, Groom, (GR), (WP) Wedding Party** $9.45

FS541 Stress Kit **(B) Bride, (GR) Groom** $13.45

FS549 BR

FS542

FS543 GR
FS543 BR

FS549 BR Set of Six Tempora Bride Tattoos **Bride** $32.45

FS542 Box of 48 Kazoos **Wh** $23.45

FS543 Coffee Mug **(BR) Bride, (GR) Groom** $11.45

SH540 GR

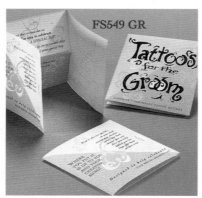

FS549 GR

CAP540 GR

SH540 GR X-Large T-Shirt **Groom** $21.45

FS549 GR Set of Six Temporary Groom Tattoos **Groom** $32.45

CAP540 GR Wedding Cap **Groom** $18.00

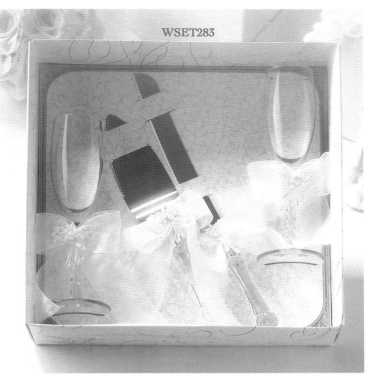
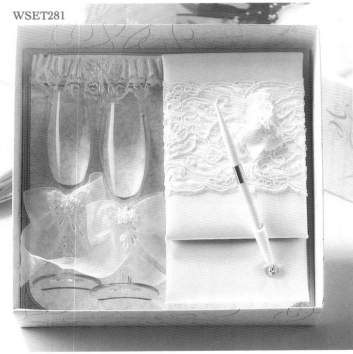
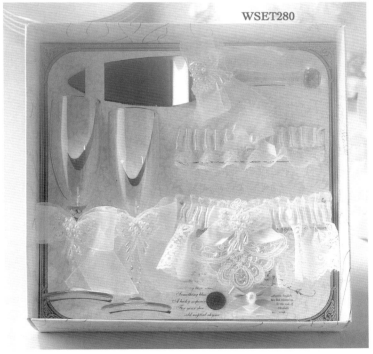

WSET282 Candle Set **White, Ivory** $44.45

WSET281 Guest Book Set $53.95

WSET283 Wedding Set $43.95

WSET280 Wedding Set $69.45

* All items on this page are available in white unless otherwise specified.

WSET452
(Candle holder
& bell sold on
page 161)

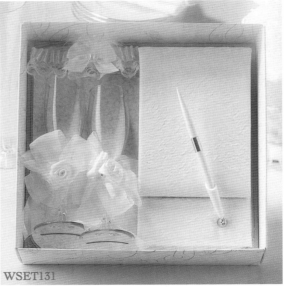

WSET131

WSET452 Candle Set $41.45

WSET131 Guest Book Set $50.95

WSET132
(Candle holders
sold on page 151)

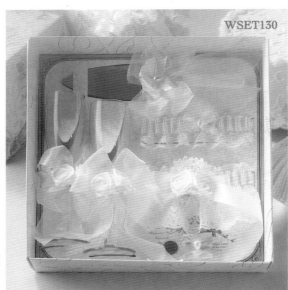

WSET130

WSET132 Candle Set $37.95

WSET130 Wedding Set $56.45

WSET283

WSET133

WSET283 Wedding Set $43.95

WSET133 Wedding Set $45.95

* All items on this page available in
white only.

FA545

CAP500 Adult Cap **(BR) Bride, (GR) Groom, (FA) Father of the Bride** $18.95

SH500 X-Large T-Shirt **(BR) Bride, (GR) Groom** $27.45

FA545 Pair of Bride & Groom Decorations $11.45

SH510 X-Large T-Shirt Set **Bride & Groom** $50.95

BUBBLES BX 0.6 oz Bottles 24 pcs $12.00

BBLCASE (Not Shown) 0.6 oz Bottles 288 pcs $94.95

BUBBLES RSBX 0.6 oz Rose Bottles 24 pcs $16.95

BBLCASE RS (Not Shown) 0.6 oz Rose Bottles 288 pcs $168.00

SP175 Treasure Box
(Sold Individually On Page 151 for $35.45)

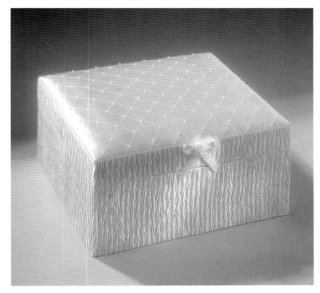

Wedding In A Box

New wedding in a box concept.
A beautiful wedding treasure keepsake box filled
with essential wedding accessories. The presentation box is large enough (11"x 13"x 6") to hold
the contents shown and described on this page,
plus several other mementos of the day. Ideal for
pictures, keepsakes, headpiece, marriage certificate, etc.

Two Versions are available:
    The Basic - Shown on this page
    The Traditional - Shown on page 208

* **The Basic Wedding in a Box**

SPSET 1 Gift Box **White** $68.45

White Satin & Pearl Treasure Box
Sequin & Pearl Knife & Server Set
Engraved Bride & Groom Toasting Glasses
Sequin & Pearl Keepsake Garter

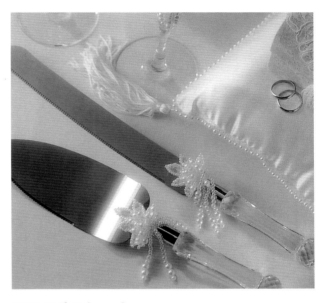

K286 Knife & Server Set
(Sold Individually On Page 154 for $25.95)

G650 Engraved Toasting Glasses
(Sold Individually On Page 188 for $19.45)

You save $30.40 when
you purchase the "Basic
Wedding in a Box"
instead of purchasing
these items separately.

LG280 Sequin Garter
(Sold Individually On Page 154 for $18.00)

HA150 Hankie, Garter & Pence Set
(Sold Individually On Page 196 for $23.95)

SPC120 5" Heart Candle
(Sold Individually On Page 172 for $18.00)

SP140 3.5" x 5" Frame
(Sold Individually On Page 151 for $8.45)

* The Traditional Wedding in a Box

SPSET 2 Gift Box White $102.95

Includes:
White Satin & Pearl Treasure Box
Chiffon & Satin Rose Toasting Glasses
Chiffon & Satin Rose Knife & Server Set
Traditions Hankie, Garter & Pence Set
Scattered Pearl Heart Candle
Scattered Pearl 3.5 x 5" Frame

G180 Toasting Glasses
(Sold Individually On Page 152 for $23.95)
K185 Knife & Server Set
(Sold Individually On Page 152 for $25.95)

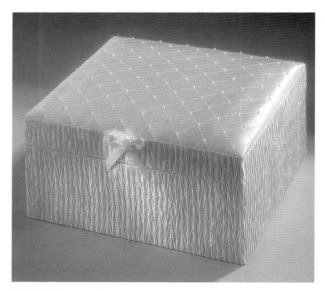

SP175 Treasure Box
(Sold Individually On Page 151 for $35.45)

You save $32.80 when you purchase the
"Traditional Wedding in a Box" instead
of purchasing these items separately.

www.YourBridalSuperstore.com

YOUR BRIDAL SUPERSTORE

proudly presents

THE

CATHY'S CONCEPTS

COLLECTION

Dazzle your wedding party with fresh and exciting jewelry styles from Cathy's Concepts. Hand-dipped glass pearls, genuine Austrian crystals, Titanic-inspired hematite and tiaras for your flower girl highlight a few of the splendid items within this exquisite collection.

*We also invite you to visit our on-line store at **www.YourBridalSuperstore.com**, featuring the most extensive collection of accessories, invitations, jewelry, gifts, favors and much more.*

YOUR BRIDAL
SUPERSTORE
...everything but the groom℠
www.YourBridalSuperstore.com

CATHY'S CONCEPTS

3mm Pearl Necklace*
N7314SW-Silver/White 14"- $21.95
N7314GI-Gold/Ivory 14"- $21.95
N7316SW-Silver/White 16"- $21.95
N7316GI-Gold/Ivory 16"-$21.95

4mm Pearl Bracelet*
B8107GI-Gold/Ivory- $18.00
B8107GW-Gold/White- $18.00
B8107SW-Silver/White- $18.00
Approx. 7"

3-6mm Graduated Pearl Necklace*
N9314SW-Silver/White 14"- $24.45
N9314GI-Gold/Ivory 14"-$24.45
N9316SW-Silver/White 16"- $24.45
N9316GI-Gold/Ivory 16"- $24.45

1. 4mm Pearl Stud*
E0014GIC - $14.45
E0014GIP - $14.45
E0014GWC- $14.45
E0014GWP- $14.45
E0014SWC- $14.45
E0014SWP- $14.45

4mm Pearl Necklace*
Available Gold/Ivory, Gold/White,
Silver/Ivory, Silver/White
N7414=14"- $25.45
N7416=16"- $25.45
N7418=18"- $25.45
N7420=20"-$25.45

2. 6mm Pearl Stud*
E0016GIC - $14.45
E0016GIP - $14.45
E0016GWC - $14.45
E0016GWP - $14.45
E0016SWC - $14.45
E0016SWP - $14.45

3. 8mm Pearl Stud*
E0018GIC - $14.45
E0018GIP - $14.45
E0018SWC - $14.45
E0018SWP - $14.45

4. 10mm Pearl Stud*
E2002GIC - $18.00
E2002GIP - $18.00
E2002SWC - $18.00
E2002SWP - $18.00

4-8mm Graduated Pearl Neck
N9616SW-Silver/White 16"- $14.45
N9616GI-Gold/Ivory 16"- $14.45
N9618SW-Silver/White 18"- $14.45
N9618GI-Gold/Ivory 18"- $14.45

6mm Pearl Bracelet*
B8106GI-Gold/Ivory- $21.95
B8106GW-Gold/White- $21.95
B8106SW-Silver/White- $21.95
Approx. 7"

6mm Pearl Necklace*
Available Gold/Ivory, Gold/White,
Silver/Ivory, Silver/White
N7614=14"- $31.45
N7616=16"- $31.45
N7618=18"- $31.45
N7620=20"- $31.45

GI=Gold Ivory
GW=Gold White
SW=Silver White
C=Clip
P=Pierced

*Sold in quantities of three.

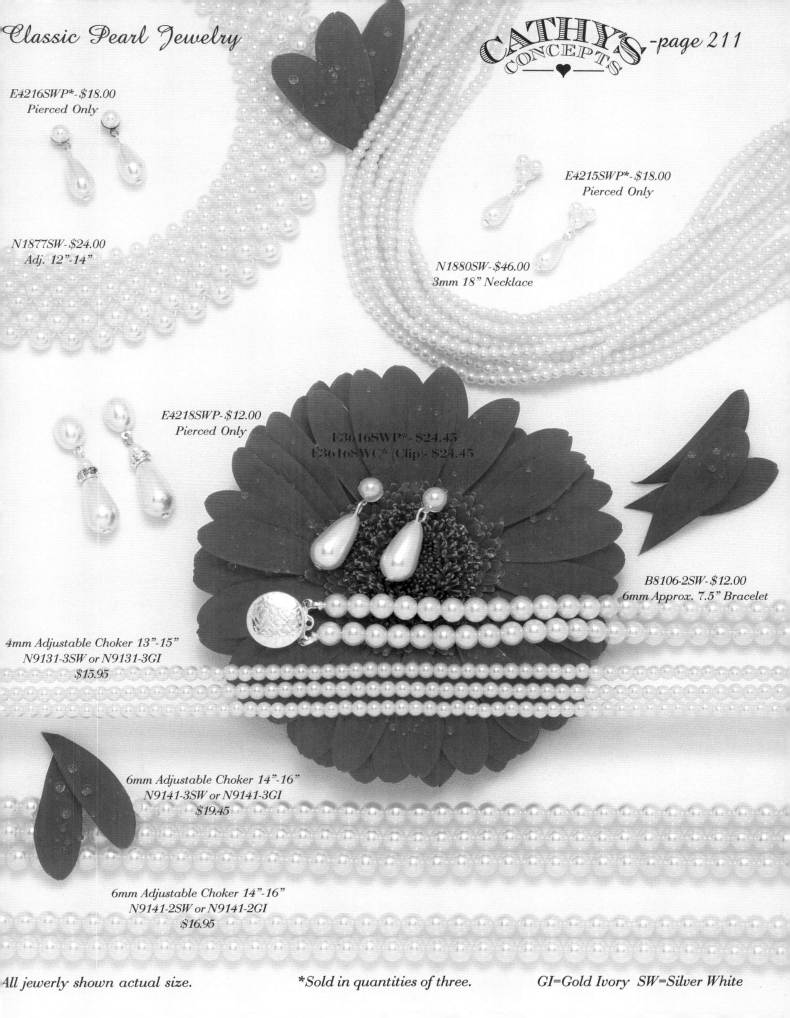

Classic Pearl Jewelry

E4216SWP*-$18.00
Pierced Only

E4215SWP*-$18.00
Pierced Only

N1877SW-$24.00
Adj. 12"-14"

N1880SW-$46.00
3mm 18" Necklace

E4218SWP-$12.00
Pierced Only

E3616SWP*-$24.45
E3616SWC* (Clip)-$24.45

B8106-2SW-$12.00
6mm Approx. 7.5" Bracelet

4mm Adjustable Choker 13"-15"
N9131-3SW or N9131-3GI
$15.95

6mm Adjustable Choker 14"-16"
N9141-3SW or N9141-3GI
$19.45

6mm Adjustable Choker 14"-16"
N9141-2SW or N9141-2GI
$16.95

All jewelry shown actual size.   *Sold in quantities of three.   GI=Gold Ivory SW=Silver White

CATHY'S CONCEPTS

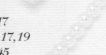

E9818
Colors 1-11,13-17, 19,23,24,26-28
$13.45

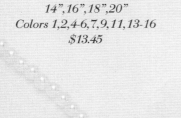

E9907
Colors 1,2,4-6,7,9,11,13-16
$13.45

E7017
Colors 1-17,19
$14.45

N7017
14",16",18",20"
Colors 1-17,19
$14.45

N9818
14",16",18",20"
Colors 1-11,13-17, 19,23,24,26-28
$13.45

N9912
14",16",18",20"
Colors 1,2,4-6,7,9,11,13-16
$13.45

E8145
Colors 1-11,13,15-17
$8.45

E8143
Colors 1-11,13,15-17
$10.95

E2743
Colors 1-11,13-17,19,23,24,26-2
$10.95

N8143
14",16",18",20"
Colors 1-11,13,15-17
$10.95

N2743
14",16",18",20"
Colors 1-11,13-17,19,23,24,26-28
$10.95

| 01 Crystal | 02 AB | 03 Blush | 28 Pink | 04 Rose | 06 Light Amethyst | 24 Lilac | 19 Purple | 07 Dark Amethyst | 05 Fuschia | 09 Ruby | 17 Bright Ruby |

| 15 Emerald | 14 Teal | 27 Lemon | 26 Ocean Blue | 23 Sky Blue | 10 Aqua | 11 Royal | 12 Dark Royal | 13 Navy | 08 Black Diamond | 16 Jet Black |

All styles available in silver/white, gold/white, gold/ivory and silver/ivory. Pierced or clip

Pearl Jewelry in GoldWhite & Silver Ivory

CATHY'S CONCEPTS

ES400GWP
ES400SIP
ES400GWC (Clip)
ES400SIC (Clip)
$12.00

E2811GWP
E2811GWC (Clip)
$9.95

E9868GWP
E9868SIP
E9868GWC (Clip)
E9868SIC (Clip)
$16.95

N8400GW
N8400SI
16" or 18"
$18.00

N2811GW
14", 16", 18", 20"
$9.95

N9867GW
N9867SI
14", 16", 18", 20"
$19.45

E9752GWP
Pierced Only
$14.45

CATHY'S CONCEPTS

An Expression of You

N9752GW
14" Adjustable Choker
$43.95

PP1002G
Ball Point Pen
$14.45

S1501GW
16" Necklace with Pierced
Only Earring
$14.45

E9947SIP
Pierced
Only
$12.00

E8141SIP
E8141GWP
E8141SIC (Clip)
E8141GWC (Clip)
$10.95

N8141SI
N8141GW
14", 16", 18", 20"
$9.95

N9947SI
14", 16", 18", 20"
$12.00

E8144SIP
E8144SIC
(Clip)
$8.45

All jewelry shown actual size.
GW=Gold White/SI=Silver Ivory

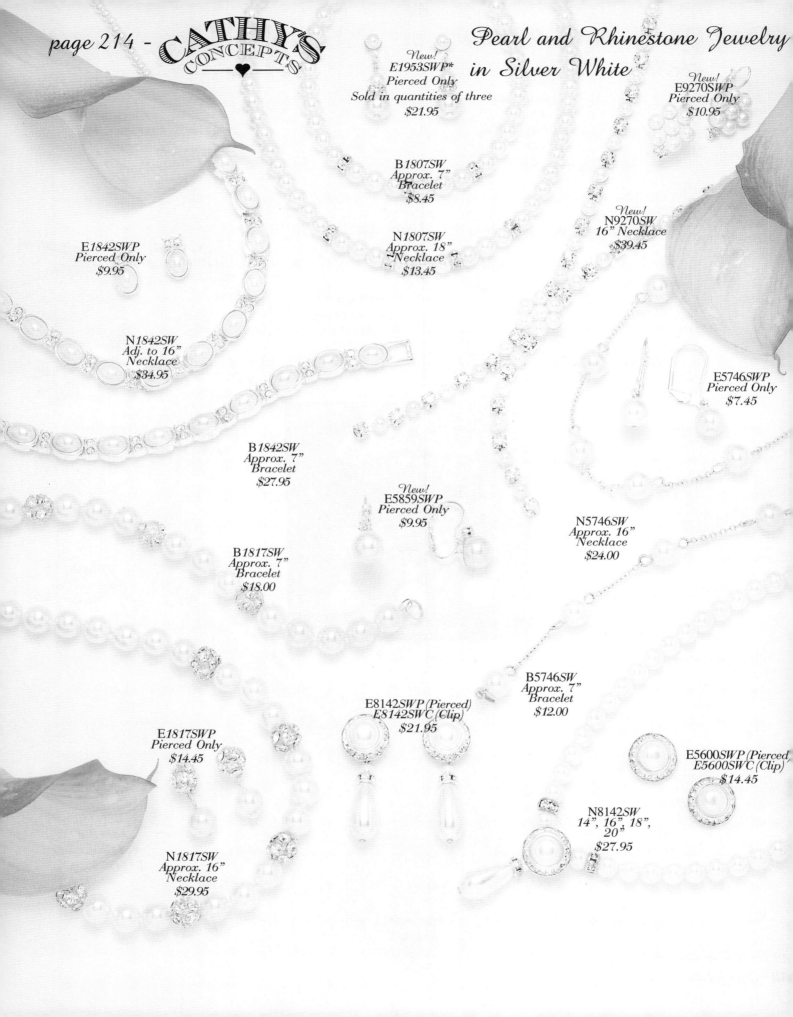

CATHY'S CONCEPTS

Pearl and Rhinestone Jewelry in Silver White

New!
E1953SWP*
Pierced Only
Sold in quantities of three
$21.95

New!
E9270SWP
Pierced Only
$10.95

B1807SW
Approx. 7"
Bracelet
$8.45

New!
N9270SW
16" Necklace
$39.45

N1807SW
Approx. 18"
Necklace
$13.45

E1842SWP
Pierced Only
$9.95

N1842SW
Adj. to 16"
Necklace
$34.95

E5746SWP
Pierced Only
$7.45

B1842SW
Approx. 7"
Bracelet
$27.95

New!
E5859SWP
Pierced Only
$9.95

N5746SW
Approx. 16"
Necklace
$24.00

B1817SW
Approx. 7"
Bracelet
$18.00

B5746SW
Approx. 7"
Bracelet
$12.00

E8142SWP (Pierced)
E8142SWC (Clip)
$21.95

E1817SWP
Pierced Only
$14.45

E5600SWP (Pierced)
E5600SWC (Clip)
$14.45

N8142SW
14", 16" 18",
20"
$27.95

N1817SW
Approx. 16"
Necklace
$29.95

Pearl Jewelry in Silver White

E9792SWP
Pierced Only
$20.45

E9798SWP
Pierced Only
$16.95

E3943SWP
Pierced Only
$16.95

N9792SW
14" or 16"
$20.45

N9798SW
14" or 16"
$14.45

N3943SW
14" or 16"
$16.95

E7007SWP
Pierced Only
$13.45

E7087SWP
Pierced Only
$9.95

N7007SW
14" or 16"
$12.00

N7087SW
14" or 16"
$9.95

E5747SWP
Pierced
Only
$15.95

E1844SWP
Pierced Only
$9.95

S1516SW $16.95
S=Pierced Earrings and Approx.
16" Necklace

N5747SW
14" or 16"
$15.95

N1844SW
14" or 16"
$9.95

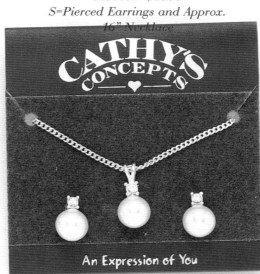

S1501SW
S=Pierced Earrings and Approx.
16" Necklace
$14.45

All jewelry shown actual size.

E7078SP
Pierced Only
Colors 1, 2, 6, 7, 9, 11, 13, 15, 16
$12.00

E9754SP
Pierced Only
Colors 1-11, 13-17, 23, 24, 26-28
$16.95

E9453SP
Pierced Only
Colors 1-17, 19
$22.95

N7078S
Colors 1, 2, 6, 7, 9, 11, 13, 15, 16
$28.95

N9754S
Approx. 16"
Colors 1-11, 13-17, 23, 24, 26-28
$24.00

E9428SP
Pierced Only
Colors 1-11, 13-17
$14.45

N9453S
Approx. 16"
Colors 1-17, 19
$52.95

E5855SP
Pierced Only
Colors 1-17, 19
$14.45

N9428S
Colors 1-11, 13-17
$36.95

EX2001S Sold in quantities of 3 2"
Extender $10.95

N5855S
Approx. 16"
Colors 1-17, 19
$27.95

EX2002S Sold in quantities of 3 2"
Extender $18.00

E9430SP
Pierced Only
Colors 1-11, 13-17, 23, 24, 26-28
$20.45

E9426SP
Pierced Only
Colors 1-17, 19
$14.45

EX4001S
Sold in quantities of 3
4" Extender $14.45

EX4002S
Sold in quantities of 3
4" Extender $24.45

N9426S
Approx. 16"
Colors 1-17, 19
$29.95

N9430S
Approx. 16"
Colors 1-11, 13-17, 23, 24, 26-28
$31.45

01 Crystal	02 AB	03 Blush	28 Pink	04 Rose	06 Light Amethyst	24 Lilac	19 Purple	07 Dark Amethyst	05 Fuschia	17 Bright Ruby	09 Ruby
15 Emerald	14 Teal	27 Lemon	26 Ocean Blue	23 Sky Blue	10 Aqua	11 Royal	12 Dark Royal	13 Navy	08 Black Diamond	16 Jet	

All jewelry shown actual size.

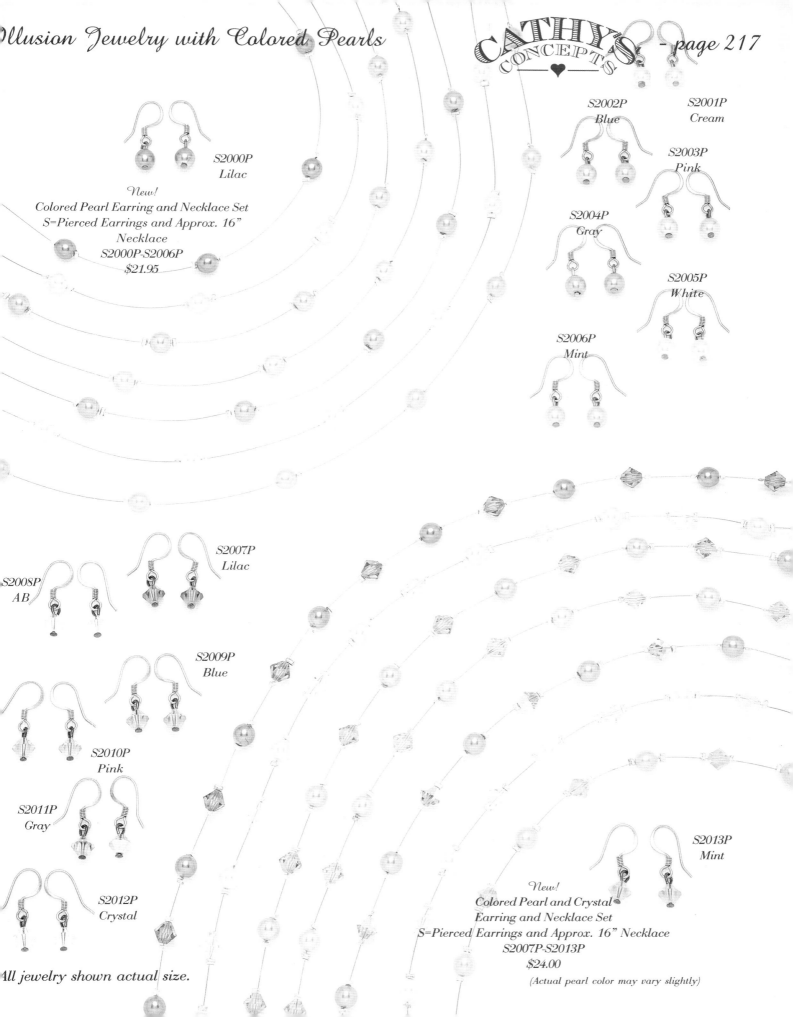

S2000P
Lilac

New!
Colored Pearl Earring and Necklace Set
S=Pierced Earrings and Approx. 16"
Necklace
S2000P-S2006P
$21.95

S2002P
Blue

S2001P
Cream

S2003P
Pink

S2004P
Gray

S2005P
White

S2006P
Mint

S2007P
Lilac

S2008P
AB

S2009P
Blue

S2010P
Pink

S2011P
Gray

S2012P
Crystal

S2013P
Mint

New!
Colored Pearl and Crystal
Earring and Necklace Set
S=Pierced Earrings and Approx. 16" Necklace
S2007P-S2013P
$24.00
(Actual pearl color may vary slightly)

All jewelry shown actual size.

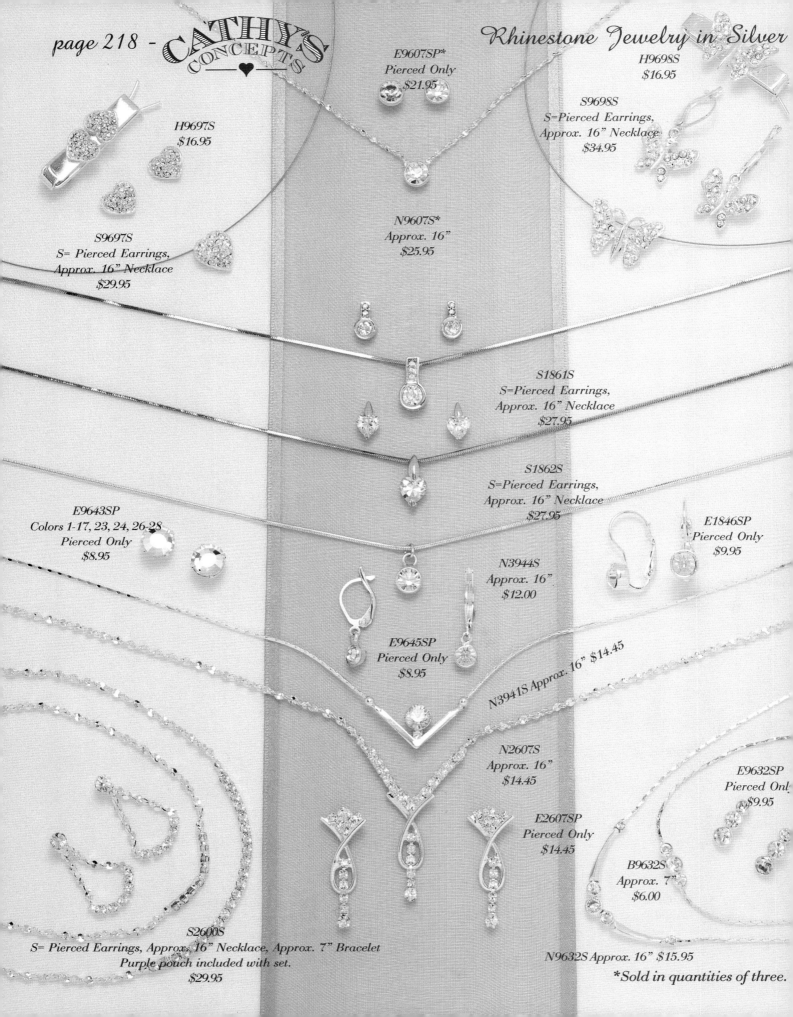

CATHY'S CONCEPTS

Rhinestone Jewelry in Silver

H9697S
$16.95

E9607SP*
Pierced Only
$21.95

H9698S
$16.95

S9698S
S=Pierced Earrings,
Approx. 16" Necklace
$34.95

S9697S
S= Pierced Earrings,
Approx. 16" Necklace
$29.95

N9607S*
Approx. 16"
$25.95

S1861S
S=Pierced Earrings,
Approx. 16" Necklace
$27.95

S1862S
S=Pierced Earrings,
Approx. 16" Necklace
$27.95

E9643SP
Colors 1-17, 23, 24, 26-28
Pierced Only
$8.95

E1846SP
Pierced Only
$9.95

N3944S
Approx. 16"
$12.00

E9645SP
Pierced Only
$8.95

N3941S Approx. 16" $14.45

N2607S
Approx. 16"
$14.45

E9632SP
Pierced Only
$9.95

E2607SP
Pierced Only
$14.45

B9632S
Approx. 7"
$6.00

S2600S
S= Pierced Earrings, Approx. 16" Necklace, Approx. 7" Bracelet
Purple pouch included with set.
$29.95

N9632S Approx. 16" $15.95

*Sold in quantities of three.

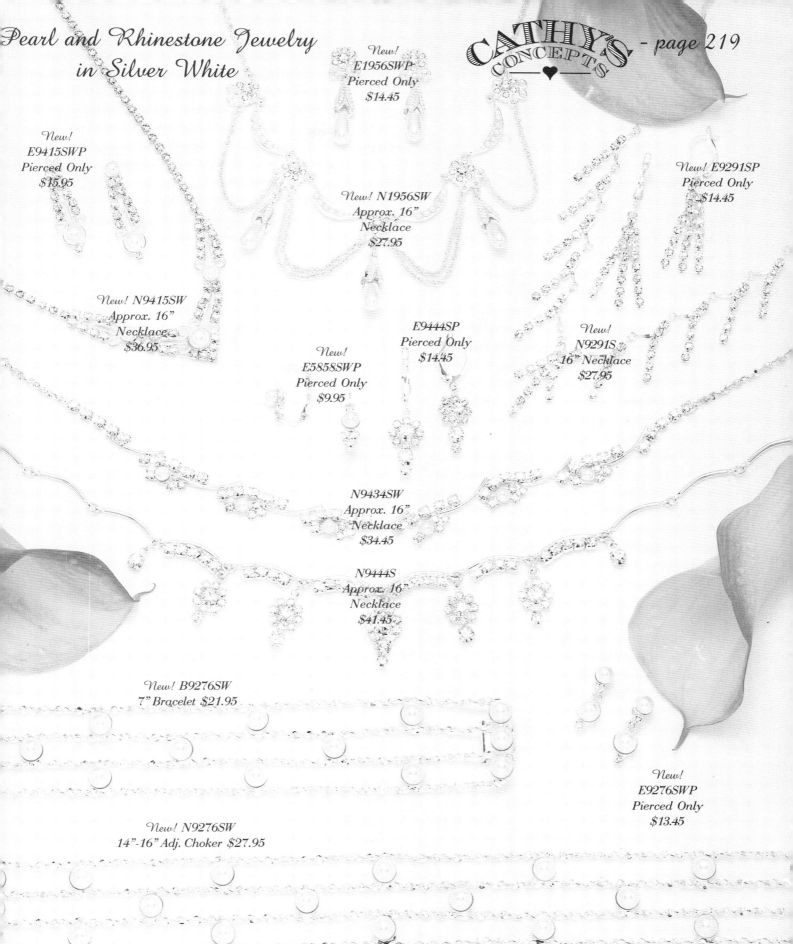

Pearl and Rhinestone Jewelry in Silver White

New!
E1956SWP
Pierced Only
$14.45

New!
E9415SWP
Pierced Only
$15.95

New! E9291SP
Pierced Only
$14.45

New! N1956SW
Approx. 16"
Necklace
$27.95

New! N9415SW
Approx. 16"
Necklace
$36.95

New!
E5858SWP
Pierced Only
$9.95

E9444SP
Pierced Only
$14.45

New!
N9291S
16" Necklace
$27.95

N9434SW
Approx. 16"
Necklace
$34.45

N9444S
Approx. 16"
Necklace
$41.45

New! B9276SW
7" Bracelet $21.95

New!
E9276SWP
Pierced Only
$13.45

New! N9276SW
14"-16" Adj. Choker $27.95

All Jewelry Shown Actual Size

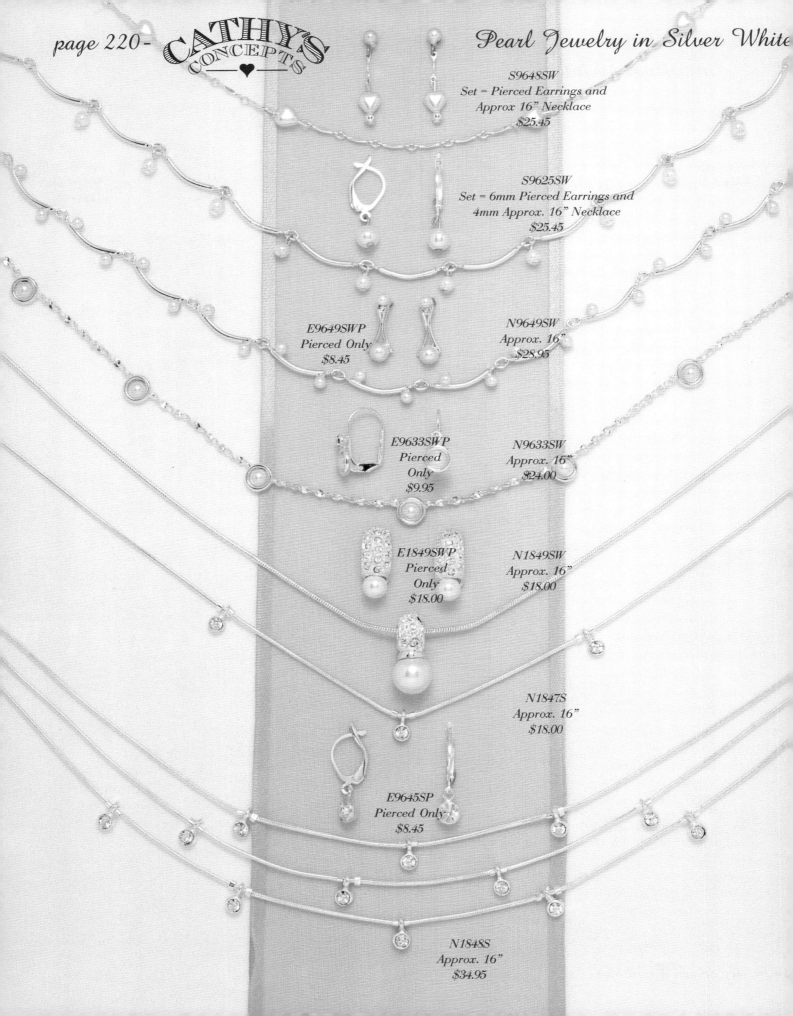

Cathy's Concepts

Pearl Jewelry in Silver White

S9648SW
Set = Pierced Earrings and
Approx 16" Necklace
$25.45

S9625SW
Set = 6mm Pierced Earrings and
4mm Approx. 16" Necklace
$25.45

E9649SWP
Pierced Only
$8.45

N9649SW
Approx. 16"
$28.95

E9633SWP
Pierced Only
$9.95

N9633SW
Approx. 16"
$24.00

E1849SWP
Pierced Only
$18.00

N1849SW
Approx. 16"
$18.00

N1847S
Approx. 16"
$18.00

E9645SP
Pierced Only
$8.45

N1848S
Approx. 16"
$34.95

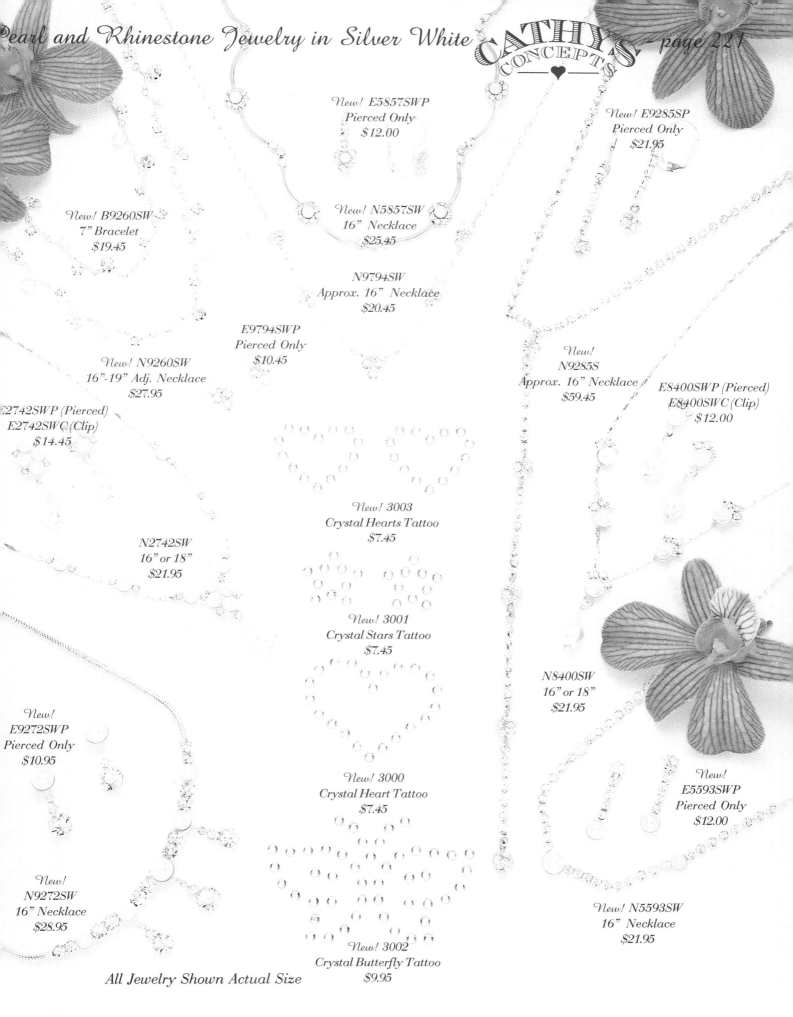

New! E5857SWP
Pierced Only
$12.00

New! E9285SP
Pierced Only
$21.95

New! B9260SW
7" Bracelet
$19.45

New! N5857SW
16" Necklace
$25.45

N9794SW
Approx. 16" Necklace
$20.45

E9794SWP
Pierced Only
$10.45

New!
N9285S
Approx. 16" Necklace
$59.45

E8400SWP (Pierced)
E8400SWC (Clip)
$12.00

New! N9260SW
16"-19" Adj. Necklace
$27.95

E2742SWP (Pierced)
E2742SWC (Clip)
$14.45

New! 3003
Crystal Hearts Tattoo
$7.45

N2742SW
16" or 18"
$21.95

New! 3001
Crystal Stars Tattoo
$7.45

N8400SW
16" or 18"
$21.95

New!
E9272SWP
Pierced Only
$10.95

New! 3000
Crystal Heart Tattoo
$7.45

New!
E5593SWP
Pierced Only
$12.00

New!
N9272SW
16" Necklace
$28.95

New! 3002
Crystal Butterfly Tattoo
$9.95

New! N5593SW
16" Necklace
$21.95

All Jewelry Shown Actual Size

CATHY'S CONCEPTS

S9618
Available Silver White or Gold Ivory
S=6mm Pierced Earring, 4-8mm 18" Necklace,
6mm 7" Bracelet
$21.95

S7416
Available Silver White or Gold Ivory
S=4mm Pierced Earrings, 16" Necklace,
7" Bracelet
$15.95

S1896
Available Silver White or Gold Ivory
S=4mm Pierced Earrings, 16" Necklace, 7" Bracelet
$21.95

S5000
Available Silver White, Gold White or Gold Ivory
S=8mm Pierced Earrings, 6mm 18" Necklace,
6mm 7" Bracelet
$21.95

S9141
Available Silver White or Gold Ivory
S=6mm Pierced Earrings, Adj 12"-14" Choker, 7" Bracelet
$27.95

S5746
Available Silver White or Gold Ivory
S=8mm Pierced Earrings, 16" Necklace,
Approx. 7" Bracelet
$27.95

All pouch sets include necklace, bracelet, earring and jewelry pouch.

Illusions

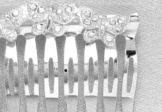

S9416S
S = Pierced Earrings and Necklace
Approx. 15"
$20.45

E7006SWP
8mm Pierced Earring
$24.00

S1876SW
S = Pierced Earrings and Approx 16" Necklace
$21.95

H9420S $14.45

N1924SW 7mm Necklace Approx. 16"
$12.00

S1863S
S = Pierced Earrings and Approx. 16" Necklace
$24.00

S9470S
S = Earrings Pierced and Approx. 16" Necklace
$16.95

N1865S Approx. 16" $14.45

N1864SW Approx. 16" $14.45

N1866SW 4mm Necklace Approx. 16" $12.00

N1867SW 4mm Necklace Approx. 16" $14.45

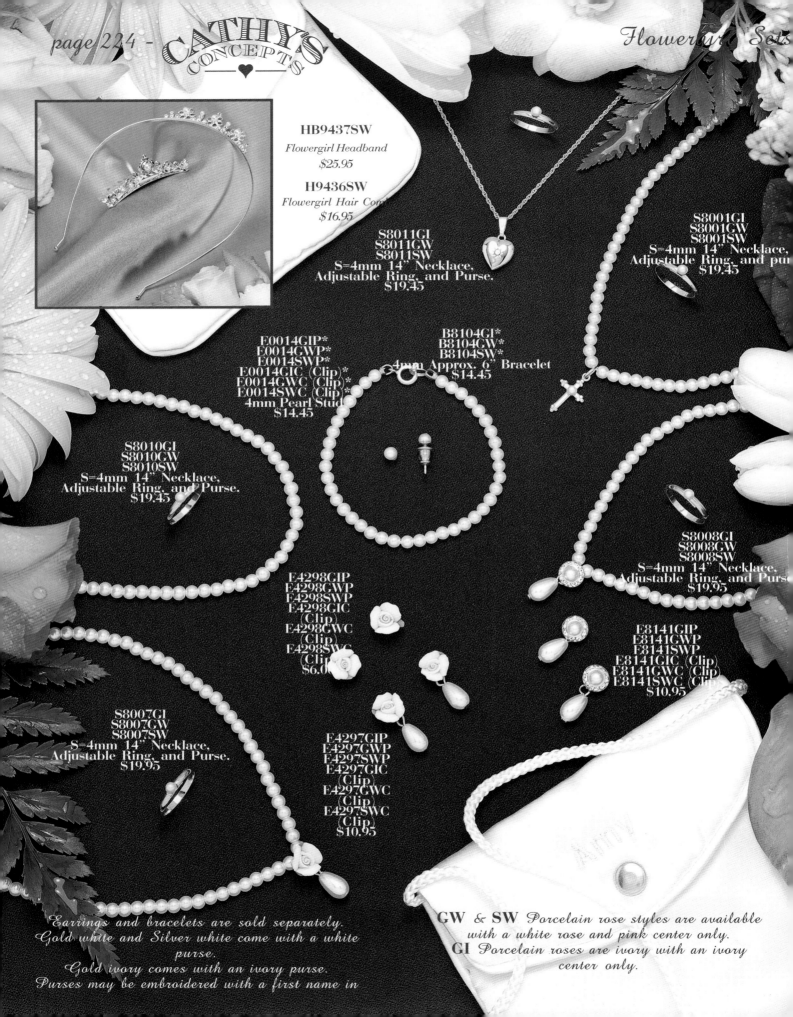

CATHY'S CONCEPTS ♥

HB9437SW
Flowergirl Headband
$25.95

H9436SW
Flowergirl Hair Comb
$16.95

S8011GI
S8011GW
S8011SW
S=4mm 14" Necklace,
Adjustable Ring, and Purse.
$19.45

S8001GI
S8001GW
S8001SW
S=4mm 14" Necklace,
Adjustable Ring, and purse
$19.45

E0014GIP*
E0014GWP*
E0014SWP*
E0014GIC (Clip)*
E0014GWC (Clip)*
E0014SWC (Clip)*
4mm Pearl Stud
$14.45

B8104GI*
B8104GW*
B8104SW*
4mm Approx. 6" Bracelet
$14.45

S8010GI
S8010GW
S8010SW
S=4mm 14" Necklace,
Adjustable Ring, and Purse.
$19.45

S8008GI
S8008GW
S8008SW
S=4mm 14" Necklace,
Adjustable Ring, and Purse
$19.95

E4298GIP
E4298GWP
E4298SWP
E4298GIC (Clip)
E4298GWC (Clip)
E4298SWC (Clip)
$6.00

E8141GIP
E8141GWP
E8141SWP
E8141GIC (Clip)
E8141GWC (Clip)
E8141SWC (Clip)
$10.95

S8007GI
S8007GW
S8007SW
S=4mm 14" Necklace,
Adjustable Ring, and Purse.
$19.95

E4297GIP
E4297GWP
E4297SWP
E4297GIC (Clip)
E4297GWC (Clip)
E4297SWC (Clip)
$10.95

Earrings and bracelets are sold separately.
Gold white and Silver white come with a white purse.
Gold ivory comes with an ivory purse.
Purses may be embroidered with a first name in

GW & SW *Porcelain rose styles are available with a white rose and pink center only.*
GI *Porcelain roses are ivory with an ivory center only.*

Tiaras

1. HB9434SW
Silver rhine-
stone adjustable
elastic headband
with pearls.
$46.45

2. T9464SW
Silver tiara with
rhinestones and
pearls.
1 3/8" Tall.
$57.45

3. T5752SW
Silver tiara with
pearls.
1" Tall.
$34.45

4. T5753SW
Silver tiara with
pearls.
1 1/2" Tall.
$34.45

5. T9461SW
Silver tiara with
rhinestones and
pearls.
1 3/8" Tall.
$66.00

6. T9466SW
T9466GI
Silver or Gold
tiara with
rhinestones and
pearls. 2" Tall.
$57.45

7. T1905SW
Silver tiara with
rhinestones and
pearls.
1 3/8" Tall.
$66.00

8. T1901SW
Silver tiara with
rhinestones and
pearls. 1 1/2"
Tall.
$66.00

All tiaras have attached combs on each side and are open in back for flexible sizing.

2

CATHY'S CONCEPTS

CATHY'S CONCEPTS

New!
E9150SP
Pierced Only
Engraving: 1 Script Initial
$9.95

New!
E9151SP
Pierced Only
Engraving: 1 Script Initial
$7.45

New!
N9150S
Necklace 16"
Engraving: 1 Script Initial
$18.00

New!
B9155S
Bracelet
Engraving: 3 Block Initials
$14.45

New!
N9156SW
Necklace 16"
Engraving: 1 Script Initial
$19.95

New! B9150S
Bracelet 7"
Engraving: 1 Script
Initial
$18.00

New!
B9154S
Bracelet
Engraving: Interlocking Monogram
$18.00

New!
B9156SW
Bracelet 7"
Engraving: 1 Script Initial
$14.45

New!
E9152SP
Pierced Only
Engraving: 1 Script Initial
$12.00

New!
B9152S
Bracelet 7"
Engraving: 1 Script Initial
$12.00

New!
B9153SW
Bracelet 7"
Engraving: 1 Script Initial
$19.95

New!
E9153SP
Pierced Only
Engraving: 1 Script Initial
$9.95

All jewelry shown is sterling silver plated.

1. *New!*
1949 $19.95
Gold Cherub Place Card Holders. Set of 4 gold cherubs with gold trimmed place cards. Approx. 6" tall. Available in gold only.

2. 2028 $25.45
Silver Plated Place Card Holders Set of six silver plated, ornate frames with place cards. Measure 3" x 4".

3. *New!*
1964 $7.45
White Porcelain Angel Card Holders Set of 6 porcelain angles with place cards. Approx. 2" tall.

4. 2041 $11.45 *Bubble Favors* Box of 24
2041-12 $9.00 12 Boxes or more
Each undecorated bottle holds 0.6 ounces of bubble solution and it's own wand. Decorate with our Favor Ribbons (2035 & 2036). Can be purchased in bulk.

5. *New!* **1948 $19.95**
Bell Place Card Holders Set of 4 silver plated bells with ringers. Approx. 2 1/4" tall. Includes silver trimmed place

6. 2035 *$16.95 White Favor Ribbons*
2036 *$16.95 Ivory Favor Ribbons*
These convenient favor ribbons are available in kits of 24. Fill with our bubble favors, rice, mints, or nuts, Everyone will love these unique favors. Each kit includes 24 pre-cut favor ribbons, matching ties and instructions.

7. *New!*
1930* $10.95
2032* $10.95
Mother of the Bride Cards
Father of the Bride Cards
The Mother and the Father of the Bride will love passing out these humorous cards at the reception. Set of 50 cards.

8. 1914 *$12.00 Vine Place Card Holder* Set of six porcelain vine place card holders with cards. 2 1/4" tall x 3" wide.

9. 1915 $13.45 *Rose Place Card Holder* Set of six porcelain rose place card holders with place cards. 1 1/4" tall x 2 1/4" wide.

I am the Father of the Bride
Nobody's paying much attention to me today, but I can assure you that I am getting my share of attention. The banks and several business firms are watching me very closely.

I am the Mother of the Bride
Today is the day my daughter weds. We've planned this wedding till we're out of our heads. We've laughed and cried and talked night and day and I wouldn't have wanted it any other way.

*Sold in quantities of three

CATHYS CONCEPTS

Tissue Holder
1926W *White/blue 4 1/2" x 3"*
Tissues included $20.45

1925W *White/blue 12" x 12" $13.45*

Tissue Holder
1927W *White 4 1/2" x 3"*
Tissues included $20.45

2050W *White only 12" x 12" $12.00*

1922W *White only 12" x 12" $21.95*

Grandmother

Mother
Thank you
mother...

Grandma with Poem Bookmark
1921W *White only 11" x 11"*
$19.95

Grandma

1923W *White 12" x 12" $10.95*

Mother with Poem Bookmark
1920W *White only 11" x 11" $19.95*

Mother

1924I *Ivory 12" x 12" $10.95*

All hankies may be embroidered free of charge with a single initial in light blue only.

Handkerchiefs

Women's Handkerchiefs with Bookmark Poem
New! **1855W** Daughter Hankie $19.95
New! **1856W** Mother-In-Law Hankie $19.95
New! **1857W** Flowergirl Hankie $19.95
New! **1858W** Stepmother Hankie $19.95

Women's Hankies measure 11" x 11 1/2"
and may be embroidered with a single block initial in blue. Bookmarks are laminated.

Men's Handkerchiefs with Bookmark Poems
New! **1851W** Father $19.95
New! **1852W** Grandfather $19.95
New! **1853W** Stepfather $19.95
New! **1854W** Father-In-Law $19.95

Men's hankies measure 17 1/2" x 16 1/2"
and may be embroidered with a block monogram in white.
Bookmarks are laminated.

Dearest Daughter

Stepmother Dear

Mother In Law

Flowergirl
*Little girl
so sweet
and small
let your flower
petals fall*

*At my
wedding
all will
see how ~ I
know you can be*

*This keepsake
hankie tucked
away can be
your "Something Old"
someday*

Dearest Grandfather
*If your eyes
should mist
a tear upon
the day I marry*

*I found this
wedding hankie
I want you
to carry*

*a token
of the bond
we share*

*I hope you
know -- Grandfather
how very much
I care*

FATHER

Father In Law

Step Father

New! **1859W** Women's Hankie
Women's Hankie may be embroidered
with a single block initial in blue.
Poem Bookmark is not included.
$16.95

New! **1850W** Men's Hankie
Men's Hankie may be embroidered
with a block monogram in white.
Poem Bookmark is not included.
$16.95

Cardholders

2006 Church Card Holder $189.00 Embellished with arched windows and silk roses, our ornate white moire church is the perfect cardholder. Cording and interlocking trim adorn this sturdy church which measures 14" x 15 1/2" x 30". Steeple and roof are detachable for the utmost convenience in shipping and storage. Add $8.00 for ground shipping.

1932 Birdcage Undecorated $46.00
1941 Birdcage Decorated $63.00
Our white metal framed birdcage with removable top is decorated with shimmer organza and satin ribbon with beautiful pearl and rhinestone embellishemnt at the heart of the bow. Measures 10" x 8" x 16 1/2".
Add $4.00 for ground shipping.

Our unique and charming church or birdcage will complete any gift table and is perfect for securing the many cards and monetary gifts given to the happy couple.

2034 *#120020345*
Ribbon Pulls
$27.95
Sterling silver plated. Instructions and ribbons are included.

New! **1963** *$24.00*
Caucasian Bride and Groom Caketop. Meaures 7" x 3 3/4".

New! **1953W** *$31.45*
Ribbon Candle Our poly resin candle has a ribbon and bow design. Tea light candle included. Measures 9"

2069W *$48.45*
English Rose Gazebo Caketop Our white gazebo caketop will look beautiful holding our bride and groom figurine (1904W) or a floral arrangement. Measures 9 1/2" x 4 1/2".

New! **1951** *$24.00*
African American Bride and Groom Caketop. Meaures 7" x 3 3/4".

1917 *$27.95*
Contemporary Caketop Our handcrafted porcelain bride and groom caketop adds a romantic look to your wedding cake. Measures 5" x 3".

Mr. & Mrs. Jay Cranwell

1915 *$13.45*
Rose Place Card Holders Set of six porcelain rose place card holders with place cards.

Caketops

CATHY'S CONCEPTS - page 231

2070W *$41.45*
English Rose Cherub Vase Caketop   Our white rose trimmed vase caketop with two attached cherubs. Measures 4 1/2" x 5". (Flowers not included.)

New! **1952W** *$34.45*
Church House Caketop   Caketop base measures 5" x 4 1/2" and is 8 1/2" tall..

1904W *$22.95*
English Rose Bride and Groom Figurine   Bride and groom figurine is 5" tall.

1906W *$20.45*
English Rose Pillar Base   Our white rose trimmed pillar base measures 4 3/4" x 2 3/4". (Pillar 7225W is sold seperately at YourBridalSuperStore.com)

2073W *$55.00*
English Rose Flutes   Our white stemmed flutes measure 8" tall. Complimentary engraving of first names and wedding date.

1907W *$9.95*
English Rose Taper Holders   Our white rose trimmed taper holders measures 3" x 2". Taper holders are sold individually. (10" Tapers 7228W sold seperately at www.YourBridalSuperStore.com)

2074W *$41.45*
English Rose Server Set   Our white server set has a delicate rose trim around each handle. Complimentary engraving of first names and wedding date.

Candelabras

New! **1958G** *Brass Plated Candelabra $22.95*
New! **1958S** *Silver Plated Candelabra $22.95*
2091 *Silver Plated Candelabra $28.95*

Truly a stunning compliment to your unity candle and tapers, Our beautiful brass and silver plated candelabras hold a single unity candle and two tapers.

Brass and silver plated candelabras (1958G and 1958S) measure 4 1/2" wide x 12 1/2" long x 4" tall. Candles are not included. Pillar and taper candles pictured with candelabra are sold at www.YourBridalSuperStore.com.

Silver plated candelabra measures 11" x 11". Candles are not included. Pillar and taper candles pictured with candelabra are sold at www.YourBridalSuperStore.com.

Angel Candle Holders

English Rose Holders

Porcelain Vine Holders

2088 *$19.95 This three piece white porcelain set features a unity candle base and two matching taper holders. Candles are not included. Candles shown are sold at www.YourBridalSuperStore.com.*

Unity base measures 4" tall x 3 1/2" wide, taper holders measure 4" tall x 2 1/2" wide.

1906W *$20.45 Our white pillar base measures 4 3/4" tall x 2 3/4" wide.*

1907W *$9.95 Our white taper holders measure 3" tall x 2" wide. Sold individually.*

Candles are not included. Candles shown are sold at www.YourBridalSuperStore.com.

1913 *$21.95 Our white porcelain set includes a unity candle holder and matching taper holders. Candles are not included. Candles shown are sold at www.YourBridalSuperStore.com.*

Base measures 4" tall x 3 1/2" wide, taper holders measure 4" tall x 2 1/2" wide.

Eternity Pillar

2095 *$33.45*

Our white porcelain oil unity candle has a floral motif trimmed in gold with gold rings. Oil is not included. Measures 9" tall.

Honeymoon Candle

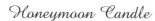

2089 *$9.95*

A soft light radiates from our honeymoon candle. A demure floral bouquet motif is embossed on the delicate off-white porcelain dome which sits on a matching saucer. A tealight beneath the dome provides a romantic glow. Tealight not included. Measures 3" tall x 4" wide.

Ribbon Candle

New!
1953W *$31.45*

Our poly resin candle has a ribbon and bow design. Tea light candle included. Measures 9" tall.

Gifts for Her

 *- page 233*

Silver Plated Envelope Compact
1501 $21.95
Complimentary engraving of a single scripted initial Measures 3 3/8" x 2 1/2".

Silver Plated Heart Key Ring
1505 $14.45
Complimentary engraving of a single scripted initial. Measures 3" x 1 1/2".

Silver Plated Tape Measure
1503 $12.00
Complimentary engraving of a single scripted initial. Measures 1 1/2".

Silver Bracelet with Heart Charm
1510 $18.00
Complimentary engraving of a single script initial. Bracelet is 7" with purple velvet pouch.

Silver Plated Address Book
1507 $20.45
Complimentary engraving on the center crest, with a single scripted initial. Measures 5 3/4" x 3 1/4"

Embroidered Tote Bag
2055 $25.45 *Our cotton canvas tote comes with a complimentary embroidered first name. Measures 20" x 13"*

Silver Heart Box
1509 $13.45
Complimentary engraving of a single script initial. Box measures 2".

Silver Plated Bookmarks
1502 *Set of Three* $9.95
Each bookmark is engraved complimentary with a single script initial. Measures 1 7/8" x 1 5/8"

Silver Plated Jewelry Box
1504 $24.00
Complimentary engraving of a scripted monogram on the lid. Measures 4" x 3 1/4" x 1 3/4"

Silver Plated Photo Frame
1508 $24.45
Complimentary engraving at the top with a scripted first name. Measures 6 1/2" x 5 1/4" and holds a 3 1/2" x 5" photograph.

ANTIQUE SILVER PHOTO FRAME

Wedding Party Pins
1900 *(3-Bride, 3-Groom)* $8.45
1901 *(3-Maid of Honor, 3-Best Man)* $8.45
1902 *(6-Bridesmaid)* $8.45
1903 *(6-Groomsmen)* $8.45

There will be no mistaking the wedding party with these clever black and white Wedding Party Pins. Sold in convenient sets of six, our pins are easy cash and carry impulse purchases. Pins measure 2 1/4" diameter.

1961W *Bride Hat* $43.95
Our decorated white bride hat will let everyone know who the bride is. This novelty hat is perfect for bachelorette parties, showers, and rehearsal dinners.

Bride and Groom Apparel
1936 *Bride T-shirt* $27.95
1937 *Groom T-shirt* $27.95
1938 *Bride Cap* $20.45
1939 *Groom Cap* $20.45
Our 100% preshrunk cotton t-shirts and adjustable ball caps make the ideal shower or engagement gift. The bride t-shirt and hat are both elegantly embroidered in metallic gold and the groom t-shirt and hat are embroidered in white. These are the perfect accessories for wedding parties, couple showers, rehearsal dinners, or honeymoons. One size fits most.

Champagne Bottle Wraps
S2021 *Set of Bride & Groom Wraps* $27.95 *Our adorable bride and groom champagne bottle wraps will be the hit of the reception. The black satin tuxedo with bow tie and boutonniere and the elegant bride complete with veil and single strand pearl necklace, will dress up any reception.*

1944W *White* $20.45 *Hard form body and soft handle are covered in satin fabric. Purse. cannot be dyed. Measures 5" x 4".*

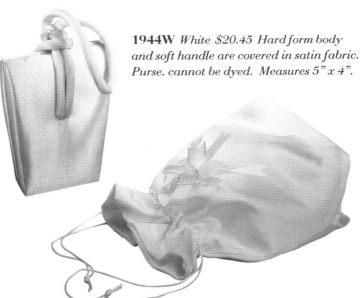

1933 *Heart Reversible Door Pillow* $28.95
"What is your mood?" Tonight or Not Tonight is embroidered, one saying on each side of the pillow in light blue satin thread on white satin with a tassel and cord handle.

1931W *Money Purse* *Matte satin fabric money purse is adorned with a romantic organza and satin bow. The perfect place to store currency or cards from your reception. Purse measures 12" x 8". White only.* $28.95

YOUR BRIDAL SUPERSTORE

proudly presents

THE
Special Day™
COLLECTION

Convey who you are by selecting lavish opulence, classic simplicity, or fun novelty from our Special Day Collection. A wide variety of everything from invitations, napkins, and matchbooks to scrolls, programs and bookmark favors awaits your selection.

*We also invite you to visit our on-line store at **www.YourBridalSuperstore.com**, featuring the most extensive collection of accessories, invitations, jewelry, gifts, favors and much more.*

YOUR BRIDAL SUPERSTORE

...everything but the groom℠

www.YourBridalSuperstore.com

PEACEFUL BLISS ▶

"From this Day Forward," that meaningful, promise-filled phrase from traditional wedding vows, is featured in glistening gold script on the front of these ecru invitations. The words are surrounded by a heart-shaped border complete with ribbons, roses and doves in flight. Your wording appears when the invitation is opened. Lined inner envelope available: gold. Displayed with wording W17 in gold ink and lettering style FLS.

SIZE: 4 1/2" x 5 7/8"

ITEM	ITEM #	25	50	75	100	Add'l 25
Invitation	WFD352	60.90	62.90	64.90	66.90	14.20
Informal Note	WF0351	43.90	44.90	45.90	46.90	10.00
Reception	WF0353	43.90	44.90	45.90	46.90	10.00
Respond	WF0354	53.90	54.90	55.90	56.90	12.20
Printed Outer Envelopes	PENV	22.00	23.00	26.70	30.40	3.70
Lined Inner Envelopes	LENV	4.90	9.80	14.70	19.60	4.90

Pricing includes black raised lettering and 14 lines of wording. For colored inks, add $7.00 to the TOTAL price of each item. Additional lines are $1.50 each.

◀ ANGEL ECHOES

Playful cherubs, classic columns and roses lend a touch of tender Victorian charm to this soft white invitation. The design is embossed to add romantic dimension to your wording. Available lined inner envelope colors: black, blue, gold, hunter, lilac, navy, peach, pearl, periwinkle, pink, plum, purple, red, rosewood (shown), sage, silver, taupe, teal and wine. Displayed with wording W36 in rosewood ink.

SIZE: 5 1/8" x 7 1/4"

ITEM	ITEM #	25	50	75	100	Add'l 25
Invitation	WFJ474	74.90	76.90	78.90	80.90	17.20
Informal Note	WF4741	43.90	44.90	45.90	46.90	10.00
Reception	WF4743	43.90	44.90	45.90	46.90	10.00
Respond	WF4744	53.90	54.90	55.90	56.90	12.20
Printed Outer Envelopes	PENV	22.00	23.00	26.70	30.40	3.70
Lined Inner Envelopes	LENV	4.90	9.80	14.70	19.60	4.90

Pricing includes black raised lettering and 14 lines of wording. For colored inks, add $7.00 to the TOTAL price of each item. Additional lines are $1.50 each.

PRISTINE CALLA LILIES ▶

Majestic, perfectly formed calla lilies surround your wording on the front of this bright white invitation card. The lilies are embossed for dramatic dimension. Lined inner envelopes available: black, gold (shown), hunter, peach, pearl, periwinkle, pink, plum, purple, rosewood, sage, silver, taupe, teal and wine. Displayed with wording W45 in gold ink and lettering style FNH.

SIZE: 5 1/2" x 7 3/4"

ITEM	ITEM #	25	50	75	100	Add'l 25
Invitation	WFU513	124.90	126.90	128.90	130.90	27.80
Informal Note	WF5131	49.90	50.90	51.90	52.90	11.20
Reception	WF5133	49.90	50.90	51.90	52.90	11.20
Respond	WF5134	59.90	60.90	61.90	62.90	13.40
Printed Outer Envelopes	PENV	22.00	23.00	26.70	30.40	3.70
Lined Inner Envelopes	LENV	4.90	9.80	14.70	19.60	4.90

Pricing includes black raised lettering and 14 lines of wording. For colored inks, add $7.00 to the TOTAL price of each item. Additional lines are $1.50 each.

1224 Edison Drive
Harewood, Maryland 21220

Sarah
and
Anthony

Mr. and Mrs. Bruce A. Marshall
invite you to share in the ceremony
uniting their daughter
Sarah Anne
and
Mr. Anthony Paul Bradley
Saturday, the tenth of May
nineteen hundred and ninety-seven
at seven o'clock in the evening
St. Paul Evangelical Lutheran Church
110 North Drake Street
Harewood, Maryland

Sarah
and
Anthony

Wedding Reception
immediately following ceremony
Venetian Room
1073 Country Club Drive

HEART BLOSSOM

A heart framed in beautifully embossed roses and lilies creates a gorgeous setting for your names on the front of this soft white invitation. The floral heart is cut from the Z-fold, which opens to reveal your wording. **Please specify names to be printed or we will use the first names from your inside wording.** Lined inner envelopes available: black, blue, fuchsia, gold, hunter, lilac, navy, peach, pearl, pink, plum, purple, red, rosewood, silver, teal and wine. Displayed with custom wording in black ink.

SIZE: 6 5/8" x 5"

ITEM	ITEM #	25	50	75	100	Add'l 25
Invitation	WFE172	84.90	86.90	88.90	90.90	19.30
Informal Note	WF1721	43.90	44.90	45.90	46.90	10.00
Reception	WF1723	43.90	44.90	45.90	46.90	10.00
Respond	WF1724	53.90	54.90	55.90	56.90	12.20
Printed Outer Envelopes	PENV	22.00	23.00	26.70	30.40	3.70
Lined Inner Envelopes	LENV	4.90	9.80	14.70	19.60	4.90

Pricing includes black raised lettering and 14 lines of wording. For colored inks, add $7.00 to the TOTAL price of each item. Additional lines are $1.50 each.

TRADITIONS OF THE HEART ▶

Three crisp panels are embossed one after the other to form a refined frame on this heavy card. The rich ecru card features your wording printed within the panels. Informals fold; reception and response enclosures are non-folding cards. Lined inner envelopes available: black (shown), gold, hunter, pearl, rosewood and wine. Displayed with wording W61 in black ink and lettering style QIL

SIZE: 5 1/8" x 7 1/4"

ITEM	ITEM #	25	50	75	100	Add'l 25
Invitation	WFJ099	70.90	72.90	74.90	76.90	16.30
Informal Note	WF5991	38.90	39.90	40.90	41.90	8.90
Reception	WF2993	38.90	39.90	40.90	41.90	8.90
Respond	WF2994	48.90	49.90	50.90	51.90	11.10
Printed Outer Envelopes	PENV	22.00	23.00	26.70	30.40	3.70
Lined Inner Envelopes	LENV	4.90	9.80	14.70	19.60	4.90

Pricing includes black raised lettering and 14 lines of wording. For colored inks, add $7.00 to the TOTAL price of each item. Additional lines are $1.50 each.

BRIDAL SPLENDOR ▶

Beautifully embossed with roses and winding filigree, this invitation evokes images of Victorian elegance. The graceful design encircles your wording on a fold of rich, smooth ecru paper. Available lined inner envelope colors: gold, hunter, pearl and wine (shown). Displayed with custom wording and wine ink and lettering style SRH

SIZE: 5" x 6 5/8"

ITEM	ITEM #	25	50	75	100	Add'l 25
Invitation	WFE618	65.90	67.90	69.90	71.90	15.30
Informal Note	WF6181	43.90	44.90	45.90	46.90	10.00
Reception	WF6183	43.90	44.90	45.90	46.90	10.00
Respond	WF6184	53.90	54.90	55.90	56.90	12.20
Printed Outer Envelopes	PENV	22.00	23.00	26.70	30.40	3.70
Lined Inner Envelopes	LENV	4.90	9.80	14.70	19.60	4.90

Pricing includes black raised lettering and 14 lines of wording. For colored inks, add $7.00 to the TOTAL price of each item. Additional lines are $1.50 each.

◀ HEART STRINGS

Pearl-embossed cherubs tug at the "heart strings" of this beautiful ecru invitation! The Z-fold is made of Forever Floral paper, which is richly embossed with an all-over pattern of rosebuds. A pair of floral hearts is embossed in pearl, delicately cut from the fold and printed with your first names. Your wording appears when the invitation is opened. **Please specify names to be printed or we will use the first names from your inside wording.** Lined inner envelope available: gold and pearl. Shown with wording W36 in wine ink.

SIZE: 7 1/4" x 5 1/8"

ITEM	ITEM #	25	50	75	100	Add'l 25
Invitation	WFJ342	130.90	132.90	134.90	136.90	29.10
Informal Note	WF3421	52.90	53.90	54.90	55.90	11.90
Reception	WF3423	52.90	53.90	54.90	55.90	11.90
Respond	WF3424	62.90	63.90	64.90	65.90	14.10
Printed Outer Envelopes	PENV	22.00	23.00	26.70	30.40	3.70
Lined Inner Envelopes	LENV	4.90	9.80	14.70	19.60	4.90

Pricing includes black raised lettering and 14 lines of wording. For colored inks, add $7.00 to the TOTAL price of each item. Additional lines are $1.50 each.

2435 Carol Court
Broad Acres, Michigan 48035

A fresh new day, and it is ours
a day of happy beginnings
when we, Jenna Marie Tanner
and Tyler John Stevenson
pledge our love as one
on Saturday, the twelfth of May
two thousand and one
at two o'clock in the afternoon
Hosanna Lutheran Church
105 Hosanna Avenue
Broad Acres, Michigan
We joyfully ask you
to share this day with us

The favor of a reply is requested
on or before April 28, 2001

M _____

_____ persons will attend

Miss Jenna Tanner
2435 Carol Court
Broad Acres, Michigan 48035

Jenna and Tyler
May 12, 2001

M _____

Table No. _____

DAISY MEADOW

Daisies "spring" from the embossed border of this large ecru invitation – lending pretty freshness to weddings held any time of year! Lined inner envelopes available: gold (shown), hunter, pearl, rosewood and wine. Displayed with wording W132 in gold ink and lettering style BIC

SIZE: 5 1/2" x 7 3/4"

ITEM	ITEM #	25	50	75	100	Add'l 25
Invitation	WFU855	92.90	94.90	96.90	98.90	21.00
Informal Note	WF8551	43.90	44.90	45.90	46.90	10.00
Reception	WF8553	43.90	44.90	45.90	46.90	10.00
Respond	WF8554	53.90	54.90	55.90	56.90	12.20
Printed Outer Envelopes	PENV	22.00	23.00	26.70	30.40	3.70
Lined Inner Envelopes	LENV	4.90	9.80	14.70	19.60	4.90

Pricing includes black raised lettering and 14 lines of wording. For colored inks, add $7.00 to the TOTAL price of each item. Additional lines are $1.50 each.

LEGEND OF LOVE ▶

"To Have & To Hold" — these beautiful words from traditional marriage vows accent the front of this French-fold invitation of white deckle-edged parchment. The front design is printed as shown in the same ink color you choose for your inside wording. Inside, your names are printed at the top in the same lettering style as your wording and are accented with the flowing "&" design shown. Your names and the same design are also printed on your enclosures. **Please specify names to be printed or we will use the first names from the invitation copy.** Lined inner envelopes available: gold, pearl, silver and wine. Displayed with wording W35 in hunter ink and lettering style UNR.

SIZE: 6 1/8" x 4 1/2"

ITEM	ITEM #	25	50	75	100	Add'l 25
Invitation	WFF819	74.90	76.90	78.90	80.90	17.20
Informal Note	WF8191	38.90	39.90	40.90	41.90	8.90
Reception	WF8193	38.90	39.90	40.90	41.90	8.90
Respond	WF8194	48.90	49.90	50.90	51.90	11.10
Printed Outer Envelopes	PENV	22.00	23.00	26.70	30.40	3.70
Lined Inner Envelopes	LENV	4.90	9.80	14.70	19.60	4.90

Pricing includes black raised lettering and 14 lines of wording. For colored inks, add $7.00 to the TOTAL price of each item. Additional lines are $1.50 each.

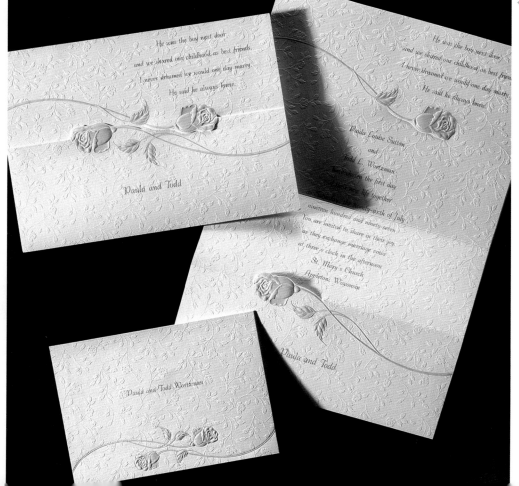

▶ RADIANT ROSES

A pair of glistening pearl roses makes a lovely closure to this uniquely folded invitation. This creamy ecru Forever Floral paper is embossed with an all-over rosebud pattern. Your names and an optional verse may be printed on the front for a personal touch; your wording appears inside. **When ordering, please be sure to specify names and choice of verse. If a verse is not indicated, we will print the verse shown. If names are not specified, we will print your names as they appear on the inside copy.** Lined inner envelope available: pearl. Displayed with wording W14 and verse F-42 in gold ink and lettering style BER.

SIZE: 6 5/8" x 5"

ITEM	ITEM #	25	50	75	100	Add'l 25
Invitation	WFE488	130.90	132.90	134.90	136.90	29.10
Informal Note	WF4881	52.90	53.90	54.90	55.90	11.90
Reception	WF4883	52.90	53.90	54.90	55.90	11.90
Respond	WF4884	62.90	63.90	64.90	65.90	14.10
Printed Outer Envelopes	PENV	22.00	23.00	26.70	30.40	3.70
Lined Inner Envelopes	LENV	4.90	9.80	14.70	19.60	4.90

Pricing includes black raised lettering and 14 lines of wording. For colored inks, add $7.00 to the TOTAL price of each item. Additional lines are $1.50 each.

SWIRL OF ROMANCE

Swirling vines and filigree in striking silver foil make this invitation irresistibly elegant! The bright white paper also features a striped border to beautifully frame your wording on the front. Lined inner envelopes available: black, hunter, peach, pearl, periwinkle, pink, plum, purple, rosewood, sage, silver, taupe, teal and wine. Displayed with wording W14 in silver ink.

SIZE: 5 1/2" x 7 3/4"

ITEM	ITEM #	25	50	75	100	Add'l 25
Invitation	WFU455	116.90	118.90	120.90	122.90	26.10
Informal Note	WF4551	52.90	53.90	54.90	55.90	11.90
Reception	WF4553	52.90	53.90	54.90	55.90	11.90
Respond	WF4554	62.90	63.90	64.90	65.90	14.10
Printed Outer Envelopes	PENV	22.00	23.00	26.70	30.40	3.70
Lined Inner Envelopes	LENV	4.90	9.80	14.70	19.60	4.90

Pricing includes black raised lettering and 14 lines of wording. For colored inks, add $7.00 to the TOTAL price of each item. Additional lines are $1.50 each.

ROMANCE

(-B) A perfect long-stemmed rose, complete with a tiny ...ud, is embossed to accent your wording. The invitation is ...vailable in your choice of creamy ecru (A) or soft white ...) paper to match the tone and the color scheme of your ...edding. Lined inner envelopes available for ecru (A): ...old, hunter, pearl and wine. Shown with wording W36 in ...ack ink and typestyle PA. Lined inner envelopes for soft ...hite (B): black, blue, fuchsia, gold, hunter (shown), lilac, ...avy, peach, pearl, pink, plum, purple, red, rosewood, ...lver, teal and wine. Displayed with wording W132 in ...unter ink and lettering style SRH.

...IZE: 5" x 6 5/8"

ECRU (A)

ITEM	ITEM #	25	50	75	100	Add'l 25
Invitation	WFE195	65.90	67.90	69.90	71.90	15.30
Informal Note	WF1951	43.90	44.90	45.90	46.90	10.00
Reception	WF1953	43.90	44.90	45.90	46.90	10.00
Respond	WF1954	53.90	54.90	55.90	56.90	12.20
Printed Outer Envelopes	PENV	22.00	23.00	26.70	30.40	3.70
Lined Inner Envelopes	LENV	4.90	9.80	14.70	19.60	4.90

...ricing includes black raised lettering and 14 lines of wording. For colored inks, ...dd $7.00 to the TOTAL price of each item. Additional lines are $1.50 each.

SOFT WHITE (B)

ITEM	ITEM #	25	50	75	100	Add'l 25
Invitation	WFE241	65.90	67.90	69.90	71.90	15.30
Informal Note	WF2411	43.90	44.90	45.90	46.90	10.00
Reception	WF2413	43.90	44.90	45.90	46.90	10.00
Respond	WF2414	53.90	54.90	55.90	56.90	12.20
Printed Outer Envelopes	PENV	22.00	23.00	26.70	30.40	3.70
Lined Inner Envelopes	LENV	4.90	9.80	14.70	19.60	4.90

...ricing includes black raised lettering and 14 lines of wording. For colored inks, ...dd $7.00 to the TOTAL price of each item. Additional lines are $1.50 each.

EXPRESSIONS ▶

Golden dots and a filigree border make this large, square invitation of sheer white paper an expression of your unique style. For a finishing touch, add a white chiffon bow. Because of the translucent quality of the paper, please allow for some natural variation in color. When writing on translucent paper, be sure to use permanent ink to prevent smearing. Because of the lavish size of this invitation, additional postage will be required. Lined inner envelopes available: black, gold (shown), pearl, pink, purple, rosewood, teal and wine. Displayed with wording W36 in gold ink.

SIZE: 7" x 7"

ITEM	ITEM #	25	50	75	100	Add'l 25
Invitation	WFX943	132.90	134.90	136.90	138.90	29.50
Informal Note	WF9421	54.90	55.90	56.90	57.90	12.30
Reception	WF9423	54.90	55.90	56.90	57.90	12.30
Respond	WF9424	64.90	65.90	66.90	67.90	14.50
Printed Outer Envelopes	PENV	22.00	23.00	26.70	30.40	3.70
Lined Inner Envelopes	LENV	4.90	9.80	14.70	19.60	4.90

Pricing includes black raised lettering and 14 lines of wording. For colored inks, add $7.00 to the TOTAL price of each item. Additional lines are $1.50 each.

◀ LUSH GARLANDS

A-B) Lush garlands of embossed roses become a statement of pure elegance on a simple soft white panel — perfect f invitations and announcements alike. Available in two si to suit your celebration. The larger invitation has the add elegance of embossed roses in the lower right corner. Lin inner envelopes available for the larger size (A): black, bl gold (shown), hunter, lilac, navy, peach, pearl, periwinkle pink, plum, purple, red, rosewood, sage, silver, taupe, teal and wine. Lined inner envelopes for the smaller size (B): black, blue, fuchsia, gold, hunter, lilac, navy, peach, pearl pink, plum, purple, red, rosewood, silver, teal and wine. Both displayed with custom wording in black ink.

SIZE: A) 5 1/8" X 7 1/4"
B) 5" X 6 5/8"

ITEM	ITEM #	25	50	75	100	Add'l 2
Invitation A (folded size 5 1/8" x 7 1/4")	WFJ772	74.90	76.90	78.90	80.90	17.20
Invitation B (folded size 5" x 6 5/8")	WFE193	70.90	72.90	74.90	76.90	16.30
Informal Note	WF7721	43.90	44.90	45.90	46.90	10.00
Reception	WF7723	43.90	44.90	45.90	46.90	10.00
Respond	WF7724	53.90	54.90	55.90	56.90	12.20
Printed Outer Envelopes	PENV	22.00	23.00	26.70	30.40	3.70
Lined Inner Envelopes	LENV	4.90	9.80	14.70	19.60	4.90

Pricing includes black raised lettering and 14 lines of wording. For colored inks, add $7.00 to the TOTAL price of each item. Additional lines are $1.50 each.

NESTLED LOVE

A pair of doves nestles together amid a border of romantic embossed filigree, symbolizing your love and commitment to each other. Soft white paper provides the perfect background for the design and your invitation wording. Lined inner envelopes available: aqua, black, blue, fuchsia, gold, hunter, lilac, navy, peach, pearl, pink, plum, purple, red, rosewood, silver, teal and wine (shown). Displayed with custom wording in wine ink and lettering style LUP.

SIZE: 5" x 6 5/8"

ITEM	ITEM #	25	50	75	100	Add'l 25
Invitation	WFE601	65.90	67.90	69.90	71.90	15.30
Informal Note	WF6011	43.90	44.90	45.90	46.90	10.00
Reception	WF6013	43.90	44.90	45.90	46.90	10.00
Respond	WF6014	53.90	54.90	55.90	56.90	12.20
Printed Outer Envelopes	PENV	22.00	23.00	26.70	30.40	3.70
Lined Inner Envelopes	LENV	4.90	9.80	14.70	19.60	4.90

Pricing includes black raised lettering and 14 lines of wording. For colored inks, add $7.00 to the TOTAL price of each item. Additional lines are $1.50 each.

SCULPTED FILIGREE

(-B) An embossed border of sculpted filigree simply and elegantly frames your wording on this lovely invitation, which is available in bright white and ecru. Add your personal touch with your choice of wording, lettering style and ink color. Lined inner envelopes available for bright white (A): gold, pearl and silver. Displayed with wording W36 in black ink and lettering style OLD. Shown with a printed outer envelope. Lined inner envelope available for ecru (B): gold (shown). Displayed with wording W17 in gold ink and typestyle PI.

SIZE: 4 1/2" x 5 7/8"

BRIGHT WHITE (A)

ITEM	ITEM #	25	50	75	100	Add'l 25
Invitation	WFD1441	58.90	60.90	62.90	64.90	13.80
Informal Note	WF24411	43.90	44.90	45.90	46.90	10.00
Reception	WF24413	43.90	44.90	45.90	46.90	10.00
Respond	WF24414	53.90	54.90	55.90	56.90	12.20
Printed Outer Envelopes	PENV	22.00	23.00	26.70	30.40	3.70
Lined Inner Envelopes	LENV	4.90	9.80	14.70	19.60	4.90

Pricing includes black raised lettering and 14 lines of wording. For colored inks, add $7.00 to the TOTAL price of each item. Additional lines are $1.50 each.

ECRU (B)

ITEM	ITEM #	25	50	75	100	Add'l 25
Invitation	WFD1442	58.90	60.90	62.90	64.90	13.80
Informal Note	WF24421	43.90	44.90	45.90	46.90	10.00
Reception	WF24423	43.90	44.90	45.90	46.90	10.00
Respond	WF24424	53.90	54.90	55.90	56.90	12.20
Printed Outer Envelopes	PENV	22.00	23.00	26.70	30.40	3.70
Lined Inner Envelopes	LENV	4.90	9.80	14.70	19.60	4.90

Pricing includes black raised lettering and 14 lines of wording. For colored inks, add $7.00 to the TOTAL price of each item. Additional lines are $1.50 each.

FLORAL SENSATION ▶

Your one-of-a-kind event deserves something special! This lavish square invitation card features a flourish of colorful flowers printed on bright white paper. Your wording is printed on a translucent overlay that neatly tucks into hidden slits in the corners of the card. Because of the size, additional postage will be required. Available lined inner envelopes: black, gold, pearl, pink, purple, rosewood, silver, teal and wine.

SIZE: 7" x 7"

ITEM	ITEM #	25	50	75	100	Add'l 25
Invitation	WFX440T	138.90	140.90	142.90	144.90	30.80
Informal Note	WF4401	52.90	53.90	54.90	55.90	11.90
Reception	WF4403	52.90	53.90	54.90	55.90	11.90
Respond	WF4404	62.90	63.90	64.90	65.90	14.10
Printed Outer Envelopes	PENV	22.00	23.00	26.70	30.40	3.70
Lined Inner Envelopes	LENV	4.90	9.80	14.70	19.60	4.90

Pricing includes black raised lettering and 14 lines of wording. For colored inks, add $7.00 to the TOTAL price of each item. Additional lines are $1.50 each.

BEAUTIFUL BEGINNINGS ▶

Deep green ribbons and rich burgundy roses surround your wording on this rich ecru invitation card – a beautiful beginning to a truly romantic wedding! Pearl embossing raises the design from the paper and creates a soft glow. Lined inner envelopes available: gold, hunter (shown), pearl, rosewood and wine. Displayed with wording W14 in hunter ink and lettering style QIL.

SIZE: 5 1/2" x 7 3/4"

ITEM	ITEM #	25	50	75	100	Add'l 25
Invitation	WFU461	124.90	126.90	128.90	130.90	27.80
Informal Note	WF4611	52.90	53.90	54.90	55.90	11.90
Reception	WF4613	52.90	53.90	54.90	55.90	11.90
Respond	WF4614	62.90	63.90	64.90	65.90	14.10
Printed Outer Envelopes	PENV	22.00	23.00	26.70	30.40	3.70
Lined Inner Envelopes	LENV	4.90	9.80	14.70	19.60	4.90

Pricing includes black raised lettering and 14 lines of wording. For colored inks, add $7.00 to the TOTAL price of each item. Additional lines are $1.50 each.

◀ CRAYON FIGURES

This delightful Z-fold invitation will bring a smile to your guests' faces. The stick figure bride and groom stand apart on the front above the verse, and the invitation opens to show them together. Verse may be printed as shown or with your choice of verse. Limit verse to two lines. **If names and verse are not specified, we will print the verse shown with your first names from the invitation copy.** Lined inner envelopes available: black, blue, fuchsia, gold, hunter, lilac, navy, peach, pearl, pink, plum, purple, rosewood (shown), silver, teal and wine. Displayed with wording W35 in rosewood ink and lettering style UNR.

SIZE: 6 5/8" x 5"

ITEM	ITEM #	25	50	75	100	Add'l 25
Invitation	WFE1368	110.90	112.90	114.90	116.90	24.80
Informal Note	WF23681	52.90	53.90	54.90	55.90	11.90
Reception	WF23683	52.90	53.90	54.90	55.90	11.90
Respond	WF23684	62.90	63.90	64.90	65.90	14.10
Printed Outer Envelopes	PENV	22.00	23.00	26.70	30.40	3.70
Lined Inner Envelopes	LENV	4.90	9.80	14.70	19.60	4.90

Pricing includes black raised lettering and 14 lines of wording. For colored inks, add $7.00 to the TOTAL price of each item. Additional lines are $1.50 each.

SHEER FLORAL

Hydrangeas and roses in soft pink, purple, gold and green are visible through the sheer white paper of this folded invitation. Your wording is printed on the front within a simple embossed border. **Because of the translucent quality of the paper, please allow for some natural variation in color. When writing on translucent paper, be sure to use permanent ink to prevent smearing.** Note: The inner envelopes included are bright white with pointed flaps. Lined inner envelopes available: black, gold, hunter, pearl, purple (shown), silver, teal and wine. Displayed with wording W132 in purple ink and lettering style BIC.

SIZE: 5 1/8" x 7 1/4"

ITEM	ITEM #	25	50	75	100	Add'l 25
Invitation	WFJ642	159.00	162.00	164.00	167.90	35.70
Informal Note	WF6421	54.90	55.90	56.90	57.90	12.30
Reception	WF6423	54.90	55.90	56.90	57.90	12.30
Respond	WF6424	64.90	65.90	66.90	67.90	14.50
Printed Outer Envelopes	PENV	22.00	23.00	26.70	30.40	3.70
Lined Inner Envelopes	LENV	4.90	9.80	14.70	19.60	4.90

Pricing includes black raised lettering and 14 lines of wording. For colored inks, add $7.00 to the TOTAL price of each item. Additional lines are $1.50 each.

TROPICAL ROMANCE ▶

Perfect for a wedding with a tropical location or theme, this Tea Length invitation card features pearl-embossed shells that form a heart at the top and a border at the bottom. The paper is bright white Forever Floral – the embossed rosebuds add an extra touch of romance. Your names are printed within the heart at the top. **Please specify names to be printed or we will use the first names from the inside wording.** Lined inner envelopes available: gold (shown) and pearl. Displayed with wording W2 in brown ink and lettering style UNR-BIC.

SIZE: 4" x 9 1/4"

ITEM	ITEM #	25	50	75	100	Add'l 25
Invitation	WFT179	116.90	118.90	120.90	122.90	26.10
Informal Note	WF1791	52.90	53.90	54.90	55.90	11.90
Reception	WF1793	52.90	53.90	54.90	55.90	11.90
Respond	WF1794	62.90	63.90	64.90	65.90	14.10
Printed Outer Envelopes	PENV	22.00	23.00	26.70	30.40	3.70
Lined Inner Envelopes	LENV	4.90	9.80	14.70	19.60	4.90

Pricing includes black raised lettering and 14 lines of wording. For colored inks, add $7.00 to the TOTAL price of each item. Additional lines are $1.50 each.

AUTUMN ROMANCE ▶

Red and gold autumn leaves have the look of fine watercolors as they float atop a wide border to frame your wording on this large, square invitation card. Your wording is showcased in the center of this non-folding card of bright white paper. Because of the lavish size of this invitation, additional postage will be required. Lined inner envelopes available: black, gold (shown), pearl and silver. Displayed with wording W36 in gold ink.

SIZE: 7" x 7"

ITEM	ITEM #	25	50	75	100	Add'l 25
Invitation	WFX868	118.90	120.90	122.90	124.90	26.50
Informal Note	WF8681	35.90	36.90	37.90	38.90	8.20
Reception	WF8683	35.90	36.90	37.90	38.90	8.20
Respond	WF8684	45.90	46.90	47.90	48.90	10.40
Printed Outer Envelopes	PENV	22.00	23.00	26.70	30.40	3.70
Lined Inner Envelopes	LENV	4.90	9.80	14.70	19.60	4.90

Pricing includes black raised lettering and 14 lines of wording. For colored inks, add $7.00 to the TOTAL price of each item. Additional lines are $1.50 each.

◀ MAJESTIC MOUNTAIN

An embossed mountain scene is a majestic backdrop for the invitation to your wedding. Your names are printed along the bottom cutaway edge of this soft white invitation for an extra personal touch. Because of the rich embossing, your inside wording will appear below the fold. **Please specify names to be printed below the cutaway edge or we will use first names from your invitation copy.** Lined inner envelopes available: black, blue, gold, hunter, lilac, navy (shown), peach, pearl, periwinkle, pink, plum, purple, red, rosewood, sage, silver, taupe, teal and wine. Displayed with navy ink in lettering style STU.

SIZE: 7 1/4" x 5 1/8"

ITEM	ITEM #	25	50	75	100	Add'l 25
Invitation	WFJ480	74.90	76.90	78.90	80.90	17.20
Informal Note	WF4801	43.90	44.90	45.90	46.90	10.00
Reception	WF4803	43.90	44.90	45.90	46.90	10.00
Respond	WF4804	53.90	54.90	55.90	56.90	12.20
Printed Outer Envelopes	PENV	22.00	23.00	26.70	30.40	3.70
Lined Inner Envelopes	LENV	4.90	9.80	14.70	19.60	4.90

Pricing includes black raised lettering and 14 lines of wording. For colored inks, add $7.00 to the TOTAL price of each item. Additional lines are $1.50 each.

PILLAR OF ROMANCE ▶

An elegant bride and groom, accented with pearl, pose amid pillars and rose garlands on this soft white Z-fold invitation. The garlands are tinted with deep pink and green. Your names are printed above the couple and a verse of your choice is printed on the center panel. **Specify names and verse when ordering, or we will use the first names from your invitation wording and print the verse shown.** Lined inner envelopes available: black, gold, hunter, pearl, periwinkle, pink, rosewood (shown), sage, silver, taupe, teal and wine. Shown with verse F51 and rosewood ink.

SIZE: 5 1/8" x 7 1/4"

ITEM	ITEM #	25	50	75	100	Add'l 25
Invitation	WFJ294	116.90	118.90	120.90	122.90	26.10
Informal Note	WF2941	52.90	53.90	54.90	55.90	11.90
Reception	WF2943	52.90	53.90	54.90	55.90	11.90
Respond	WF2944	62.90	63.90	64.90	65.90	14.10
Printed Outer Envelopes	PENV	22.00	23.00	26.70	30.40	3.70
Lined Inner Envelopes	LENV	4.90	9.80	14.70	19.60	4.90

Pricing includes black raised lettering and 14 lines of wording. For colored inks, add $7.00 to the TOTAL price of each item. Additional lines are $1.50 each.

◀ ## THE FUTURE IS OURS

Innocence and first love are captured in the touching black-and-white photo on this invitation's sheer overlay, while the gold foil verse expresses how inspiring the new millennium is to your love. The verse reads: "Take my hand in walking through a new century. Together we will build it, the future is ours to see." The photo is also enhanced with a single red rose. Your wording is printed on a white card beneath; you join the two pieces with the sheer white ribbon that is included. Lined inner envelopes available: black, gold, hunter, pearl, red and silver. Displayed with wording W42 in gold ink.

SIZE: 5 1/8" x 7 1/4"

ITEM	ITEM #	25	50	75	100	Add'l 25
Invitation	WFJ617	169.00	173.00	177.00	181.90	38.70
Informal Note	WF0181	52.90	53.90	54.90	55.90	11.90
Reception	WF0183	52.90	53.90	54.90	55.90	11.90
Respond	WF0184	62.90	63.90	64.90	65.90	14.10
Printed Outer Envelopes	PENV	22.00	23.00	26.70	30.40	3.70
Lined Inner Envelopes	LENV	4.90	9.80	14.70	19.60	4.90

Pricing includes black raised lettering and 14 lines of wording. For colored inks, add $7.00 to the TOTAL price of each item. Additional lines are $1.50 each.

SYMBOL OF MATRIMONY ▶

A simple gold foil cross is accented with a garland of pearl-embossed ribbons and roses. These traditional symbols of matrimony beautifully adorn this soft white invitation. Lined inner envelopes available: black, blue, fuchsia, gold (shown), hunter, lilac, navy, peach, pearl, pink, plum, purple, red, rosewood, teal and wine. Displayed with custom wording in gold ink and lettering style FLS.

SIZE: 5" x 6 5/8"

ITEM	ITEM #	25	50	75	100	Add'l 25
Invitation	WFE271	90.90	92.90	94.90	96.90	20.60
Informal Note	WF2711	52.90	53.90	54.90	55.90	11.90
Reception	WF2713	52.90	53.90	54.90	55.90	11.90
Respond	WF2714	62.90	63.90	64.90	65.90	14.10
Printed Outer Envelopes	PENV	22.00	23.00	26.70	30.40	3.70
Lined Inner Envelopes	LENV	4.90	9.80	14.70	19.60	4.90

Pricing includes black raised lettering and 14 lines of wording. For colored inks, add $7.00 to the TOTAL price of each item. Additional lines are $1.50 each.

1505 Cliff Drive
Walsh, Colorado 81090

Courtney
and
Marcus

Mr. and Mrs. Marcus Bentilla

A fresh new day, and it is ours
a day of happy beginnings
when we, Courtney Ann Jameson
and Marcus Jeffrey Bentilla
pledge our love as one
on Saturday, the second of June
two thousand one
at two o'clock in the afternoon
St. Theresa Catholic Church
13500 Mulberry Street
Walsh, Colorado
We joyfully ask you
to share this day with us

Reception following ceremony
Lakewood Country Club
983 Lakewood Court

DAISY CHEER

Pearl-embossed white daisies with cheery yellow centers add fresh elegance to this sheer white invitation.
Because of the translucent quality of the paper, please allow for some natural variation in paper color.
When writing on translucent paper, be sure to use permanent ink to prevent smearing. Lined inner
envelopes available: black, gold (shown), hunter, pearl and silver. Displayed with wording W132 in gold ink
and lettering style ISA.
SIZE: 5 1/8" x 7 1/4"

ITEM	ITEM #	25	50	75	100	Add'l 25
Invitation	WFJ473	124.90	126.90	128.90	130.90	27.80
Informal Note	WF4731	54.90	55.90	56.90	57.90	12.30
Reception	WF4733	54.90	55.90	56.90	57.90	12.30
Respond	WF4734	64.90	65.90	66.90	67.90	14.50
Printed Outer Envelopes	PENV	22.00	23.00	26.70	30.40	3.70
Lined Inner Envelopes	LENV	4.90	9.80	14.70	19.60	4.90

Pricing includes black raised lettering and 14 lines of wording. For colored inks,
add $7.00 to the TOTAL price of each item. Additional lines are $1.50 each.

JOINED BY LOVE

Your hearts are entwined forever – and the pair of interlocking gold foil hearts at the top of this invitation symbolize your emotions beautifully! The non-folding invitation is made of sheer, bright white paper. An embossed panel at the edges further distinguishes your wording. Because of the translucent quality of the paper, please allow for some natural color variation. When writing on translucent paper, be sure to use permanent ink to prevent smearing. Lined inner envelopes available: black, gold (shown), hunter, pearl, periwinkle, purple, red, silver, teal and wine. Shown with wording W46 in gold ink and lettering style VOL.

SIZE: 5 1/8" x 7 1/4"

ITEM	ITEM #	25	50	75	100	Add'l 25
Invitation	WFJ1401	114.90	116.90	118.90	120.90	25.70
Informal Note	WF24011	54.90	55.90	56.90	57.90	12.30
Reception	WF24013	54.90	55.90	56.90	57.90	12.30
Respond	WF24014	64.90	65.90	66.90	67.90	14.50
Printed Outer Envelopes	PENV	22.00	23.00	26.70	30.40	3.70
Lined Inner Envelopes	LENV	4.90	9.80	14.70	19.60	4.90

Pricing includes black raised lettering and 14 lines of wording. For colored inks, add $7.00 to the TOTAL price of each item. Additional lines are $1.50 each.

▷ QUAINT HYDRANGEA ▷

...beautiful periwinkle blue hydrangea printed on a folded, sheer white insert is framed by an ...mbossed window on the front of the bright white folded wrap. Your wording is printed inside the ...eer insert. You simply join the two-piece invitation with the pretied silver cord, which is included. ...ned inner envelopes available: gold, pearl, purple and silver. Displayed with wording W132 in ...riwinkle ink and lettering style PEN.

...ZE: 5" x 6 5/8"

TEM	ITEM #	25	50	75	100	Add'l 25
...nvitation	WFE874	161.00	164.00	167.00	170.90	36.30
...nformal Note	WF8741	43.90	44.90	45.90	46.90	10.00
...eception	WF8743	43.90	44.90	45.90	46.90	10.00
...espond	WF8744	53.90	54.90	55.90	56.90	12.20
...rinted Outer ...nvelopes	PENV	22.00	23.00	26.70	30.40	3.70
...ined Inner ...nvelopes	LENV	4.90	9.80	14.70	19.60	4.90

...ricing includes black raised lettering and 14 lines of wording. For colored inks, ...dd $7.00 to the TOTAL price of each item. Additional lines are $1.50 each.

◁ UNIQUELY SWEET

Silver foil hearts entwine at the top of this invitation, sending a message of true love. The invitation is made from sheer, bright white paper embossed with a crisp single panel. When writing on translucent paper, be sure to use permanent ink to prevent smearing. Lined inner envelopes available: black, hunter, pearl, periwinkle, purple, red, silver (shown), teal and wine. Displayed with wording W46 in silver ink and lettering style BIC.

SIZE: 5 1/8" x 7 1/4"

ITEM	ITEM #	25	50	75	100	Add'l 25
Invitation	WFJ187	114.90	116.90	118.90	120.90	25.70
Informal Note	WF1871	54.90	55.90	56.90	57.90	12.30
Reception	WF1873	54.90	55.90	56.90	57.90	12.30
Respond	WF1874	64.90	65.90	66.90	67.90	14.50
Printed Outer Envelopes	PENV	22.00	23.00	26.70	30.40	3.70
Lined Inner Envelopes	LENV	4.90	9.80	14.70	19.60	4.90

Pricing includes black raised lettering and 14 lines of wording. For colored inks, add $7.00 to the TOTAL price of each item. Additional lines are $1.50 each.

DIMENSIONS ▶

White roses and leaves accent your names and wording on this unique invitation. It has the look of texture and embossing but is actually smoothly printed on soft white paper. Your names are printed within a white square on the front, and when the lovely Z-fold is opened, your wording and more roses are revealed inside. **If names are not specified, we will use the first names from the inside copy.** Lined inner envelopes available: black, blue, fuchsia, gold, hunter, lilac, navy, peach, pearl (shown), pink, plum, purple, red, rosewood, silver, teal and wine. Displayed with wording W45 in black ink and lettering style MAH.

SIZE: folded 6 5/8" x 5"

ITEM	ITEM #	25	50	75	100	Add'l 25
Invitation	WFE285	116.90	118.90	120.90	122.90	26.10
Informal Note	WF2851	52.90	53.90	54.90	55.90	11.90
Reception	WF2853	52.90	53.90	54.90	55.90	11.90
Respond	WF2854	62.90	63.90	64.90	65.90	14.10
Printed Outer Envelopes	PENV	22.00	23.00	26.70	30.40	3.70
Lined Inner Envelopes	LENV	4.90	9.80	14.70	19.60	4.90

Pricing includes black raised lettering and 14 lines of wording. For colored inks, add $7.00 to the TOTAL price of each item. Additional lines are $1.50 each.

◀ SIMPLICITY OF LOVE

Smooth soft white paper forms our most economically elegant invitation; your wording receives full attention! Perfect for the most extravagant and the most intimate celebrations alike. Lined inner envelopes available: gold, pearl, pink and silver. Displayed with wording W36 in black ink and lettering style QIL-FNH. (All other elements of your ensemble may be printed with lettering style QIL or FNH.) Lettering style QIL is shown on the respond card.

SIZE: folded 4 1/2" x 5 7/8"

ITEM	ITEM #	25	50	75	100	Add'l 25
Invitation	WFD038	46.90	48.90	50.90	52.90	11.20
Informal Note	WF0321	35.90	36.90	37.90	38.90	8.20
Reception	WF0323	35.90	36.90	37.90	38.90	8.20
Respond	WF0324	45.90	46.90	47.90	48.90	10.40
Printed Outer Envelopes	PENV	22.00	23.00	26.70	30.40	3.70
Lined Inner Envelopes	LENV	4.90	9.80	14.70	19.60	4.90

Pricing includes black raised lettering and 14 lines of wording. For colored inks, add $7.00 to the TOTAL price of each item. Additional lines are $1.50 each.

CASCADING ROSES ▶

Your invitation message is elegantly framed with cascading roses embossed in the corners of a classic panel. On our richest ecru paper, this invitation speaks eloquently of tradition and true love. Lined inner envelopes available: black, gold, hunter, pearl, rosewood and wine (shown). Displayed with wording W17 in wine ink and lettering style PEN.

SIZE: folded 5 1/8" x 7 1/4"

ITEM	ITEM #	25	50	75	100	Add'l 25
Invitation	WFJ598	74.90	76.90	78.90	80.90	17.20
Informal Note	WF5921	43.90	44.90	45.90	46.90	10.00
Reception	WF5923	43.90	44.90	45.90	46.90	10.00
Respond	WF5924	53.90	54.90	55.90	56.90	12.20
Printed Outer Envelopes	PENV	22.00	23.00	26.70	30.40	3.70
Lined Inner Envelopes	LENV	4.90	9.80	14.70	19.60	4.90

Pricing includes black raised lettering and 14 lines of wording. For colored inks, add $7.00 to the TOTAL price of each item. Additional lines are $1.50 each.

► HEARTS OF BLUE

Navy pearl-embossed roses and hunter leaves add unique beauty to this large, bright white Z-fold invitation. Stylized pearl hearts swirl on the front above a verse of your choice. One heart is sculpted from the fold and cut to form a frame for your names, which are printed inside above your wording. **If names and verse are not specified, we will print the verse shown and use first names from the invitation copy.** Lined inner envelopes available: black, gold, hunter, pearl, sage, silver, taupe and teal. Displayed with wording W36 and verse F90 in grey ink and lettering style MAH.

SIZE: folded 7 1/4" x 5 1/2"

ITEM	ITEM #	25	50	75	100	Add'l 25
Invitation	WFU280	126.90	128.90	130.90	132.90	28.20
Informal Note	WF2801	52.90	53.90	54.90	55.90	11.90
Reception	WF2803	52.90	53.90	54.90	55.90	11.90
Respond	WF2804	62.90	63.90	64.90	65.90	14.10
Printed Outer Envelopes	PENV	22.00	23.00	26.70	30.40	3.70
Lined Inner Envelopes	LENV	4.90	9.80	14.70	19.60	4.90

Pricing includes black raised lettering and 14 lines of wording. For colored inks, add $7.00 to the TOTAL price of each item. Additional lines are $1.50 each.

BOUND BY LOVE ►

Interlocking hearts printed with your names are just the beginning of this soft white invitation's romance. Pearl-embossed roses and ribbons accent the hearts, while sculpted edges lend a graceful touch. Inside, your wording is topped by a tiny pearl rose – perfection to the last detail! **Please specify names when ordering, or we will use the first names from your invitation copy.** Lined inner envelopes available: black, blue, fuchsia, gold, hunter, lilac, navy, peach, pearl, pink, plum, purple, red, rosewood, silver, teal and wine. Displayed with wording W42 in grey ink. Informal is shown with monogram M4.

SIZE: folded 5" x 6 5/8"

ITEM	ITEM #	25	50	75	100	Add'l 25
Invitation	WFE152	130.90	132.90	134.90	136.90	29.10
Informal Note	WF1521	49.90	50.90	51.90	52.90	11.20
Reception	WF1523	49.90	50.90	51.90	52.90	11.20
Respond	WF1524	59.90	60.90	61.90	62.90	13.40
Printed Outer Envelopes	PENV	22.00	23.00	26.70	30.40	3.70
Lined Inner Envelopes	LENV	4.90	9.80	14.70	19.60	4.90

Pricing includes black raised lettering and 14 lines of wording. For colored inks, add $7.00 to the TOTAL price of each item. Additional lines are $1.50 each.

CELTIC ROMANCE

The Celtic knot design bordering this bright white invitation beautifully symbolizes never-ending love. The border is embossed in pearl for elegant shimmer. Lined inner envelopes available: black (shown), gold, hunter, peach, pearl, periwinkle, pink, plum, purple, rosewood, sage, silver, taupe, teal and wine. Displayed with wording W14 in black ink and lettering style PA.

SIZE: 5 1/2" x 7 3/4"

ITEM	ITEM #	25	50	75	100	Add'l 25
Invitation	WFU180	122.90	124.90	126.90	128.90	27.40
Informal Note	WF1801	49.90	50.90	51.90	52.90	11.20
Reception	WF1803	49.90	50.90	51.90	52.90	11.20
Respond	WF1804	59.90	60.90	61.90	62.90	13.40
Printed Outer Envelopes	PENV	22.00	23.00	26.70	30.40	3.70
Lined Inner Envelopes	LENV	4.90	9.80	14.70	19.60	4.90

Pricing includes black raised lettering and 14 lines of wording. For colored inks, add $7.00 to the TOTAL price of each item. Additional lines are $1.50 each.

PEARL-EMBOSSED NAPKINS

A-E) Make your good taste evident at each place setting with pearl-embossed napkins. Your names and wedding date are printed in the lettering style shown. Choose an ink or foil color listed below. Napkins are available only with the pearl designs shown; ink or foil color applies to personalization. Available in luncheon (13" x 13") and beverage (9 1/2" x 9 1/2") sizes. **Please specify names, date and ink or foil color.**

A-E

Pearl Beverage Napkins	50	42.00
Pearl Beverage Napkins	add'l 50	18.00
Pearl Luncheon Napkins	50	42.00
Pearl Luncheon Napkins	add'l 50	18.00

INK COLORS
Black, brown, fuchsia, hunter, lilac, navy, periwinkle, pink, plum, purple, red, rosewood, sage, taupe, teal, wine

FOIL COLORS
Blue, gold, hunter, pink, purple, red, silver, teal, white

Please note: For best results, choose gold or silver foil for black, navy, purple, teal and wine napkins.

B,C) A pearl-embossed floral heart adorns ecru or white napkins. Your names and date are printed within the heart design. Please note: Beverage napkins feature your names and wedding date printed in the elegant block lettering shown. See pricing at left. Please specify names, date and ink or foil color. Ink and foil colors listed above.

B) WF197B Ecru Pearl Floral Heart Beverage
WF197L Ecru Pearl Floral Heart Luncheon

C) WF194B White Pearl Floral Heart Beverage
WF194L White Pearl Floral Heart Luncheon

A) White napkins feature a pearl-embossed bouquet your names and wedding date are printed beneath the design. See pricing at left. Please specify names date and ink or foil color. Ink and foil colors listed above.

WF188B White Pearl Bouquet Beverage
WF188L White Pearl Bouquet Luncheon

D) White napkins are embossed with fresh and fun daisies in pearl. Your names and wedding date are printed beneath the design. See pricing above. Please specify names, date and ink or foil color. Ink and foil colors listed above.

WF161B White Pearl Daisy Beverage
WF161L White Pearl Daisy Luncheon

E) A pearl couple design adds romance to these white napkins. Your names and wedding date are printed beneath the design. See pricing above. Please specify names, date and ink or foil color. Ink and foil colors listed above.

WF290B White Pearl Couple Beverage
WF290L White Pearl Couple Luncheon

F

Sweetheart Beverage Napkins	50	46.50
Sweetheart Beverage Napkins	add'l 50	22.50
Sweetheart Luncheon Napkins	50	46.50
Sweetheart Luncheon Napkins	add'l 50	22.50

F) A sweet image of young love is printed in black and white on white napkins. A single red rose adds color. Your names and date are printed beneath the design. Choose an ink or foil color listed above for personalization. Available in luncheon (13" x 13") and beverage (9 1/2" x 9 1/2") sizes. Please specify names, date and ink or foil color. Please specify names, date and ink or foil color. Ink and foil colors listed above.

WF215B White Sweetheart Beverage
WF215L White Sweetheart Luncheon

◄ PERSONALIZED NAPKINS

WHITE NAPKINS AT COST SAVINGS!

Select our supersoft white napkins and save! White complements any ink or foil color and makes your design, names and wedding date stand out. Mix with a solid color sold above for a striking effect. Select a design from those shown on page 288 and choose your ink or foil color from those listed below. The colored inks listed are available at no additional charge. Available in beverage size (9 1/2" x 9 1/2" unfolded) and luncheon size (13" x 13" unfolded). Lettering style available as shown. Please specify names, wedding date, design choice and ink or foil color for personalization.

WF102B White Beverage Napkins
WF102L White Luncheon Napkins

Prices include imprinting of first names, wedding date and choice of design for both the white and colorful napkins. If you would not like a design on your napkins, please state "No Design" when ordering.

COLORFUL NAPKINS

Our supersoft three-ply napkins are available in a wide variety of colors with your choice of design to coordinate with your wedding theme. Your napkins will also be personalized with your names and wedding date in the lettering style shown. Select a design from page 288 and an ink or foil color from those listed below. The colored inks listed are available at no additional charge. Also be sure to order napkins for the groom's dinner and gift opening to coordinate your entire wedding weekend. Napkins are available in two sizes: beverage napkins (9 1/2" x 9 1/2" unfolded) and luncheon napkins (13" x 13" unfolded). Please specify names, wedding date, design choice and ink or foil color for personalization. To obtain an accurate count when ordering napkins, we recommend you double the number of invitations ordered, assuming two guests will attend per invitation.

NAPKIN COLORS	ITEM NUMBERS	
	Beverage Size	Luncheon Size
A) Red	WF109B	WF109L
B) Silver Grey	WF119B	WF119L
C) Black	WF141B	WF141L
D) White	WF102B	WF102L
E) Navy	WF135B	WF135L
F) Yellow	WF105B	WF105L
G) Purple	WF117B	WF117L
H) Lavender	WF115B	WF115L
I) Periwinkle	WF176B	WF176L
J) Teal	WF122B	WF122L
K) Sage	WF160B	WF160L
L) Peach	WF136B	WF136L
M) Rose	WF118B	WF118L
N) Pastel Pink	WF106B	WF106L
O) Wine	WF116B	WF116L
P) Hunter	WF138B	WF138L
Q) Ecru	WF111B	WF111L

A-Q

Colored Beverage Napkins	100	29.00
Colored Luncheon Napkins	100	29.00
White Beverage Napkins	100	27.00
White Luncheon Napkins	100	27.00

INK COLORS

Black, brown, fushia, gold, grey, hunter, lilac, navy, plum, purple, red, rosewood, periwinkle, pink, sage, silver, taupe, teal, wine

FOIL COLORS

Blue, gold, hunter, pink, purple, rainbow, red, silver, teal, white

Rainbow foil combines several foil colors and is available for an additional charge of $5.00 for every 100 napkins ordered.

Please note: For best results, choose gold or silver foil for black, navy, purple, teal and wine napkins.

Note: Napkins can be printed with a maximum of 26 characters per line including spaces. Capital letters count as two characters.

ACCESSORIES

A) Personalized matchbooks are a traditional, affordable keepsake for your guests. Available in 15 colors to brighten up every table, matchbooks are printed in foil with your first names, wedding date and choice of design at no additional cost. Select a foil color from those listed below and a design from page 288. Please specify names, wedding date, design and foil color when ordering.

WF02M White
WF33M Silver*
WF138M Purple
WF88M Black
WF66M Pink
WF99M Red
WF100M Rose
WF105M Dark Blue

WF95M Teal
WF376M Ecru
WF103M Peach
WF348M Hunter
WF101M Lavender
WF102M Wine
WF22M Gold*

* NOTE: Gold and silver matches are available with black imprint only.

A

White Matchbooks	50	23.90
Colored Matchbooks	50	23.90

B) Personalized matchboxes make great favors for your guests. These useful favors are imprinted with your names, wedding date and choice of design from those on page 288 in a foil color from those listed below. Each matchbox contains 40 stick matches. Please specify names, wedding date, design and foil color when ordering. Assembly required.

WFSLM Favor Matchboxes

B

Favor Matchboxes	50	31.90
Favor Matchboxes	add'l 50	20.90

C) Place card matchbooks combine two useful accessories into one convenient item. The white matchbooks are personalized with your names, wedding date, and name and table number lines in the design shown. Select a foil color from those listed below. Please specify names, wedding date and foil color when ordering.

WF302BM Place Card Matchbooks

C

Place Card Matchbooks	50	28.90

D) They look like matchbooks, but actually contain tiny notepads inside instead of matches! The notepad covers are personalized with your first names and wedding date in your choice of foil color from those listed below. Choose a design from those shown on page 288 to be printed above your personalization. Each 2" x 2" notepad contains 15 perforated pages. Please specify names, wedding date, design number and foil color when ordering.

WFMBPK Pink
WFMBRO Rose
WFMBBK Black
WFMBWH White
WFMBGD Gold

WFMBPU Purple
WFMBPE Peach
WFMBHG Hunter
WFMBMR Wine
WFMBTL Teal (shown open)

D

Notepads	50	27.90

FOIL COLORS AVAILABLE FOR PERSONALIZED MATCHES AND FAVOR NOTEPADS

foil colors Available for your Matches and Notepads: black, brown, gold, hunter, lilac, navy, periwinkle, pink, purple, rainbow*, red, rosewood, silver, teal and white

*Rainbow foil combines several foil colors and is available for an additional charge of $1.50 for every 50 matches or notepads. Will be printed in black foil in the lettering style shown. Please specify names, wedding date and design.

THANK YOU NOTES

for gracious expressions of gratitude

A-L) For gifts as special as your wedding presents, thank you notes are essential. Preprinted notes let you respond quickly; however, more personal handwritten notes should be sent later. Choose from the verses shown on page 255 or create a verse of your own for a note that expresses your style. You may also select a lettering style from those shown on page 284 for your inside verse. Thank you designs are available only as shown. Prices for black ink and up to five lines of copy are shown. For a colorful ink add $7.00. When ordering printed notes, include your verse, lettering style and ink color. Also, specify if names are to be printed beneath the verse. Mailing envelopes are included.

A,B) An ornate filigree border is embossed on ecru or white paper for romance. "Thank You" appears in sparkling gold foil script.
A) WF0105 Ecru Filigree or B) WF0115 White Filigree

C,D) Our rich white and ecru thank you notes feature a triple panel with roses in subtle embossing and a lustrous gold foil "Thank You."
C) WF1135 White Roses or D) WF5735 Ecru Roses

E) Beautifully embossed ivy entwines the border of these bright white notes with "Thank You" in gold foil. WF4935 Ivy Design

F) An embossed floral heart surrounds the words "Thank You" in gold foil on this white note. WF1075 Floral Heart

A-F

	50	100	add'l 25
Thank you - Printed	48.90	52.90	11.30
Thank you - Blank	18.00		8.50

G) Silver hearts add sparkle to this white thank you note.
WF0015 Hearts

H) Young love is captured in this black-and-white portrait on white paper accented by a gold foil verse and a red rose.
WF7995 Young Love

I) Rich burgundy roses and green leaves are embossed in pearl on these ecru notes. "Thank You" glistens in gold foil.
WF1085 Burgundy Roses

J) An ornate pearl-embossed border frames a gold foil "Thank You" on this bright white note.
WF1245 Pearl Embossed

K) Translucent white paper* is embossed with a swirling filigree pattern and features a gold foil "Thank You."
WF1395 Translucent Embossed Swirls

L) Beautiful pastel flowers are printed on sheer white paper*, and "Thank You" sparkles in gold foil.
WF6425 Translucent Floral.

* Because of the unique, translucent quality of the paper, please allow for some natural color variation. Be sure to use permanent ink when writing on these notes to prevent smearing.

G

	50	100	add'l 25
Thank you - Printed	53.90	57.90	12.30
Thank you - Blank	19.50		9.00

H-J

	50	100	add'l 25
Thank you - Printed	53.90	57.90	12.50
Thank you - Blank	19.50		9.00

K-L

	50	100	add'l 25
Thank you - Printed	62.90	66.90	14.25
Thank you - Blank	21.00		10.00

A,B) A double band of shimmering pearl highlights the embossed border of these elegant bright white thank you notes. "Thank You" gleams in your choice of gold or silver foil.
A) WF1525 Gold/Pearl Panel
B) WF1535 Silver/Pearl Panel

	50	100	add'l 25
Thank you - Printed	53.90	57.90	12.30
Thank you - Blank	19.50		9.00

C-J) These traditional thank you notes could not be more lovely. For added elegance, an embossed rose adorns notes H-J.
C) WF8655 White/rainbow foil
D) WF1235 White/purple foil
E) WF9995 White/hunter foil
F) WF5015 White/navy foil
G) WF7075 Ecru/gold foil
H) WF1475 White/black foil/rose
I) WF1145 White/gold foil/rose
J) WF0465 Ivory/gold foil/rose

	50	100	add'l 25
Thank you - Printed	43.90	47.90	10.20
Thank you - Blank	15.50		7.00

L) Pretty pastel flowers and titles in gold foil make these white notes a lovely way to express your thanks to your wedding party and others. The set includes 29 blank cards and 30 blank envelopes: one card titled "To my Best Man," one "To my Maid of Honor," one "To my Matron of Honor," one "To my Personal Attendant," one "To my Flowergirl," one "To my Ringbearer," five cards with "To my Bridesmaid," five cards with "To my Groomsman," four cards with "To my Usher," and nine cards with "Thank You for Your Services."
WF3805

Thank you - Wedding Party	set	8.95

POPULAR THANK YOU VERSES

These verses may be used on the inside of your thank you cards. You may choose from those shown below or write your own. Specify the verse number in the Verse No. box on the order form. If you choose to write your own thank you verse, write "custom" in the Verse No. box and write your verse in the space provided.

TY5

With sincere appreciation,
we both send thanks to you
for your very lovely gift
and for your thoughtful wishes, too.

Bethany and Roger Zimmerman

TY6

A loving note can barely say
all we felt that magic day.
A heartfelt thanks is sent to you
for your thoughtful gift and wishes, too.

Maria and Jerry Steinback

TY8

Words cannot express
the joy that we feel
remembering that you shared
the beginning of our new life together.
Thank you for your very thoughtful gift.

Mr. and Mrs. Russell Jackson

TY38

Being remembered
In such a nice way
Means a lot more than
Just "thank you" can say!
Mr. and Mrs. Kenneth Isder

FAVOR BOOKMARKS AND SCROLLS
meaningful, memorable keepsakes

BOOKMARKS
Printed with your names, wedding date and choice of verse, bookmarks are an elegant, personal way to thank your guests! Each bookmark may also be printed with a design of your choice from page 288 to coordinate with your wedding theme. Select a verse from those shown on the bookmarks, or write your own verse for an additional $25.00 charge. Please be sure to specify the verse number in the blank provided on the order form when ordering. Pricing is for black ink. Your verse, names, design and wedding date may be printed on the 2 1/4" x 8 1/4" bookmarks in a colorful ink for an additional $7.00 charge. The following colored inks are available: brown, fuchsia, gold, grey, hunter, lilac, navy, periwinkle, pink, plum, purple, red, rosewood, sage, silver, taupe, teal and wine. Verses available only in the lettering style shown on the bookmarks. Satin tassels are free with your bookmarks. Please specify the tassel color when ordering. Choose from silver, teal, white, emerald, black, ecru, gold, purple or pink tassels or hunter. If a tassel color is not noted, tassels that match the paper color will be sent. Tassels are not attached.
Please specify your names, wedding date, verse, design, ink color and tassel color.

A-C

Bookmark - WF605BKMK	50	47.90
Bookmark - WF605BKMK	add'l 25	18.50
Bookmark - WF603BKMK	50	45.90
Bookmark - WF603BKMK	add'l 25	18.00
Bookmark - WF30122BKMK	50	43.90
Bookmark - WF30122BKMK	add'l 50	35.00

A-C) Translucent white bookmarks are available with a colorful floral pattern, an embossed filigree pattern or smooth to suit your wedding style. **Because of the translucent quality of the paper, please allow for some natural color variation.**
A) WF605BKMK Floral Translucent, shown with verse FB108
B) WF603BKMK Embossed Filigree Translucent, shown with verse FB106 and design 1035C
C) WF30122BKMK Smooth Translucent, shown with verse FB1 and design 1104C

SCROLLS
Scrolls are a popular way to thank guests for making your day special. Choose a verse from those shown on page 255, or you may write your own verse for an additional $25.00. Each 5" x 7" scroll will also be personalized with your names and wedding date. Scrolls D-G may also be printed with a design from page 288. Your design, verse, names and wedding date will be printed in the same ink color. Prices shown are for printing in black ink; for printing in a colored ink, add $7.00. Choose an ink color from page 283 and lettering style from page 284. Scrolls may be rolled and secured with scroll rings (item K sold on page 257) and handed to guests before the ceremony or placed at each plate at the reception. **Please indicate names, wedding date, design (items D-G), lettering style, verse and ink color.**

D,E) Scrolls made from Forever Floral paper let you thank guests with style.
Choose creamy ecru or bright white paper.
D) WF8006 Ecru Forever Floral, shown with verse SC107 and design 2637C
E) WF9006 White Forever Floral, shown with verse SC113 and design 1930C

Scroll - WF8006	100	45.9
Scroll - WF8006	add'l 50	19.5
Scroll - WF9006	100	45.9
Scroll - WF9006	add'l 50	19.5

F,G) Rich, smooth vellum papers give these scrolls traditional appeal.
F) WF1466 Ecru Vellum (no deckle edge), shown with verse SC107 and design 1064C
G) WF2026 White Vellum Deckle, shown with verse SC102 and design 1464C

Scroll - WF1466	100	40.90
Scroll - WF1466	add'l 50	18.50
Scroll - WF2026	100	40.90
Scroll - WF2026	add'l 50	18.50

H,I) Scrolls of sheer white paper are printed with an all-over filigree pattern in glossy ink or with a colorful floral pattern for unique elegance. **Because of the translucent quality of the paper, please allow for some natural variation in color.**
H) WF9426 Filigree Translucent
I) WF6426 Floral Translucent

Scroll - WF9426	100	47.90
Scroll - WF9426	add'l 50	20.50
Scroll - WF6426	100	47.90
Scroll - WF6426	add'l 50	20.50

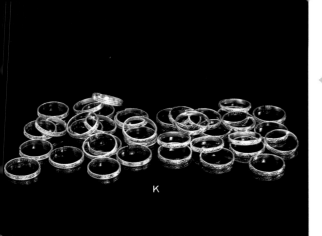

K) Gold and silver rings are perfect for securing your scrolls, decorating favors, using as napkin rings...and more! Sold in packages of 144.
WFP92G Gold Rings
WFP92S Silver Rings

Gold Rings - WFP92G	7.90
Silver Rings - WFP92S	7.90

PLACE CARDS
seating your guests in style

A-J) Personalized place cards direct your guests to their places at the table with beautiful designs that reflect your wedding theme. Prices include printing in black ink with your first names, wedding date and lines to write guests' names and table number. Items C, D, I and J may also be printed with your choice of design from page 288. For printing in a colorful ink, add $7.00. See page 283 for ink selection and page 284 for lettering style-choices. **Please specify names, wedding date and ink color.**

A) Add a unique touch to each place setting with these personalized heart-shaped place cards designed to attach to the stems of your toasting flutes. Each 3 3/4" X 2 3/4" white card features a pearl heart outline and rose design. A slot and opening at the top makes it easy for you to secure the cards around the stems of your flutes.
WF1808 Flute Stem Place Cards

A

Place card - WF1808	50	40.90
Place card - WF1808	add'l 25	17.50

B) Sheer white paper with a subtle pinstripe design creates these clearly elegant place cards. An embossed scroll frame surrounds your personalization on the front. Place cards measure 41/4" x 2 1/8" **Because of the translucent quality of the paper, please allow for some natural color variation. When writing on translucent place cards, be sure to use permanent ink to prevent smearing. Design only as shown.**
WF6428 Translucent Place Cards

C,D) Forever Floral paper is an elegant backdrop for place cards. Choose a design from page 288. Your names, date and design are printed in the same ink color. Place cards measure 4 1/4" x 2 1/8"
C) WF9008 White
D) WF8008 Ecru

E,F) An ornate border is embossed around the edges of these white or ecru place cards. Place cards measure 4 3/8" x 2 1/8" **Design only as shown.**
E) WF2248 White Embossed
F) WF3018 Ecru Embossed

G,H) Three embossed panels surround large bright white or ecru place cards with elegance. Place cards measure 4 3/8" x 2 1/4". **Design only as shown.**
G) WF91 White
H) WF976PC Ecru

I,J) Crisp ecru, white or bright white (not shown) place cards let you create the look! Choose a design from page 288. Your names, wedding date and design are printed in the same ink color. Place cards measure 4 3/8" x 2 1/8"
 I) WF0328 White Vellum
J) WF2388 Ecru Vellum
   WF9108 Bright White Vellum.

B

Place card - WF6428	50	47.90
Place card - WF6428	add'l 25	11.50

C-D

Place card - WF9008	50	47.90
Place card - WF9008	add'l 25	11.50
Place card - WF8008	50	47.90
Place card - WF8008	add'l 25	11.50

E-F

Place card - WF2248	50	47.90
Place card - WF2248	add'l 25	11.50
Place card - WF3018	50	47.90
Place card - WF3018	add'l 25	11.50

G-H

Place card - WF91	50	47.90
Place card - WF91	add'l 25	11.50
Place card - WF976PC	50	47.90
Place card - WF976PC	add'l 25	11.50

I-J

Place card - WF0328	50	44.90
Place card - WF0328	add'l 25	10.50
Place card - WF2388	50	44.90
Place card - WF2388	add'l 25	10.50
Place card - WF9108	50	44.90
Place card - WF9108	add'l 25	10.50

WEDDING PROGRAMS
elegant guides to your ceremony

A-E) Wedding programs welcome guests to your ceremony and provide important information. Prices are for 70 lines of copy in black ink; for a colorful ink add $7.00. A message up to 14 lines long may be printed on the back for $25.00 extra. Choose a lettering style from page 284 for your introductory wording; the remaining copy is printed in block lettering. If you would like a proof copy of your programs, there will be a $25.00 charge. Please allow 48 hours for processing of your proof copy once received, plus shipping time. This also applies to your program order. Because of the amount of wording, we cannot accept phone orders for programs. For complete ordering information, see the order form at the end of the book.

A) Pearl-embossed hearts, roses and ribbons gleam on this soft white Z-fold program, and "Our Wedding Service" sparkles in gold foil. Your first names are printed within the hearts in the same lettering style and ink color as your introductory inside wording. **Please specify names.** Folded size: 3 3/4" x 8 1/2"

	50	75	100	add'l 25
Program - WFP1050	92.90	95.90	98.90	21.90

B) A beautiful bouquet of white flowers is captured on this soft white program. "Love One Another" is printed in black beside the floral design. Your program wording is printed inside. Coordinate with any invitation. Folded size: 5 1/2" x 8 1/2"

	50	75	100	add'l 25
Program - WFP657P Printed	77.90	80.90	83.90	18.90
Program - WFP657B Blank			40.90	9.00

C) A black-and-white photograph of charming young sweethearts is enhanced by touches of color to create adorable programs. "This Day I'll Marry My Friend..." appears in white on the front; your program wording is printed inside. Folded size: 5 1/2" x 8 1/2"

	50	75	100	add'l 25
Program - WFP0112P Printed	77.90	80.90	83.90	18.90
Program - WFP0112B Blank			40.90	9.00

D) Wrap your wedding programs in sheer elegance! A fold of sheer white paper printed with "Our Wedding Service" your names, wedding date and location covers a fold of ecru parchment, which is printed inside with your ceremony information. The two pieces are scored and punched at the sides, making it easy for you to fold and join them with the ecru satin ribbon included. **Because of the unique quality of the translucent paper, please allow for some natural color variation. Please specify names, wedding date and ceremony location for printing on the front.** Folded size: 5 1/2" x 8 1/2"

	50	75	100	add'l 25
Program - WFP1360	133.90	143.90	155.90	33.90

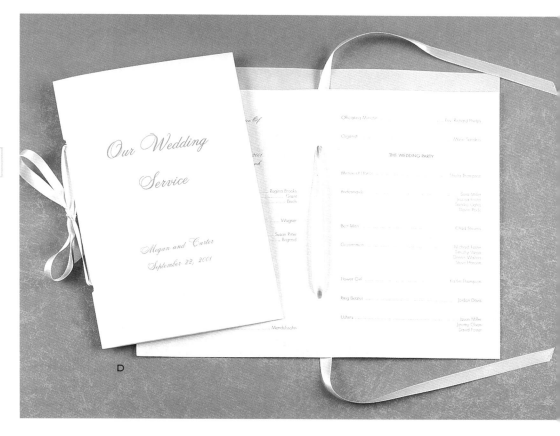

E) A romantic pattern of pearl leaves and filigree covers the outside of this beautiful tri-fold program of translucent white paper. The front is printed with "The Marriage Service of," your names and wedding date. The inside two panels are printed with your introductory wording and your ceremony information. **Because of the unique quality of the translucent paper, please allow for some natural color variation. Please specify names and wedding date for printing on the front.** Folded size: 4" x 9".

	50	75	100	add'l 25
Program - WFP436	84.00	86.00	88.00	19.70

DECORATIONS...*for reception flair*

A) Our white pew bows are an easy and elegant way to reserve pews for special family members and friends or add a decorative touch to all the pews at your ceremony. The 5" bows are made of a sheer-finished plastic and form magically in seconds by pulling the small ribbon ends. No fussing — just perfect bows every time.
WFF392 White Pew Bows ....$10.95 *per pkg. of 4*

B) Add romantic touches to your wedding with beautiful ecru or white ribbon and netting bows. The bows are perfect accents for pews, floral arrangements, chairs, reception tables and much more. The bows, which are shipped flat to prevent crushing, form easily by pulling and securing the small ribbon ends. When formed, the bows measure 6½" in diameter and have two 12" streamers.
WF024 Ecru Bow ....$4.95 *each*
WF040 White Bow ....$4.95 *each*

C) Add romantic glimmer to your wedding decor with our white bridal lights. The 31-foot, 70-bulb strands have outlets at each end for stringing together. The lights are perfect for indoor and outdoor use.
WF15652 White Bridal Lights $14.95

D) Provide a safe and convenient way to collect cards and monetary gifts during your reception with this wishing well. The corrugated cardboard well is 27½" x 12" and holds approximately 250 cards. Two 5" white tissue bells are included. ***Because of its size, we will ship this item separately.***
WF702 Wishing Well $38.95

E) Your bouquet is such a special part of your bridal attire — so proudly display it on your reception table in a handy bouquet clamp! The white clamps are made of sturdy plastic and secure easily to your tables. Each clamp comes with two interchangeable attachments to hold most bouquet styles. A hook at the bottom of the clamp allows you to attractively drape your table covering behind your bouquet. Be sure to order a clamp to hold each bridesmaid's bouquet for a colorful, uniquely decorated head table. ***Each clamp holds one bouquet.***
WF88 Bouquet Holder ....$15.95 *each*

F) Decorate the windows of your getaway car easily and without damage using white temporary paint. The paint goes on effortlessly with the sponge applicator built into the tube and wipes off with a wet cloth. Perfect for indoor and outdoor use, the sponge marker can be used on windows, posters, banners and more.
WF05 Sponge Marker $9.00

www.YourBridalSuperstore.com

A) Let the world know you're "Just Married" with this sheer plastic banner featuring white and silver bells and white lettering. Moisten the 7¾" x 29" reusable banner and apply to any flat surface. Perfect for your getaway car.
WF06 "Just Married" Banner $16.50

B) Beautifully printed and sculpted, this black-and-white "Just Married" banner will be a romantic accent to your getaway car. Cutout doves "carry" the banner and white hearts add sweet detail. The 38" x 16" banner is made of sturdy water-resistant paperboard. Foam strips on the back lock into your trunk, securing the banner to the back of your car.
WFJMDOV Dove-Design Car Banner $27.50

C) Inspired by all the elegance of the Victorian era, this beautiful marriage certificate will document your wedding with style and grace. The 11" x 14" certificate is made of thick, high quality paper and is ready to complete and frame.
WF39700 Victorian Marriage Certificate $19.50

D) Stylish sunglasses with a white "Just Married" design on the lens are essential for wearing during the getaway and on your honeymoon. Sunglasses are available in your choice of black or white and include a neck strap.
WF30JMB Black Sunglasses $13.95
WF30JMW White Sunglasses $13.95

E) Document your marriage with a certificate preserved in this white folder. The folder displays a beautiful certificate (ready to complete) and a 7" x 10" portrait. Personalize the cover with your names engraved on a gold-tone plate. The folder is a special keepsake for you and a touching gift for parents and grandparents. **Specify names and wedding date**.
WF837B Marriage Certificate Folder $17.50
WF837P Personalized ....$5.00 Engraving Fee + $17.50

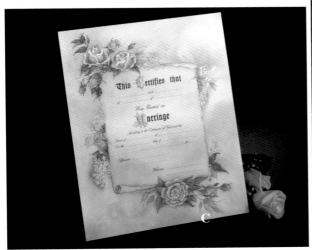

www.YourBridalSuperstore.com

Special Day ™

BALLOONS...
for festive and "uplifting" decorations

A-G) Carry through your wedding theme with these fun decorator balloons. Each balloon inflates to 11" and may be filled with helium to make stunning arrangements. The white balloons have a pearly finish and feature the design in black printing; item E features the design in pearl. Balloons are sold in packages of 20.

A) *WF10009 White Balloons / "This Day"*...*$11.95 pkg.*
B) *WF2109 White Balloons / "Just Married"*..................................*$11.95 pkg.*
C) *WF660 White Balloons / Doves* ....*$11.95 pkg.*
D) *WF4110WH White Balloons / Black Silhouette* ....*$11.95 pkg.*
E) *WF32003 White Balloons / Pearl Hearts and "Just Married"*........*$13.95 pkg.*
F) *WF077WN White Balloons / Western* ....*$11.95 pkg.*
G) *WF4109WH White Balloons / Sweetheart Couple* ....*$11.95 pkg.*

H) A heart design framed in roses and lilies features "Just Married" in black on 11" pearl balloons.
WFHFB Rose Heart Balloons .... *$11.95 per pkg. of 20*

I) Vines of lovely green ivy on clear 11" balloons are an elegantly unique decoration.
WFGIB Ivy Balloons... *$13.95 per pkg. of 20*

J) A white "Just Married" design is accented with flowers, hearts, doves, rings, bells and toasting glasses on these soft white 11" balloons.
WFJMB Floral Just Married Balloons.................................. *$13.95 per pkg. of 20*

K) Touching, colorful photos by popular photographer Kim Anderson are printed in full color on both sides of these heart-shaped Mylar balloons. One side features a bride and groom with the words "It's just the beginning," and the other side features the same couple and the word "Celebrate." The silver balloons measure 18" x 18" and are perfect for filling with helium. *Kim Anderson© NBM Bahner Studios*
WF036 Kim Anderson Heart-Shaped Mylar Balloons ....*$24.95 per 10*

L) Silver foil hearts cover these clear, heart-shaped Mylar balloons with romance. The sturdy balloons are dramatically beautiful on their own and also make lovely complements to the colorful balloons we offer on page 263. Each measures 18" x 18" and is suitable for filling with helium.
WF42013 Heart-Shaped Mylar Balloons with Silver Hearts ....*$24.95 per 10*

www.YourBridalSuperstore.com

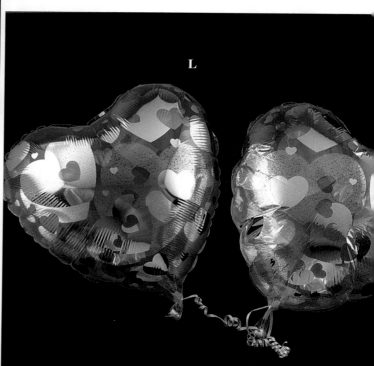

A) Our fabulous kit contains everything you need to create a beautiful 36" x 40" balloon heart sculpture. The kit comes with easy-to-follow instructions, 180 five-inch pearl balloons, two sizing templates and a three-piece metal frame.
WF48007 Balloon Heart Kit *$33.50*

B) Pearly 11" balloons in a variety of romantic colors add elegance to all of your wedding decorations! Choose from blue, emerald, hot pink, ivory, peach, pearl, pink, purple and teal. Note: Each package contains one color. **Please specify color(s).**
WFC650 Pearlized Balloons ....*$27.50 per pkg. of 144*

C) Create an impressive balloon arch quickly and easily with this balloon decorating strip. Helium-filled balloons instantly form the arch. No wires needed – just secure the ends with weights. A 25-foot strip of durable clear plastic holds up to 12 balloons per foot.
WF32007 Balloon Decorating Strip *$11.95*

D) Pearly white balloons will add a bridal touch to your entire celebration – from showers to parties to reception! Balloons measure 11" when inflated. **Please specify pearl white when ordering.**
WFC650 Pearl White Balloons ....*$27.50 per pkg. of 144*

E) White, easy-to-assemble tissue bells make decorating a breeze. They are available in four sizes for creating beautifully balanced arrangements.
WFBC5205 5" White Tissue Bells ....*$17.95 per pkg. of 12*
WFTB7 7" White Tissue Bells ....*$21.95 per pkg. of 12*
WFBC5209 9" White Tissue Bells ....*$17.95 per pkg. of 6*
WFTB12 12" White Tissue Bells ....*$21.95 per pkg. of 6*

F) Curling ribbon is a lovely way to tie favors, hang balloons and accent gifts. The 3/16" white ribbon is available on 500-yard rolls.
WFC3505 White Curling Ribbon ....*$7.95 per roll*

G) Create an elegant canopy, decorations for your tables and other festive touches with white crepe paper streamers. The 2" wide streamers are available on 500-foot rolls.
WFSC501 White Crepe Paper Streamers ....*$9.00 per roll*

www.YourBridalSuperstore.com

Special Day - page 263

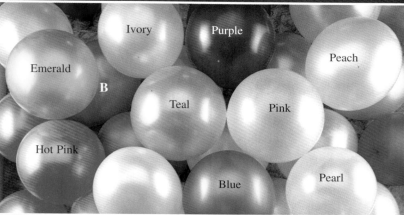

Ivory Purple Peach Emerald B Teal Pink Hot Pink Blue Pearl

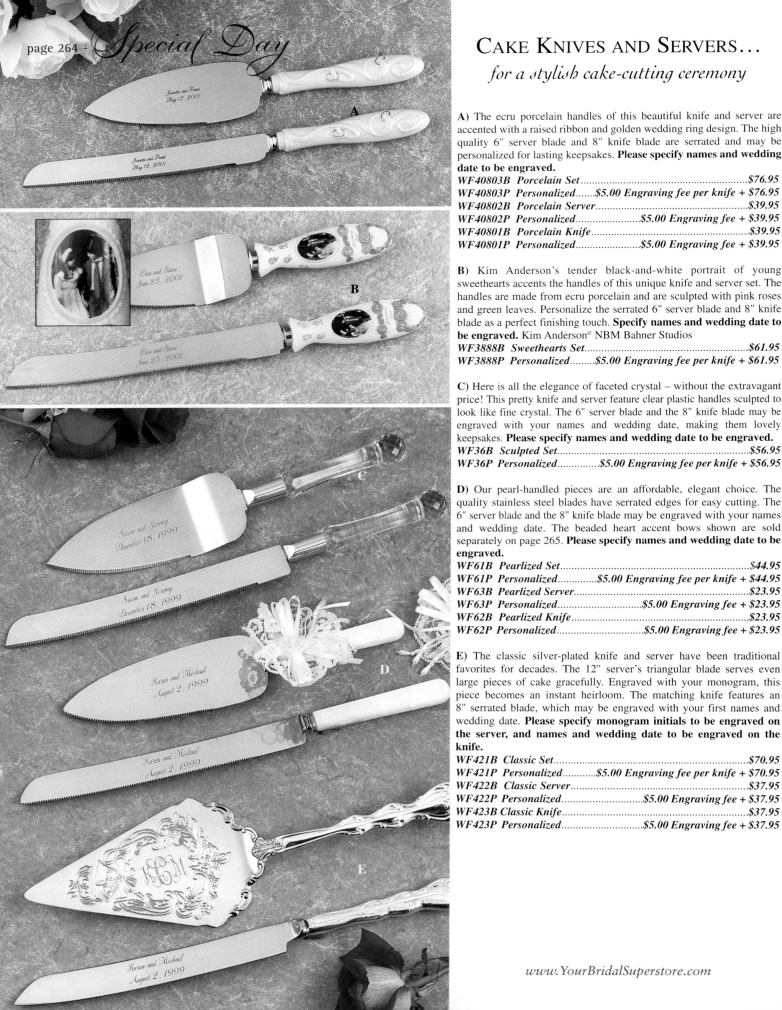

CAKE KNIVES AND SERVERS...
for a stylish cake-cutting ceremony

A) The ecru porcelain handles of this beautiful knife and server are accented with a raised ribbon and golden wedding ring design. The high quality 6" server blade and 8" knife blade are serrated and may be personalized for lasting keepsakes. **Please specify names and wedding date to be engraved.**

WF40803B Porcelain Set...$76.95
WF40803P Personalized.......$5.00 Engraving fee per knife + $76.95
WF40802B Porcelain Server...$39.95
WF40802P Personalized.......................$5.00 Engraving fee + $39.95
WF40801B Porcelain Knife..$39.95
WF40801P Personalized.......................$5.00 Engraving fee + $39.95

B) Kim Anderson's tender black-and-white portrait of young sweethearts accents the handles of this unique knife and server set. The handles are made from ecru porcelain and are sculpted with pink roses and green leaves. Personalize the serrated 6" server blade and 8" knife blade as a perfect finishing touch. **Specify names and wedding date to be engraved.** Kim Anderson© NBM Bahner Studios

WF3888B Sweethearts Set...$61.95
WF3888P Personalized.........$5.00 Engraving fee per knife + $61.95

C) Here is all the elegance of faceted crystal – without the extravagant price! This pretty knife and server feature clear plastic handles sculpted to look like fine crystal. The 6" server blade and the 8" knife blade may be engraved with your names and wedding date, making them lovely keepsakes. **Please specify names and wedding date to be engraved.**

WF36B Sculpted Set...$56.95
WF36P Personalized...............$5.00 Engraving fee per knife + $56.95

D) Our pearl-handled pieces are an affordable, elegant choice. The quality stainless steel blades have serrated edges for easy cutting. The 6" server blade and the 8" knife blade may be engraved with your names and wedding date. The beaded heart accent bows shown are sold separately on page 265. **Please specify names and wedding date to be engraved.**

WF61B Pearlized Set..$44.95
WF61P Personalized...............$5.00 Engraving fee per knife + $44.95
WF63B Pearlized Server...$23.95
WF63P Personalized..........................$5.00 Engraving fee + $23.95
WF62B Pearlized Knife..$23.95
WF62P Personalized..........................$5.00 Engraving fee + $23.95

E) The classic silver-plated knife and server have been traditional favorites for decades. The 12" server's triangular blade serves even large pieces of cake gracefully. Engraved with your monogram, this piece becomes an instant heirloom. The matching knife features an 8" serrated blade, which may be engraved with your first names and wedding date. **Please specify monogram initials to be engraved on the server, and names and wedding date to be engraved on the knife.**

WF421B Classic Set..$70.95
WF421P Personalized...........$5.00 Engraving fee per knife + $70.95
WF422B Classic Server..$37.95
WF422P Personalized..........................$5.00 Engraving fee + $37.95
WF423B Classic Knife..$37.95
WF423P Personalized..........................$5.00 Engraving fee + $37.95

A) A raised filigree design graces handles of white porcelain for a cake knife and server of pure elegance. The 8" knife blade and 6" server blade are made of quality stainless steel and are serrated for effortless cutting and serving. Personalize your serving set with your first names and wedding date engraved on each blade. Create a beautifully coordinated wedding with the porcelain guest book and pen sold on page 278. **Please specify names and wedding date to be engraved.**

WF24B White Porcelain Set...*$52.95*
WF24P Personalized......................*$5.00 Engraving fee per knife + $52.95*

B) Richly sculpted flowers adorn the handles of this silver-plated set, adding richness and elegance to your cake-cutting ceremony. The uniquely shaped 6" server blade makes serving easy, and the 8" knife blade is gently serrated for smooth cutting. Each blade may be engraved with your first names and wedding date, creating heirlooms to be treasured and used for years of celebrations to come. The set arrives in a beautiful box covered in deep burgundy velvet. The beaded heart accent bows shown are sold separately below. **Please specify names and wedding date to be engraved.**

WF85B Silver Floral Set...*$58.95*
WF85P Personalized....................*$5.00 Engraving fee per knife + $58.95*

C) Sleek, classic serving pieces will accent your cake-cutting ceremony beautifully, and will be lovely when used for entertaining in the future. These rounded silver-plated handles are topped with a band of gold plating for unique elegance. The 6" server blade and the 8" knife blade may be engraved, making them heirloom quality mementos of your wedding. **Please specify names and wedding date to be engraved.**

WF3281B Silver and Gold Set...*$52.95*
WF3281P Personalized...................*$5.00 Engraving fee per knife + $52.95*

D) Bows of satin-edged white chiffon add a lovely touch to your serving pieces, glasses, floral arrangements, gifts and more. The 4" wide bows are accented with a strand of faux pearls and attach easily to your accessories with adhesive-backed Velcro tabs. Sold in pairs.

WF717 Accent Bows...*$20.95 pair*

E) Accent the stems of your toasting glasses, serving pieces, candles, guest book pens, vases and more with these pretty accent bows. Each bow features a sequined heart amid a flourish of ribbon and a white circle of lace measuring 3" in diameter. The bows attach easily with adhesive-backed Velcro tabs and are sold in pairs.

WF716 Sequined Heart Accent Bows...*$17.95 pair*

Special Day™ - page 265

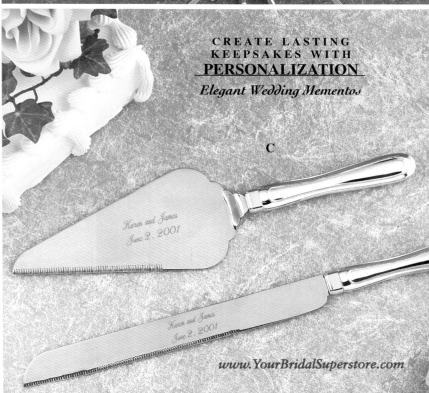

CREATE LASTING KEEPSAKES WITH PERSONALIZATION
Elegant Wedding Mementos

www.YourBridalSuperstore.com

A

B

MUST-HAVE ITEMS...
for creating and preserving wedding memories

A) Protect your cake top for years of memories with our cake top dome. Made of sturdy, crystal-clear plastic, the dome measures 10" tall and 7½" in diameter to accommodate most cake tops. A white plastic base forms a secure fit to prevent dust and moisture from getting inside. Order several to hold and display other fragile keepsakes, such as corsages, dried flowers and bouquets, and figurines. *Cake tops sold separately.*
WF100A Cake Top Dome...$20.95

B,C) According to tradition, a bride and groom should save the top portion of their wedding cake to share on their first anniversary. Our cake storage boxes let you easily and beautifully observe this tradition. Each features a protective inner bag to prevent freezer burn, keeping your cake fresh and delicious for your first anniversary celebration. Afterwards, the 8" x 8" x 5" keepsake boxes may be used to store your garter, napkins, invitations and other mementos. Choose from two styles.

B) Our Memories cake box features a softly colored, beautifully photographed background collage of wedding cake and flowers. The touching verse* on the top reads: "Memories of our wedding day...the top layer of our cake to share after our first year...the glasses we raised to everyone's "Cheers!"...Our announcement from the hometown news...our invitation...a bow from the pews...the boutonniere...the garter...some lace...the cards that marked the bride's and groom's place...some petals from the bride's bouquet...the confetti that flew as we drove away...our very first photo as husband and wife...keepsakes we'll cherish all our lives!"
*WF4420 Memories Cake Box $20.95
Under license from Special Day. All rights reserved.

C) A sweet, pretty pattern of vines and colorful flowers trails across this white box, creating a romantic place to store your keepsakes after your cake is finished.
WF444 Sweet Memories Cake Box $20.95

D) Which bridesmaid will lead a life of adventure? Who will be the next to be wed? Who will be blessed with good luck? Find out with the fun tradition of "ribbon pulling." Dating back to the Victorian era, cake pulling involves tying ribbons to silver-plated charms and hiding the charms between layers of your wedding cake. At the reception, each bridesmaid pulls a ribbon and discovers the charm that will tell her fortune. The custom is also fun to do at your bridesmaid luncheon or rehearsal dinner. Our set includes six silver-plated charms: a heart for love everlasting; a ring telling of an upcoming wedding; a clover for good luck; a rocking horse predicting a happy home; a flower for love that flourishes; and an anchor for an adventurous life. A card giving history, information and ideas for incorporating the custom into your celebration is included.
WF90 Cake Charms $46.95

E) You spent a great deal of time and money selecting the perfect wedding dress. Protect your investment for the benefit of future generations of brides. Our heavy vinyl gown bag protects your gown from moths and years of accumulated dust and moisture. The 32" x 70" bag accommodates the most elaborate trains and veils.
WFGB95 Bridal Gown Bag..$20.95

C

D

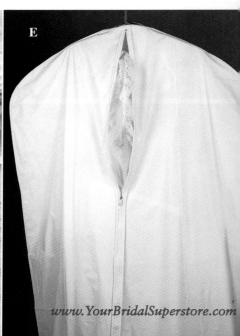

E

WEDDING ESSENTIALS...
making the event unforgettable

A) Light up your reception with these pretty votive holders printed with "Sweet Memories" in gold script. The clear glass holders are 2½" x 2½" and hold white votive candles (sold separately). Arrange the votives and holders throughout your reception – around your wedding cake, punch bowl, buffet table and more – for a romantic glow. They also make thoughtful gifts for your hostesses, servers and others who help at the reception.

WF1967 Glass Votive Holders ....$21.95 per 6
WF5150 White Votive Candles ....$5.95 per 6

B) Welcome to 96 pages of ideas for creating the perfect wedding cake. This full-color book shows cake styles to fit a variety of wedding themes and provides suggestions for accessories. If you're a baker and want to make your own wedding cake, detailed instructions are also included. Softcover book.
WF10 Cake Book $15.50

C) A lacy aisle runner of soft white fabric not only creates a stunning entrance, it also protects your wedding gown and train from dirt and moisture brought in on guests' shoes. The runner measures 36" x 100' with a sturdy cord for easy unrolling. *Because of its size, we will ship your aisle runner separately at no additional cost.*
WFFL100RP Lacy Aisle Runner...............................$47.95

D) Save on rental costs with our affordable plastic aisle runner. The durable white plastic runner has the look of fine linen and will protect your gown and train from mud and moisture. The runner measures 36" x 100' with a satin ribbon to make unrolling effortless. *Because of its size, we will ship your aisle runner separately at no additional cost.*
WFG3009 Plastic Aisle Runner...............................$39.95

E) Dance the night away in style and comfort wearing shoes decorated with this easy-to-use kit. This decorating kit works with your tennis shoes (canvas works best) and includes everything you need to create footwear that complements your trousseau: craft glue and lacy sequined appliques. For an added touch of elegance, use the white satin ribbon included in place of your shoe laces.
WFSK031 Shoe Decorating Kit...............................$25.50

www.YourBridalSuperstore.com

Special Day™ - page 267

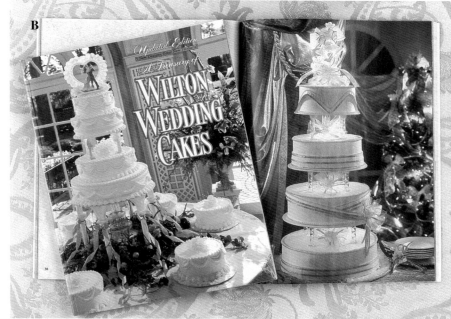

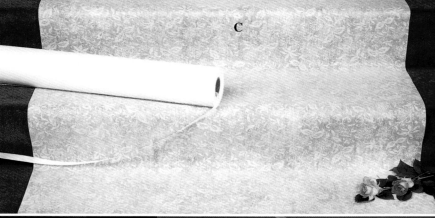

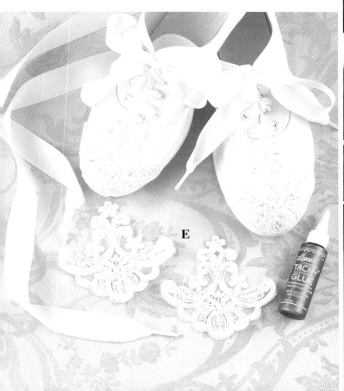

A

B

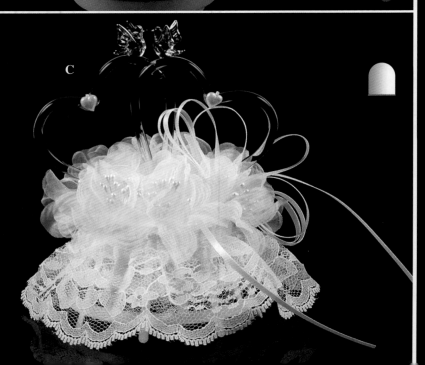

C

CAKE TOPS...
the finishing touch to your wedding cake

A) Cows have been taking the decorating world by storm — and they have arrived in time to add a touch of fun to your wedding cake! These porcelain cow figurines, painted in wonderful detail, stand 3" tall and are 1¾" x 2" at the base. The "groom" sports a painted black bow tie and the "bride" wears a veil of real netting. After the wedding, they will be an adorable reminder of your wedding day.
WF64 Cow Cake Top Figurines ....**$14.50** *per pair*

B) A Precious Moments® "Bless You Two" bride and groom figurine will lend tender innocence to your wedding cake. The figurine is made from fine, white porcelain bisque and is accented with touches of soft pastel paint. This sweet couple stands 5½" tall and measures 3" in diameter at the base. It will make a lovely keepsake long after your wedding cake is gone!
WF9255 Precious Moments® Cake Top Figurine **$69.95**

C) Your wedding theme of romance will be complete with this double-heart cake top on your wedding cake. Charming glass doves with gold accents rest atop finely crafted blown glass hearts to create a beautiful cake top. Adorned with sprays of iridescent pearls, soft fabric roses, flowing satin ribbon and a lace ruffle, this stunning white cake top stands 8" tall with a 4" sturdy plastic base.
WF32001 White Hand-Blown Cake Top **$46.95**

D) Glass butterflies with golden wings bring delicate beauty to this cake top. The butterflies nestle amid ruffles of white lace, clusters of silk flowers and flourishes of satin ribbon. A heart-shaped arch in the background features gold-accented bells to add more sparkle. The cake top stands 7" tall and has a 3¾" diameter base of sturdy plastic.
WFT12 Butterfly Cake Top **$56.50**

This symbol tells you the cake top featured fits in the Cake Top Dome *sold on page 266.*

www.YourBridalSuperstore.com

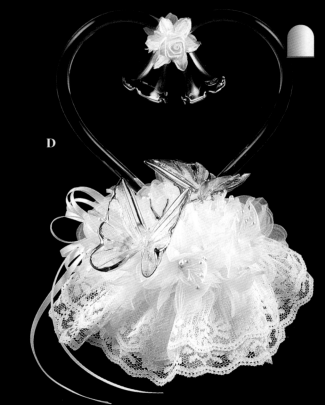

D

A) Hand-sculpted porcelain calla lilies and petite blossoms make this cake top uniquely beautiful. The porcelain flowers are nestled in netting and lace at the base of a glass heart-shaped arch. A pair of glass wedding bells are also accented with a bouquet of the porcelain flowers. The cake top stands 7½" tall and stands on a 3¾" diameter white plastic base covered in white lace.
WF10367 Porcelain Calla Lily Cake Top *$46.00*

B) Young sweethearts sculpted from ecru porcelain bisque will be an adorable finishing touch to your wedding cake. The couple is accented with netting, pearls, ribbons and lace — and the bride wears a veil of real netting! The keepsake-worthy figurine stands 6½" tall. A ruffle of ecru lace surrounds the 4½" diameter base.
WF0511 Porcelain Sweethearts Cake Top...........................*$35.95*

C) This elegant porcelain couple figurine is both a beautiful addition to your wedding cake and a lovely keepsake of your day. Intricate sculpting brings every detail to life — from the bride's bouquet to the floral pattern on her skirt. A rich, creamy ecru glaze and accents of glistening gold provide the final romantic touches. The cake top stands 7½" tall; the base measures 3¾" x 4¾". A coordinating cake serving set is sold on page 266.
WF89 Ecru Porcelain Cake Top Figurine *$47.95*

D) For the perfect finishing touch to your fairy tale wedding cake, choose this dreamy castle cake top. Sparkling, crystal-clear glass forms the peaks and turrets, and gold provides gleaming accents. The castle stands under an 8½" clear arch and is surrounded by white flowers and netting. A ruffle of white lace conceals the sturdy plastic 4½" diameter base.
WFT101 Castle Cake Top..*$79.95*

This symbol tells you the cake top featured fits in the Cake Top Dome *sold on page 266.*

www.YourBridalSuperstore.com

A

B

D

C

ELEGANT GLASSWARE...
for sparkling wedding toasts

A) What could be better for toasting your love and your new life together than toasting flutes with sculpted heart stems? The 9¼" tall flutes hold a generous 8 ounces. Personalize the flutes with your first names engraved on the front and your wedding date on the back. Set of two. **Please specify your first names and wedding date to be engraved.**
WF4579B Heart Stem Flutes *$39.95*
WF4579P Personalized ....*$5.00 Engraving fee per glass + $39.95*

B) Create unique and unforgettable wedding toasts with these interlocking silver-plated flutes. The two flutes become "one" to form a heart shape and symbolize the joining of your two lives. These flutes stand 8½" tall and the bowls hold 5 ounces each. Set of two. **These flutes cannot be engraved.**
WF3001B Interlocking Heart Flutes..*$79.50*

C) Faceted stems swirl at the top to hold the gracefully shaped bowls of these toasting flutes. Each 8¾" tall flute holds 6 ounces. They may be engraved with your names and wedding date to make them lasting keepsakes. Set of two.
Please specify your first names and wedding date to be engraved.
WF8999B Faceted Stem Toasting Flutes..*$37.95*
WF8999P Personalized......................................*$5.00 Engraving fee per glass + $37.95*

D) Soft periwinkle hydrangeas bloom next to "Bride" and "Groom" on these romantic toasting flutes. Each 8¾" tall flute holds 5 ounces. They may be engraved with your names and wedding date on the back to make them lasting keepsakes. Set of two.
Please specify first names and wedding date to be engraved.
WF6064B Hydrangea Toasting Flutes...*$41.50*
WF6064P Personalized......................................*$5.00 Engraving fee per glass + $41.50*

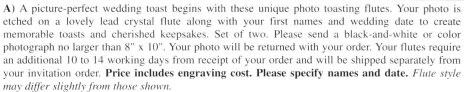

A) A picture-perfect wedding toast begins with these unique photo toasting flutes. Your photo is etched on a lovely lead crystal flute along with your first names and wedding date to create memorable toasts and cherished keepsakes. Set of two. Please send a black-and-white or color photograph no larger than 8" x 10". Your photo will be returned with your order. Your flutes require an additional 10 to 14 working days from receipt of your order and will be shipped separately from your invitation order. **Price includes engraving cost. Please specify names and date.** *Flute style may differ slightly from those shown.*
WF5331P *Photo Flutes Personalized*...*$102.50*

B) Your romantic theme is expressed in your wedding toasts with these flutes accented with a rose-embellished heart design. The 8¾" flutes hold 5 ounces and may be personalized with your first names and wedding date on the back. Set of two. **Please specify names and wedding date.**
WF9637B *Rose Heart Toasting Flutes* *$40.95*
WF9637P *Personalized*...*$5.00 Engraving fee per glass + $40.95*

C) Treat all the special people in your wedding to a personalized bowl-shaped glass. The front is engraved with any title you choose (Soloist, Grandmother, Personal Attendant, etc.) and the back is engraved with the recipient's name. Glasses stand 4" tall and hold 5½ ounces each. **Price includes engraving cost. Please specify title and first name.**
WF84790P *Bowl-Shaped Glasses Personalized*...*$17.95 each*

D) Keepsake tulip glasses are etched with your names and wedding date.
Each stands 7¾" tall and holds 6 ounces. Set of two. **Price includes engraving cost. Please specify names and wedding date.**
WFT8477P *Tulip Glasses Personalized*..*$37.95*

E) A touching portrait of childhood sweethearts is reproduced on the front of lead crystal toasting flutes for sentimental wedding toasts. Your names and wedding date may be engraved on the back of the flutes for a personal touch. Set of two.
Please specify names and wedding date. *Flute style may differ slightly from those shown.*
WF2431B *Sweetheart Flutes*...*$55.95*
WF2431P *Personalized*..*$5.00 Engraving fee per glass + $55.95*

www.YourBridalSuperstore.com

A) Create a stunning head table with personalized tulip-shaped glasses for you, all of you[r] attendants and your parents. Etched with titles in delicate white lettering, these fine crysta[l] glasses make beautiful keepsakes and provide a perfect way to thank your attendants. For an eve[n] more personal gift and keepsake, each glass may be personalized with a first name on the back[.] Toasting glasses are 7¾" tall and hold 6 ounces.
Please specify first name when ordering personalized glasses.

Tulip Glasses for the Bride and Groom
WF323B Bride and Groom Glasses ....$27.95 *set of twe[lve]*
WF323P Personalized.....................................$5.00 Engraving fee per glass + $27.95 *set of twe[lve]*
Tulip Glasses for the Bridal Party (sold individually)

WF8477BM Best Man	WF8477U Usher
WF8477MDH Maid of Honor	WF8477MB Mother of the Bride
WF8477G Groomsman	WF8477FB Father of the Bride
WF8477B Bridesmaid	WF8477MG Mother of the Groom
WF8477MTH Matron of Honor	WF8477FG Father of the Groom

Blank Glasses ....$15.95 *eac[h]*
Personalized..$5.00 Engraving fee + $15.95 *each*

B) Our graceful brass-stemmed goblets stand 7½" tall and the silver-plated bowls hold 6 ounces[.] Each may be engraved with your names and wedding date for an heirloom that will be cherishe[d] for generations. When clinked together, the elegant goblets resound a melodious chime. Set o[f] two. **Please specify names and date.**
WF2255B Silver and Brass Goblets ....$65.9[5]
WF2255P Personalized...$5.00 Engraving fee per glass + $65.9[5]

C) Accent the stems of your toasting glasses, serving pieces, candles, guest book pens, vases and[d] more with these pretty accent bows. Each bow features a sequined heart amid a flourish of ribbo[n] and a white circle of lace measuring 3" in diameter. The bows attach easily with Velcro tabs an[d] are sold in pairs.
WF716 Sequined Heart Accent Bows...$17.95 *pai[r]*

D) Bows of sheer white chiffon edged in satin will beautifully accent your toasting glasses[,] serving pieces, guest book pen and more. Each measures 4" across, features dangling faux pearl[s] and attaches easily with Velcro tabs. Sold in pairs.
WF717 Chiffon Accent Bows.. $20.95 *pai[r]*

A) Your wedding toasts will be even more joyful when you raise flutes accented in gold with "This Day I Married My Friend!" The crystal-clear flutes may be engraved on the back with your first names and wedding date. Flutes stand 8³⁄₄" tall and hold 5 ounces each. Set of two. **Please specify first names and wedding date to be engraved.**
WF3796B "This Day" Flutes...$40.95
WF3796P Personalized.....................................$5.00 Engraving fee per glass + $40.95

B) The open-weave stems, graceful bowls and gold rims of these tall crystal flutes will make your wedding toasts elegant and unique. Each 9" flute holds 5 ounces. When personalized with your first names and wedding date, the flutes will become keepsakes you'll cherish. Set of two. **Please specify first names and wedding date to be engraved.**
WF0290B Open-Weave Crystal Flutes..$53.50
WF0290P Personalized.....................................$5.00 Engraving fee per glass + $53.50

C) Genuine pewter doves and roses are accented with "Bride" or "Groom" in shimmering gold lettering, lending romance to your wedding toasts. Gold rims and gold filigree around the pewter designs add to the elegance. These crystal-clear toasting flutes stand 7³⁄₄" tall and hold 5 ounces each. Personalize them with your names and wedding date etched on the back. Set of two. **Please specify your first names and wedding date.**
WF2619B Pewter Doves Flute...$52.95
WF2619P Personalized...$5.00 Engraving fee per glass+ $52.95

D) The look of delicate flower petals is captured in the sculpted stems of these lead crystal toasting flutes. The petal-like design is frosted where the stems meet the bowls for a romantic accent. Each 8¹⁄₂" flute holds 5³⁄₄ ounces and may be personalized with a first name etched on one side and your wedding date on the opposite side. Set of two. **Please specify your first names and wedding date.**
WF9019B Frosted Stem Flutes..$57.95
WF9019P Personalized.......................................$5.00 Engraving fee per glass + $57.95

www.YourBridalSuperstore.com

SATIN AND LACE...
romantic accents for your special day

A) Covered with delicate white lace, this 5" x 7" flower girl basket is lightweight, easy to carry and features a flat vinyl base to retain moisture for flowers. *Flowers not included.*
WFF611 Lace Flower Girl Basket $17.95

B) For the perfect complement to your wedding gown, choose our pearl-trimmed drawstring bag made from elegant white satin brocade. The bag measures $4\frac{1}{2}$" tall and $5\frac{1}{2}$" in diameter for holding your lipstick, powder, handkerchief, comb and other essentials on your wedding day.
WF182301 White Beaded Bag..$45.50

C) A soft flower basket of white satin trimmed in exquisite matching lace will make your flowers and your flower girl even more beautiful. A plastic dish inside retains moisture for fresh flowers, making the basket perfect for bridesmaids' bouquets and centerpieces, too. Each basket stands 7" tall and is 5" in diameter. *Flowers not included.*
WF401 White Flower Basket.......................................$32.95

D,E) For a pretty accent to your flower girl's attire and a lovely way to set off her flowers, choose a beautiful wicker basket accented with satin, lace, faux pearls and chiffon. The white basket has white accents and the ecru basket has ecru accents. Each basket stands 12" tall and has a 4" diameter opening. The baskets also look pretty holding favors or floral arrangements on your reception tables and make lovely gifts for bridesmaids when filled with scented soaps, flavored coffees or other items.
D) WF080 White Wicker Basket...............................$33.95
E) WF008 Ecru Wicker Basket $33.95

F) *Something old, something new, something borrowed, something blue...and a lucky sixpence for your shoe!* All of the ingredients to ensure a happy marriage are creatively combined on this handcrafted sixpence shoe bow. The old, rare sixpence is decked in blue satin ribbon, white lace borrowed from a garter and a white netting blossom – signifying the newness of your life together. The sixpence will increase in value because it is no longer being produced. This one-of-a-kind accessory measures 2" x 3" and easily clips on to your shoe or garter.
WFX6666 Sixpence Shoe Clip..................................$20.50

G-J) Pure white satin and beautiful lace create a bridal set of elegance. Choose a lovely 11" x 11" heart-shaped or 12" x 10" rectangular ring bearer pillow trimmed with lace and satin ribbon. The 11" x 12" satin handbag is trimmed with lace and has a satin ribbon drawstring. A 1" ruffle of soft iridescent lace and an iridescent bow create an elegant garter. *Engraved heart charms are sold separately on page 275.*
G) WF3672WE Large Heart-Shaped Pillow $19.50
H) WFP136   White Satin Handbag...................................$20.95
I) WFRP132   White Rectangular Pillow $22.50
J) WF40   Satin and Lace Garter...................................$10.95
**   WF1312   Bridal Set with Heart Pillow**..........................$46.50
**   WF1313   Bridal Set with Rectangular Pillow** $47.50

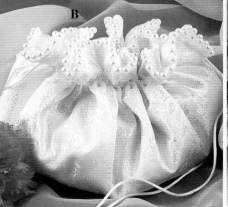

Something old.
Something new.
Something borrowed.
Something blue.

All wrapped up with a
Six Pence for your shoe.

A) Rich satin cord trim and tassels add a regal touch to this square ring bearer pillow — making it the perfect accent to your fairy tale walk down the aisle! The 8" x 8" white satin pillow is also covered with iridescent lace and features a white lace applique, beaded charms and white satin ribbon streamers.

WF125901 Square Tassel Pillow $45.50

B) Bring back the tradition of the ring bearer actually carrying the rings down the aisle with this exquisite ring bearer box. Your rings will safely and elegantly rest between sheer satin pillows in this brocade-covered chest trimmed with iridescent pearl beads and lavish 3" white lace. Box measures 3" x 4" x 2".

WFTC2950 Ring Bearer Box..$55.50

C,D) The graceful chiffon and satin trim on this white pillow and garter set will be a romantic complement to your wedding. A satin bow, and chiffon and satin ribbon accent each piece. The heart-shaped satin ring bearer pillow measures 10" x 10" and comes complete with a satin hand strap on the back. The matching garter completes the elegant look.

C) *WF179103 Chiffon and Satin Pillow* $38.95
D) *WF1799   Chiffon and Satin Garter* $15.95

E-G) Lovely, lacy white butterfly appliqués accent this white satin ring bearer pillow, bridal garter and flower basket set. For a finishing touch of romance, a sparkling rhinestone bead and satin ribbon adorn each. The pillow measures 7½" x 7½". The flower basket is 7½" tall and 4" x 3" at the base. The garter features a butterfly-patterned chiffon ruffle and a blue satin ribbon.

E) *WF47008 Butterfly Pillow*...$57.50
F) *WF87008 Butterfly Basket* $50.50
G) *WF27008 Butterfly Garter* $22.95

H) A satin ring bearer pillow embroidered with your first names, wedding date and the elegant design shown will add a personal touch to your ceremony and make a lovely wedding keepsake. The white heart-shaped pillow measures 10½" x 9½" and is trimmed with a lace ruffle and satin ribbon. Choose up to three thread colors for embroidering the design and personalization. *Note: Names and wedding date will be printed in one color only; please specify which of your color choices you prefer.* Thread colors (see below): 81 metallic silver; 80 metallic gold; 47 navy; 41 dusty rose; 39 mint green; 37 fuchsia; 33 purple; 26 peacock; 23 teal; 16 royal blue; 13 peach; 11 mauve; 10 burgundy; 09 lavender; 40 hunter; 07 light blue; 06 pink; 01 white; 04 red; 03 ecru; 02 black; or 52 rust (not shown). **Specify names, wedding date and thread colors.** Please allow 14 days for processing. Pillow will be shipped separately from the rest of your order. **Price includes engraving cost.**

WFC75P Embroidered Pillow...$50.95

I,J) Beautifully formed ecru porcelain roses decliately adorn this ring bearer pillow and garter set. The 8" x 8" ecru satin pillow is covered with a sheer layer of striped ecru chiffon. Tiny porcelain roses complete each corner, and the center is accented with satin ribbon streamers. The matching garter features a ruffle of the striped ecru chiffon and a tiny porcelain rose on the satin ribbon streamers.

I) *WF6803 Porcelain Rose Pillow* $57.50
J) *WF6903 Porcelain Rose Garter* $17.50

K) Heart charms engraved with your first names and wedding date add a personal touch to your bridal handbag, ring bearer pillow and garter. Threaded with ribbon, the charms also add a personal touch to your cake knife, toasting glasses and more! Available in gold and silver. **Price includes engraving cost. Specify your names and wedding date to be engraved.**

WFJ1400P Gold Charm ....$4.80 *each*
WFJ1410P Silver Charm..$4.80 *each*

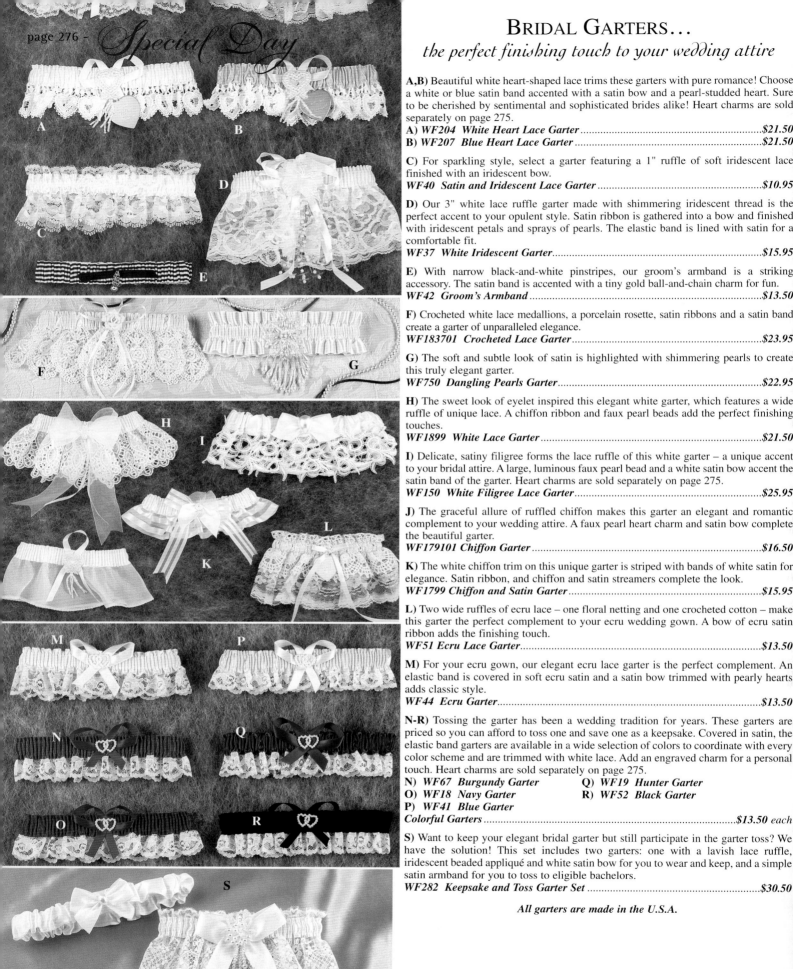

BRIDAL GARTERS...
the perfect finishing touch to your wedding attire

A,B) Beautiful white heart-shaped lace trims these garters with pure romance! Choose a white or blue satin band accented with a satin bow and a pearl-studded heart. Sure to be cherished by sentimental and sophisticated brides alike! Heart charms are sold separately on page 275.
A) *WF204 White Heart Lace Garter* **$21.50**
B) *WF207 Blue Heart Lace Garter* **$21.50**

C) For sparkling style, select a garter featuring a 1" ruffle of soft iridescent lace finished with an iridescent bow.
WF40 Satin and Iridescent Lace Garter **$10.95**

D) Our 3" white lace ruffle garter made with shimmering iridescent thread is the perfect accent to your opulent style. Satin ribbon is gathered into a bow and finished with iridescent petals and sprays of pearls. The elastic band is lined with satin for a comfortable fit.
WF37 White Iridescent Garter **$15.95**

E) With narrow black-and-white pinstripes, our groom's armband is a striking accessory. The satin band is accented with a tiny gold ball-and-chain charm for fun.
WF42 Groom's Armband **$13.50**

F) Crocheted white lace medallions, a porcelain rosette, satin ribbons and a satin band create a garter of unparalleled elegance.
WF183701 Crocheted Lace Garter **$23.95**

G) The soft and subtle look of satin is highlighted with shimmering pearls to create this truly elegant garter.
WF750 Dangling Pearls Garter **$22.95**

H) The sweet look of eyelet inspired this elegant white garter, which features a wide ruffle of unique lace. A chiffon ribbon and faux pearl beads add the perfect finishing touches.
WF1899 White Lace Garter **$21.50**

I) Delicate, satiny filigree forms the lace ruffle of this white garter – a unique accent to your bridal attire. A large, luminous faux pearl bead and a white satin bow accent the satin band of the garter. Heart charms are sold separately on page 275.
WF150 White Filigree Lace Garter **$25.95**

J) The graceful allure of ruffled chiffon makes this garter an elegant and romantic complement to your wedding attire. A faux pearl heart charm and satin bow complete the beautiful garter.
WF179101 Chiffon Garter **$16.50**

K) The white chiffon trim on this unique garter is striped with bands of white satin for elegance. Satin ribbon, and chiffon and satin streamers complete the look.
WF1799 Chiffon and Satin Garter **$15.95**

L) Two wide ruffles of ecru lace – one floral netting and one crocheted cotton – make this garter the perfect complement to your ecru wedding gown. A bow of ecru satin ribbon adds the finishing touch.
WF51 Ecru Lace Garter **$13.50**

M) For your ecru gown, our elegant ecru lace garter is the perfect complement. An elastic band is covered in soft ecru satin and a satin bow trimmed with pearly hearts adds classic style.
WF44 Ecru Garter **$13.50**

N-R) Tossing the garter has been a wedding tradition for years. These garters are priced so you can afford to toss one and save one as a keepsake. Covered in satin, the elastic band garters are available in a wide selection of colors to coordinate with every color scheme and are trimmed with white lace. Add an engraved charm for a personal touch. Heart charms are sold separately on page 275.

N) *WF67 Burgundy Garter*   **Q)** *WF19 Hunter Garter*
O) *WF18 Navy Garter*   **R)** *WF52 Black Garter*
P) *WF41 Blue Garter*
Colorful Garters ....**$13.50** *each*

S) Want to keep your elegant bridal garter but still participate in the garter toss? We have the solution! This set includes two garters: one with a lavish lace ruffle, iridescent beaded appliqué and white satin bow for you to wear and keep, and a simple satin armband for you to toss to eligible bachelors.
WF282 Keepsake and Toss Garter Set **$30.50**

All garters are made in the U.S.A.

www.YourBridalSuperstore.com

ELEGANT PENS...
for a beautiful guest registry

A) Covered in white satin and accented with a satin bow, braided trim and a large faux pearl, this pen base will accent your guest book beautifully. A white swivel holder supports a pen with a 12" white ostrich plume. The oval base measures $3\frac{3}{4}$" x $5\frac{1}{2}$". A matching guest book is sold on page 279.
WF1150   Satin Bow and Pearl Base with Plume Pen...............................**$31.95**

B) A heart-shaped white porcelain base is covered in embossed scrolls and filigree. A gold-tone pen rests securely in a swivel holder attached to the $3\frac{1}{2}$" x $3\frac{1}{2}$" base; the pen and base together measure 8" tall. The pen set makes a lovely complement to the porcelain-accented guest book sold on page 278.
WF10007   Porcelain Heart Base Pen **$34.95**

C) A gold-tone pen in a heart-shaped crystal base is a lovely accessory for your guest book and a perfect keepsake after the wedding. It also makes special gifts for attendants and friends. Pen and base measure 8" tall; base is $3\frac{1}{4}$" across.
WF188G   Gold Pen with Crystal Heart Base **$23.95**

D) Accent your Western wedding with this 3" x $2\frac{1}{2}$" pen base covered in white satin and trimmed with satin cord, ribbon, hearts and a gold-tone Western hat charm. A white pen with gold accents rests in the gold swivel holder. The base and pen stand $8\frac{1}{2}$" tall.
WF28   Western Base Pen...**$34.50**

E) Faceted lead crystal forms a guest book pen base of exquisite quality and sparkle — your guest book table will certainly be eye-catching! The $3\frac{1}{4}$" diameter base features a silver-tone swivel stand to hold a silver-tone pen. Together, the base and pen measure 8" tall.
WF1317   Silver Pen with Round Crystal Base **$25.95**

F) Genuine pewter is sculpted with hearts and flowers for a uniquely romantic guest book pen. The $2\frac{1}{4}$" diameter base features a foam-lined bottom to protect the surface of your guest book table. A $6\frac{3}{4}$" pen sculpted with the same pretty design rests in the swivel holder attached to the base. Together, the base and pen stand $8\frac{3}{4}$" tall.
WF807   Pewter Pen and Base **$31.95**

G) Plume pens add tradition to your guest book. Gold-tone filigree bases hold pens with 14" ostrich plumes, which are available in emerald, burgundy, purple, mauve, pink, white, peach, red, royal blue, teal, ecru, black and hot pink. Pens write in blue ink. **Specify plume color choice.**
WFAPC25   Plume Pen...**$19.50**

H) A white or ecru pen with a 14" matching ostrich plume rests in a contemporary Lucite base. The base is available personalized with a gold-tone plate engraved with your names and wedding date. **Specify color, names and wedding date.**
WFPC27B   Lucite Base Pen..**$22.95**
WFPC27P   Personalized.....................**$5.00 Engraving fee + $22.95**

I) Silver plating makes this sleek and elegant pen set shimmer. The heavy oval base measures $2\frac{3}{4}$" x 3" x $1\frac{1}{4}$" and features a felt-covered bottom to protect your table. The base and pen together stand $5\frac{1}{2}$" tall.
WF3201   Silver-Plated Base and Pen **$43.50**

www.YourBridalSuperstore.com

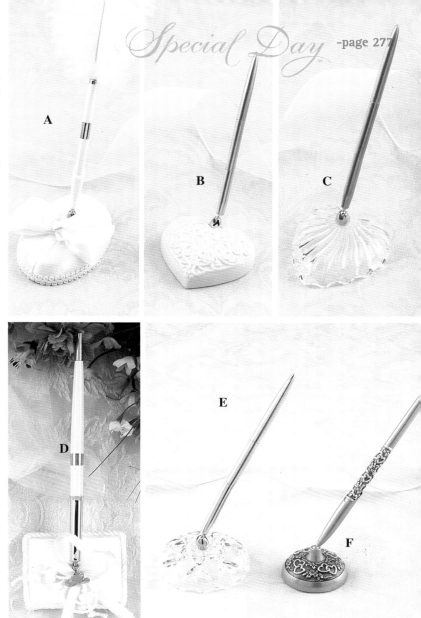

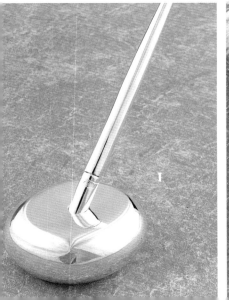

The Invitation

The Rehearsal

A

B

Our Wedding

Our Wedding

Our Guests

Our Guests

C

D

A-D) Pearl-embossed flowers form a heart on the covers of these albums, lending romance to your wedding memories. Choose white or ecru covers to match your wedding. Personalize the albums with your names and wedding date engraved on a gold-tone plate to match the gold titles. **Please specify names and wedding date to be engraved.**

A,B) The bookbound album measures 9" x 11" and contains 52 pages, including space to record 240 guests and 224 gifts.
A) *WF8W52B* **White Pearl Heart Album**..............................$38.50
   WF8W52P **Personalized**....................$5.00 Engraving fee + $38.50
B) *WF10003B* **Ecru Pearl Heart Album** $38.50
   WF10003P **Personalized**....................$5.00 Engraving fee + $38.50

C,D) The matching guest book measures $7\frac{3}{4}$" x $5\frac{3}{4}$" and contains space to hold the signatures of 600 guests.
C) *WFW52B* **White Pearl Heart Guest Book** $20.50
   WFW52P **Personalized**....................$5.00 Engraving fee + $20.50
D) *WF10006B* **Ecru Pearl Heart Guest Book**............................$20.50
   WF10006P **Personalized**....................$5.00 Engraving fee + $20.50

E) White raw silk and a beaded, white satin floral appliqué create a look of fresh beauty on this guest book. Inside are pages to hold the signatures of up to 650 guests. The 9" x 7" book may be personalized with your names and wedding date engraved on a gold-tone plate. **Please specify names and wedding date.** A matching pen is sold below.
WF3900B **Floral Appliqué Guest Book** $70.95
WF3900P **Personalized**.........................$5.00 Engraving fee + $70.95

F) An oval pen base is covered in white raw silk, trimmed with satin cord and adorned with a beaded, white satin floral appliqué. The base measures 6" x 4" and features a swivel holder for the 6" gold-tone pen included.
WF0220 **Floral Appliqué Pen** $38.50

G) Make registering your guests an elegant experience with this beautiful guest book. Covered in white moiré satin, it is adorned with a plaque of richly sculpted white porcelain on the front and may be personalized with your names and wedding date engraved on a gold-tone plate inside. Gold-accented pages hold the signatures of nearly 900 guests. The guest book is 8" x $5\frac{1}{2}$" and ties securely closed with white satin ribbon. **Please specify names and wedding date to be engraved.** Matching pen is sold below.
WF10004B **Porcelain Guest Book** $51.50
WF10004P **Personalized**.........................$5.00 Engraving fee + $51.50

H) A heart-shaped white porcelain base is covered in embossed scrolls and filigree. A gold-tone pen rests securely in a swivel holder attached to the $3\frac{1}{2}$" x $3\frac{1}{2}$" base; the pen and base together measure 8" tall. The pen set makes a lovely complement to the porcelain-accented guest book sold above.
WF10007 **Gold Pen with Porcelain Base** $34.95

Guests

Guests

F

E

G

This is the Keepsake

H

WEDDING ALBUMS...
capturing those precious memories

A,B) Express your love and friendship and record the memories of your wedding with this white bookbound album and guest book. The white padded covers feature gold foil lettering and an adorable black-and-white portrait of young sweethearts. Embossing enhances all 52 pages, which include space to record all of your precious memories — from your first date to your honeymoon — and space to record 224 gifts and 240 guests. The matching guest book has space to record 600 guests. Each book may be personalized with your names and wedding date engraved on a gold-tone plate. **Please specify first names and wedding date.**

A) WF2-W53B Young Love Album $39.50
    WF2-W53P Personalized..............................$5.00 Engraving fee + $39.50
B) WF7-W53B Guest Book $21.50
    WF7-W53P Personalized..............................$5.00 Engraving fee + $21.50

C) Available with "Guests" in gold or silver, our 7¾" x 5¾" guest books record 1,000 names. They may be personalized with your names and wedding date on a gold- or silver-tone plate to match the title. **Please specify names and wedding date.**

WF774GB Gold or WF774SB Silver $20.50
WF774GP or WF774SP Personalized................$5.00 Engraving fee + $20.50

D) Your guest registry table will look beautiful with this white guest book accented with a lacy white butterfly appliqué. A sparkling rhinestone bead adds the finishing touch. The 8½" x 6¼" book has space for the signatures and addresses of more than 900 guests. It may be personalized with your names and wedding date engraved on a gold-tone plate inside the front cover. **Please specify names and wedding date.**

WF7780B Butterfly Appliqué Guest Book..................................$73.95
WF7780P Personalized.................................$5.00 Engraving fee + $73.95

E) A lavish bow of wide white satin and a faux pearl bead make this guest book a pleasure to sign. The book is covered in padded white satin. Inside are gold-tinted pages for the signatures, addresses and best wishes of more than 400 guests. Personalize the book with your first names and wedding date engraved on a gold-tone plate inside the front cover. **Please specify names and wedding date.** Matching pen is sold below.

WF11502B Satin Bow Guest Book $40.95
WF11502P Personalized.................................$5.00 Engraving fee + $40.95

F) An oval base of white satin is accented with a wide satin bow and a faux pearl. The 3¾" x 5½" base features a pen with a 12" white ostrich plume. Order the guest book sold above for a perfect match.

WF1150 Satin Bow Pen $31.95

G,H) A gold foil cross design accented with pearl-embossed flowers and ribbon adds a beautiful touch to these pure white albums. Our 9" x 11¼" bookbound album has 52 embossed pages and registers 240 guests and 224 gifts. Up to 600 guests' signatures can be registered with the matching 7½" x 5¾" guest book. Albums may be personalized with your names and wedding date on a gold-tone plate to match the gold titles. **Please specify names and wedding date to be engraved.**

G) WF2W52B Cross Bookbound Album $38.95
    WF2W52P Personalized..............................$5.00 Engraving fee + $38.95
H) WF7W54B Cross Guest Book $19.95
    WF7W54P Personalized..............................$5.00 Engraving fee + $19.95

page 280 – *Special Day*™

UNITY CANDLES...
a beautiful symbol of two becoming one

A) A large, handcrafted unity candle and white, slow-burning taper candles will create a beautiful ceremony. The 3" x 9" unity candle will last for many anniversaries to come. The 12" tapers are also perfect for centerpieces.
WFC112W Sculpted Unity Candle..*$45.95*
WF84 Taper Candles ....*$3.50 each*

B) This wedding bell candleholder set is perfect for both the altar and your reception tables. The high quality, three-piece set is brass-plated and holds two tapers and a center candle up to 4" in diameter. Candles are sold separately above.
WF238BR Wedding Bells Unity Set *$44.50*

C) A lovely brass-plated candle snuffer extinguishes candle flames easily and prevents wax from being blown onto tablecloths. Snuffer measures 7" long.
WF118BR Candle Snuffer *$7.50*

D) Lifelike flowers and ornate scrolls are sculpted on this beautiful white candle, creating the perfect addition to your unity candle ceremony. The 7½" tall, 4" diameter candle also makes a lovely centerpiece and will become a treasured keepsake.
WF600 White Sculpted Floral Candle *$43.50*

E) These ecru candles will make a lovely addition to your unity candle ceremony. The center candle is 8" tall and 2¼" in diameter. Tapers are 9½" tall.
WF1756 Ecru Unity Candle *$30.50*
WF5102 Ecru Taper Candles ....*$4.50 each*

F) Celebrated photographer Kim Anderson has captured childhood sweethearts in black and white, adding an adorable touch to these ecru porcelain candleholders. Each holder is adorned with pink rosebuds. The center holder, which also features the words "Promises of Love" in pink script, stands 3¾" tall and will accommodate a candle up to 3" in diameter. The matching taper holders are 3" tall and hold standard taper candles. Kim Anderson© NBM Bahner Studios. Candles are sold separately above.
WF2389 Kim Anderson Unity Set *$67.50*

G) Our hand-blown glass chimney and wood base will last for years of reminiscing — simply replace the wax candle when necessary. The 8" chimney is engraved with your invitation wording for a lasting keepsake.* To receive the unity candle at a cost savings, order it when you order your invitations. When assembled, the chimney and base are 13" tall. One 6" white candle is included. Flowers not included.
WF3022 Unity Candle (ordered w/invitations) *$79.50*
WF3021 Unity Candle (ordered separately)...............................*$89.50*
*Engraved chimneys require an additional 10-14 days from the receipt of order; therefore, your candle will be shipped separately from your invitation order.

H) Celebrate your love with this distinctive unity candle set. The shimmering pewter base is gracefully designed with two hearts and the phrase "Two Become One." The set includes two 12" white tapers and a white 9" tall, 3" diameter unity candle with the inscription "And The Two Shall Become One" in silver script. The set will be a lovely reminder of your wedding day when proudly displayed in your home.
WF1310 "Two Become One" Unity Set................................*$69.00 set*

I) A touching verse is inscribed in gold lettering on our popular 10" white unity candle. The verse reads: "This day I will marry my friend. The one I laugh with, live for, and love." Candle is 3" in diameter.
WFU311 Unity Candle with Verse *$43.50*

www.YourBridalSuperstore.com

APPRECIATION GIFTS...
for those who made your day unforgettable

A) Your bridesmaids are some of your best friends, and each will cherish this lovely photo mat designed to display wedding pictures in the cutout frames. Each 10" x 8" mat of thick ecru paper is printed in taupe ink with "Bridesmaid / Best of Friends" and is perfect for framing (frame and photos not included).

WFPM Bridesmaid Photo Mat..**$16.50**

B) Each time they use this beautiful cherry wood box, your friends and attendants will be reminded of your friendship and wedding. The 7¼" x 5½" box is 2" deep. On the hinged lid is a pewter plaque accented with sculpted flowers and "Friendship Comes From The Heart." The recipient's first and last name may be engraved on a silver-tone plate attached inside. **Please specify name.**

WF08B Cherry Wood and Pewter Box **$44.95**
WF08P Personalized.....................................**$5.00 Engraving fee + $44.95**

C) Show your bridesmaids your heartfelt appreciation with this vanilla-scented candle in a covered glass jar. This candle features a meaningful verse printed within a heart design in lustrous gold foil: "a Bridesmaid…Close by at your wedding, Close to your heart forever." Candle is 4½" tall and 3¾" in diameter.

WFBMC Bridesmaid Candle...**$19.50**

D) Slender enough to fit in the smallest evening bag, this heart-shaped compact mirror is a gift your attendants and special friends will love. The top of the 2½" x 2¼" silver-plated compact may be engraved with a three-initial monogram. **Please specify initials with the last name initial in the middle.**

WF79B Heart-Shaped Compact..**$16.95**
WF79P Personalized.....................................**$5.00 Engraving fee + $16.95**

E) An intricately sculpted porcelain oil unity candle will illuminate your wedding with warmth and elegance. The 9" tall, 3¼" diameter white candle uses lamp oil (not included), and will last for years. A wick is included.

WFA373W Porcelain Oil Unity Candle **$46.00**

F) Beautiful and useful, this calendar will be a daily reminder of your wedding and friendship! The calendar arrives in a slim, 5" x 5¼" clear plastic case that opens to form an easel stand. Thick white calendar pages inside are dated and feature stunning black-and-white photos. The front page is printed in black with the following verse: *Thank You — You've shared with me so many special times. On this day, I'm so glad to have you by my side and thankful to have you as my friend.** Space is allowed beneath the verse for you to write your name and a personal message.

WF1263 Bridesmaid Calendar...**$16.50**
* Under license from Special Day. All rights reserved.

G) Here's the perfect card to convey your sincere thanks to your bridesmaids and maid of honor. The verse, written especially for this special time in your life, is printed in gold foil and purple, and surrounded by a colorful floral border. The inside verse reads: "At this most special time as my marriage and new life begin, I'm glad to have you by my side, and thankful to have you as my friend." Matching envelopes included.

WFTY30 Bridesmaid Appreciation Cards....................................**$9.50 per 3**
WFAC Maid of Honor Appreciation Card.....................................**$3.50 each**

www.YourBridalSuperstore.com

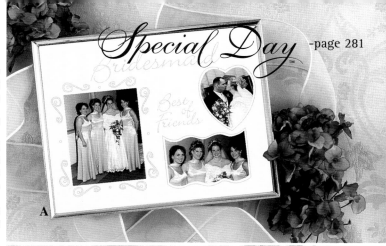

A

B

A,B) Give your groomsmen and best man a gift that is elegant and useful. Thes wide-bowled mugs have a genuine pewter plaque with "World's Greatest" engraved i Latin. The sturdy mugs stand 5" tall and hold 20 ounces each. Mugs may be engrave with a first and last name on a silver nameplate. **Please specify names to be engrave**
A) WF1122B Groomsman Mug...$40.50
    WF1122P *Personalized*..*$5.00 Engraving fee + $40.50*
B) WF1121B Best Man Mug..$40.50
    WF1121P *Personalized*..*$5.00 Engraving fee + $40.50*

C) Your attendants will love these silver-plated can coolers to keep their beverage cold. This foam-lined can holder may be personalized with up to three initials to mak it an even more thoughtful gift. **Please specify initials with the last name initial i the middle.**
WF1116B Can Cooler $30.5
WF1116P *Personalized*...*$5.00 Engraving fee + $30.5*

D) Our striking money clip is a gift attendants will appreciate. The sculpted, gold-ton clip may be engraved with a first name or three initials in block lettering. **Pleas specify name or three initials for engraving.**
WF390B Keepsake Money Clip $17.5
WF390P *Personalized*..*$5.00 Engraving fee + $17.5*

E) This handsome multi-use pen and key ring flashlight set is a gift the men in you wedding will surely use and appreciate. The silver-tone pen writes in black, orang and red ink, and is also equipped with a mechanical pencil insert. The set is held in 7" x 2½" brushed metal case, which may be personalized with three initials on the top **Please specify initials with the last name initial in the middle.**
WF30103B Pen and Light w/ Case $53.50
WF30103P *Personalized*...*$5.00 Engraving fee + $53.50*

F) Perfect for holding rings, watches, tie tacs and spare change, this solid wood bo is a thoughtful gift for your distinguished groomsmen. Inside are four compartment lined in rich green velveteen. The hinged lid of the 9½" x 5¼" box may b personalized with a first name engraved on a gold-tone plate in the block letterin shown. **Please specify name.**
WF5310B Wood Box...$33.5
WF5310P *Personalized*..*$5.00 Engraving fee + $33.50*

G) Your groomsmen will love these colonial-style tankards. The thick glass mug hold 16 ounces each and may be engraved with two initials as shown. **Please specif two initials to be engraved.**
WF5027B Colonial Tankard...$17.50
WF5027P *Personalized*..*$5.00 Engraving fee + $17.50*

www.YourBridalSuperstore.com

C

D

E

F

G

Ink &Liner Colors

Brown · Fuchsia · Gold · Grey

Hunter · Lilac · Navy · Plum · Purple

Red · Rosewood · Periwinkle · Pink

Sage · Silver · Taupe · Teal · Wine

Periwinkle · Peach · Lilac · Rosewood · Pink · Fuchsia · Blue

Sage · Taupe · Gold · Silver · Purple · Teal · Navy

Pearl · Plum · Wine · Hunter · Black · Red

Monograms

The following monograms may be used on Informal Notes shown with Invitations in the Special Day Collection. Monogram 4 is available only as shown. Monograms 5 and 6 are available in any typestyle. Specify monogram number followed by the lettering style (eg: M5-ISA).

M4 · M6 *Mackenzie V Jordan* · M5 *Anastacia & Michael* K

Lettering Styles

BER

Aa Bb Cc Dd Ee Ff Gg Hh Ii Jj Kk Ll Mm
Nn Oo Pp Qq Rr Ss Tt Uu Vv Ww Xx Yy Zz
1 2 3 4 5 6 7 8 9 0
The honour of your presence…

BIC

Aa Bb Cc Dd Ee Ff Gg Hh Ii Jj Kk Ll Mm
Nn Oo Pp Qq Rr Ss Tt Uu Vv Ww Xx Yy Zz
1 2 3 4 5 6 7 8 9 0
The honour of your presence…

CIT

Aa Bb Cc Dd Ee Ff Gg Hh Ii Jj Kk Ll Mm
Nn Oo Pp Qq Rr Ss Tt Uu Vv Ww Xx Yy Zz
1 2 3 4 5 6 7 8 9 0
The honour of your presence…

CSP

Aa Bb Cc Dd Ee Ff Gg Hh Ii Jj Kk Ll Mm
Nn Oo Pp Qq Rr Ss Tt Uu Vv Ww Xx Yy Zz
1 2 3 4 5 6 7 8 9 0
The honour of your presence…

FLS

Aa Bb Cc Dd Ee Ff Gg Hh Ii Jj Kk Ll Mm
Nn Oo Pp Qq Rr Ss Tt Uu Vv Ww Xx Yy Zz
1 2 3 4 5 6 7 8 9 0
The honour of your presence…

FNH

Aa Bb Cc Dd Ee Ff Gg Hh Ii Jj Kk Ll Mm
Nn Oo Pp Qq Rr Ss Tt Uu Vv Ww Xx Yy Zz
1 2 3 4 5 6 7 8 9 0
The honour of your presence…

ISA

Aa Bb Cc Dd Ee Ff Gg Hh Ii Jj Kk Ll Mm
Nn Oo Pp Qq Rr Ss Tt Uu Vv Ww Xx Yy Zz
1 2 3 4 5 6 7 8 9 0
The honour of your presence…

LUP

Aa Bb Cc Dd Ee Ff Gg Hh Ii Jj Kk Ll Mm
Nn Oo Pp Qq Rr Ss Tt Uu Vv Ww Xx Yy Zz
1 2 3 4 5 6 7 8 9 0
The honour of your presence…

MAH

Aa Bb Cc Dd Ee Ff Gg Hh Ii Jj Kk Ll Mm
Nn Oo Pp Qq Rr Ss Tt Uu Vv Ww Xx Yy Zz
1 2 3 4 5 6 7 8 9 0
The honour of your presence…

MUR

Aa Bb Cc Dd Ee Ff Gg Hh Ii Jj Kk Ll Mm
Nn Oo Pp Qq Rr Ss Tt Uu Vv Ww Xx Yy Zz
1 2 3 4 5 6 7 8 9 0
The honour of your presence…

PA

Aa Bb Cc Dd Ee Ff Gg Hh Ii Jj Kk Ll Mm
Nn Oo Pp Qq Rr Ss Tt Uu Vv Ww Xx Yy Zz
1 2 3 4 5 6 7 8 9 0
The honour of your presence…

PEN

Aa Bb Cc Dd Ee Ff Gg Hh Ii Jj Kk Ll Mm
Nn Oo Pp Qq Rr Ss Tt Uu Vv Ww Xx Yy Zz
1 2 3 4 5 6 7 8 9 0
The honour of your presence…

PI

Aa Bb Cc Dd Ee Ff Gg Hh Ii Jj Kk Ll Mm
Nn Oo Pp Qq Rr Ss Tt Uu Vv Ww Xx Yy Zz
1 2 3 4 5 6 7 8 9 0
The honour of your presence…

QIL

Aa Bb Cc Dd Ee Ff Gg Hh Ii Jj Kk Ll Mm
Nn Oo Pp Qq Rr Ss Tt Uu Vv Ww Xx Yy Zz
1 2 3 4 5 6 7 8 9 0
The honour of your presence…

SRH

Aa Bb Cc Dd Ee Ff Gg Hh Ii Jj Kk Ll Mm
Nn Oo Pp Qq Rr Ss Tt Uu Vv Ww Xx Yy Zz
1 2 3 4 5 6 7 8 9 0
The honour of your presence…

STU

Aa Bb Cc Dd Ee Ff Gg Hh Ii Jj Kk Ll Mm
Nn Oo Pp Qq Rr Ss Tt Uu Vv Ww Xx Yy Zz
1 2 3 4 5 6 7 8 9 0
The honour of your presence…

UNR

Aa Bb Cc Dd Ee Ff Gg Hh Ii Jj Kk Ll Mm
Nn Oo Pp Qq Rr Ss Tt Uu Vv Ww Xx Yy Zz
1 2 3 4 5 6 7 8 9 0
The honour of your presence…

VOL

Aa Bb Cc Dd Ee Ff Gg Hh Ii Jj Kk Ll Mm
Nn Oo Pp Qq Rr Ss Tt Uu Vv Ww Xx Yy Zz
1 2 3 4 5 6 7 8 9 0
The honour of your presence…

Invitation Verses

W2
With joyful hearts
we ask you to be present
at the ceremony uniting
Rose Marie Gullio
and
Richard Mark Jackson
Saturday, the twenty-fourth of July
two thousand four
at *four o'clock in the afternoon*
Hope Baptist Church
1422 West Bell Street
Anaheim, California

Mr. and Mrs. Stephan Guillo

W14
Lydia Marie Peterson
and
Joshua John Foxworth
have chosen the first day
of their new life together
as *Saturday, the ninth of October*
two thousand four
You are invited to share in their joy
as they exchange marriage vows
at *two o'clock in the afternoon*
First Lutheran Church
579 West Wayne Street
Sculville, California

W17
Erin Janelle Violet
and
Neil Douglas Johnson
request the honour of your presence
at their marriage
on *Saturday, the twenty-fourth of July*
two thousand four
at *four o'clock in the afternoon*
Faith Church of Christ
29897 Seventeenth Avenue
Burlwood, California

W35
Charles and Frances Williams
invite you to share in the joy
of the marriage uniting their daughter
Katherine Elizabeth
and
Michael Geoffrey Black
on *Saturday, the sixth of November*
two thousand four
at *St. Phillips Church*
Fourth Street and Highland Drive
Fillmore, California

W36
Mr. and Mrs. Tyler McDonald
request the honour of your presence
at the marriage of their daughter
Hannah Charlotte
to
Mr. Squire Ross Ferguson
on *Saturday, the ninth of October*
at *three o'clock in the afternoon*
Our Savior Methodist Church
County Road B
Columbia Heights, California

W42
This day I will marry my best friend,
the one I laugh with, live for, love
Courtney Elizabeth Kropp
daughter of
Mr. and Mrs. David Kropp
and
Brian James Norman
son of
Mr. and Mrs. Nicholas Norman
hope that you will join in this celebration
on *Saturday, the twenty-fourth of July*
two thousand four
at *four o'clock in the afternoon*
St. Peter's Catholic Church
718 Range Street
Sacramento, California

W45
Together with our parents
Mr. and Mrs. Michael Ankeny
and
Mr. and Mrs. Andrew Wendland
we,
Kimberly Jo Ankeny
and
Bradley Louis Wendland
invite you to share in the joy
of the beginning of our new life together
when we exchange marriage vows
on *Saturday, the twenty-second day of May*
at *one o'clock in the afternoon*
Evangelical Free Church
879 Broadway
San Diego, California

W46
Two lives, two hearts
joined together in friendship
united forever in love.
It is with joy that we,
Amanda Clare Murphy
and
Tony Anton Brown
invite you to share
in a celebration of love
as we exchange our marriage vows
on *Saturday, the tenth of April*
two thousand four
at *seven o'clock in the evening*
Church of Our Lord
6638 Highway Nine
Hemet, California

W61
The most joyous of occasions
is the union of man and woman
in celebration of life ...
Mr. and Mrs. Kevin Zelter
invite you to share in the ceremony
uniting their daughter
Denise Rose
and
Mr. Cody Crimmins
on *Saturday, the twenty-first of August*
two thousand four
at *four o'clock in the afternoon*
Oak Forest Country Club
Riverside Drive and Maple Street
San Diego, California

W132
A fresh new day, and it is ours
a day of happy beginnings
when we, *Sharon Anne Wilson*
and *Byron Joseph Schmidt*
pledge our love as one
on *Saturday, the thirteenth of November*
two thousand four
at *two o'clock in the afternoon*
Seventh Day Adventists
100 Second Street
San Francisco, California
We joyfully ask you
to share this day with us

WCustom example:
(create your own verse)

Substitute words in italics with your specific information

Reception Verses

R10
To help us celebrate,
please join us for the Reception
immediately following the ceremony
Carmel Ranch Country Club
55239 Carmel Ranch Road
San Diego, California

R11
The pleasure of your company is requested
at the Reception
immediately following the ceremony
Carmel Ranch Country Club
55239 Carmel Ranch Road
San Diego, California

R30
Please join us
for Dinner and Reception
at *five o'clock in the afternoon*
Carmel Ranch Country Club
55239 Carmel Ranch Road
San Diego, California

R4
Reception, Dinner and Dance
immediately following ceremony
Carmel Ranch Country Club
55239 Carmel Ranch Road
San Diego, California

R6
Reception
immediately following ceremony
Carmel Ranch Country Club
55239 Carmel Ranch Road
San Diego, California

R8
Cocktails served at *5:00 p.m.*
Dinner served at *6:30 p.m.*
Dancing *8:00 p.m. until 12:00 a.m.*
Carmel Ranch Country Club
55239 Carmel Ranch Road
San Diego, California

RCustom example:
(create your own verse)

Respond Verses

E2
The favor of a
reply is requested
on or before *July 24, 2004*
M _____
Number of persons __

E21
The favor of a reply is requested
on or before *July 24, 2004*
M _____
Number of persons __

E24
We are looking forward
to celebrating with you.
Please reply by *July 24, 2004*
M _____
Number of persons __

E4
Kindly respond on or before
July 24, 2004
M _____
__ persons will attend

E5
The courtesy of a reply is requested by
July 24, 2004
M _____
Please indicate number of each
Filet Mignon ___ *Chicken Kiev*___

E6
The favor of a reply is requested
before *July 24, 2004*
M _____
__ will attend
__ will not be able to attend

ECustom example:
(create your own verse)

Substitute words in italics with your specific information

Scroll verses

Verse SC102

On this day of happy beginnings,
we thank you for being with us
at this celebration of our love
and the beginning of our life together.

As the years come and go,
our thoughts will give us pleasure
remembering this enchanted day
and all your good wishes.

Adrian and Trevor
December 15, 2002

Verse SC108

We thank you, each and every one,
for joining us this day.
You've added to our happiness
in a very special way.

As the years shall come and go,
our dreams will give us pleasure
and bring you back to us again
in memories to treasure.

Debbie and Chad
May 12, 2002

Verse SC113

Love . . .
is patient and kind; love is not
jealous, or conceited, or proud,
or provoked; love does not keep
a record of wrongs; love is not
happy with evil, but is pleased
with the truth. Love never gives
up; its faith, hope and patience never fail.

Thank you
for sharing with us
the precious moments of this day

Ruth and Jacob
October 13, 2002.

Verse SC106

This is only a tiny message,
but it's written just for you
for finding time in your busy life
to give us a moment or two.

We hope that you can feel as we,
lighthearted and gay,
and share with us the magic
of this enchanting day.

Kayla and Jeff
September 8, 2002

Verse SC107
This Day I will Marry My Friend

This day is filled with happiness,
and joy is ours to share
with all our friends and relatives
who came to show they care.
The prayer we carry in our hearts
of love and faith and peace
we give to you with every hope
that these will never cease.

Sherri and Adam
August 25, 2002

Bookmark verses

Verse FB101

Words can never tell
the joy that
is ours today,
knowing that
our shared
the beginning of
our life together.

We hope you can feel
the magic of
this enchanting day,
which will become
more memorable
because you were
here with us.

Linda and Thomas
October 12, 2002

Verse FB102

On this day
of happy beginning,
we thank you
for being with us
at this celebration
of our love
and the beginning
of our life together.

As the years
come and go,
our thoughts will
give us pleasure
remembering this
enchanted day
and all your
good wishes.

Marie and Jim
June 15, 2002

Verse FB106

This is only
a tiny message,
but it's written
just for you
for finding time
in your busy life
to give us a
moment or two.

We hope that
you can feel, as we,
light-hearted and gay,
and share with us
the magic of
this enchanting day.

Cindy and Michael
May 9, 2002

Verse FB107

This day is filled
with happiness,
and joy is ours
to share
with all our friends
and relatives
who came to
show they care.

The prayer we carry
in our hearts
of love and faith
and peace
we give to you
with every hope
that these
will never cease.

Amber and Shane
September 28, 2002

Verse FB108

We thank you,
each and every one,
for joining us
this day.
You've added
to our happiness
in a very
special way.

As the years
shall come and go,
our dreams
will give us pleasure
and bring you back
to us again
in memories
to treasure.

Carrie and Brad
June 30, 2002

Verse FB110

When our daughter
was a little girl,
we often used to say
how proud and happy
we would be
on this, her wedding day.
Our daughter
is not lost to us;
in fact we've gained a son.
We're happy
you can share our joy
and see them joined as one.
So, may we
welcome all of you,
and may this whole day be
a happy and a joyous one
for friends and family.

Kari and Brad
September 7, 2002

Substitute words in italics with your specific information

Select a design from those shown here to be printed on bookmarks, matches, napkins,
notepads, place cards and scrolls. To order these items blank (without a design), please specify "no design" on your order form.

DESIGN 1002C | DESIGN 1007C | DESIGN 1017C | DESIGN 1029C | DESIGN 1033C | DESIGN 1035C

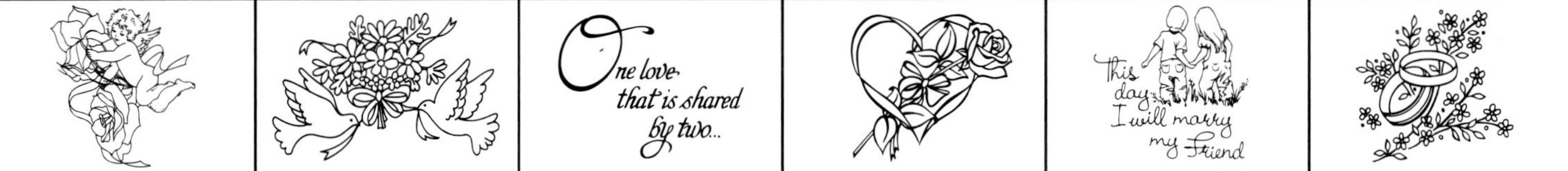

DESIGN 1040C | DESIGN 1043C | DESIGN 1054C | DESIGN 1061C | DESIGN 1064C | DESIGN 1068C

DESIGN 1075C | DESIGN 1077C | DESIGN 1098C | DESIGN 1104C | DESIGN 1130C | DESIGN 1140C

DESIGN 1168C | DESIGN 1174C | DESIGN 1192C | DESIGN 1200C | DESIGN 1251C | DESIGN 1261C

DESIGN 1267C | DESIGN 1329C | DESIGN 1414C | DESIGN 1460C | DESIGN 1464C | DESIGN 1493C

DESIGN 1614C | DESIGN 1654C | DESIGN 1938C | DESIGN 1939C | DESIGN 1970C | DESIGN 2461C

DESIGN 2466C | DESIGN 2467C | DESIGN 2480C | DESIGN 2631C | DESIGN 2632C | DESIGN 2634C

DESIGN 2635C | DESIGN 2637C | DESIGN 2641C | DESIGN 2648C | DESIGN 2649C | DESIGN 2651C

DESIGN 2712C | DESIGN 2770C | DESIGN 2807C | DESIGN 2809C | DESIGN 2812C

MONOGRAM M55
Please specify initial desired.

YOUR BRIDAL SUPERSTORE

proudly presents

THE

Carlson Craft®

COLLECTION

Create an inspiring memory with personal correspondence from Carlson Craft's Personalized Stationery Collection. Offering a rich assortment from traditional, contemporary or novelty styles, Carlson Craft brings you impeccably designed and printed items at the highest quality available.

*We also invite you to visit our on-line store at **www.YourBridalSuperstore.com,** featuring the most extensive collection of accessories, invitations, jewelry, gifts, favors and much more.*

YOUR BRIDAL
SUPERSTORE
...everything but the groom℠

www.YourBridalSuperstore.com

TRADITIONAL WHITE ▶

This traditional single panel is featured on a soft white vellum folder. This ensemble features an informal folder. Respond and reception will be a card. 5 1/8" x 7 3/4"
WA203-71

LINER CHOICES:

Plum, Navy, Hunter, Wine, Black, Purple, Rosewood, Silver, Taupe, Pearl, Gold, Sage, Lilac, Peach, Periwinkle, Pink, Red, Sky, Teal

ITEM	ITEM NUMBER	25	50	75
Invitation	WA203-71	51.90	56.90	61.90
Invitation Envelope Flaps	PRTENV	22.00	23.00	26.70
Invitation Liner Envelopes	LINEDENV	4.90	9.80	14.70
Reception Cards	WARW22	31.70	34.10	36.50
Respond Cards	WAEW22-01	39.60	42.70	45.80
Note	WAI406-01	31.70	34.10	36.50
Note Envelope Flaps	PRTENV	22.00	23.00	26.70
Thank You Folder – Blank Inside	WAU406-01	31.70	34.10	36.50

ITEM (cont.)	100	125	150	Add'l 25
Invitation	66.90	81.30	95.70	14.40
Invitation Envelope Flaps	30.40	34.10	37.80	3.70
Invitation Liner Envelopes	19.60	24.50	29.40	4.90
Reception Cards	38.90	47.20	55.50	8.30
Respond Cards	48.90	59.30	69.70	10.40
Note	38.90	47.20	55.50	8.30
Note Envelope Flaps	30.40	34.10	37.80	3.70
Thank You Folder – Blank Inside	38.90	47.20	55.50	8.30

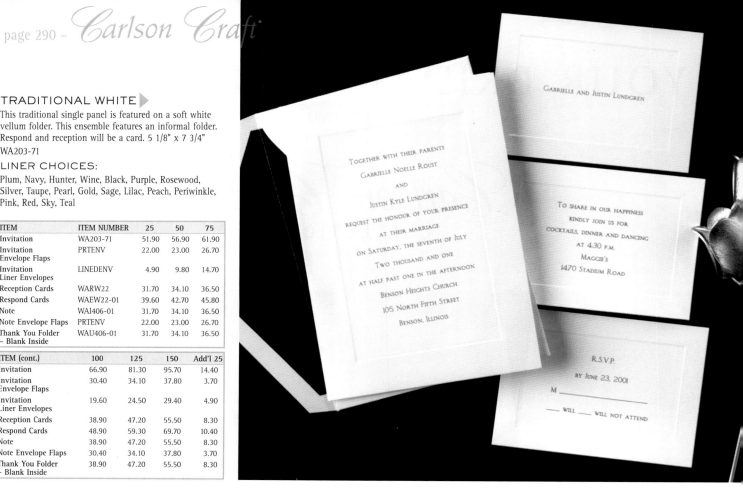

◀ CRISP PANEL

This elegant embossed triple panel card is featured on a soft white vellum. This ensemble features an informal folder. Respond and reception will be a card. 5 1/8" x 7 3/4"
WA1341-71

LINER CHOICES:

Plum, Navy, Hunter, Wine, Black, Purple, Rosewood, Silver, Taupe, Pearl, Gold, Sage, Lilac, Peach, Periwinkle, Pink, Red, Sky, Teal

ITEM	ITEM NUMBER	25	50	75
Invitation	WA1341-71	58.90	64.90	70.90
Invitation Envelope Flaps	PRTENV	22.00	23.00	26.70
Invitation Liner Envelopes	LINEDENV	4.90	9.80	14.70
Reception Cards	WAR1631	37.30	40.50	43.70
Respond Cards	WAE1631-01	45.20	49.10	53.00
Note	WAI3890-01	37.30	40.50	43.70
Note Envelope Flaps	PRTENV	22.00	23.00	26.70
Thank You Folder – Blank Inside	WAU3890-01	37.30	40.50	43.70

ITEM (cont.)	100	125	150	Add'l 25
Invitation	76.90	93.50	110.10	16.60
Invitation Envelope Flaps	30.40	34.10	37.80	3.70
Invitation Liner Envelopes	19.60	24.50	29.40	4.90
Reception Cards	46.90	56.90	66.90	10.00
Respond Cards	56.90	69.00	81.10	12.10
Note	46.90	56.90	66.90	10.00
Note Envelope Flaps	30.40	34.10	37.80	3.70
Thank You Folder – Blank Inside	46.90	56.90	66.90	10.00

INTRICATE FILIGREE

A soft white folder with a delicate embossed flourish.
4 1/2" x 5 7/8"
WA735-30

LINER CHOICES:

Silver, Pearl, Gold

ITEM	ITEM NUMBER	25	50	75
Invitation	WA735-30	49.50	54.30	59.10
Invitation Envelope Flaps	PRTENV	22.00	23.00	26.70
Invitation Liner Envelopes	LINEDENV	4.90	9.80	14.70
Reception Cards	WAR7350	36.30	39.50	42.70
Respond Cards	WAE7350-01	44.20	48.10	52.00
Note	WAI7350-01	36.30	39.50	42.70
Note Envelope Flaps	PRTENV	22.00	23.00	26.70
Thank You Folder – Blank Inside	WAU7350-01	36.30	39.50	42.70

ITEM (cont.)	100	125	150	Add'l 25
Invitation	63.90	77.70	91.50	13.80
Invitation Envelope Flaps	30.40	34.10	37.80	3.70
Invitation Liner Envelopes	19.60	24.50	29.40	4.90
Reception Cards	45.90	55.70	65.50	9.80
Respond Cards	55.90	67.80	79.70	11.90
Note	45.90	55.70	65.50	9.80
Note Envelope Flaps	30.40	34.10	37.80	3.70
Thank You Folder – Blank Inside	45.90	55.70	65.70	9.80

CLASSIC ROSE

A white rose is embossed on this traditional folder.
5" x 6 5/8"
WA241-40

LINER CHOICES:

Plum, Navy, Hunter, Wine, Black, Purple, Rosewood, Silver, Taupe, Pearl, Gold, Aqua, Fuchsia, Lilac, Peach, Pink, Red, Royal, Sky, Teal

ITEM	ITEM NUMBER	25	50	75
Invitation	WA241-40	55.40	60.90	66.40
Invitation Envelope Flaps	PRTENV	22.00	23.00	26.70
Invitation Liner Envelopes	LINEDENV	4.90	9.80	14.70
Reception Cards	WAR2410	37.30	40.50	43.70
Respond Cards	WAE2410-01	45.20	49.10	53.00
Note	WAI2410-01	37.30	40.50	43.70
Note Envelope Flaps	PRTENV	22.00	23.00	26.70
Thank You Folder – Blank Inside	WAU2410-01	37.30	40.50	43.70

ITEM (cont.)	100	125	150	Add'l 25
Invitation	71.90	87.40	102.90	15.50
Invitation Envelope Flaps	30.40	34.10	37.80	3.70
Invitation Liner Envelopes	19.60	24.50	29.40	4.90
Reception Cards	46.90	56.90	66.90	10.00
Respond Cards	56.90	69.00	81.10	12.10
Note	46.90	56.90	66.90	10.00
Note Envelope Flaps	30.40	34.10	37.80	3.70
Thank You Folder – Blank Inside	46.90	56.90	66.90	10.00

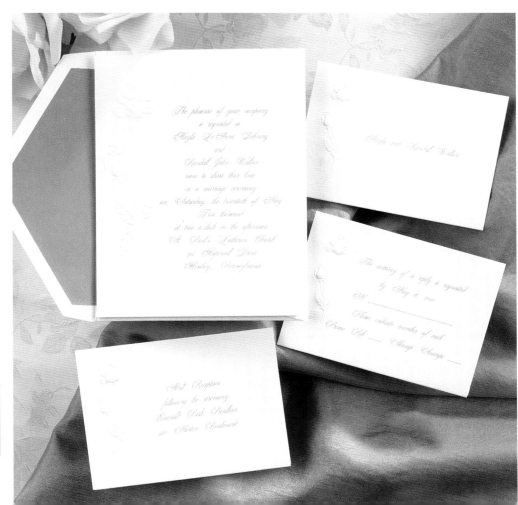

ELEGANT WHITE ON WHITE

This soft white z-fold features a pearl embossed vine pattern. Your names will be printed on the front. Specify first names. The elegant satin adhesive bow is included in the price of this invitation. Customer assembly is required. 5" x 6 5/8"
WAF5631-40

LINER CHOICES:

Plum, Navy, Hunter, Wine, Black, Purple, Rosewood, Silver, Taupe, Pearl, Gold, Starlite, Aqua, Fuchsia, Lilac, Peach, Pink, Red, Royal, Sky, Teal

ITEM	ITEM NUMBER	25	50	75	100	125	150	Add'l 25
Invitation	WAF5631-40	103.00	130.30	157.60	184.90	226.80	268.70	41.90
Invitation Envelope Flaps	PRTENV	22.00	23.00	26.70	30.40	34.10	37.80	3.70
Invitation Liner Envelopes	LINEDENV	4.90	9.80	14.70	19.60	24.50	29.40	4.90
Reception Cards	WAR2563	41.50	45.30	49.10	52.90	64.20	75.50	11.30
Respond Cards	WAE2563-01	49.40	53.90	58.40	62.90	76.30	89.70	13.40
Note	WAI2563-01	41.50	45.30	49.10	52.90	64.20	75.50	11.30
Note Envelope Flaps	PRTENV	22.00	23.00	26.70	30.40	34.10	37.80	3.70
Thank You Folder – Blank Inside	WAU2563-01	41.50	45.30	49.10	52.90	64.20	75.50	11.30

◄ "YOUNG LOVE"

"Young Love" A touch of red accents a black and white photo on a soft white tri-fold. "This day I will marry my Friend; the one I laugh with, live for, dream with, Love." will appear in gold foil on front and inside panel. 5" x 6 5/8"
WA8201-40

LINER CHOICES:

Plum, Navy, Hunter, Wine, Black, Purple, Rosewood, Silver, Taupe, Pearl, Gold, Starlite, Aqua, Fuchsia, Lilac, Peach, Pink, Red, Royal, Sky, Teal

ITEM	ITEM NUMBER	25	50	75
Invitation	WA8201-40	97.00	108.30	119.60
Invitation Envelope Flaps	PRTENV	22.00	23.00	26.70
Invitation Liner Envelopes	LINEDENV	4.90	9.80	14.70
Reception Cards	WAR7902	41.50	45.30	49.10
Respond Cards	WAE7902-01	49.40	53.90	58.40
Note	WAI7902-01	41.50	45.30	49.10
Note Envelope Flaps	PRTENV	22.00	23.00	26.70
Thank You Folder – Blank Inside	WAU7902-01	41.50	45.30	49.10

ITEM (cont.)	100	125	150	Add'l 25
Invitation	130.90	158.90	186.90	28.00
Invitation Envelope Flaps	30.40	34.10	37.80	3.70
Invitation Liner Envelopes	19.60	24.50	29.40	4.90
Reception Cards	52.90	64.20	75.50	11.30
Respond Cards	62.90	76.30	89.70	13.40
Note	52.90	64.20	75.50	11.30
Note Envelope Flaps	30.40	34.10	37.80	3.70
Thank You Folder – Blank Inside	52.90	64.20	75.50	11.30

DELICATE ROSES ►

Garlands of embossed roses appear on this creamy ecru folder. 5 1/8" x 7 1/4"
WA598-70

LINER CHOICES:

Hunter, Bright Gold, Wine, Rosewood, Taupe, Pearl

ITEM	ITEM NUMBER	25	50	75
Invitation	WA598-70	61.70	68.10	74.50
Invitation Envelope Flaps	PRTENV	22.00	23.00	26.70
Invitation Liner Envelopes	LINEDENV	4.90	9.80	14.70
Reception Cards	WAR5980	37.30	40.50	43.70
Respond Cards	WAE5980-21	45.20	49.10	53.00
Note	WAI5980-21	37.30	40.50	43.70
Note Envelope Flaps	PRTENV	22.00	23.00	26.70
Thank You Folder – Blank Inside	WAU5980-21	37.30	40.50	43.70

ITEM (cont.)	100	125	150	Add'l 25
Invitation	80.90	98.10	115.30	17.20
Invitation Envelope Flaps	30.40	34.10	37.80	3.70
Invitation Liner Envelopes	19.60	24.50	29.40	4.90
Reception Cards	46.90	56.90	66.90	10.00
Respond Cards	56.90	69.00	81.10	12.10
Note	46.90	56.90	66.90	10.00
Note Envelope Flaps	30.40	34.10	37.80	3.70
Thank You Folder – Blank Inside	46.90	56.90	66.90	10.00

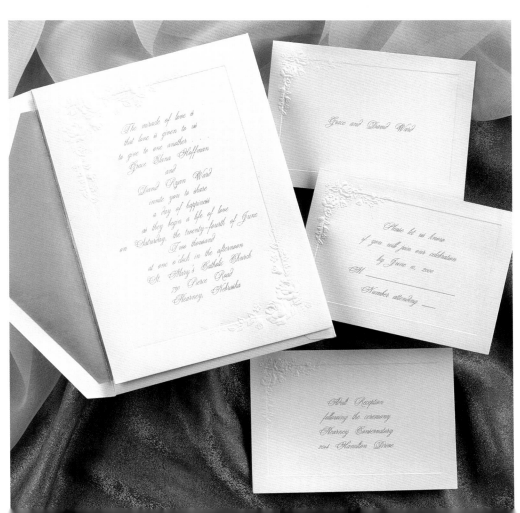

GRACEFUL ROSES AND VINES ▶

This soft white folder has embossed roses with vine accents.
5 1/8" x 7 1/4"

WA718-71

LINER CHOICES:

Plum, Navy, Hunter, Wine, Black, Purple, Rosewood, Silver, Taupe, Pearl, Gold, Sage, Lilac, Peach, Periwinkle, Pink, Red, Sky, Teal

ITEM	ITEM NUMBER	25	50	75
Invitation	WA718-71	61.70	68.10	74.50
Invitation Envelope Flaps	PRTENV	22.00	23.00	26.70
Invitation Liner Envelopes	LINEDENV	4.90	9.80	14.70
Reception Cards	WAR7180	37.30	40.50	43.70
Respond Cards	WAE7180-01	45.20	49.10	53.00
Note	WAI7180-01	37.30	40.50	43.70
Note Envelope Flaps	PRTENV	22.00	23.00	26.70
Thank You Folder – Blank Inside	WAU7180-01	37.30	40.50	43.70

ITEM (cont.)	100	125	150	Add'l 25
Invitation	80.90	98.30	115.70	17.40
Invitation Envelope Flaps	30.40	34.10	37.80	3.70
Invitation Liner Envelopes	19.60	24.50	29.40	4.90
Reception Cards	46.90	56.90	66.90	10.00
Respond Cards	56.90	69.00	81.10	12.10
Note	46.90	56.90	66.90	10.00
Note Envelope Flaps	30.40	34.10	37.80	3.70
Thank You Folder – Blank Inside	46.90	56.90	66.90	10.00

◀ SCULPTURED HEARTS

This soft white z-fold has interlocking pink roses with hunter leaves and pearl ribbon. Your names will be printed in the hearts. Specify first names.
5" x 6 5/8"

WA1511-40

LINER CHOICES:

Hunter, Wine, Rosewood, Silver, Starlite, Pearl, Pink, Teal

ITEM	ITEM NUMBER	25	50	75
Invitation	WA1511-40	89.20	99.10	109.00
Invitation Envelope Flaps	PRTENV	22.00	23.00	26.70
Invitation Liner Envelopes	LINEDENV	4.90	9.80	14.70
Reception Cards	WAR1514	41.60	45.70	49.80
Respond Cards	WAE1514-01	49.50	54.30	59.10
Note	WAI1514-01	41.60	45.70	49.80
Note Envelope Flaps	PRTENV	22.00	23.00	26.70
Thank You Folder – Blank Inside	WAU1514-01	41.60	45.70	49.80

ITEM (cont.)	100	125	150	Add'l 2
Invitation	118.90	144.10	169.30	25.20
Invitation Envelope Flaps	30.40	34.10	37.80	3.70
Invitation Liner Envelopes	19.60	24.50	29.40	4.90
Reception Cards	53.90	65.40	76.90	11.50
Respond Cards	63.90	77.50	91.10	13.60
Note	53.90	65.40	76.90	11.50
Note Envelope Flaps	30.40	34.10	37.80	3.70
Thank You Folder – Blank Inside	53.90	65.40	76.90	11.50

EXQUISITE PLUM ROSES

This soft white card features elegant pearl embossed roses, leaves and ribbon in plum and hunter. 5 1/8" x 7 1/4"
WA1246-71

LINER CHOICES:
Plum, Hunter, Wine, Black, Pearl, Sage

ITEM	ITEM NUMBER	25	50	75
Invitation	WA1246-71	90.80	102.50	112.20
Invitation Envelope Flaps	PRTENV	22.00	23.00	26.70
Invitation Liner Envelopes	LINEDENV	4.90	9.80	14.70
Reception Cards	WAR2246	42.60	46.70	50.80
Respond Cards	WAE2246-01	50.50	55.30	60.10
Note	WAI2246-01	42.60	46.70	50.80
Note Envelope Flaps	PRTENV	22.00	23.00	26.70
Thank You Folder – Blank Inside	WAU2246-01	42.60	46.70	50.80

ITEM (cont.)	100	125	150	Add'l 25
Invitation	122.90	149.20	175.50	26.30
Invitation Envelope Flaps	30.40	34.10	37.80	3.70
Invitation Liner Envelopes	19.60	24.50	29.40	4.90
Reception Cards	54.90	66.60	78.30	11.70
Respond Cards	64.90	78.70	92.50	13.80
Note	54.90	66.60	78.30	11.70
Note Envelope Flaps	30.40	34.10	37.80	3.70
Thank You Folder – Blank Inside	54.90	66.60	78.30	11.70

BUTTERSOFT CALLA LILY BOUQUET

An elegant calla lily card with your wedding invitation printed on the translucent overlay, all tied together with metallic gold ribbon. Customer assembly is required. 5 1/8" x 7 1/4"
WAN1247-71

LINER CHOICES:
Hunter, Black, Pearl, Gold

ITEM	ITEM NUMBER	25	50	75
Invitation	WAN1247-71	112.70	126.10	139.50
Invitation Envelope Flaps	PRTENV	22.00	23.00	26.70
Invitation Liner Envelopes	LINEDENV	4.90	9.80	14.70
Reception Cards	WAR2247	43.50	47.30	51.10
Respond Cards	WAE2247-01	51.40	55.90	60.40
Note	WAI2247-01	43.50	47.30	51.10
Note Envelope Flaps	PRTENV	22.00	23.00	26.70
Thank You Folder Blank Inside	WAU2247-01	43.50	47.30	51.10

ITEM (cont.)	100	125	150	Add'l 25
Invitation	152.90	185.60	218.30	32.70
Invitation Envelope Flaps	30.40	34.10	37.80	3.70
Invitation Liner Envelopes	19.60	24.50	29.40	4.90
Reception Cards	54.90	66.60	78.30	11.70
Respond Cards	64.90	78.70	92.50	13.80
Note	54.90	66.60	78.30	11.70
Note Envelope Flaps	30.40	34.10	37.80	3.70
Thank You Folder Blank Inside	54.90	66.60	78.30	11.70

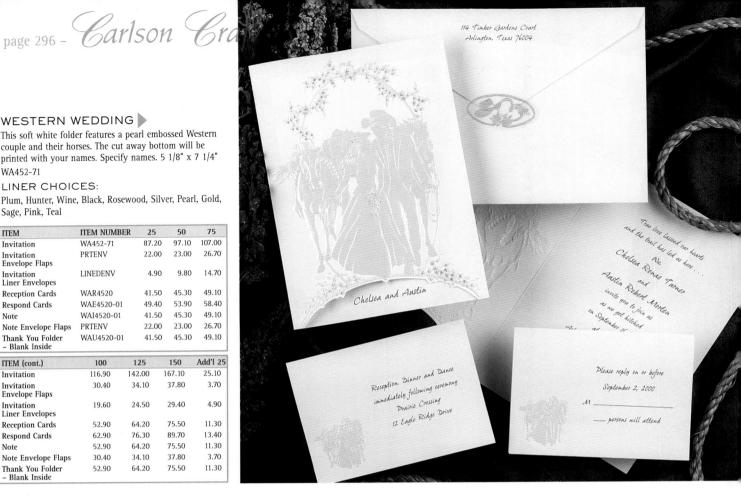

WESTERN WEDDING ▶

This soft white folder features a pearl embossed Western couple and their horses. The cut away bottom will be printed with your names. Specify names. 5 1/8" x 7 1/4"

WA452-71

LINER CHOICES:

Plum, Hunter, Wine, Black, Rosewood, Silver, Pearl, Gold, Sage, Pink, Teal

ITEM	ITEM NUMBER	25	50	75
Invitation	WA452-71	87.20	97.10	107.00
Invitation Envelope Flaps	PRTENV	22.00	23.00	26.70
Invitation Liner Envelopes	LINEDENV	4.90	9.80	14.70
Reception Cards	WAR4520	41.50	45.30	49.10
Respond Cards	WAE4520-01	49.40	53.90	58.40
Note	WAI4520-01	41.50	45.30	49.10
Note Envelope Flaps	PRTENV	22.00	23.00	26.70
Thank You Folder – Blank Inside	WAU4520-01	41.50	45.30	49.10

ITEM (cont.)	100	125	150	Add'l 25
Invitation	116.90	142.00	167.10	25.10
Invitation Envelope Flaps	30.40	34.10	37.80	3.70
Invitation Liner Envelopes	19.60	24.50	29.40	4.90
Reception Cards	52.90	64.20	75.50	11.30
Respond Cards	62.90	76.30	89.70	13.40
Note	52.90	64.20	75.50	11.30
Note Envelope Flaps	30.40	34.10	37.80	3.70
Thank You Folder – Blank Inside	52.90	64.20	75.50	11.30

◀ SIMPLY ELEGANT

A traditional, simple bright white card features an embossed double panel border. 5 1/2" x 7 1/4"

WA1478-87

LINER CHOICES:

Plum, Hunter, Wine, Black, Purple, Rosewood, Silver, Taupe, Pearl, Gold, Sage, Peach, Periwinkle, Pink, Sky, Teal

ITEM	ITEM NUMBER	25	50	75
Invitation	WA1478-87	76.80	85.50	94.2
Invitation Envelope Flaps	PRTENV	22.00	23.00	26.7
Invitation Liner Envelopes	LINEDENV	4.90	9.80	14.7
Reception Cards	WAR2476	39.30	42.50	45.7
Respond Cards	WAE2476-15	47.20	51.10	55.0
Note	WAI2476-15	39.30	42.50	45.7
Note Envelope Flaps	PRTENV	22.00	23.00	26.7
Thank You Folder – Blank Inside	WAU2476-15	39.30	42.50	45.7

ITEM (cont.)	100	125	150	Add'l
Invitation	102.90	125.00	147.10	22.1
Invitation Envelope Flaps	30.40	34.10	37.80	3.7
Invitation Liner Envelopes	19.60	24.50	29.40	4.9
Reception Cards	48.90	59.40	69.90	10.5
Respond Cards	58.90	71.50	84.10	12.6
Note	48.90	59.40	69.90	10.5
Note Envelope Flaps	30.40	34.10	37.80	3.7
Thank You Folder – Blank Inside	48.90	59.40	69.90	10.5

Please join our families
on this special occasion
when our children
Rachelle Christina
and
Benjamin Edward
will be married
on Saturday, the tenth of June
Two thousand
at four o'clock in the afternoon
Centenary Methodist Church
432 South Madison Avenue
Silver Creek, Ohio

Mr. and Mrs. John Bergin
Mr. and Mrs. Lawrence Kennedy

M _____
____ will ____ will not attend
Number of persons ____
R.s.v.p. by May 27, 2000

Rachelle and Benjamin Kennedy

The pleasure of your company is requested
at the Reception
immediately following the ceremony
La Hacienda
32 Calle de Oro

TIME HONORED PEARL
A soft white pearl embossed panel card is truly traditional and elegant.
5 1/8" x 7 1/4"

WA5553-71

LINER CHOICES:
Plum, Navy, Hunter, Wine, Black, Purple, Rosewood, Silver, Taupe, Pearl, Gold, Sage, Lilac, Peach, Periwinkle, Pink, Red, Sky, Teal

ITEM	ITEM NUMBER	25	50	75	100	125	150	Add'l 25
Invitation	WA5553-71	78.90	87.90	96.60	105.90	128.60	151.30	22.70
Invitation Envelope Flaps	PRTENV	22.00	23.00	26.70	30.40	34.10	37.80	3.70
Invitation Liner Envelopes	LINEDENV	4.90	9.80	14.70	19.60	24.50	29.40	4.90
Reception Cards	WAR2551	41.50	45.30	49.10	52.90	64.20	75.50	11.30
Respond Cards	WAE2551-01	49.40	53.90	58.40	62.90	76.30	89.70	13.40
Note	WAI2551-01	41.50	45.30	49.10	52.90	64.20	75.50	11.30
Note Envelope Flaps	PRTENV	22.00	23.00	26.70	30.40	34.10	37.80	3.70
Thank You Folder – Blank Inside	WAU2551-01	41.50	45.30	49.10	52.90	64.20	75.50	11.30

Because you have shared in our lives
by your friendship and love, we
Aimee Rachelle Christenson
and
Robert Andrew Charpetier
together with our parents
invite you to share
the beginning of our new life together
when we exchange marriage vows
on Saturday, the twenty-second of July
Two thousand
at half past one in the afternoon
Forest Hills Church
70 Durant Avenue
Forest Hills, Kentucky

Mr. and Mrs. Robert Charpetier

M
___ will ___ will not attend
Number of persons ___
R.s.v.p. by July 8, 2000

Join us for the Reception
immediately following the ceremony
Country Inn
6490 East Second Street

LUXURIOUS ROSES AND PEARLS

Embossed roses and ribbon in shimmering pearl highlight the
border of this creamy ecru invitation folder. 5 1/8" x 7 1/4"
WA584-70

LINER CHOICES:

Bright Gold, Hunter, Wine, Rosewood, Taupe, Pearl

ITEM	ITEM NUMBER	25	50	75	100	125	150	Add'l 25
Invitation	WA584-70	82.20	91.10	100.00	108.90	132.00	155.10	23.10
Invitation Envelope Flaps	PRTENV	22.00	23.00	26.70	30.40	34.10	37.80	3.70
Invitation Liner Envelopes	LINEDENV	4.90	9.80	14.70	19.60	24.50	29.40	4.90
Reception Cards	WAR5840	41.50	45.30	49.10	52.90	64.20	75.50	11.30
Respond Cards	WAE5840-21	49.40	53.90	58.40	62.90	76.30	89.70	13.40
Note	WAI5840-21	41.50	45.30	49.10	52.90	64.20	75.50	11.30
Note Envelope Flaps	PRTENV	22.00	23.00	26.70	30.40	34.10	37.80	3.70
Thank You Folder – Blank Inside	WAU5840-21	41.50	45.30	49.10	52.90	64.20	75.50	11.30

◄ SOPHISTICATED FILIGREE

This pearl embossed triple panel includes an elegant border of filigree on this bright white card. 5 1/2" x 7 3/4"
WA9152-226

LINER CHOICES:
Navy, Pearl

ITEM	ITEM NUMBER	25	50	75
Invitation	WA9152-226	102.70	114.90	125.50
Invitation Envelope Flaps	PRTENV	22.00	23.00	26.70
Invitation Liner Envelopes	LINEDENV	4.90	9.80	14.70
Reception Cards	WAR9521	41.50	45.30	49.10
Respond Cards	WAE9521-203	49.40	53.90	58.40
Note	WAI9520-203	41.50	45.30	49.10
Note Envelope Flaps	PRTENV	22.00	23.00	26.70
Thank You Folder – Blank Inside	WAU9520-203	41.50	45.30	49.10

ITEM (cont.)	100	125	150	Add'l 25
Invitation	136.90	165.90	194.90	29.00
Invitation Envelope Flaps	30.40	34.10	37.80	3.70
Invitation Liner Envelopes	19.60	24.50	29.40	4.90
Reception Cards	52.90	64.20	75.50	11.30
Respond Cards	62.90	76.30	89.70	13.40
Note	52.90	64.20	75.50	11.30
Note Envelope Flaps	30.40	34.10	37.80	3.70
Thank You Folder – Blank Inside	52.90	64.20	75.50	11.30

SHIMMERING STARS ►

Clusters of gold foil stars fall on a creamy ecru card.
5 1/2" x 7 3/4"
WA1189-99

LINER CHOICES:
Hunter, Wine, Pearl, Gold

ITEM	ITEM NUMBER	25	50	75
Invitation	WA1189-99	90.50	101.30	112.10
Invitation Envelope Flaps	PRTENV	22.00	23.00	26.70
Invitation Liner Envelopes	LINEDENV	4.90	9.80	14.70
Reception Cards	WAR2189	43.50	47.30	51.10
Respond Cards	WAE2189-21	51.40	55.90	60.40
Note	WAI2189-21	43.50	47.30	51.10
Note Envelope Flaps	WAU2189-21	43.50	47.30	51.10
Thank You Folder – Blank Inside	PRTENV	22.00	23.00	26.70

ITEM (cont.)	100	125	150	Add'l 25
Invitation	122.90	149.30	175.70	26.40
Invitation Envelope Flaps	30.40	34.10	37.80	3.70
Invitation Liner Envelopes	19.60	24.50	29.40	4.90
Reception Cards	54.90	66.60	78.30	11.70
Respond Cards	64.90	78.70	92.50	13.80
Note	54.90	66.60	78.30	11.70
Note Envelope Flaps	30.40	34.10	37.80	3.70
Thank You Folder – Blank Inside	54.90	66.60	78.30	11.70

Isabel Anne Moretti
and
Patrick James Eaton
have chosen the first day
of their new life together
as Saturday, the second of September
Two thousand
You are invited to share in their joy
as they exchange marriage vows
at half past two in the afternoon
St. John's Catholic Church
320 Belgrade Avenue
Olympia, Washington

Isabel & Patrick

Cocktails served at 4:30 p.m.
Dinner served at 6:00 p.m.
Dancing 8:00 p.m. until 12:00 a.m.
Olympia Country Club
7450 Carlisle Boulevard

The favour of a reply is requested
before August 19, 2000

M _____
___ will attend
___ not able to attend

WISPY TRANSLUCENT

A blind embossed border of swirled filigree softly falls on this translucent card. When writing on translucent paper, permanent pen is recommended to prevent smearing. 5 1/2" x 7 3/4"
WA4811-87

LINER CHOICES:
Plum, Hunter, Wine, Black, Purple, Rosewood, Silver, Starlite, Taupe, Pearl, Gold, Sage, Peach, Periwinkle, Pink, Sky, Teal

ITEM	ITEM NUMBER	25	50	75	100	125	150	Add'l 25
Invitation	WA4811-87	94.70	106.10	117.50	128.90	156.50	184.10	27.60
Invitation Envelope Flaps	PRTENV	22.00	23.00	26.70	30.40	34.10	37.80	3.70
Invitation Liner Envelopes	LINEDENV	4.90	9.80	14.70	19.60	24.50	29.40	4.90
Reception Cards	WAR2481	45.60	49.70	53.80	57.90	70.30	82.70	12.40
Respond Cards	WAE2481-15	54.50	59.30	64.10	68.90	83.60	98.30	14.70
Note	WAI2481-15	45.60	49.70	53.80	57.90	70.30	82.70	12.40
Note Envelope Flaps	PRTENV	22.00	23.00	26.70	30.40	34.10	37.80	3.70
Thank You Folder – Blank Inside	WAU2481-15	45.60	49.70	53.80	57.90	70.30	82.70	12.40

◀ DELICATE PEARL HEARTS

Pearl embossed plum roses, hunter leaves and flowing ribbon appear on this bright white z-fold. Printed on the front, a quotation of your choice and your names will be highlighted inside the die cut heart. Please specify your names.
7 3/4" x 5 1/2"
WA1255-87

LINER CHOICES:

Plum, Hunter, Black, Silver, Pearl, Teal

ITEM	ITEM NUMBER	25	50	75
Invitation	WA1255-87	98.40	109.90	121.40
Invitation Envelope Flaps	PRTENV	22.00	23.00	26.70
Invitation Liner Envelopes	LINEDENV	4.90	9.80	14.70
Reception Cards	WAR2255	43.60	47.70	51.80
Respond Cards	WAE2255-15	51.50	56.30	61.10
Note	WAI2255-15	43.60	47.70	51.80
Note Envelope Flaps	PRTENV	22.00	23.00	26.70
Thank You Folder – Blank Inside	WAU2255-15	43.60	47.70	51.80

ITEM (cont.)	100	125	150	Add'l 25
Invitation	132.90	161.40	189.90	28.50
Invitation Envelope Flaps	30.40	34.10	37.80	3.70
Invitation Liner Envelopes	19.60	24.50	29.40	4.90
Reception Cards	55.90	67.80	79.70	11.90
Respond Cards	65.90	80.00	94.10	14.10
Note	55.90	67.80	79.70	11.90
Note Envelope Flaps	30.40	34.10	37.80	3.70
Thank You Folder – Blank Inside	55.90	67.80	79.70	11.90

ROMANTIC LOVE ▶

A bridal couple shown under a trellis decorated with purple, pearl embossed roses on a bright white z-fold. Your names appear on the front. Please specify names. A quotation of your choice is printed on the center panel and your invitation wording appears on the right.
7 3/4" x 5 1/2"
WA8258-87

LINER CHOICES:

Black, Purple, Silver, Pearl, Gold, Starlite, Periwinkle

ITEM	ITEM NUMBER	25	50	75
Invitation	WA8258-87	98.40	109.90	121.40
Invitation Envelope Flaps	PRTENV	22.00	23.00	26.70
Invitation Liner Envelopes	LINEDENV	4.90	9.80	14.70
Reception Cards	WAR8580	43.60	47.70	51.80
Respond Cards	WAE8580-15	51.50	56.30	61.10
Note	WAI8580-15	43.60	47.70	51.80
Note Envelope Flaps	PRTENV	22.00	23.00	26.70
Thank You Folder – Blank Inside	WAU8580-15	43.60	47.70	51.80

ITEM (cont.)	100	125	150	Add'l 25
Invitation	132.90	161.40	189.90	28.50
Invitation Envelope Flaps	30.40	34.10	37.80	3.70
Invitation Liner Envelopes	19.60	24.50	29.40	4.90
Reception Cards	55.90	67.80	79.70	11.90
Respond Cards	65.90	80.00	94.10	14.10
Note	55.90	67.80	79.70	11.90
Note Envelope Flaps	30.40	34.10	37.80	3.70
Thank You Folder – Blank Inside	55.90	67.80	79.70	11.90

SIMPLE CLASSIC SQUARE ▶

Rich bands of shimmering pearl border
this bright white square. 5 1/2" x 5 1/2"
Extra postage is required.

WA1254-37

LINER CHOICES:

Hunter, Taupe, Pearl, Gold

ITEM	ITEM NUMBER	25	50	75
Invitation	WA1254-37	81.00	90.30	99.60
Invitation Envelope Flaps	PRTENV	22.00	23.00	26.70
Invitation Liner Envelopes	LINEDENV	4.90	9.80	14.70
Reception Cards	WAR2254	40.50	44.30	48.10
Respond Cards	WAE2254-15	48.40	52.90	57.40
Note	WAI2254-15	40.50	44.30	48.10
Note Envelope Flaps	PRTENV	22.00	23.00	26.70
Thank You Folder – Blank Inside	WAU2254-15	40.50	44.30	48.10

ITEM (cont.)	100	125	150	Add'l 25
Invitation	108.90	132.30	155.70	23.40
Invitation Envelope Flaps	30.40	34.10	37.80	3.70
Invitation Liner Envelopes	19.60	24.50	29.40	4.90
Reception Cards	51.90	63.00	74.10	11.10
Respond Cards	61.90	75.10	88.30	13.20
Note	51.90	63.00	74.10	11.10
Note Envelope Flaps	30.40	34.10	37.80	3.70
Thank You Folder – Blank Inside	51.90	63.00	74.10	11.10

◀ FOREVER FLORAL

A beautiful pearl embossed heart appears on this "tea
length" bright white forever floral card. Your first
names will be printed at the top. Specify first names.
4" x 9 1/4"

WA1399-224

LINER CHOICES:

Bright Gold, Taupe, Pearl

ITEM	ITEM NUMBER	25	50	75
Invitation	WA1399-224	95.90	106.90	117.90
Invitation Envelope Flaps	PRTENV	22.00	23.00	26.70
Invitation Liner Envelopes	LINEDENV	4.90	9.80	14.70
Reception Cards	WAR2399	43.60	47.70	51.80
Respond Cards	WAE2399-27	51.50	56.30	61.10
Note	WAI2399-27	43.60	47.70	51.80
Note Envelope Flaps	PRTENV	22.00	23.00	26.70
Thank You Folder – Blank Inside	WAU2399-27	43.60	47.70	51.80

ITEM (cont.)	100	125	150	Add'l 25
Invitation	128.90	156.50	184.10	27.60
Invitation Envelope Flaps	30.40	34.10	37.80	3.70
Invitation Liner Envelopes	19.60	24.50	29.40	4.90
Reception Cards	55.90	67.80	79.70	11.90
Respond Cards	65.90	80.00	94.10	14.10
Note	55.90	67.80	79.70	11.90
Note Envelope Flaps	30.40	34.10	37.80	3.70
Thank You Folder – Blank Inside	55.90	67.80	79.70	11.90

ROMANTIC GLOW

Shimmering pearl bands richly sculpture this bright white square. 7" x 7"
Extra postage is required.
WA923-68

LINER CHOICES:

Wine, Black, Purple, Rosewood, Silver, Taupe, Pearl, Gold, Periwinkle, Pink, Teal, Peach, Sky, Starlite

ITEM	ITEM NUMBER	25	50	75
Invitation	WA923-68	97.00	108.30	119.60
Invitation Envelope Flaps	PRTENV	22.00	23.00	26.70
Invitation Liner Envelopes	LINEDENV	4.90	9.80	14.70
Reception Cards	WAR9230	41.50	45.30	49.10
Respond Cards	WAE9230-15	49.40	53.90	58.40
Note	WAI9230-15	41.50	45.30	49.10
Note Envelope Flaps	PRTENV	22.00	23.00	26.70
Thank You Folder – Blank Inside	WAU9230-15	41.50	45.30	49.10

ITEM (cont.)	100	125	150	Add'l 25
Invitation	130.90	158.90	186.90	28.00
Invitation Envelope Flaps	30.40	34.10	37.80	3.70
Invitation Liner Envelopes	19.60	24.50	29.40	4.90
Reception Cards	52.90	64.20	75.50	11.30
Respond Cards	62.90	76.30	89.70	13.40
Note	52.90	64.20	75.50	11.30
Note Envelope Flaps	30.40	34.10	37.80	3.70
Thank You Folder – Blank Inside	52.90	64.20	75.50	11.30

SOPHISTICATED FLOURISH

This bright white square is highlighted with pearl embossed flourishes around the border. 7" x 7"
Extra postage is required.
WA8052-68

LINER CHOICES:

Wine, Black, Purple, Rosewood, Silver, Taupe, Pearl, Gold, Periwinkle, Pink, Teal

ITEM	ITEM NUMBER	25	50	75
Invitation	WA8052-68	96.40	107.90	119.40
Invitation Envelope Flaps	PRTENV	22.00	23.00	26.70
Invitation Liner Envelopes	LINEDENV	4.90	9.80	14.70
Reception Cards	WAR2258	40.50	44.30	48.10
Respond Cards	WAE2258-15	48.40	52.90	57.40
Note	WAI2258-15	40.50	44.30	48.10
Note Envelope Flaps	PRTENV	22.00	23.00	26.70
Thank You Folder – Blank Inside	WAU2258-15	40.50	44.30	48.10

ITEM (cont.)	100	125	150	Add'l 25
Invitation	130.90	158.90	186.90	28.00
Invitation Envelope Flaps	30.40	34.10	37.80	3.70
Invitation Liner Envelopes	19.60	24.50	29.40	4.90
Reception Cards	51.90	63.00	74.10	11.10
Respond Cards	61.90	75.10	88.30	13.20
Note	51.90	63.00	74.10	11.10
Note Envelope Flaps	30.40	34.10	37.80	3.70
Thank You Folder – Blank Inside	51.90	63.00	74.10	11.10

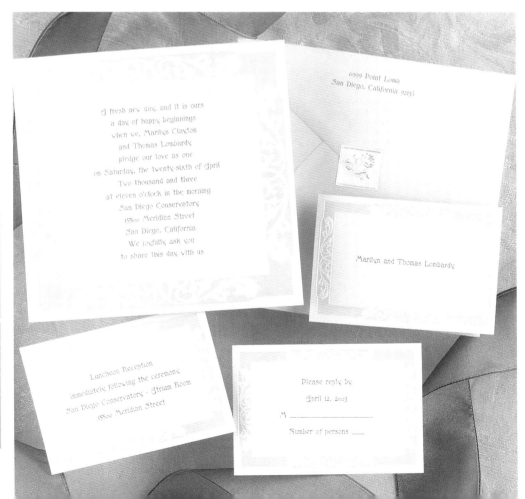

I DO ▶

Two youngsters share tender moments on the front of this white z-fold invitation. The brown-tone portraits are highlighted by a red rose and preprinted gold foil wording; He asked ... She said "Yes!" which follows through inside with the caption; They'll say "I do!" 5" x 6 5/8"

WA4481-40

LINER CHOICES:

Hunter, Wine, Black, Rosewood, Pearl, Gold, Pink, Red

ITEM	ITEM NUMBER	25	50	75
Invitation	WA4481-40	100.60	112.70	124.80
Invitation Envelope Flaps	PRTENV	22.00	23.00	26.70
Invitation Liner Envelopes	LINEDENV	4.90	9.80	14.70
Reception Cards	WAR2480	43.50	47.30	51.10
Respond Cards	WAE2480-01	51.40	55.90	60.40
Note	WAI2480-01	43.50	47.30	51.10
Note Envelope Flaps	PRTENV	22.00	23.00	26.70
Thank You Folder – Blank Inside	WAU2480-01	43.50	47.30	51.10

ITEM (cont.)	100	125	150	Add'l 25
Invitation	136.90	166.20	195.50	29.30
Invitation Envelope Flaps	30.40	34.10	37.80	3.70
Invitation Liner Envelopes	19.60	24.50	29.40	4.90
Reception Cards	54.90	66.60	78.30	11.70
Respond Cards	64.90	78.70	92.50	13.80
Note	54.90	66.60	78.30	11.70
Note Envelope Flaps	30.40	34.10	37.80	3.70
Thank You Folder – Blank Inside	54.90	66.60	78.30	11.70

◀ ONE LOVE

A simple, but elegant design with interlocking gold stemmed white roses on a translucent short z-fold. For a personal touch, your names and a quotation of your choice appear on the front of this invitation, please specify names. Silver and other light ink colors are not recommended. When writing on translucent paper, permanent pen is recommended to prevent smearing. 5" x 6 5/8"

WA6651-40

LINER CHOICES:

Plum, Navy, Hunter, Wine, Black, Purple, Rosewood, Silver, Taupe, Pearl, Gold, Aqua, Fuchsia, Lilac, Peach, Pink, Red, Royal, Sky, Starlite, Teal

ITEM	ITEM NUMBER	25	50	75
Invitation	WA6651-40	105.50	117.30	129.10
Invitation Envelope Flaps	PRTENV	22.00	23.00	26.70
Invitation Liner Envelopes	LINEDENV	4.90	9.80	14.70
Reception Cards	WAR2566	45.00	49.30	53.60
Respond Cards	WAE2566-01	52.90	57.90	62.90
Note	WAI2566-01	45.00	49.30	53.60
Note Envelope Flaps	PRTENV	22.00	23.00	26.70
Thank You Folder – Blank Inside	WAU2566-01	45.00	49.30	53.60

ITEM (cont.)	100	125	150	Add'l 2
Invitation	140.90	170.80	200.70	29.90
Invitation Envelope Flaps	30.40	34.10	37.80	3.70
Invitation Liner Envelopes	19.60	24.50	29.40	4.90
Reception Cards	57.90	70.30	82.70	12.40
Respond Cards	67.90	82.40	96.90	14.50
Note	57.90	70.30	82.70	12.40
Note Envelope Flaps	30.40	34.10	37.80	3.70
Thank You Folder – Blank Inside	57.90	70.30	82.70	12.40

◄ FAIRY TALE ROMANCE

A romantic pearl embossed castle scene rises out of the distance on the front of this bright white z-fold. Your names appear on the front. Please specify names. Inside two panels are revealed: your choice of a quotation in the center and your invitation wording on the right. 5 1/2" x 7 3/4"
WA9459-87

LINER CHOICES:

Plum, Hunter, Wine, Black, Purple, Rosewood, Silver, Taupe, Pearl, Gold, Sage, Peach, Pink, Starlite, Periwinkle, Teal

ITEM	ITEM NUMBER	25	50	75
Invitation	WA9459-87	96.50	107.30	118.10
Invitation Envelope Flaps	PRTENV	22.00	23.00	26.70
Invitation Liner Envelopes	LINEDENV	4.90	9.80	14.70
Reception Cards	WAR4592	41.50	45.30	49.10
Respond Cards	WAE4592-15	49.40	53.90	58.40
Note	WAI4592-15	41.50	45.30	49.10
Note Envelope Flaps	PRTENV	22.00	23.00	26.70
Thank You Folder – Blank Inside	WAU4592-15	41.50	45.30	49.10

ITEM (cont.)	100	125	150	Add'l 25
Invitation	128.90	156.30	183.70	27.40
Invitation Envelope Flaps	30.40	34.10	37.80	3.70
Invitation Liner Envelopes	19.60	24.50	29.40	4.90
Reception Cards	52.90	64.20	75.50	11.30
Respond Cards	62.90	76.30	89.70	13.40
Note	52.90	64.20	75.50	11.30
Note Envelope Flaps	30.40	34.10	37.80	3.70
Thank You Folder – Blank Inside	52.90	64.20	75.50	11.30

TENDER LOVE ►

The innocence of first love is portrayed with this detailed brown tone pencil sketch on a French fold ivory paper with a delicate deckle edge. The friendship you share is reflected in the gold foil front verse. The front verse is available only as shown. 4 1/2" x 5 7/8"
WA734-55
Lined inner envelopes are not available with this invitation.

ITEM	ITEM NUMBER	25	50	75
Invitation	WA734-55	70.70	78.10	85.50
Invitation Envelope Flaps	PRTENV	22.00	23.00	26.70
Reception Cards	WAR7340	39.40	42.90	46.40
Respond Cards	WAE7340-19	47.30	51.50	55.70
Note	WAI7340-19	39.40	42.90	46.40
Note Envelope Flaps	PRTENV	22.00	23.00	26.70
Thank You Folder – Blank Inside	WAU7340-19	39.40	42.90	46.40

ITEM (cont.)	100	125	150	Add'l 25
Invitation	92.90	112.60	132.30	19.70
Invitation Envelope Flaps	30.40	34.10	37.80	3.70
Reception Cards	49.90	60.60	71.30	10.70
Respond Cards	59.90	72.70	85.50	12.80
Note	49.90	60.60	71.30	10.70
Note Envelope Flaps	30.40	34.10	37.80	3.70
Thank You Folder – Blank Inside	49.90	60.60	71.30	10.70

A CHERISHED MOMENT ▶

A bridal couple embraces amid columns, pearl swag and burgundy tinted calla lilies. Your names are printed on the front of this white z-fold. Please specify names. Opening your z-fold invitation reveals a left inside quotation of your choice and your invitation wording amidst burgundy calla lilies on the right. 5 1/2"x 7 1/4"

WA3820-71

LINER CHOICES:

Hunter, Wine, Silver, Pearl

ITEM	ITEM NUMBER	25	50	75
Invitation	WA3820-71	90.60	100.70	110.80
Invitation Envelope Flaps	PRTENV	22.00	23.00	26.70
Invitation Liner Envelopes	LINEDENV	4.90	9.80	14.70
Reception Cards	WAR3822	39.50	43.30	47.10
Respond Cards	WAE3822-01	47.40	51.90	56.90
Note	WAI3822-01	39.50	43.30	47.10
Note Envelope Flaps	PRTENV	22.00	23.00	26.70
Thank You Folder – Blank Inside	WAU3822-01	41.50	45.30	49.10

ITEM (cont.)	100	125	150	Add'l 25
Invitation	120.90	146.60	172.30	25.70
Invitation Envelope Flaps	30.40	34.10	37.80	3.70
Invitation Liner Envelopes	19.60	24.50	29.40	4.90
Reception Cards	50.90	61.80	72.70	10.90
Respond Cards	60.90	73.90	86.90	13.00
Note	50.90	61.80	72.70	10.90
Note Envelope Flaps	30.40	34.10	37.80	3.70
Thank You Folder – Blank Inside	52.90	64.20	75.50	11.30

◀ LASTING MEMORIES

A sophisticated bright white forever floral invitation will reflect your commitment. Your names and date are featured on the front. Please specify names and wedding date. The inside left panel reads; "Shall I Compare Thee To A Summer's Day?" William Shakespeare, Sonnet XVII "You Are My Warmth, My Light, My Love, All The Year Through..." Your invitation wording is printed flush left and highlighted by a pearl band of filigree on the right side that shows on front when the invitation is closed. 5 1/8"x 7 1/4"

WA2741-79

LINER CHOICES:

Black, Purple, Rosewood, Taupe, Pearl, Teal

ITEM	ITEM NUMBER	25	50	75
Invitation	WA2741-79	105.50	117.30	129.10
Invitation Envelope Flaps	PRTENV	22.00	23.00	26.70
Invitation Liner Envelopes	LINEDENV	4.90	9.80	14.70
Reception Cards	WAR2274	43.60	47.70	51.80
Respond Cards	WAE2274-27	51.50	56.30	61.10
Note	WAI2274-27	43.60	47.70	51.80
Note Envelope Flaps	PRTENV	22.00	23.00	26.70
Thank You Folder – Blank Inside	WAU2274-27	43.60	47.70	51.80

ITEM (cont.)	100	125	150	Add'l 25
Invitation	140.90	170.80	200.70	29.90
Invitation Envelope Flaps	30.40	34.10	37.80	3.70
Invitation Liner Envelopes	19.60	24.50	29.40	4.90
Reception Cards	55.90	67.80	79.70	11.90
Respond Cards	65.90	80.00	94.10	14.10
Note	55.90	67.80	79.70	11.90
Note Envelope Flaps	30.40	34.10	37.80	3.70
Thank You Folder – Blank Inside	55.90	67.80	79.70	11.90

◀ELEGANT COUPLE

A beautifully detailed couple stands amidst pearl embossed roses and candlelight on the front of this bright white z-fold invitation. For a personal touch your names appear on the front, please specify names. Inside two panels are revealed, your choice of a quotation in the center and your invitation wording on the right. 5 3/8" x 7 3/4"

WA9359-87

LINER CHOICES:

Plum, Hunter, Wine, Black, Purple, Rosewood, Silver, Taupe, Pearl, Gold, Sage, Peach, Periwinkle, Pink, Teal, Starlite

ITEM	ITEM NUMBER	25	50	75
Invitation	WA9359-87	95.90	106.90	117.90
Invitation Envelope Flaps	PRTENV	22.00	23.00	26.70
Invitation Liner Envelopes	LINEDENV	4.90	9.80	14.70
Reception Cards	WAR3590	41.50	45.30	49.10
Respond Cards	WAE3590-15	49.40	53.90	58.40
Note	WAI3590-15	41.50	45.30	49.10
Note Envelope Flaps	PRTENV	22.00	23.00	26.70
Thank You Folder – Blank Inside	WAU3590-15	41.50	45.30	49.10

ITEM (cont.)	100	125	150	Add'l 25
Invitation	128.90	156.50	184.10	27.60
Invitation Envelope Flaps	30.40	34.10	37.80	3.70
Invitation Liner Envelopes	19.60	24.50	29.40	4.90
Reception Cards	52.90	64.20	75.50	11.30
Respond Cards	62.90	76.30	89.70	13.40
Note	52.90	64.20	75.50	11.30
Note Envelope Flaps	30.40	34.10	37.80	3.70
Thank You Folder – Blank Inside	52.90	64.20	75.50	11.30

JUMPING THE BROOM ▶

The cover design illustrates Nigerian wedding attire. The bride's dress is inspired by "asooke" fabric which is traditional in formal wear. The cowrie shells are used for adornment and are symbolic of fertility. On the back of the invitation, your guests will find this description noted so they may share in the African-American experience. The invitation opens to showcase a quotation of your choice in the center and your invitation wording to the right. 5" x 6 5/8"

WA3271-40

LINER CHOICES:

Plum, Navy, Hunter, Wine, Black, Purple, Taupe, Pearl, Gold, Teal

ITEM	ITEM NUMBER	25	50	75
Invitation	WA3271-40	96.40	107.90	119.40
Invitation Envelope Flaps	PRTENV	22.00	23.00	26.70
Invitation Liner Envelopes	LINEDENV	4.90	9.80	14.70
Reception Cards	WAR3272	39.40	42.90	46.40
Respond Cards	WAE3272-01	47.30	51.50	55.70
Note	WAI3272-01	39.40	42.90	46.40
Note Envelope Flaps	PRTENV	22.00	23.00	26.70
Thank You Folder – Blank Inside	WAU3272-01	39.40	42.90	46.40

ITEM (cont.)	100	125	150	Add'l 25
Invitation	130.90	158.90	186.90	28.00
Invitation Envelope Flaps	30.40	34.10	37.80	3.70
Invitation Liner Envelopes	19.60	24.50	29.40	4.90
Reception Cards	49.90	60.60	71.30	10.70
Respond Cards	59.90	72.70	85.50	12.80
Note	49.90	60.60	71.30	10.70
Note Envelope Flaps	30.40	34.10	37.80	3.70
Thank You Folder – Blank Inside	49.90	60.60	71.30	10.70

GARDEN-FRESH FLOWERS ▶

This lavish, bright white square card features a flourish of vivid flowers printed on the border. Your invitation wording is surrounded by the floral border. Due to the generous size of this invitation, additional postage is required. 7" x 7"
WA5841-68

LINER CHOICES:

Black, Gold, Pearl, Periwinkle, Pink, Purple, Rosewood, Silver, Sky, Taupe, Teal, Wine

ITEM	ITEM NUMBER	25	50	75	100	125	150	Add'l 25
Invitation	WA5841-68	97.80	109.50	121.20	132.90	161.40	189.90	28.50
Invitation Envelope Flaps	PRTENV	22.00	23.00	26.70	30.40	34.10	37.80	3.70
Invitation Liner Envelopes	LINEDENV	4.90	9.80	14.70	19.60	24.50	29.40	4.90
Reception Cards	WAR7084	45.60	49.70	53.80	57.90	70.30	82.70	12.40
Respond Cards	WAE7084-15	54.50	59.30	64.10	68.90	83.60	98.30	14.70
Note	WAI7084-15	45.60	49.70	53.80	57.90	70.30	82.70	12.40
Note Envelope Flaps	PRTENV	22.00	23.00	26.70	30.40	34.10	37.80	3.70
Thank You Folder – Blank Inside	WAU7084-15	45.60	49.70	53.80	57.90	70.30	82.70	12.40

◀ AUTUMN HUES

An autumn array of leaves and trees adorn the front and inside panels of this ecru z-fold invitation. Your first names and wedding date will be printed on the front. Please specify first names and wedding date. The invitation opens to showcase a quotation of your choice in the center and your invitation wording will be printed flush left on the right panel. 5" x 6 5/8"
WA5871-40

LINER CHOICES:

Gold, Black, Hunter, Pearl, Taupe, Wine

ITEM	ITEM NUMBER	25	50	75	100	125	150	Add'l 25
Invitation	WA5871-40	100.60	112.70	124.80	136.90	166.20	195.50	29.30
Invitation Envelope Flaps	PRTENV	22.00	23.00	26.70	30.40	34.10	37.80	3.70
Invitation Liner Envelopes	LINEDENV	4.90	9.80	14.70	19.60	24.50	29.40	4.90
Reception Cards	WAR7871	43.50	47.30	51.10	54.90	66.60	78.30	11.70
Respond Cards	WAE7871-01	51.40	55.90	60.40	64.90	78.70	92.50	13.80
Note	WAI7871-01	43.50	47.30	51.10	54.90	66.60	78.30	11.70
Note Envelope Flaps	PRTENV	22.00	23.00	26.70	30.40	34.10	37.80	3.70
Thank You Folder – Blank Inside	WAU7871-01	43.50	47.30	51.10	54.90	66.60	78.30	11.70

SONG OF CELEBRATION ▶

You are celebrating your love and the start of your new life. The swirling wording; "This Day I Will Marry My Friend" in silver foil accents the cutaway heart. Behind the heart is an array of pastel colors which opens to display your invitation wording. 5" x 6 5/8"
WA5873-40

LINER CHOICES:

Aqua, Black, Gold, Hunter, Lilac, Pearl, Pink, Purple, Rosewood, Silver, Teal

ITEM	ITEM NUMBER	25	50	75	100	125	150	Add'l 25
Invitation	WA5873-40	107.90	120.90	133.90	146.90	178.30	209.70	31.40
Invitation Envelope Flaps	PRTENV	22.00	23.00	26.70	30.40	34.10	37.80	3.70
Invitation Liner Envelopes	LINEDENV	4.90	9.80	14.70	19.60	24.50	29.40	4.90
Reception Cards	WAR7873	43.50	47.30	51.10	54.90	66.60	78.30	11.70
Respond Cards	WAE7873-01	51.40	55.90	60.40	64.90	78.70	92.50	13.80
Note	WAI7873-01	43.50	47.30	51.10	54.90	66.60	78.30	11.70
Note Envelope Flaps	PRTENV	22.00	23.00	26.70	30.40	34.10	37.80	3.70
Thank You Folder – Blank Inside	WAU7873-01	43.50	47.30	51.10	54.90	66.60	78.30	11.70

◄ 2 LIVES 1 LOVE

A white z-fold features sterling silver wording; "2 Lives Be Come 1 Love" Your first names appear on the front; open to your last names and invitation wording inside over the sterling silver wording. This is truly a unique invitation and gives the feeling of romance. Due to the unique design of this invitation, the invitation wording is only available as shown. The invitation wording will be sampled after your wedding profile information. 4" x 9 1/4"
WA5894-223

LINER CHOICES:

Black, Bright Gold, Pearl, Sage, Taupe

ITEM	ITEM NUMBER	25	50	75	100	125	150	Add'l 25
Invitation	WA5894-223	126.90	142.90	158.90	174.90	212.30	249.70	37.40
Invitation Envelope Flaps	PRTENV	22.00	23.00	26.70	30.40	34.10	37.80	3.70
Invitation Liner Envelopes	LINEDENV	4.90	9.80	14.70	19.60	24.50	29.40	4.90
Reception Cards	WAR7894	43.50	47.30	51.10	54.90	66.60	78.30	11.70
Respond Cards	WAE7894-15	51.40	55.90	60.40	64.90	78.70	92.50	13.80
Note	WAI7894-15	43.50	47.30	51.10	54.90	66.60	78.30	11.70
Note Envelope Flaps	PRTENV	22.00	23.00	26.70	30.40	34.10	37.80	3.70
Thank You Folder – Blank Inside	WAU7894-15	43.50	47.30	51.10	54.90	66.60	78.30	11.70

STAR CROSSED LOVERS ►

Your invitation wording is revealed when you open the white window. The translucent stars and hearts are tied to the window cut out with a delicate, white chiffon ribbon. Customer assembly is required. 5" x 6 5/8"

WAN5896-40

LINER CHOICES:

Wine, Aqua, Black, Fuchsia, Gold, Hunter, Lilac, Navy, Peach, Pearl, Pink, Plum, Purple, Red, Rosewood, Royal Blue, Silver, Sky, Starlite, Taupe, Teal

ITEM	ITEM NUMBER	25	50	75	100	125	150	Add'l 25
Invitation	WAN5896-40	123.40	137.90	152.40	166.90	202.60	238.30	35.70
Invitation Envelope Flaps	PRTENV	22.00	23.00	26.70	30.40	34.10	37.80	3.70
Invitation Liner Envelopes	LINEDENV	4.90	9.80	14.70	19.60	24.50	29.40	4.90
Reception Cards	WAR7896	39.30	42.50	45.70	48.90	59.40	69.90	10.50
Respond Cards	WAE7896-01	47.20	51.10	55.00	58.90	71.50	84.10	12.60
Note	WAI7896-01	39.30	42.50	45.70	48.90	59.40	69.90	10.50
Note Envelope Flaps	PRTENV	22.00	23.00	26.70	30.40	34.10	37.80	3.70
Thank You Folder – Blank Inside	WAU7896-01	39.30	42.50	45.70	48.90	59.40	69.90	10.50

◄ WHIMSICAL PERIWINKLE

A band of periwinkle flowers border the edge of this bright white card. A soft periwinkle tinted overlay covers your invitation wording with sheer beauty. The two layers are tied together with delicate sheer white ribbon. Customer assembly is required. 5 3/8" x 7 3/4"
WAN0901-87

LINER CHOICES:

Black, Pearl, Periwinkle, Purple, Silver

ITEM	ITEM NUMBER	25	50	75	100	125	150	Add'l 25
Invitation	WAN0901-87	131.10	147.70	164.30	180.90	219.60	258.30	38.70
Invitation Envelope Flaps	PRTENV	22.00	23.00	26.70	30.40	34.10	37.80	3.70
Invitation Liner Envelopes	LINEDENV	4.90	9.80	14.70	19.60	24.50	29.40	4.90
Reception Cards	WAR7901	45.60	49.70	53.80	57.90	70.30	82.70	12.40
Respond Cards	WAE7901-15	54.50	59.30	64.10	68.90	83.60	98.30	14.70
Note	WAI7901-15	45.60	49.70	53.80	57.90	70.30	82.70	12.40
Note Envelope Flaps	PRTENV	22.00	23.00	26.70	30.40	34.10	37.80	3.70
Thank You Folder – Blank Inside	WAU7901-15	45.60	49.70	53.80	57.90	70.30	82.70	12.40

ALL THE TRIMMINGS ▶

This bright white, forever floral paper is a symbol of eternal love. The cut out heart, with a delicate chiffon ribbon pulled through the heart opening, gives a unique feeling of romance. Your first names and wedding date appear on the bottom of the invitation. Please specify first names and wedding date. A two-line quotation of your choice is printed above your names to add to the invitation's charm and speaks volumes about your love and who you are. 5" x 6 5/8"

WAF5902-49

LINER CHOICES:

Pearl, Bright Gold

ITEM	ITEM NUMBER	25	50	75
Invitation	WAF5902-49	117.80	131.50	145.20
Invitation Envelope Flaps	PRTENV	22.00	23.00	26.70
Invitation Liner Envelopes	LINEDENV	4.90	9.80	14.70
Reception Cards	WAR7090	45.60	49.70	53.80
Respond Cards	WAE7090-27	54.50	59.30	64.10
Note	WAI7090-27	45.60	49.70	53.80
Note Envelope Flaps	PRTENV	22.00	23.00	26.70
Thank You Folder – Blank Inside	WAU7090-27	45.60	49.70	53.80

ITEM (cont.)	100	125	150	Add'l 25
Invitation	158.90	192.90	226.90	34.00
Invitation Envelope Flaps	30.40	34.10	37.80	3.70
Invitation Liner Envelopes	19.60	24.50	29.40	4.90
Reception Cards	57.90	70.30	82.70	12.40
Respond Cards	68.90	83.60	98.30	14.70
Note	57.90	70.30	82.70	12.40
Note Envelope Flaps	30.40	34.10	37.80	3.70
Thank You Folder – Blank Inside	57.90	70.30	82.70	12.40

◀ COLORFUL TREASURE

Your invitation wording is printed amidst soft pink and white stripes. A pretty translucent overlay with roses folds around your base card and is sure to capture the hearts of your guests! Customer assembly is required. 5 1/8" x 7 1/4"

WAN5903-71

LINER CHOICES:

Rosewood, Black, Gold, Hunter, Pearl, Pink, Plum, Sage, T

ITEM	ITEM NUMBER	25	50	75
Invitation	WAN5903-71	123.40	137.90	152.40
Invitation Envelope Flaps	PRTENV	22.00	23.00	26.70
Invitation Liner Envelopes	LINEDENV	4.90	9.80	14.70
Reception Cards	WANR7903	47.00	51.30	55.60
Respond Cards	WANE7903-01	54.90	59.90	64.90
Note	WANI7903-01	47.00	51.30	55.60
Note Envelope Flaps	PRTENV	22.00	23.00	26.70
Thank You Folder – Blank Inside	NA	47.00	51.30	55.60

ITEM (cont.)	100	125	150	Add'l 2
Invitation	166.90	202.60	238.30	35.70
Invitation Envelope Flaps	30.40	34.10	37.80	3.70
Invitation Liner Envelopes	19.60	24.50	29.40	4.90
Reception Cards	59.90	72.70	85.50	12.80
Respond Cards	69.90	84.80	99.70	14.90
Note	59.90	72.70	85.50	12.80
Note Envelope Flaps	30.40	34.10	37.80	3.70
Thank You Folder – Blank Inside	59.90	72.70	85.50	12.80

◄ EPICAL ROMANCE

Absolutely stunning...this pink and white tea length invitation
sets off the elegant sterling silver flourishes. A delicate, petite
chiffon bow combines to create a wedding invitation of
breathtaking beauty. Please specify first names for the front
of the invitation. Customer assembly is required. 4" x 9 1/4"
WAF5916-223

LINER CHOICES:

Pearl, Black, Bright Gold

ITEM	ITEM NUMBER	25	50	75
Invitation	WAF5916-223	144.90	178.90	212.90
Invitation Envelope Flaps	PRTENV	22.00	23.00	26.70
Invitation Liner Envelopes	LINEDENV	4.90	9.80	14.70
Reception Cards	WAR7916	45.60	49.70	53.80
Respond Cards	WAE7916-15	54.50	59.30	64.10
Note	WAI7916-15	45.60	49.70	53.80
Note Envelope Flaps	PRTENV	22.00	23.00	26.70
Thank You Folder – Blank Inside	WAU7916-15	45.60	49.70	53.80

ITEM (cont.)	100	125	150	Add'l 25
Invitation	246.90	302.30	357.70	55.40
Invitation Envelope Flaps	30.40	34.10	37.80	3.70
Invitation Liner Envelopes	19.60	24.50	29.40	4.90
Reception Cards	57.90	70.30	82.70	12.40
Respond Cards	68.90	83.60	98.30	14.70
Note	57.90	70.30	82.70	12.40
Note Envelope Flaps	30.40	34.10	37.80	3.70
Thank You Folder – Blank Inside	57.90	70.30	82.70	12.40

WATERCOLOR PASTELS ►

This bright white tea length folder is wrapped within a floral
watercolor translucent wrap. The wrap softly folds over your
invitation wording inside the folder. A bright white name
card with your first names is tied to this invitation with a
delicate white chiffon ribbon. Customer assembly is required.
Please specify your first names. When writing on translucent
paper, permanent pen is recommended to prevent smearing.
4" x 9 1/2"
WAN5915-223

LINER CHOICES:

Black, Bright Gold, Pearl, Sage

ITEM	ITEM NUMBER	25	50	75
Invitation	WAN5915-223	183.00	218.30	253.60
Invitation Envelope Flaps	PRTENV	22.00	23.00	26.70
Invitation Liner Envelopes	LINEDENV	4.90	9.80	14.70
Reception Cards	WAR7915	47.00	51.30	55.60
Respond Cards	WAE7915-15	54.90	59.90	64.90
Note	WAI7915-15	47.00	51.30	55.60
Note Envelope Flaps	PRTENV	22.00	23.00	26.70
Thank You Folder - Blank Inside	WAU7915-15	47.00	51.30	55.60

ITEM (cont.)	100	125	150	Add'l 25
Invitation	288.90	350.50	412.10	61.60
Invitation Envelope Flaps	30.40	34.10	37.80	3.70
Invitation Liner Envelopes	19.60	24.50	29.40	4.90
Reception Cards	59.90	72.70	85.50	12.80
Respond Cards	69.90	84.80	99.70	14.90
Note	59.90	72.70	85.50	12.80
Note Envelope Flaps	30.40	34.10	37.80	3.70
Thank You Folder - Blank Inside	59.90	72.70	85.50	12.80

BY THE SEA ▶

Dreaming of a seaside wedding? Shimmering, pearl embossed seashells bring the elegance and beauty of the shore to your wedding invitation. Your wording is framed by a double, textured band of pearl on this bright white card.
5 3/8" x 7 3/4"
WA5917-87

LINER CHOICES:

Taupe, Black, Bold, Hunter, Peach, Pearl, Periwinkle, Pink, Plum, Purple, Rosewood, Sage, Silver, Sky, Starlite, Teal, Wine

ITEM	ITEM NUMBER	25	50	75
Invitation	WA5917-87	102.90	114.90	126.90
Invitation Envelope Flaps	PRTENV	22.00	23.00	26.70
Invitation Liner Envelopes	LINEDENV	4.90	9.80	14.70
Reception Cards	WAR7917	45.60	49.70	53.80
Respond Cards	WAE7917-15	54.50	59.30	64.10
Note	WAI7917-15	45.60	49.70	53.80
Note Envelope Flaps	PRTENV	22.00	23.00	26.70
Thank You Folder – Blank Inside	WAU7917-15	45.60	49.70	53.80

ITEM (cont.)	100	125	150	Add'l 25
Invitation	138.90	168.60	198.30	29.70
Invitation Envelope Flaps	30.40	34.10	37.80	3.70
Invitation Liner Envelopes	19.60	24.50	29.40	4.90
Reception Cards	57.90	70.30	82.70	12.40
Respond Cards	68.90	83.60	98.30	14.70
Note	57.90	70.30	82.70	12.40
Note Envelope Flaps	30.40	34.10	37.80	3.70
Thank You Folder – Blank Inside	57.90	70.30	82.70	12.40

◀ DAISY DIMENSION

A folded square of sheer translucent paper is wrapped within a white corrugated folder. The corrugated outside folder has a cut-out frame to highlight the splendid embossed daisy. The daisy is on the front of the translucent folder with your invitation wording inside. A silver pre-tied cord holds the ensemble together. Customer assembly is required. Due to the invitation's unique size, additional postage is required. When writing on translucent paper, permanent pen is recommended to prevent smearing.
5 1/2" x 5 1/2"

WAN5919-37

LINER CHOICES:

Hunter, Gold, Pearl, Silver, Taupe

ITEM	ITEM NUMBER	25	50	75
Invitation	WAN5919-37	173.20	207.10	241.00
Invitation Envelope Flaps	PRTENV	22.00	23.00	26.70
Invitation Liner Envelopes	LINEDENV	4.90	9.80	14.70
Reception Cards	WAR7919	45.60	49.70	53.80
Respond Cards	WAE7919-15	54.50	59.30	64.10
Note	WAI7919-15	45.60	49.70	53.80
Note Envelope Flaps	PRTENV	22.00	23.00	26.70
Thank You Folder – Blank Inside	WAU7919-15	45.60	49.70	53.80

ITEM (cont.)	100	125	150	Add'l 25
Invitation	274.90	333.50	392.10	58.60
Invitation Envelope Flaps	30.40	34.10	37.80	3.70
Invitation Liner Envelopes	19.60	24.50	29.40	4.90
Reception Cards	57.90	70.30	82.70	12.40
Respond Cards	68.90	83.60	98.30	14.70
Note	57.90	70.30	82.70	12.40
Note Envelope Flaps	30.40	34.10	37.80	3.70
Thank You Folder – Blank Inside	57.90	70.30	82.70	12.40

Liner & Ink Colors

STARLITE
AQUA
TEAL
HUNTER
LILAC
PURPLE
PEACH
SKY
ROYAL
NAVY
SAGE

PERIWINKLE
RED
ROSEWOOD
WINE
PINK
GOLD
SILVER
FUCHSIA
BLACK
PEARL
PLUM
TAUPE

Aqua *Black* *Blue* *Brown* *Fuchsia* *Gold* *Grey*

Hunter *Lilac* *Navy* *Peach* *Periwinkle* *Pink* *Plum*

Purple *Red* *Rosewood* *Sage* *Silver* *Sky* *Taupe*

Teal *Wine*

Lettering Styles

AMZ

Aa Bb Cc Dd Ee Ff Gg Hh Ii Jj Kk Ll Mm
Nn Oo Pp Qq Rr Ss Tt Uu Vv Ww Xx Yy Zz
1 2 3 4 5 6 7 8 9 0
The honour of your presence...

AVA

Aa Bb Cc Dd Ee Ff Gg Hh Ii Jj Kk Ll Mm
Nn Oo Pp Qq Rr Ss Tt Uu Vv Ww Xx Yy Zz
1 2 3 4 5 6 7 8 9 0
The honour of your presence...

BIC

Aa Bb Cc Dd Ee Ff Gg Hh Ii Jj Kk Ll Mm
Nn Oo Pp Qq Rr Ss Tt Uu Vv Ww Xx Yy Zz
1 2 3 4 5 6 7 8 9 0
The honour of your presence...

BIN

Aa Bb Cc Dd Ee Ff Gg Hh Ii Jj Kk Ll Mm
Nn Oo Pp Qq Rr Ss Tt Uu Vv Ww Xx Yy Zz
1 2 3 4 5 6 7 8 9 0
The honour of your presence...

BLV

Aa Bb Cc Dd Ee Ff Gg Hh Ii Jj Kk Ll Mm
Nn Oo Pp Qq Rr Ss Tt Uu Vv Ww Xx Yy Zz
1 2 3 4 5 6 7 8 9 0
The honour of your presence...

CAS

Aa Bb Cc Dd Ee Ff Gg Hh Ii Jj Kk Ll Mm
Nn Oo Pp Qq Rr Ss Tt Uu Vv Ww Xx Yy Zz
1 2 3 4 5 6 7 8 9 0
The honour of your presence...

CHM

Aa Bb Cc Dd Ee Ff Gg Hh Ii Jj Kk Ll Mm
Nn Oo Pp Qq Rr Ss Tt Uu Vv Ww Xx Yy Zz
1 2 3 4 5 6 7 8 9 0
The honour of your presence...

CSP

Aa Bb Cc Dd Ee Ff Gg Hh Ii Jj Kk Ll Mm
Nn Oo Pp Qq Rr Ss Tt Uu Vv Ww Xx Yy Zz
1 2 3 4 5 6 7 8 9 0
The honour of your presence...

GRM

Aa Bb Cc Dd Ee Ff Gg Hh Ii Jj Kk Ll Mm
Nn Oo Pp Qq Rr Ss Tt Uu Vv Ww Xx Yy Zz
1 2 3 4 5 6 7 8 9 0
The honour of your presence...

ISA

Aa Bb Cc Dd Ee Ff Gg Hh Ii Jj Kk Ll Mm
Nn Oo Pp Qq Rr Ss Tt Uu Vv Ww Xx Yy Zz
1 2 3 4 5 6 7 8 9 0
The honour of your presence...

LCR

AA BB CC DD EE FF GG HH II JJ KK LL MM
NN OO PP QQ RR SS TT UU VV WW XX YY ZZ
1 2 3 4 5 6 7 8 9 0
THE HONOUR OF YOUR PRESENCE...

LUP

Aa Bb Cc Dd Ee Ff Gg Hh Ii Jj Kk Ll Mm
Nn Oo Pp Qq Rr Ss Tt Uu Vv Ww Xx Yy Zz
1 2 3 4 5 6 7 8 9 0
The honour of your presence...

MOP

Aa Bb Cc Dd Ee Ff Gg Hh Ii Jj Kk Ll Mm
Nn Oo Pp Qq Rr Ss Tt Uu Vv Ww Xx Yy Zz
1 2 3 4 5 6 7 8 9 0
The honour of your presence...

NAD

Aa Bb Cc Dd Ee Ff Gg Hh Ii Jj Kk Ll Mm
Nn Oo Pp Qq Rr Ss Tt Uu Vv Ww Xx Yy Zz
1 2 3 4 5 6 7 8 9 0
The honour of your presence...

NUP

Aa Bb Cc Dd Ee Ff Gg Hh Ii Jj Kk Ll Mm
Nn Oo Pp Qq Rr Ss Tt Uu Vv Ww Xx Yy Zz
1 2 3 4 5 6 7 8 9 0
The honour of your presence...

OXF

Aa Bb Cc Dd Ee Ff Gg Hh Ii Jj Kk Ll Mm
Nn Oo Pp Qq Rr Ss Tt Uu Vv Ww Xx Yy Zz
1 2 3 4 5 6 7 8 9 0
The honour of your presence...

PAX

Aa Bb Cc Dd Ee Ff Gg Hh Ii Jj Kk Ll Mm
Nn Oo Pp Qq Rr Ss Tt Uu Vv Ww Xx Yy Zz
1 2 3 4 5 6 7 8 9 0
The honour of your presence...

RKS

Aa Bb Cc Dd Ee Ff Gg Hh Ii Jj Kk Ll Mm
Nn Oo Pp Qq Rr Ss Tt Uu Vv Ww Xx Yy Zz
1 2 3 4 5 6 7 8 9 0
The honour of your presence...

SAR

Aa Bb Cc Dd Ee Ff Gg Hh Ii Jj Kk Ll Mm
Nn Oo Pp Qq Rr Ss Tt Uu Vv Ww Xx Yy Zz
1 2 3 4 5 6 7 8 9 0
The honour of your presence...

SHA

Aa Bb Cc Dd Ee Ff Gg Hh Ii Jj Kk Ll Mm
Nn Oo Pp Qq Rr Ss Tt Uu Vv Ww Xx Yy Zz
1 2 3 4 5 6 7 8 9 0
The honour of your presence...

Monograms

MONOGRAM M4

MONOGRAM M20

Marissa and Brandon

MONOGRAM P91

Respond Verses

E8
M _____
____ will ____ will not attend
Number of persons ____
R.s.v.p. by *July 5, 2004*

E9
The favor of a reply is requested
on or before *July 5, 2004*
M _____
___ persons will attend

E13
Please reply on or before
July 5, 2004
M _____
___ persons will attend
___ *beef* ___ *chicken*

E14
Please respond on or before
July 5, 2004
M _____
Number of persons ___

E15
Kindly respond by
July 5, 2004
M _____
___ persons will attend

E30
The courtesy of a reply is requested
by *July 5, 2004*
M _____
Number of persons ____

Reception Verses

R7
Dinner and Dance
immediately following the ceremony
Carmel Country Club
5562 Carmel Ranch Road
San Diego, California

R9
Join us for the Reception
immediately following the ceremony
Carmel Country Club
5562 Carmel Ranch Road
San Diego, California

R12
Luncheon Reception
immediately following the ceremony
Carmel Country Club
5562 Carmel Ranch Road
San Diego, California

R15
Reception
following the ceremony
Carmel Country Club
5562 Carmel Ranch Road
San Diego, California

R18
Adult Reception
following the ceremony
Carmel Country Club
5562 Carmel Ranch Road
San Diego, California

R24
We invite you to share with us
our joy at the Reception
immediately following the ceremony
Carmel Country Club
5562 Carmel Ranch Road
San Diego, California

Substitute words in italics with your specific information

Invitation Verses

W140
With joyous hearts
we invite you to attend
our wedding
on *Saturday, the seventh of July*
two thousand four
at *two o'clock in the afternoon*
Hope Baptist Church
1422 West Bell Street
Anaheim, California
Janet Marie Rose
and
Richard Allen Melton

W25
How beautiful is the day
that is touched by love
Mr. and Mrs. George Shepard
request the honour of your presence
at the marriage of their daughter
Katherine Rose
to
Michael Goeffrey White
on *Saturday, the twenty-fourth of August*
two thousand four
at *four o'clock in the afternoon*
St. Peter's Catholic Church
718 Midway Street
Sacramento, California

W37
Mr. and Mrs. Michael Ankeny
request the pleasure of your company
at the marriage of their daughter
Alexandria Leigh
to
Mr. Jeffrey Smith
on *Saturday, the tenth of April*
two thousand four
at *four o'clock in the afternoon*
Oak Forest Country Club
Riverside Drive and Maple Street
San Diego, California

W38
Mr. and Mrs. Mark VanHorn
and
Mr. and Mrs. Kevin Zelter
request the honour of your presence
at the marriage of their children
Hannah Charlotte
and
James Thomas
on *Saturday, the fifth of June*
two thousand four
at *three o'clock in the afternoon*
Our Savior Methodiist Church
County Road B
Columbia Heights, California

W41
The miracle of love is
that love is given to us
to give to one another . . .
Lydia Marie Peterson
and
Joshua John Fox
invite you to share
a day of happiness
as they begin a life of love
on *Saturday, the seventh of August*
two thousand four
at *one o'clock in the afternoon*
Church of Our Lord
6638 Maple Street
Hemet, California

W42
This day I will marry my best friend,
the one I laugh with, live for, love
Brooke Leigh
daughter of
Mr. and Mrs. John R. Ellis
and
David Nelson
son of
Mr. and Mrs. King
hope that you will join in this celebration
on *Saturday, the second of May*
two thousand four
at *seven o'clock in the evening*
St. Phillips Church
579 West Wayne Street
Sculville, California

W44
Together with their parents
Brenda May Roberts
and
Paul Mark Jones
request the honour of your presence
at their marriage
on *Saturday, the twenty-first of August*
two thousand four
at *seven o'clock in the evening*
Preston Country Club
100 Second Street
San Francisco, California

W56
Mr. and Mrs. James DeJovorie
and
Mr. and Mrs. Richard Franklin
invite you to witness as their children
Stephanie Lee and *Jeffrey Allen*
share the Sacrament of Matrimony
with each other
A Wedding Mass will celebrate this union
on *Saturday, the first of May*
two thousand four
at *St. Peter's Catholic Church*
2897 Seventeenth Avenue
Burbank, California

W67
Please join our family
on this joyous occasion
when our daughter
Courtney Lea
will be married to
Mark Anthony Drill
on *Saturday, the fifth of August*
at *four o'clock in the afternoon*
two thousand four
Evangelical Free Church
877 Broadway
Black Hills, South Dakota
Mr. and Mrs. Luke Thompson

W9
Jennifer Leigh Sonders
and
Bryan Johnathan DePew
invite you to share in the joy
when they exchange marriage vows
and begin their new life together
on *Saturday, the fifth of June*
two thousand four
at *four o'clock in the afternoon*
Hope Lutheran Church
1266 West Byrne Avenue
West Lafayette, Indiana

Substitute words in italics with your specific information

YOUR BRIDAL SUPERSTORE

proudly presents

THE
Regency®
COLLECTION

Exclusively unique designs, genuine engraving and quality thermography set our Regency Collection apart. Offering an extensive variety of traditional and contemporary invitations, the Regency Collection includes a wide variety of designs that appeal to all brides.

*We also invite you to visit our on-line store at **www.YourBridalSuperstore.com**, featuring the most extensive collection of accessories, invitations, jewelry, gifts, favors and much more.*

YOUR BRIDAL
SUPERSTORE
...everything but the groom℠

www.YourBridalSuperstore.com

**LOWEST PRICE GUARANTEE
& FREE SHIPPING**
See Order Form for details

 *Regency*®

WRAPPED IN ELEGANCE (WHITE) ▶

A sheet of translucent white paper is printed with your first names to form an elegant wrap for the bright white, non-folding invitation card inside. Your names are printed in the same lettering and ink color as your wording, which is printed on the inside card. Please specify names; if not specified, we will use the first names from the invitation wording.

ON THE INVITATION:
Lettering Style #160
Black Ink
Printed Return Envelope

LINER CHOICES:
Aqua, Black (shown), Burgundy, Gold, Hunter, Lilac, Navy, Peach, Pearl, Periwinkle, Pink, Purple, Red, Rosewood, Silver, Taupe, Teal, Wedgewood
SIZE: 5 1/8" x 7 5/16"

ITEM	ITEM NUMBER	25	50	75	100	125	150	Add'l 25
Invitation	0IA-KIT13W	95.90	104.90	113.90	122.90	151.20	179.50	28.30
Printed Invitation								
Envelope Flaps	0IA-VBWJO	22.90	26.90	28.90	30.90	35.40	39.90	4.50
Lined Inner Envelopes	Specify Color	4.90	9.80	14.70	19.60	24.50	29.40	4.90
Reception Folder	0IA-F9160R	32.90	34.90	36.90	38.90	47.50	56.10	8.60
Respond Folder	0IA-F9160E	40.90	42.90	44.90	46.90	57.30	67.70	10.40
Informal Notes	0IA-F9160N	32.90	34.90	36.90	38.90	47.50	56.10	8.60
Thank You Folder – Blank Inside	0IA-F9160T	32.90	34.90	36.90	38.90	47.50	56.10	8.60
Thank You Folder – Printed Inside	0IA-F9160T2	53.40	55.40	63.60	71.80	86.60	101.40	14.80
Printed Envelope Flaps	0IA-VBW200	22.90	26.90	28.90	30.90	35.40	39.90	4.50

WRAPPED IN ELEGANCE (ECRU) ◀

A sheet of translucent ecru paper is printed with your first names to form an elegant wrap for the ecru non-folding invitation card inside. Your names are printed in the same lettering and ink color as your wording, which is printed on the inside card. Please specify names; if not specified, we will use the first names from the invitation

ON THE INVITATION:
Lettering Style #074
Gold Ink

LINER CHOICES:
Gold (shown), Pearl, Taupe
SIZE: 5 1/8" x 7 5/16"

ITEM	ITEM NUMBER	25	50	75	100	125	150	Add'l 25
Invitation	0IA-KIT03W	95.90	104.90	113.90	122.90	151.20	179.50	28.30
Printed Invitation								
Envelope Flaps	0IA-ERJO	22.90	26.90	28.90	30.90	35.40	39.90	4.50
Lined Inner Envelopes	Specify Color	4.90	9.80	14.70	19.60	24.50	29.40	4.90
Reception Folder	0IA-W8888R	35.90	37.90	39.90	41.90	51.10	60.30	9.20
Respond Folder	0IA-W8888E	43.90	45.90	47.90	49.90	60.90	71.90	11.00
Informal Notes	0IA-W401N	35.90	37.90	39.90	41.90	51.10	60.30	9.20
Thank You Folder – Blank Inside	0IA-W401T	35.90	37.90	39.90	41.90	51.10	60.30	9.20
Thank You Folder – Printed Inside	0IA-W401T2	56.40	58.40	66.60	74.80	90.20	105.60	15.40
Printed Envelope Flaps	0IA-ER200	22.90	26.90	28.90	30.90	35.40	39.90	4.50

PANELS OF PEARL ▶

A bright white folded invitation is bordered with embossed panels, adding dimension to your wording on the front. Two bands of pearl foil add unforgettable luster. Invitations include tissues, unlined inner envelopes and blank outer envelopes. Respond folders include printed return envelopes. Note paper and thank you note folders include blank envelopes. Prices are for black ink. For a colorful ink, add $7.00 to the total price of each printed item.

ON THE INVITATION:
Lettering Style #238
Black Ink

LINER CHOICES:
Aqua, Black (shown), Burgundy, Gold, Hunter, Lilac, Navy, Peach, Pearl, Periwinkle, Pink, Purple, Red, Rosewood, Silver, Taupe, Teal, Wedgewood
SIZE: 5 1/8" x 7 5/16"

ITEM	ITEM NUMBER	25	50	75	100	125	150	Add'l 25
Invitation	0IA-W559W	82.90	91.90	100.90	108.90	134.00	159.10	25.10
Printed Invitation								
Envelope Flaps	0IA-VBWJO	22.90	26.90	28.90	30.90	35.40	39.90	4.50
Lined Inner Envelopes	Specify Color	4.90	9.80	14.70	19.60	24.50	29.40	4.90
Reception Folder	0IA-W8790R	46.90	48.90	50.90	52.90	64.50	76.10	11.60
Respond Folder	0IA-W8790E	54.90	56.90	58.90	60.90	74.30	87.70	13.40
Informal Notes	0IA-W8790N	46.90	48.90	50.90	52.90	64.50	76.10	11.60
Thank You Folder – Blank Inside	0IA-W8790T	46.90	48.90	50.90	52.90	64.50	76.10	11.60
Thank You Folder – Printed Inside	0IA-W8790T2	67.40	69.40	77.60	85.80	103.60	121.40	17.80
Printed Envelope Flaps	0IA-VBW200	22.90	26.90	28.90	30.90	35.40	39.90	4.50

PEARL PERFECTION

Bands of glistening pearl foil set the stage for your elegant wedding. Your wording is displayed on the front of this folded ecru invitation. Invitations include tissues, unlined inner envelopes and blank outer envelopes. Respond folders include printed return envelopes. Note paper and thank you note folders include blank envelopes. Prices are for black ink. For a colorful ink, add $7.00 to the total price of each printed item.

ON THE INVITATION:
Lettering Style #010
Black Ink

LINER CHOICES:
Gold, Pearl (shown), Taupe
SIZE: 5 1/8" x 7 5/16"

ITEM	ITEM NUMBER	25	50	75	100	125	150	Add'l 25
Invitation	OIA-W1157W	84.90	93.90	102.90	110.90	136.40	161.90	25.50
Printed Invitation Envelope Flaps	OIA-ERJO	22.90	26.90	28.90	30.90	35.40	39.90	4.50
Lined Inner Envelopes	Spec. Color	4.90	9.80	14.70	19.60	24.50	29.40	4.90
Reception Folder	OIA-W2157R	46.90	48.90	50.90	52.90	64.50	76.10	11.60
Respond Folder	OIA-W2157E	54.90	56.90	58.90	60.90	74.30	87.70	13.40
Informal Notes	OIA-W2157N	46.90	48.90	50.90	52.90	64.50	76.10	11.60
Thank You Folder – Blank Inside	OIA-W2157T	46.90	48.90	50.90	52.90	64.50	76.10	11.60
Thank You Folder – Printed Inside	OIA-W2157T2	67.40	69.40	77.60	85.80	103.60	121.40	17.80
Printed Envelope Flaps	OIA-ER200	22.90	26.90	28.90	30.90	35.40	39.90	4.50

JOYOUS LOVE

The whimsical wedding couple design on this bright white invitation is a touching expression of joy. The design is accented with pastel pink, purple, yellow and green. Your first names are printed on the front of the z-fold; a quotation of your choice is on the center panel and your wording is on the right, bordered by hearts and flowers. Please specify names and quotation; if not specified, we will use the first names from the invitation wording and quotation Q35. Invitations include tissues, unlined inner envelopes and blank outer envelopes.

ON THE INVITATION:
Lettering Style #007
Gray Ink

LINER CHOICES:
Black, Gold, Hunter, Lilac, Pearl,
Pink, Purple (shown), Silver, Teal
SIZE: 5" x 6 5/8"

ITEM	ITEM NUMBER	25	50	75	100	125	150	Add'l 25
Invitation	OIA-W1432W	76.90	84.90	92.90	100.90	124.10	147.30	23.20
Printed Invitation Envelope Flaps	OIA-VBWEO	22.90	26.90	28.90	30.90	35.40	39.90	4.50
Lined Inner Envelopes	Spec. Color	4.90	9.80	14.70	19.60	24.50	29.40	4.90
Reception Folder	OIA-W2432R	43.90	45.90	47.90	49.90	60.90	71.90	11.00
Respond Folder	OIA-W2432E	51.90	53.90	55.90	57.90	70.70	83.50	12.80
Informal Notes	OIA-W2432N	43.90	45.90	47.90	49.90	60.90	71.90	11.00
Thank You Folder – Blank Inside	OIA-W2432T	43.90	45.90	47.90	49.90	60.90	71.90	11.00
Thank You Folder – Printed Inside	OIA-W2432T2	64.40	66.40	74.60	82.80	100.00	117.20	17.20
Printed Envelope Flaps	OIA-VBW200	22.90	26.90	28.90	30.90	35.40	39.90	4.50

HEART OF MY HEART

Deeply embossed hearts are printed with your names and cut to form an interlocking closure to this unique fold of bright white, linen-textured paper. The hearts are surrounded by embossed flowers. Your wording is printed inside. Please specify names; if not specified, we will use the first names from the invitation wording. Invitations include tissues, unlined inner envelopes and blank outer envelopes.

ON THE INVITATION:
Lettering Style #028
Lilac Ink
Printed Return Envelope

LINER CHOICES:
Black, Burgundy, Gold, Hunter, Lilac, Peach, Pearl, Pink,
Purple (shown), Silver, Teal, Wedgewood
SIZE: 5" x 6 5/8"

ITEM	ITEM NUMBER	25	50	75	100	125	150	Add'l 25
Invitation	OIA-W1347W	74.90	82.90	90.90	98.90	121.70	144.50	22.80
Printed Invitation Envelope Flaps	OIA-VBWEO	22.90	26.90	28.90	30.90	35.40	39.90	4.50
Lined Inner Envelopes	Specify Color	4.90	9.80	14.70	19.60	24.50	29.40	4.90
Reception Folder	OIA-W2347R	40.90	42.90	44.90	46.90	57.20	67.50	10.30
Respond Folder	OIA-W2347E	48.90	50.90	52.90	54.90	67.00	79.10	12.10
Informal Notes	OIA-W2347N	40.90	42.90	44.90	46.90	57.20	67.50	10.30
Thank You Folder – Blank Inside	OIA-W2347T	40.90	42.90	44.90	46.90	57.20	67.50	10.30
Thank You Folder – Printed Inside	OIA-W2347T2	61.40	63.40	71.60	79.80	96.30	112.80	16.50
Printed Envelope Flaps	OIA-VBW200	22.90	26.90	28.90	30.90	35.40	39.90	4.50

MOMENT TO CHERISH (PEARL) ▶

An embossed couple, sculpted columns and rose garlands – all accented with luminous pearl foil – give a romantic look to this invitation. Your first names are printed on the front, a quotation of your choice appears on the center panel of this bright white z-fold invitation and your wording is printed on the right. Please specify names and quotation; if not specified, we will use the first names from the invitation.

ON THE INVITATION:
Lettering Style #061
Gray Ink

LINER CHOICES:
Aqua, Black, Burgundy, Gold, Hunter, Lilac, Navy, Peach, Pearl, Periwinkle, Pink, Purple, Red, Rosewood, Silver (shown), Taupe.
SIZE: 5 1/8" x 7 5/16"

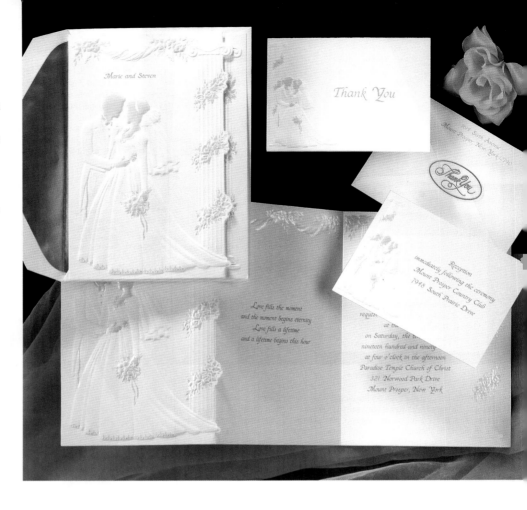

ITEM	ITEM NUMBER	25	50	75
Invitation	OIA-W1266W	95.90	104.90	113.90
Printed Invitation Envelope Flaps	OIA-VBWJO	22.90	26.90	28.90
Lined Inner Envelopes	Spec. Color	4.90	9.80	14.70
Reception Folder	OIA-W2266R	46.90	48.90	50.90
Respond Folder	OIA-W2266E	54.90	56.90	58.90
Informal Notes	OIA-W2266N	46.90	48.90	50.90
Thank You Folder – Blank Inside	OIA-W2266T	46.90	48.90	50.90
Thank You Folder – Printed Inside	OIA-W2266T2	67.40	69.40	77.60
Printed Envelope Flaps	OIA-VBW200	22.90	26.90	28.90

ITEM (cont.)	100	125	150	Add'l 25
Invitation	122.90	151.20	179.50	28.30
Printed Invitation Envelope Flaps	30.90	35.40	39.90	4.50
Lined Inner Envelopes	19.60	24.50	29.40	4.90
Reception Folder	52.90	64.50	76.10	11.60
Respond Folder	60.90	74.30	87.70	13.40
Informal Notes	52.90	64.50	76.10	11.60
Thank You Folder – Blank Inside	52.90	64.50	76.10	11.60
Thank You Folder – Printed Inside	85.80	103.60	121.40	17.80
Printed Envelope Flaps	30.90	35.40	39.90	4.50

◀ UNITED IN LOVE

Two embossed hearts are joined by a gold foil wedding band - a romantic closure to this uniquely folded, soft white invitation. Embossing adds to this invitation's appeal. Invitations include tissues, unlined inner envelopes and blank outer envelopes. Respond folders include printed return envelopes. Note paper and thank you note folders include blank envelopes. Prices are for black ink.

ON THE INVITATION:
Lettering Style #001
Gold Ink

LINER CHOICES:
Gold, Pearl, Silver
SIZE: 4 7/16" x 5 13/16"

ITEM	ITEM NUMBER	25	50	75
Invitation	OIA-F19993W	59.90	65.90	71.90
Printed Invitation Envelope Flaps	OIA-VWD0	22.90	26.90	28.90
Lined Inner Envelopes	Specify Color	4.90	9.80	14.70
Reception Folder	OIA-W24R	32.90	34.90	36.90
Respond Folder	OIA-W24E	40.90	42.90	44.90
Informal Notes	OIA-W32N	32.90	34.90	36.90
Thank You Folder – Blank Inside	OIA-W32T	32.90	34.90	36.90
Thank You Folder – Printed Inside	OIA-W32T2	53.40	55.40	63.60
Printed Envelope Flaps	OIA-VW200	22.90	26.90	28.90

ITEM (cont.)	100	125	150	Add'l 25
Invitation	76.90	94.60	112.30	17.70
Printed Invitation Envelope Flaps	30.90	35.40	39.90	4.50
Lined Inner Envelopes	19.60	24.50	29.40	4.90
Reception Folder	38.90	47.50	56.10	8.60
Respond Folder	46.90	57.30	67.70	10.40
Informal Notes	38.90	47.50	56.10	8.60
Thank You Folder – Blank Inside	38.90	47.50	56.10	8.60
Thank You Folder – Printed Inside	71.80	86.60	101.40	14.80
Printed Envelope Flaps	30.90	35.40	39.90	4.50

LOVE AT FIRST SIGHT

Two youngsters share a tender kiss on the front of this Victorian-style z-fold invitation. The colorful portrait is framed by delicate embossing, which also decorates each corner of the ecru paper. Your first names are printed at the bottom and your wording is revealed inside. Please specify names; if not specified, we will use the first names from the invitation wording. Invitations include tissues, unlined inner envelopes and blank outer envelopes. Respond folders include printed return envelopes. Note paper and thank you note folders include blank envelopes.

ON THE INVITATION:
Lettering Style #238
Gold Ink
Printed Return Envelope

LINER CHOICES:
Gold (shown), Pearl
SIZE: 6 5/8" x 5"

ITEM	ITEM NUMBER	25	50	75
Invitation	OIA-W1691W	87.90	96.90	105.90
Printed Invitation Envelope Flaps	OIA-EREO	22.90	26.90	28.90
Lined Inner Envelopes	Specify Color	4.90	9.80	14.70
Reception Folder	OIA-W2691R	40.90	42.90	44.90
Respond Folder	OIA-W2691E	48.90	50.90	52.90
Informal Notes	OIA-W2691N	40.90	42.90	44.90
Thank You Folder – Blank Inside	OIA-W2691T	40.90	42.90	44.90
Thank You Folder – Printed Inside	OIA-W2691T2	61.40	63.40	71.60
Printed Envelope Flaps	OIA-ER200	22.90	26.90	28.90

ITEM (cont.)	100	125	150	Add'l 25
Invitation	114.90	141.30	167.70	26.40
Printed Invitation Envelope Flaps	30.90	35.40	39.90	4.50
Lined Inner Envelopes	19.60	24.50	29.40	4.90
Reception Folder	46.90	57.20	67.50	10.30
Respond Folder	54.90	67.00	79.10	12.10
Informal Notes	46.90	57.20	67.50	10.30
Thank You Folder – Blank Inside	46.90	57.20	67.50	10.30
Thank You Folder – Printed Inside	79.80	96.30	112.80	16.50
Printed Envelope Flaps	30.90	35.40	39.90	4.50

LUSTROUS SILVER

A shimmering silver filigree pattern is printed over a band of rich black. The design creates a stunning frame for your wording on this non-folding invitation card of bright white paper. Invitations include tissues, unlined inner envelopes and blank outer envelopes. Respond folders include printed return envelopes. Note paper and thank you note folders include blank envelopes. Prices are for black ink. For a colorful ink, add $7.00 to the total price of each printed item.

ON THE INVITATION:
Lettering Style #007
Black Ink
Printed Return Envelope

LINER CHOICES:
Black (shown), Burgundy, Deep Teal, Gold, Hunter, Navy, Pearl, Periwinkle, Rosewood, Sage, Silver
SIZE: 5 1/8" x 7 5/16"

ITEM	ITEM NUMBER	25	50	75
Invitation	OIA-W1604WV	99.90	109.90	119.90
Printed Invitation Envelope Flaps	OIA-VBWTO	22.90	26.90	28.90
Lined Inner Envelopes	Specify Color	4.90	9.80	14.70
Reception Folder	OIA-W2604R	49.90	51.90	53.90
Respond Folder	OIA-W2604E	57.90	59.90	61.90
Informal Notes	OIA-W2604N	49.90	51.90	53.90
Thank You Folder – Blank Inside	OIA-W2604T	49.90	51.90	53.90
Thank You Folder – Printed Inside	OIA-W2604T2	70.40	72.40	80.60
Printed Envelope Flaps	OIA-VBW200	22.90	26.90	28.90

ITEM (cont.)	100	125	150	Add'l 25
Invitation	128.90	158.60	188.30	29.70
Printed Invitation Envelope Flaps	30.90	35.40	39.90	4.50
Lined Inner Envelopes	19.60	24.50	29.40	4.90
Reception Folder	55.90	68.20	80.50	12.30
Respond Folder	63.90	78.00	92.10	14.10
Informal Notes	55.90	68.20	80.50	12.30
Thank You Folder – Blank Inside	55.90	68.20	80.50	12.30
Thank You Folder – Printed Inside	88.80	107.30	125.80	18.50
Printed Envelope Flaps	30.90	35.40	39.90	4.50

ROSES AND RINGS

Your first names, embossed rings and rosebuds appear through a rose-covered, cameolike cutout on the front of this tri-fold invitation. The design is embossed on bright white paper and accented with soft pink and gray. Your wording is printed inside. Please specify names; if not specified, we will use the first names from the invitation wording.

ON THE INVITATION:
Lettering Style #077
Silver Ink
Printed Return Envelope

LINER CHOICES:
Black, Pearl, Pink (shown), Silver
SIZE: 6 5/8" x 5"

ITEM	ITEM NUMBER	25	50	75	100	125	150	Add'l 25
Invitation	0IA-W1371RW	93.90	102.90	111.90	120.90	148.70	176.50	27.80
Printed Invitation Envelope Flaps	0IA-VBWEO	22.90	26.90	28.90	30.90	35.40	39.90	4.50
Lined Inner Envelopes	Specify Color	4.90	9.80	14.70	19.60	24.50	29.40	4.90
Reception Folder	0IA-W2371R	46.90	48.90	50.90	52.90	64.50	76.10	11.60
Respond Folder	0IA-W2371E	54.90	56.90	58.90	60.90	74.30	87.70	13.40
Informal Notes	0IA-W2371N	46.90	48.90	50.90	52.90	64.50	76.10	11.60
Thank You Folder – Blank Inside	0IA-W2371T	46.90	48.90	50.90	52.90	64.50	76.10	11.60
Thank You Folder – Printed Inside	0IA-W2371T2	67.40	69.40	77.60	85.80	103.60	121.40	17.80
Printed Envelope Flaps	0IA-VBW200	22.90	26.90	28.90	30.90	35.40	39.90	4.50

CLASSIC TRADITION IN ECRU ▶

A single panel is embossed on a fold of rich ecru paper for a traditional invitation with impeccable style. Choose from three sizes to suit the style of your celebration. The matching reception and respond enclosures are unique non-folding cards. Invitations include tissues, unlined inner envelopes and blank outer envelopes. Respond cards include printed return envelopes. Note paper and thank you note folders include blank envelopes. Prices are for black ink. For a colorful ink, add $7.00 to the total price of each printed item.

A) ON THE INVITATION:
Lettering Style #299
Black Ink
Printed Return Envelope

A) LINER CHOICES:
Gold, Pearl, Taupe
SIZE: 5 1/8" x 7 5/16"

ITEM A	ITEM NUMBER	25	50	75	100	125	150	Add'l 25
Invitation	0IA-W23W	52.90	57.90	62.90	66.90	82.30	97.70	15.40
Printed Invitation Envelope Flaps	0IA-ERJ0	22.90	26.90	28.90	30.90	35.40	39.90	4.50
Lined Inner Envelopes	Specify Color	4.90	9.80	14.70	19.60	24.50	29.40	4.90
Reception Folder	0IA-W9999R	35.90	37.90	39.90	41.90	51.10	60.30	9.20
Respond Folder	0IA-W9999E	43.90	45.90	47.90	49.90	60.90	71.90	11.00
Informal Notes	0IA-W400N	35.90	37.90	39.90	41.90	51.10	60.30	9.20
Thank You Folder – Blank Inside	0IA-W400T	35.90	37.90	39.90	41.90	51.10	60.30	9.20
Thank You Folder – Printed Inside	0IA-W400T2	56.40	58.40	66.60	74.80	90.20	105.60	15.40
Printed Envelope Flaps	0IA-ER200	22.90	26.90	28.90	30.90	35.40	39.90	4.50

CLASSIC TRADITION IN ECRU ▶

A single panel is embossed on a fold of rich ecru paper for a traditional invitation with impeccable style. Choose from three sizes to suit the style of your celebration. The matching reception and respond enclosures are unique non-folding cards. Invitations include tissues, unlined inner envelopes and blank outer envelopes. Respond cards include printed return envelopes. Note paper and thank you note folders include blank envelopes. Prices are for black ink. For a colorful ink, add $7.00 to the total price of each printed item.

B) ON THE INVITATION:
Lettering Style #001
Black Ink

B) LINER CHOICES:
Gold, Pearl
SIZE: A 5" x 6 5/8"

C) ON THE INVITATION:
Lettering Style #059
Gold Ink

C) LINER CHOICE:
Gold (shown)
SIZE: B 4 7/16" x 5 13/16"

ITEM B	ITEM NUMBER	25	50	75	100	125	150	Add'l 25
Invitation	0IA-W43W	50.90	55.90	60.90	64.90	79.80	94.70	14.90
Printed Invitation Envelope Flaps	0IA-ERE0	22.90	26.90	28.90	30.90	35.40	39.90	4.50
Lined Inner Envelopes	Specify Color	4.90	9.80	14.70	19.60	24.50	29.40	4.90
Reception Folder	0IA-W9999R	35.90	37.90	39.90	41.90	51.10	60.30	9.20
Respond Folder	0IA-W9999E	43.90	45.90	47.90	49.90	60.90	71.90	11.00
Informal Notes	0IA-W400N	35.90	37.90	39.90	41.90	51.10	60.30	9.20
Thank You Folder – Blank Inside	0IA-W400T	35.90	37.90	39.90	41.90	51.10	60.30	9.20
Thank You Folder – Printed Inside	0IA-W400T2	56.40	58.40	66.60	74.80	90.20	105.60	15.40
Printed Envelope Flaps	0IA-ER200	22.90	26.90	28.90	30.90	35.40	39.90	4.50

ITEM C	ITEM NUMBER	25	50	75	100	125	150	Add'l 25
Invitation	0IA-W11W	43.90	47.90	51.90	55.90	68.80	81.70	12.90
Printed Invitation Envelope Flaps	0IA-ERD0	22.90	26.90	28.90	30.90	35.40	39.90	4.50
Lined Inner Envelopes	Specify Color	4.90	9.80	14.70	19.60	24.50	29.40	4.90
Reception Folder	0IA-W9999R	35.90	37.90	39.90	41.90	51.10	60.30	9.20
Respond Folder	0IA-W9999E	43.90	45.90	47.90	49.90	60.90	71.90	11.00
Informal Notes	0IA-W400N	35.90	37.90	39.90	41.90	51.10	60.30	9.20
Thank You Folder – Blank Inside	0IA-W400T	35.90	37.90	39.90	41.90	51.10	60.30	9.20
Thank You Folder – Printed Inside	0IA-W400T2	56.40	58.40	66.60	74.80	90.20	105.60	15.40
Printed Envelope Flaps	0IA-ER200	22.90	26.90	28.90	30.90	35.40	39.90	4.50

 *Regency*®

CELEBRATION ▶

Start your special celebration with this elegant square invitation. Bands of pearl foil border this large, non-folding card of thick, bright white paper. Because of the unique size and shape of this invitation, extra postage is required. Invitations include tissues, unlined inner envelopes and blank outer envelopes. Respond folders include printed return envelopes. Note paper and thank you note folders include blank envelopes. Prices are for black ink. For a colorful ink, add $7.00 to the total price of each printed item.

ON THE INVITATION:
Lettering Style #014
Black Ink
Printed Return Envelope

LINER CHOICES:
Black, Dark Blue, Gold, Pearl (shown), Periwinkle, Pink, Purple, Silver, Teal
SIZE: 7" x 7"

ITEM	ITEM NUMBER	25	50	75
Invitation	0IA-356WH	60.90	66.90	72.90
Printed Invitation Envelope Flaps	0IA-ERJO	22.90	26.90	28.90
Lined Inner Envelopes	Specify Color	4.90	9.80	14.70
Reception Folder	0IA-7905R	40.90	42.90	44.90
Respond Folder	0IA-7905E	48.90	50.90	52.90
Informal Notes	0IA-7905N	40.90	42.90	44.90
Thank You Folder – Blank Inside	0IA-7905T	40.90	42.90	44.90
Thank You Folder – Printed Inside	0IA-7905T2	61.40	63.40	69.60
Printed Envelope Flaps	0IA-ER200	22.90	26.90	28.90

ITEM (cont.)	100	125	150	Add'l 25
Invitation	78.90	97.10	115.30	18.20
Printed Invitation Envelope Flaps	30.90	35.40	39.90	4.50
Lined Inner Envelopes	19.60	24.50	29.40	4.90
Reception Folder	46.90	57.20	67.50	10.30
Respond Folder	54.90	67.00	79.10	12.10
Informal Notes	46.90	57.20	67.50	10.30
Thank You Folder – Blank Inside	46.90	57.20	67.50	10.30
Thank You Folder – Printed Inside	75.80	82.00	88.20	6.20
Printed Envelope Flaps	30.90	35.40	39.90	4.50

WISPS OF WATERCOLOR ▶

Soft strokes of yellow, purple, fuchsia and hunter watercolor have created the romantic little flowers that crown this bright white folded invitation. Your wording is printed beneath the floral design on the front. Invitations include tissues, unlined inner envelopes and blank outer envelopes. Respond folders include printed return envelopes. Note paper and thank you note folders include blank envelopes. Prices are for black ink. For a colorful ink, add $7.00

ON THE INVITATION:
Lettering Style #337
Purple Ink

LINER CHOICES:
Black, Gold, Hunter, Lilac, Pearl, Periwinkle, Purple (shown), Rosewood, Silver, Taupe
SIZE: 5 1/8" x 7 5/16"

ITEM	ITEM NUMBER	25	50	75
Invitation	0IA-W2314W	72.90	80.90	88.90
Printed Invitation Envelope Flaps	0IA-VBWJO	22.90	26.90	28.90
Lined Inner Envelopes	Spec. Color	4.90	9.80	14.70
Reception Folder	0IA-W2314R	43.90	45.90	47.90
Respond Folder	0IA-W2314E	51.90	53.90	55.90
Informal Notes	0IA-W2314N	43.90	45.90	47.90
Thank You Folder – Blank Inside	0IA-W2314T	43.90	45.90	47.90
Thank You Folder – Printed Inside	0IA-W2314T2	64.40	66.40	74.60
Printed Envelope Flaps	0IA-VBW200	22.90	26.90	28.90

ITEM (cont.)	100	125	150	Add'l 25
Invitation	96.90	119.20	141.50	22.30
Printed Invitation Envelope Flaps	30.90	35.40	39.90	4.50
Lined Inner Envelopes	19.60	24.50	29.40	4.90
Reception Folder	49.90	60.90	71.90	11.00
Respond Folder	57.90	70.70	83.50	12.80
Informal Notes	49.90	60.90	71.90	11.00
Thank You Folder – Blank Inside	49.90	60.90	71.90	11.00
Thank You Folder – Printed Inside	82.80	100.00	117.20	17.20
Printed Envelope Flaps	30.90	35.40	39.90	4.50

FIRST ROSE

A black-and-white portrait captures the moment before a young girl receives her first red rose. The sweet design is printed on a large z-fold of bright white paper. Your first names are printed beneath the fold and your wording appears inside. Please specify names; if not specified, we will use the first names from the invitation wording. Invitations include tissues, unlined inner envelopes and blank outer envelopes. Respond folders include printed return envelopes. Note paper and thank you note folders include blank envelopes.

ON THE INVITATION:
Lettering Style #238
Black Ink
Printed Return Envelope

LINER CHOICES:
Black, Burgundy, Deep Teal, Gold, Hunter, Navy, Pearl, Periwinkle, Pink, Purple, Rosewood, Sage, Silver
SIZE: 7 1/4" x 5 1/2"

ITEM	ITEM NUMBER	25	50	75	100	125	150	Add'l 25
Invitation	0IA-J905W	95.90	104.90	113.90	122.90	151.20	179.50	28.30
Printed Invitation Envelope Flaps	0IA-VBWTO	22.90	26.90	28.90	30.90	35.40	39.90	4.50
Lined Inner Envelopes	Specify Color	4.90	9.80	14.70	19.60	24.50	29.40	4.90
Reception Folder	0IA-J9050R	43.90	45.90	47.90	49.90	60.90	71.90	11.00
Respond Folder	0IA-J9050E	51.90	53.90	55.90	57.90	70.70	83.50	12.80
Informal Notes	0IA-J9050N	43.90	45.90	47.90	49.90	60.90	71.90	11.00
Thank You Folder – Blank Inside	0IA-J9050T	43.90	45.90	47.90	49.90	60.90	71.90	11.00
Thank You Folder – Printed Inside	0IA-J9050T2	64.40	66.40	74.60	82.80	100.00	117.20	17.20
Printed Envelope Flaps	0IA-VBW20O	22.90	26.90	28.90	30.90	35.40	39.90	4.50

Mr. and Mrs. John Neville
invite you to share in the ceremony
uniting their daughter
Cassandra Marie
and
Mr. Jacob Benjamin Giefer
Saturday, the ninth of January
nineteen hundred and ninety-nine
at two o'clock in the afternoon
Old Landmark Church
2601 North Meadow Avenue
Indian Springs, Nevada

3186 West Sunset Drive
Indian Springs, Nevada 89018

Reception following ceremony
Rolling Hills Supper Club
1954 Catalina Drive
Indian Springs, Nevada

BEAUTIFUL BLOSSOMS

A pearl-embossed band of spring flowers gives this square invitation a delicately fresh look. The border frames your wording on the front of the non-folding card of bright white paper. Because of the size and shape of this invitation, extra postage will be required. Invitations include tissues, unlined inner envelopes and blank outer envelopes. Respond folders include printed return envelopes. Note paper and thank you note folders include blank envelopes. Prices are for black ink. For a colorful ink, add $7.00 to the total price of each printed item.

ON THE INVITATION:
Lettering Style #238
Burgundy Ink
Printed Return Envelope

LINER CHOICES:
Black, Gold, Navy, Pearl, Periwinkle,
Pink, Purple, Silver, Teal
SIZE: 7" x 7"

ITEM	ITEM NUMBER	25	50	75	100	125	150	Add'l 25
Invitation	OIA-W1322W	103.90	113.90	123.90	132.90	163.50	194.10	30.60
Printed Invitation Envelope Flaps	OIA-VBWQO	22.90	26.90	28.90	30.90	35.40	39.90	4.50
Lined Inner Envelopes	Spec. Color	4.90	9.80	14.70	19.60	24.50	29.40	4.90
Reception Folder	OIA-W2322R	46.90	48.90	50.90	52.90	64.50	76.10	11.60
Respond Folder	OIA-W2322E	54.90	56.90	58.90	60.90	74.30	87.70	13.40
Informal Notes	OIA-W2322N	46.90	48.90	50.90	52.90	64.50	76.10	11.60
Thank You Folder – Blank Inside	OIA-W2322T	46.90	48.90	50.90	52.90	64.50	76.10	11.60
Thank You Folder – Printed Inside	OIA-W2322T2	67.40	69.40	77.60	85.80	103.60	121.40	17.80
Printed Envelope Flaps	OIA-VBW200	22.90	26.90	28.90	30.90	35.40	39.90	4.50

TRADITIONAL STYLE

A crisply embossed triple-panel border gracefully surrounds your wedding wording. This non-folding invitation card is available in a horizontal or vertical format on rich ecru paper. Invitations include tissues, unlined inner envelopes and blank outer envelopes. Respond folders include printed return envelopes. Note paper and thank you note folders include blank envelopes.

ON THE INVITATION: Lettering Style #001

LINER CHOICES: Gold (shown), Pearl, Taupe
SIZE: 7 5/16" x 5 1/8"

ITEM	ITEM NUMBER	25	50	75
Invitation (Horizontal)	OIA-F133WH	60.90	66.90	72.90
Invitation (Vertical)	OIA-F113WV	60.90	66.90	72.90
Printed Invitation Envelope Flaps	OIA-FERJO	22.90	26.90	28.90
Lined Inner Envelopes	Specify Color	4.90	9.80	14.70
Reception Folder	OIA-F3570R	40.90	42.90	44.90
Respond Folder	OIA-F3570E	48.90	50.90	52.90
Informal Notes	OIA-F3570N	40.90	42.90	44.90
Thank You Folder – Blank Inside	OIA-F3570T	40.90	42.90	44.90
Thank You Folder – Printed Inside	OIA-F3570T2	61.40	63.40	71.60
Printed Envelope Flaps	OIA-FER200	22.90	26.90	28.90

ITEM (cont.)	100	125	150	Add'l 25
Invitation	78.90	97.10	115.30	18.20
Printed Invitation Envelope Flaps	30.90	35.40	39.90	4.50
Lined Inner Envelopes	19.60	24.50	29.40	4.90
Reception Folder	46.90	57.20	67.50	10.30
Respond Folder	54.90	67.00	79.10	12.10
Informal Notes	46.90	57.20	67.50	10.30
Thank You Folder – Blank Inside	46.90	57.20	67.50	10.30
Thank You Folder – Printed Inside	79.80	96.30	112.80	16.50
Printed Envelope Flaps	30.90	35.40	39.90	4.50

COUNTRY SWEETHEARTS ▶

Two country sweethearts hand-in-hand add romance and innocence to this natural parchment, French-fold invitation finished with a deckle edge. The touching gold foil verse on the front is available as shown and will not change with your choice of ink color. Invitations include tissues, unlined inner envelopes and blank outer envelopes. Respond folders include printed return envelopes. Note paper and thank you note folders include blank envelopes.

ON THE INVITATION: Lettering Style #077
Gold Ink

LINER CHOICES: Gold (shown),
SIZE: 6 1/8" x 4 1/2"

ITEM	ITEM NUMBER	25	50	75
Invitation	OIA-A4589W	71.90	78.90	85.90
Printed Invitation Envelope Flaps	OIA-PWUO	22.90	26.90	28.90
Lined Inner Envelopes	Spec. Color	4.90	9.80	14.70
Reception Folder	OIA-A45891R	40.90	42.90	44.90
Respond Folder	OIA-A45891E	48.90	50.90	52.90
Informal Notes	OIA-A45891N	40.90	42.90	44.90
Thank You Folder – Blank Inside	OIA-A45891T	40.90	42.90	44.90
Thank You Folder – Printed Inside	OIA-A45891T2	61.40	63.40	71.60
Printed Envelope Flaps	OIA-PW200	22.90	26.90	28.90

ITEM (cont.)	100	125	150	Add'l 25
Invitation	92.90	114.30	135.70	21.40
Printed Invitation Envelope Flaps	30.90	35.40	39.90	4.50
Lined Inner Envelopes	19.60	24.50	29.40	4.90
Reception Folder	46.90	57.20	67.50	10.30
Respond Folder	54.90	67.00	79.10	12.10
Informal Notes	46.90	57.20	67.50	10.30
Thank You Folder – Blank Inside	46.90	57.20	67.50	10.30
Thank You Folder – Printed Inside	79.80	96.30	112.80	16.50
Printed Envelope Flaps	30.90	35.40	39.90	4.50

INSPIRATION ▶

Invite guests to your wedding with this lovely, inspirational invitation. A Bible and candle design is embossed in pearl beside the quotation of your choice on the front of this bright white z-fold. Your first names are printed below the sculpted fold. Please specify names and quotation; if not specified, we will use the first names from the invitation wording and the quotation from the photo. Invitations include tissues, unlined inner envelopes and blank outer envelopes.

ON THE INVITATION:
Lettering Style #074
Black Ink

LINER CHOICES:
Gold, Pearl (shown)
SIZE: 5" x 6 5/8"

ITEM	ITEM NUMBER	25	50	75
Invitation	OIA-J690W	93.90	102.90	111.90
Printed Invitation Envelope Flaps	OIA-VBWPO	22.90	26.90	28.90
Lined Inner Envelopes	Spec. Color	4.90	9.80	14.70
Reception Folder	OIA-J7550R	46.90	48.90	50.90
Respond Folder	OIA-J7550E	54.90	56.90	58.90
Informal Notes	OIA-J7550N	46.90	48.90	50.90
Thank You Folder – Blank Inside	OIA-J7550T	46.90	48.90	50.90
Thank You Folder – Printed Inside	OIA-J7550T2	67.40	69.40	77.60
Printed Envelope Flaps	OIA-VBW200	22.90	26.90	28.90

ITEM (cont.)	100	125	150	Add'l 25
Invitation	120.90	148.70	176.50	27.80
Printed Invitation Envelope Flaps	30.90	35.40	39.90	4.50
Lined Inner Envelopes	19.60	24.50	29.40	4.90
Reception Folder	52.90	64.50	76.10	11.60
Respond Folder	60.90	74.30	87.70	13.40
Informal Notes	52.90	64.50	76.10	11.60
Thank You Folder – Blank Inside	52.90	64.50	76.10	11.60
Thank You Folder – Printed Inside	85.80	103.60	121.40	17.80
Printed Envelope Flaps	30.90	35.40	39.90	4.50

◀ PROMISE OF LOVE

Entwined pearl-embossed hearts and tiny pearl flowers accent the front of this z-fold invitation of bright white, floral-patterned paper. The quotation of your choice is printed on the front and your first names appear below the sculpted fold. Specify names and quotation; if not specified, we will use the first names from the invitation wording and the quotation from the photo.

ON THE INVITATION:
Lettering Style #074

LINER CHOICES
Gold, Pearl (shown),
SIZE: 6 1/8" x 4 3/4"

ITEM	ITEM NUMBER	25	50	75
Invitation	OIA-J680W	93.90	102.90	111.90
Printed Invitation Envelope Flaps	OIA-VBWPO	22.90	26.90	28.90
Lined Inner Envelopes	Spec. Color	4.90	9.80	14.70
Reception Folder	OIA-J6800R	49.90	51.90	53.90
Respond Folder	OIA-J6800E	57.90	59.90	61.90
Informal Notes	OIA-J6800N	49.90	51.90	53.90
Thank You Folder – Blank Inside	OIA-J6800T	49.90	51.90	53.90
Thank You Folder – Printed Inside	OIA-J6800T2	70.40	72.40	80.60
Printed Envelope Flaps	OIA-VBW200	22.90	26.90	28.90

ITEM (cont.)	100	125	150	Add'l 2
Invitation	120.90	148.70	176.50	27.80
Printed Invitation Envelope Flaps	30.90	35.40	39.90	4.50
Lined Inner Envelopes	19.60	24.50	29.40	4.90
Reception Folder	55.90	68.20	80.50	12.30
Respond Folder	63.90	78.00	92.10	14.10
Informal Notes	55.90	68.20	80.50	12.30
Thank You Folder – Blank Inside	55.90	68.20	80.50	12.30
Thank You Folder – Printed Inside	88.80	107.30	125.80	18.50
Printed Envelope Flaps	30.90	35.40	39.90	4.50

Teal

Lilac

Burgundy

Pearl

Hunter

Navy

Silver

Sage

Black

Red

Pink

Taupe

Wedgewood

Rosewood

Periwinkle

Lined Inner Envelopes

Inner envelopes lined with color create a gorgeous backdrop for your invitations. Choose the hue that matches the design of the invitation or one that matches your ink color. Regency offers 17 envelope lining colors. Look for the "Liner Choices" column under the invitation of your choice to see which envelope liners are available. See pricing section under the invitation of your choice for additional envelopes.

Ink Colors

Black ink is a sophisticated and timeless choice for your wedding invitations. But today's couples are creating new traditions with colorful inks that express their unique sense of style. Regency offers 21 ink colors — one will be perfect for your wedding ensemble. The pricing listed for each invitation includes printing in black ink. For a colorful ink from those shown below, please add $7.00 to the total price of each printed item.

Black	Brown	Burgundy	Gold	Gray	Hunter	Lilac
Navy	Periwinkle	Pink	Plum	Purple	Red	Rosewood
Aqua	Sage	Silver	Taupe	Teal	Wedgewood	Peach

Purple

Gold

Lettering Styles

001
Aa Bb Cc Dd Ee Ff Gg Hh Ii Jj Kk Ll Mm
Nn Oo Pp Qq Rr Ss Tt Uu Vv Ww Xx Yy Zz
1 2 3 4 5 6 7 8 9 0
The honour of your presence…

003
Aa Bb Cc Dd Ee Ff Gg Hh Ii Jj Kk Ll Mm
Nn Oo Pp Qq Rr Ss Tt Uu Vv Ww Xx Yy Zz
1 2 3 4 5 6 7 8 9 0
The honour of your presence…

007
Aa Bb Cc Dd Ee Ff Gg Hh Ii Jj Kk Ll Mm
Nn Oo Pp Qq Rr Ss Tt Uu Vv Ww Xx Yy Zz
1 2 3 4 5 6 7 8 9 0
The honour of your presence…

009
Aa Bb Cc Dd Ee Ff Gg Hh Ii Jj Kk Ll Mm
Nn Oo Pp Qq Rr Ss Tt Uu Vv Ww Xx Yy Zz
1 2 3 4 5 6 7 8 9 0
The honour of your presence…

011
Aa Bb Cc Dd Ee Ff Gg Hh Ii Jj Kk Ll Mm
Nn Oo Pp Qq Rr Ss Tt Uu Vv Ww Xx Yy Zz
1 2 3 4 5 6 7 8 9 0
The honour of your presence…

030
Aa Bb Cc Dd Ee Ff Gg Hh Ii Jj Kk Ll Mm
Nn Oo Pp Qq Rr Ss Tt Uu Vv Ww Xx Yy Zz
1 2 3 4 5 6 7 8 9 0
The honour of your presence…

033
Aa Bb Cc Dd Ee Ff Gg Hh Ii Jj Kk Ll Mm
Nn Oo Pp Qq Rr Ss Tt Uu Vv Ww Xx Yy Zz
1 2 3 4 5 6 7 8 9 0
The honour of your presence…

059
Aa Bb Cc Dd Ee Ff Gg Hh Ii Jj Kk Ll Mm
Nn Oo Pp Qq Rr Ss Tt Uu Vv Ww Xx Yy Zz
1 2 3 4 5 6 7 8 9 0
The honour of your presence…

061
Aa Bb Cc Dd Ee Ff Gg Hh Ii Jj Kk Ll Mm
Nn Oo Pp Qq Rr Ss Tt Uu Vv Ww Xx Yy Zz
1 2 3 4 5 6 7 8 9 0
The honour of your presence…

074
Aa Bb Cc Dd Ee Ff Gg Hh Ii Jj Kk Ll Mm
Nn Oo Pp Qq Rr Ss Tt Uu Vv Ww Xx Yy Zz
1 2 3 4 5 6 7 8 9 0
The honour of your presence…

077
Aa Bb Cc Dd Ee Ff Gg Hh Ii Jj Kk Ll Mm
Nn Oo Pp Qq Rr Ss Tt Uu Vv Ww Xx Yy Zz
1 2 3 4 5 6 7 8 9 0
The honour of your presence…

238
Aa Bb Cc Dd Ee Ff Gg Hh Ii Jj Kk Ll Mm
Nn Oo Pp Qq Rr Ss Tt Uu Vv Ww Xx Yy Zz
1 2 3 4 5 6 7 8 9 0
The honour of your presence…

345
Aa Bb Cc Dd Ee Ff Gg Hh Ii Jj Kk Ll Mm
Nn Oo Pp Qq Rr Ss Tt Uu Vv Ww Xx Yy Zz
1234567890
THE HONOUR OF YOUR PRESENCE…

386
Aa Bb Cc Dd Ee Ff Gg Hh Ii Jj Kk Ll Mm
Nn Oo Pp Qq Rr Ss Tt Uu Vv Ww Xx Yy Zz
1 2 3 4 5 6 7 8 9 0
The honour of your presence…

505
Aa Bb Cc Dd Ee Ff Gg Hh Ii Jj Kk Ll Mm
Nn Oo Pp Qq Rr Ss Tt Uu Vv Ww Xx Yy Z
1 2 3 4 5 6 7 8 9 0
The honour of your presence…

831
Aa Bb Cc Dd Ee Ff Gg Hh Ii Jj Kk Ll Mm
Nn Oo Pp Qq Rr Ss Tt Uu Vv Ww Xx Yy Zz
1234567890
The honour of your presence…

Monograms

Monogram No.: **P-71**
Available only as shown

Monogram No.: **1**
Available only as shown

Monogram No.: **3**
Shown with Lettering 831

Respond Verses

E1
Please respond on or before
Saturday, the twenty-fourth of July
M_____
___ accept with pleasure
___ decline with regret

E14
The favour of a reply is requested
before*Saturday, the twenty-fourth of July*
Name _____
Please indicate dinner preference:
___ Entree 1 ___ Entree 2

E2
The favour of a reply is requested
before *Saturday, the twenty-fourth of July*
M_____
___ accept with pleasure
___ decline with regret

E5
Please respond on or before
Saturday, the twenty-fourth of July
M_____
___ will attend
___ not able to attend

E6
The favour of a reply is requested
before *Saturday, the twenty-fourth of July*
M_____
___ will attend
___ not able to attend

E8
The favour of a reply is requested
before *Saturday, the twenty-fourth of July*
M_____
Number of persons ___

ECustom example:
(create your own verse)

Substitute words in italics with your specific information

Reception Verses

R12
Reception Brunch
immediately following the ceremony
Carmel Ranch Country Club
55239 Carmel Ranch Road
San Diego, California

R4
Reception and Dinner
immediately following ceremony
Carmel Ranch Country Club
55239 Carmel Ranch Road
San Diego, California

R5
Reception
at *four o'clock in the afternoon*
Carmel Ranch Country Club
55239 Carmel Ranch Road
San Diego, California

R6
Reception
immediately following ceremony
Carmel Ranch Country Club
55239 Carmel Ranch Road
San Diego, California

R8
Reception following ceremony
at the home and garden of
Mr. and Mrs. Smith
6349 Apple Road
San Bernadino, California

R9
Adult Reception
at *seven o'clock*
Carmel Ranch Country Club
55239 Carmel Ranch Road
San Diego, California

RCustom example:
(create your own verse)

Invitation Verses

L1
Mr. and Mrs. Mark VanHorn
request the honor of your presence
at the marriage of their daughter
Hannah Charlotte
to
Mr. Zachary Allen Taylor
on *Saturday, the seventh of July*
two thousand three
at *two o'clock in the afternoon*
Hope Lutheran Church
1566 West Dime Street
Anaheim, California

L10
Together with their parents
Brenda May Roberts
and
Paul Mark Jones
request the honour of your presence
at their marriage
on *Saturday, the eighth of April*
two thousand two
at *five o'clock in the afternoon*
Evangelical Free Church
850 Broadway
San Diego, California

L12
Alexandria Leigh
and
Patrick Henry Roberts
have chosen the first day
of their new life together
as *Saturday, the tenth of August*
two thousand four
You are invited to share in their joy
as they exchange marriage vows
at *Church of Our Lord*
6655 Wood Street
Lafayette, Indiana

L16
Jennifer Leigh Baker
and
Bryan Jonathan Depew
will pledge their love as one
on *Saturday, the second of May*
two thousand three
at *three o'clock in the afternoon*
St. Phillips Church
560 West Wind Street
Atlanta, Georgia
Our joy will be more complete
if you can share this celebration with us
Mr. and Mrs. Thomas Baker
Mr. and Mrs. Jonathan Depew

L19
A fresh new day and it is ours
a day of happy beginnings
when we, *Amanda Clare Brown*
and *Joseph Damon Crighton*
pledge our love as one
on *Saturday, the fifteenth of May*
two thousand three
at *one o'clock in the afternoon*
Our joy will be more complete
if you can join in this celebration of life

L22
Mr. and Mrs. Domingo R. Lopez
request the honour of your presence
at the marriage of their daughter
Christina Rosa
to
Raul Lee
son of
Mr. and Mrs. Miguel Gomez
on *Saturday, the eighth of June*
two thousand three
at *two o'clock in the afternoon*
St. Peter's Catholic Church
516 East Church Street
Sacramento, California

L4
Mr. and Mrs. Eric P. Johnson
and
Mr. and Mrs. Steven Channing
invite you to share in the joy of
the marriage uniting their children
Katherine Rose
and
Eric Lee
This celebration of love will be
on *Saturday, the tenth of August*
two thousand four
at *four o'clock in the afternoon*
Our Saviour Methodist Church
100 Third Street
Chicago, Illinois

*Substitue words in italics with your
specific information*

L5
Carolyn Ann Smith
and
Steven Gregory Hanson
invite you to share in the joy
of the beginning of their new life
together
when they exchange marriage vows
on *Saturday, the eleventh of August*
two thousand three
at *two o'clock in the afternoon*
Faith Church of Christ
2163 Fourteenth Avenue
Albany, New York

L8
We invite you to be with us
as we begin our new life together
on *Saturday, the twenty-first of July*
two thousand four
at *four o'clock in the afternoon*
Preston Country Club
2886 Glenwood Drive
Trinidad, Colorado
Kimberly Leigh Critton
and
David Lee Townsend

LCustom example:
(create your own verse)

Thank You Verses

TY5
You brought joy to our day,
warmth to our lives,
and happiness to our hearts...
Thank you for your thoughtful gift!
Kim and Bernie White

TY19
We sincerely thank you
for your lovely gift and
all of your good wishes.
Carrie and Bob Anderson

TY20
ONE "THANK YOU" FOR THE LOVELY GIFT
ANOTHER FOR THE THOUGHT
A DOZEN COULDN'T TELL ALL THE
HAPPINESS IT BROUGHT
KATHY AND STEVE FREEMAN

TY21
We sincerely thank you
for your very lovely gift and
for all of your good wishes.
Barb and Ryan Jacob

Your Invitation Ensemble

A) YOUR INVITATION serves as an important guide for your wedding guests. Not only does it include information such as the hosts, date, time and location of the ceremony, it also sets the style for your entire wedding. So select a design and wording for your invitation to reflect your personality! Mail all of your invitations on the same day, four to six weeks before your wedding date. We advise you to have your ensemble weighed at the post office for proper postage. Postage will vary depending on the invitation size, the weight of paper and number of enclosure cards included.

ANNOUNCEMENTS are sent to friends and relatives you are unable to invite to the wedding. Select any invitation to serve as an announcement and include the information printed on your invitations, *excluding the time of the ceremony.* Announcements should be mailed immediately following the wedding, preferably the same day.

B) PRINTED RETURN ADDRESSES ensure that undeliverable invitations are returned to you so you may personally contact those individuals. Printed in raised lettering on the outer envelope flaps, return addresses add elegance to your envelopes while saving you addressing time.

C) LINED INNER ENVELOPES add a rich and colorful finishing touch to your invitations. Available colors are listed at the end of each collection.

D) INFORMAL THANK YOU CARDS are printed with your names on the front. Blank interiors provide room for a personal handwritten note of thanks. Informal cards may also be used long after the wedding for daily correspondence and notes. FREE blank envelopes are included.

E) RECEPTION CARDS inform guests of the time and location of festivities following the ceremony. These cards may also be used to invite guests to dances, gift openings and other celebrations, and to let guests know where you will be "at home" after the wedding. Since these cards are enclosed with the invitations, envelopes are not necessary.

F) RESPOND CARDS often accompany reception cards to help you arrive at an accurate guest count. Respond cards are enclosed with the invitation and should be returned two weeks prior to the wedding date. FREE printed return envelopes are included to ensure a quick reply. Remember to specify the name and return address to be printed on the respond envelopes.

Accessories

Coordinate your entire wedding with beautiful accessories. *The Special Day collection* offers printed accessories like those shown at right. *Shown: bookmarks (sold on page 256); napkins (sold on page 252); place cards (sold on page 257); thank you notes (sold on pages 255 and with collection if shown).*

YOUR BRIDAL SUPERSTORE
...everything but the groom℠
www.YourBridalSuperstore.com

CALL
1-800-286-2806
For Friendly Customer Service

Invitation Order Form

Completing Your Invitation Ensemble

Invitations: Front and inside wording will be printed in the same ink color. Specify the Bride and Groom names to be printed on the front and inside copy. If names are not indicated when a verse is chosen, we will print the first names you have specified on the Invitation Order Form. Invitations with a foil verse on the front may not be changed.

Colored Inks $7.00
The price listed for each invitation, enclosure card and printed envelope includes raised printing in BLACK ink; for printing in colored ink, add $7.00 to the price of each item ordered. Colored ink choices are available at the end of each collection.

Additional Lines.......................$1.50 per line
Invitation prices include up to 14 lines of wording, unless otherwise indicated, excluding corner copy. Reception cards, response cards, printed thank you notes and at home cards include up to five lines. Informal cards include one line of copy.

Corner Copy $8.00
Up to five lines of reception or ceremony information may be printed in the lower left or right corner of your invitation. For two corner copies, (i.e. left and right hand copy) the price is $12.00 total.

Quantity: Order enough invitations for guests you may have overlooked. If you place a second order, you will be billed the original price per 25 invitations, not the price for the

additional 25 invitations. Example:
Original order of **100** with reorder of 25:$69.90 + $63.90 =133.80
Original order of **125** invitations: $69.90 + $15.00 = 84.90
                                             Total Savings = $48.90

Non-English Language..............$10.00/item
Invitations may be printed in Spanish, French or any non-English language that uses the English alphabet for $10.00 per item. Spanish and French accent marks are printed at no charge. Non-English wording must be printed or typed with accent marks indicated.

Special Setup.......................................$25.00
If an invitation is shown with printing on one side only, and you would like printing on both the front and back, we will design a special setup. Front copy will be printed in raised lettering; back copy will be printed flat. Gold and silver inks are not available. Attach a separate page with the copy you would like and where you want it printed.

Proofs ....$25.00 per item
Request a black-and-white copy of your wording to check spelling and positioning. This is **not** a printed invitation. Please indicate a daytime phone number in case we have questions. Proofs will be sent within 3-4 working days. Please remember that we will not process your order until we receive your acceptance of the proof. Please sign the proof indicating that you accept the proof and fax it to 619-287-1019.

Lined Inner Envelopes: You may enhance

your inner envelope with elegant liners. Liner color selections are available at the end of each collection. Lined inner envelopes are available in the colors and styles listed by each invitation. Prices are listed with each item.

Printed Outer Envelopes: We recommend that you have your return address printed on the outer envelope to ensure the return of undeliverable invitations. Return addresses will be printed in raised lettering on the flap in the same lettering style as your invitation. Prices shown are for raised printing in black ink and are listed with each item. Envelopes may be printed in a colored ink for an additional charge of $7.00. Colored ink choices are available at the end of each collection.

Samples ....$4.00 per sample
A sample of any item may be ordered at a cost of $4.00 for each sample you would like to view. The samples are printed with generic wording. Requests for samples can be made via email at Orders@YourBridalSuper Store.com or over the phone. Please be sure to include the item number(s) you would like to receive along with your name, address and telephone number where you can be reached.

Recommendations: We highly recommend that you order at least 25 extra invitations and envelopes in case you think of additional guests, make mistakes, or if you want to save a few as keepsakes.

Invitation Ordering Instructions

PRE-ORDER: For your convenience, we have included a Practice Order Form page. Also, please note that each step is numbered on the invitation and wedding program form for easy ordering.

STEP 1: Start by checking the box for which collection your invitation ensemble is from. Please type or print clearly your name and address in the *"Sold and Ship To"* section. Fill in telephone numbers, the bride's full name, groom's full name, the date of your order and your wedding date under this section.

STEP 2: In the *"Invitations or Announcements"* section, enter quantity, item number, lettering style, verse (if you have chosen one from our

selections), ink color and price for each item you are ordering.

STEP 3: Use the *"Special Instructions"* section for any special requests (i.e. "Please put the bride's name in all capital letters" or "Please print the verse with no justification").

STEP 4: In the *"Front Copy"* section, use the spaces provided for the copy you wish to be imprinted on the front of the invitations that feature this option. This section is most often used for names, dates, and front copy verses. A front copy verse is available only on invitations shown with one.

STEP 5: In the *"Invitation Copy"* section, use the spaces provided for the copy of the verse you have chosen from Step 2. Type or print clearly the verse, using the appropriate information for your wedding and any customized wording you would like to use. Remember to check the box to the left of the *"Invitation Copy"* box if you would like us to follow your wording exactly or make changes for wording that is socially incorrect. Use the *"Etiquette Guidelines for Wedding Invitations"* page for examples of verse wording for special circumstances. Your wording will be centered line by line. Otherwise, use the *"Special Instructions"* section to explain how you would like your copy to be printed.

Invitation Ordering Instructions (Continued)

STEP 6: In the "*Bottom Corner Copy*" section, list any copy that you would like to use on the same panel as the "*Invitation Copy*". This section can be used for any additional copy you would like printed on the bottom of the main "*Invitation Copy*" panel (i.e." Dinner and Dance following Ceremony"). Remember to select either the left or right box, depending on where you would like the copy to be printed.

STEP 7: In the "*Invitation Envelopes*" section, please type or print clearly the quantity, item number, lettering style, ink color and price in the spaces provided. Below that, type or print clearly your return address. The return address will be printed without a name unless you print or type your name here. There is a $1.50 extra line charge if you wish to have your name printed here.

STEP 8: In the "*Lined Inner Envelopes*" section, type or print clearly the quantity, color, item number, and the total price in the spaces provided.

STEP 9: In the "*Reception*" section, type or print clearly the quantity, item number, lettering style, verse number, ink color and price in the spaces provided. Below that, type or print clearly the verse, using the appropriate

information for your wedding. Verse selections are located at the back of each collection. Indicate any custom wording here as well.

STEP 10: In the "*Respond Cards/Envelopes*" section, type or print clearly the quantity, item number, lettering style, verse number, ink color and price. Below that, type or print clearly the verse, using the appropriate information for your wedding and any customized wording you would like to use. Verse selections are located at the back of each collection.

STEP 11: In the "*Copy for Respond Envelopes*" section, type or print clearly the name and return address you would like to use on the front of the Respond envelope. This address is where your guests will send their RSVP's for your ceremony and reception.

STEP 12: In the "*Informal Notes or Matching Thank You Notes*" section, type or print clearly the quantity, item number, lettering style, ink color, monogram number, verse number, and price in the spaces provided. Type or print clearly the names (Bride/Groom) you would like printed on the notes. Informal Notes or Matching Thank You Notes come with free non-printed envelopes. If you would like your envelopes to be printed, please go to Step 13.

STEP 13: If you would like pre-printed envelopes for *Informal Notes* and *Thank You Cards*, type or print clearly the quantity, item number, lettering style, ink color and price in the spaces provided in the "*Informal Notes & Thank You Envelopes*" section. Below that, type or print clearly the return address to be used on the envelopes. There is a $1.50 extra line charge if you wish to have your name printed here. The return address will be printed without a name unless you print or type your name here.

STEP 14: Sign the Order Form.

STEP 15: Be sure you have entered all pertinent prices in the Order Form and complete the "*Invitation Order Summary*". Add sales tax (where applicable) and shipping charges to the amount of your order to calculate the total amount due. Select "*Method of Payment*" and complete the billing information. Mail the completed Order Form, along with your check or money order, to Your Bridal Super Store at the address indicated on the Order Form. Be sure to include the complete Order Form when submitting your order. Orders may be faxed to 619-287-1019. Faxed orders must be paid by credit card. Sorry, because of the amount of copy, we cannot accept phone orders for invitations.

Wedding Program Order Form

Program Ordering Instructions

STEP 1: Please type or print clearly your name and address in the "*Sold and Ship To*" section located at the upper left side of the order form.

STEP 2: Choose a lettering style and enter it in the space provided in the "*Order Summary*" section. Only your names on the front (where available) and the program introduction are printed in your lettering style choice. Remaining copy is printed in block type, as shown in the picture. Prices include black ink. For colored ink, add $7.00 to the total price of your programs. Add any extra line or printing charges to the total cost of your programs. Programs allow for up to 70 lines of copy. Enter quantity, item number, price, ink color, colored ink charge and the total cost in the spaces provided. Enter shipping charges and sales tax and add them to the subtotal for total amount due.

STEP 3: Type or print clearly the item number, quantity, ink color, and lettering style in the spaces

provided. Type or print clearly your program wording on the Program Order Form. Be sure to call attention to any unusual spelling, capitalization or spacing such as Jon, Maryann, Henri, La Gow, LaGow, Lagow, etc., by indicating "Spelling OK." Cross out any section that you will not be using in your wedding. For example, if you don't have a flower girl, just cross out the flower girl section to indicate that this should not be printed. The wedding programs are printed on the inside and are usually one page in length. If there is more than one page, it will be printed like the sample shown.

STEP 4: Continue to type or print clearly the wedding party information in the spaces provided. All information (not in parentheses) in the wording portion of the Program Order Form will be printed unless you have drawn a line through it. If you wish to add additional

information, fill in the blanks provided on the Order Form. If you need more space, type or clearly print your additional wording on a blank sheet of paper and attach it to the form. Should you choose to print a poem or thank you verse on the back page of your program, an additional charge of $25.00 will be applied for up to 14 lines of copy. Type or print clearly your back page wording on a blank sheet of paper and indicate that it is "Back Copy".

STEP 5: Indicate the method of payment you will be using. If a credit card is used, be sure to enter your card number and expiration date. Be sure the cardholder signs your Order Form. If the order is faxed, payment must be made by credit card. Sorry, because of the amount of copy, we cannot accept phone orders for wedding programs. Fax your order to 619-287-1019. For questions, call Your Bridal Super Store at 1-800-286-2806.

336

Etiquette Guidelines for Wedding Invitations

INVITATIONS ISSUED BY BRIDE'S PARENTS

Standard Form
Mr. and Mrs. William Lewis Baker
request the honour of your presence
at the marriage of their daughter
Barbara Ann
to
Richard Dean Smith
on Saturday, the fourteenth of June
Two thousand and three
at three o'clock in the afternoon
First Presbyterian Church
101 Main Street
Edina, Minnesota

Nuptial Mass
Mr. and Mrs. William Lewis Baker
request the honour of your presence
at the marriage of their daughter
Barbara Ann
to
Richard Dean Smith
on Saturday, the fourteenth of June
Two thousand and three
at an eleven o'clock Nuptial Mass
Saint John's Catholic Church
11188 Church Street
Edina, Minnesota

INVITATIONS ISSUED BY BRIDE AND GROOM'S PARENTS

Mr. and Mrs. William Lewis Baker
and
Mr. and Mrs. Roger Vernon Smith
request the honour of your presence
at the marriage of their children

INVITATIONS ISSUED BY GROOM'S PARENTS

Mr. and Mrs. Roger Vernon Smith
request the honour of your presence
at the marriage of
Barbara Ann Baker
to their son
Richard Dean Smith

INVITATIONS ISSUED BY BRIDE AND GROOM

Barbara Ann Baker
and
Richard Dean Smith
request the honour of your presence
at their marriage

INVITATIONS ISSUED BY FRIENDS

Mr. and Mrs. Steven Karl Schmidt
request the honour of your presence
at the marriage of
Barbara Ann Baker

INVITATIONS ISSUED BY ADULT CHILDREN

William J. Leonard, Jr.
David L. Leonard
Barbara A. Smith
request the honour of your presence
at the marriage of their mother
Sharon Marie
to
Thomas Gardiner

SECOND MARRIAGES

Divorcee uses combination of maiden and married names
Mr. and Mrs. William Lewis Baker
request the honour of your presence
at the marriage of their daughter
Barbara Ann Baker Smith

Widow uses married name
Mr. and Mrs. William Lewis Baker
request the honour of your presence
at the marriage of their daughter
Barbara Ann Smith

PARENTS DIVORCED

Divorced Parents
Mrs. Nelson Baker
Mr. William Lewis Baker
request the honour of your presence
OR
Mrs. Joyce Nelson Baker
and
Mr. William Lewis Baker
request the honour of your presence

Bride's Divorced Mother (if not remarried) uses combination of her maiden and married names
Mrs. Joyce Nelson Baker
requests the honour of your presence
at the marriage of her daughter
Barbara Ann

Bride's Divorced Father (if not remarried)
Mr. William Lewis Baker
requests the honour of your presence
at the marriage of his daughter
Barbara Ann

Divorced Mother and Stepfather
Mr. and Mrs. Thomas C. Cooley
request the honour of your presence
at the marriage of her daughter
Barbara Ann Baker
OR
Mr. and Mrs. Thomas C. Cooley
request the honour of your presence
at the marriage of Mrs. Cooley's daughter
Barbara Ann Baker
OR (Mother only invites)
Mrs. Thomas C. Cooley
requests the honour of your presence
at the marriage of her daughter
Barbara Ann Baker

Divorced Father and Stepmother
Mr. and Mrs. William Lewis Baker
request the honour of your presence
at the marriage of his daughter
Barbara Ann Baker
OR
Mr. and Mrs. William Lewis Baker
request the honour of your presence
at the marriage of Mr. Baker's daughter
Barbara Ann Baker

INVITATIONS ISSUED BY MORE THAN 2 SETS OF PARENTS

Mr. and Mrs. William Lewis Baker
Mr. and Mrs. Thomas C. Cooley
and
Mr. and Mrs. Roger Vernon Smith
request the honour of your presence
at the marriage of their children

RECALLING INVITATIONS

Wording may be adjusted to fit the circumstances
Mr. and Mrs. William Lewis Baker
are obliged to recall the invitations
for the marriage of their daughter
Barbara Ann
to
Richard Dean Smith
as the marriage will not take place

ONE PARENT DECEASED

Living parent not remarried
Mrs. William Lewis Baker
requests the honour of your presence
at the marriage of her daughter
Barbara Ann

Living parent has remarried
Mr. and Mrs. John T. Huber
request the honour of your presence
at the marriage of her daughter
Barbara Ann Baker
OR
Mr. and Mrs. John T. Huber
request the honour of your presence
at the marriage of their daughter
Barbara Ann Baker

BOTH PARENTS DECEASED

Invitations issued by unmarried older brother and/or sister
Mr. Roger Vernon Baker
requests the honour of your presence
at the marriage of his sister
Barbara Ann

Invitations issued by married older brother or sister
Mr. and Mrs. John J. Keller
request the honour of your presence
at the marriage of her sister
Barbara Ann Baker

Invitation issued by grandparents or uncle and aunt
Mr. and Mrs. Oliver J. Olson
request the honour of your presence
at the marriage of their granddaughter
Barbara Ann Baker

DOUBLE WEDDINGS

When brides are sisters, the older sister is mentioned first
Mr. and Mrs. William Lewis Baker
request the honour of your presence
at the marriage of their daughters
Barbara Ann
to
Richard Dean Smith
and
Dawn Eloise
to
Allen Henry Mercer

RECEPTION INVITATIONS

The phrase "request the pleasure of your company" is used here and on invitations to other social functions
Mr. and Mrs. William Lewis Baker
request the pleasure of your company
at the wedding reception
for their daughter

USE OF HONOR AND HONOUR

HONOR
You are cordially invited to attend
a Retirement Party
in honor of Bob Johnson

HONOUR
Mr. and Mrs. Robert Johnson
request the honour of your presence
at the marriage of their daughter

WEDDING ANNOUNCEMENTS

Announcements must always have a year line, and time of ceremony is never mentioned
Mr. and Mrs. William Lewis Baker
have the honour of announcing
the marriage of their daughter
Barbara Ann
to
Richard Dean Smith
on Saturday, the fourteenth of June
Two thousand and three
First Presbyterian Church
Edina, Minnesota

REAFFIRMATION OF VOWS

The honour of your presence
is requested at the reaffirmation
of the wedding vows of
Mr. and Mrs. Vincent Forbes

SUFFIXES

Jr., junior, II, III, IV are all properly preceded by a comma

Jr. is capitalized when abbreviated
Richard Dean Smith, Jr.

Junior is not capitalized when spelled in full
Richard Dean Smith, junior

Roman numerals are properly preceded by a comma
Richard Dean Smith, III

TITLES

Reverend, Doctor, Captain, etc. are not abbreviated unless lack of space necessitates it
Reverend and Mrs. William L. Baker
request the honour of your presence
at the marriage of their daughter
Barbara Ann
to
Doctor Richard Dean Smith

MILITARY WEDDINGS

Officers above the rank of Lieutenant have title preceding name
Major and Mrs. William Lewis Baker
request the honour of your presence
at the marriage of their daughter
Barbara Ann
to
Captain Richard Dean Smith
United States Army

Junior Officers have title placed on next line preceding branch of service
Mr. and Mrs. William Lewis Baker
request the honour of your presence
at the marriage of their daughter
Barbara Ann
to
Richard Dean Smith
First Lieutenant, United States Army

Rank below Sergeant is not indicated, and branch of service is placed below name
Mr. and Mrs. William Lewis Baker
request the honour of your presence
at the marriage of their daughter
Barbara Ann
to
Richard Dean Smith
United States Army

Wedding Program Order Form

Please Type or Print Clearly   See Page 258-259 for Samples of Wedding Programs

Name		Date of Order	
Address	Apt. #	Wedding Date	
City	State	Zip	
Bride's name		Groom's Name	
Home Phone ( )		Bride's Email address	
Work Phone ( )			

ORDER SUMMARY

Quantity	Item No.	Price	Lettering Style	Ink Color	Colored Ink Charge	Total Cost
Extra Lines (Additional charge of $1.50 per line over 70 lines of copy)						
Back Copy Printing Charges - (Additional charge of $25.00 for up to 14 lines of copy)						
❏ Print Proof $25						
Subtotal						
Sales Tax Orders shipped to CA, add 7.75% sales tax						
Shipping Charges (See charges at right)						
TOTAL AMOUNT DUE						

Please fax this order form to 619-287-1019

(5)   **METHOD OF PAYMENT**

Note: If order is faxed, payment must be made by credit card.

❏ My check or money order is enclosed for the full amount including shipping charges.

❏ Please charge my order to my

❏ Visa   ❏ Mastercard   ❏ American Express

Card No. [ ][ ][ ][ ][ ][ ][ ][ ][ ][ ][ ][ ][ ][ ][ ][ ]

Expiration Date _____

Cardholder's
Signature _____

For shipping rates, please refer to shipping charges on page 340.

---

(3)

Item No.
Quantity
Ink Color
Lettering Style

(Introduction and names on front – where available – printed in your choice of lettering style.)

THE MARRIAGE SERVICE OF

_____ (bride's name)
_____ (groom's name)
_____ (day, month, year)
_____ (time)
_____ (church or place)
_____ (city)

(The main program wording will be printed in block lettering style. Please cross out any wording not wanted.)

PRELUDE
_____ (song) _____ (composer)
_____ (song) _____ (composer)
_____ (song) _____ (composer)
_____ (song) _____ (composer)
_____ (insert additional line)

PROCESSIONAL
_____ (song) _____ (composer)
_____ (song) _____ (composer)
_____ (insert additional line)

GREETING AND PRAYER
_____ (song) _____ (composer)
_____ (insert additional line)

READINGS
_____ (song) _____ (composer)
_____ (insert additional line)

EXCHANGE OF VOWS

BLESSING AND EXCHANGE OF RINGS
_____ (song) _____ (composer)
_____ (insert additional line)

LIGHTING OF THE UNITY CANDLE
_____ (song) _____ (composer)
_____ (insert additional line)

LITURGY OF THE EUCHARIST
_____ (song) _____ (composer)
_____ (insert additional line)

COMMUNION
_____ (song) _____ (composer)
_____ (insert additional line)
_____ (insert additional line)

RECESSIONAL
_____ (song) _____ (composer)

---

(4)   Names to be printed on front:_____and_____

Date to be printed on front (if applicable): _____

THE WEDDING PARTY
(NAME / RELATIONSHIP – relationship optional)

(TITLE)

Officiant _____
Organist _____
Musician _____
Soloist _____

Maid of Honor _____
Matron of Honor _____
Bridesmaids _____
_____
_____
_____
_____

Best Man _____
Groomsmen _____
_____
_____
_____
_____

Flower Girl _____
Ring Bearer _____

Ushers _____
_____
_____
_____

Additional Wording (optional)
_____
_____

❏ See the enclosed page for additional wording and/or Back Copy wording. (Additional charge of $25.00 for up to 14 lines of back copy)

338

Practice Invitation Order Form

BE SURE TO READ INVITATION ORDERING INSTRUCTIONS ON PAGE 334 AND 335 CAREFULLY BEFORE COMPLETING ORDER FORM TO ENSURE ACCURATE DELIVERY. PLEASE TYPE OR PRINT CLEARLY IN INK.

FOR OFFICE USE ONLY

YOUR BRIDAL SUPERSTORE
...everything but the groom™
www.YourBridalSuperstore.com
6347 Caminito Tenedor
San Diego, CA 92120
Tel: 1-800-286-2806

Account No.

P.O No.

Date

Proof $25.00
☐ Fax to (   )
☐ Mail

(1) SOLD and SHIP TO:

Name

Street Address   Apt. #
It is important to include your street address (not a Post Office Box). Many shipping carriers cannot deliver to a P.O. Box.

City   State   Zip Code

Work Phone (   )   Home Phone (   )

Bride's Full Name   Date of Order

Groom's Full Name   Wedding Date

(2) INVITATIONS or ANNOUNCEMENTS

Qty.	Item No	Lettering Style	Verse No.	Ink Color	Price*

Proof (add $25.00) Yes ☐ No ☐

(3) Special Instructions:

(4) Front Copy: (only available if catalog shows copy on the front. State names, date and/or quotation):

Invitation Collection
(Please check one)
☐ Carlson Craft
☐ Regency
☐ Special Day

CHECK APPLICABLE BOX
☐ Change wording that is socially incorrect.
☐ Follow wording exactly.

(5) Invitation Copy:
1. 2. 3. 4. 5. 6. 7. 8. 9. 10. 11. 12. 13. 14. 15. 16.

Add $1.50 per line over 14 lines

*Prices shown are for black ink only. For raised colored ink, add $7.00 to the total price of each printed item.

(6) Left Bottom Corner Copy ($8.00) ☐ Add $1.50 per line over 5 lines   Right Bottom Corner Copy ($8.00) ☐ Add $1.50 per line over 5 lines
1. 2. 3. 4. 5.

(7) INVITATION ENVELOPE FLAPS or PRINTED OUTER ENVELOPES

Qty.	Item No.	Lettering Style	Ink Color	Price*

Return Address on Flaps:
Street:
City/State/Zip:

(8) LINED INNER ENVELOPES

Qty.	Color	Item No.	Price*

(9) RECEPTION CARDS/FOLDERS

Qty.	Item No.	Lettering Style	Verse No.	Ink Color	Price*
1.					
2.					
3.					
4.					
5.					

Add $1.50 for each line over 5 lines   Attach a separate sheet for extra lines

(10) RESPOND CARDS/ENVELOPES

Qty.	Item No.	Lettering Style	Verse No.	Ink Color	Price*
1.					
2.					
3.					
4.					
5.					

Add $1.50 for each line over 5. If name & address not given, copy will be taken from Ship To Information

(11) Copy for Respond Envelopes (FREE)

Name / Names (required):
Street:
City / State / Zip Code:

(12)INFORMAL NOTES OR MATCHING THANK YOU NOTES/FOLDER

Qty.	Item No.	Lettering Style	Ink Color	Monogram No. (if applicable)	Verse No.	Price*

Names or Initials for Monogram (if applicable)

(13)INFORMAL NOTES & THANK YOU ENVELOPES

Qty.	Item No.	Lettering Style	Ink Color	Price*

Return Address on Flaps:
Street:
City/State/Zip:

(14) SIGNATURE:

Invitation Order Form

BE SURE TO READ INVITATION ORDERING INSTRUCTIONS ON PAGE 334 AND 335 CAREFULLY BEFORE COMPLETING ORDER FORM TO ENSURE ACCURATE DELIVERY. PLEASE TYPE OR PRINT CLEARLY IN INK.

FOR OFFICE USE ONLY

YOUR BRIDAL SUPERSTORE
...everything but the groom™
www.YourBridalSuperstore.com
6347 Caminito Tenedor
San Diego, CA 92120
Tel: 1-800-286-2806

Account No.		
P.O. No.		
Date		

Proof $25.00
- ☐ Fax to ( )
- ☐ Mail

Invitation Collection
(Please check one)
- ☐ Carlson Craft
- ☐ Regency
- ☐ Special Day

CHECK APPLICABLE BOX
- ☐ **Change wording that is socially incorrect.**
- ☐ **Follow wording exactly.**

*Prices shown are for black ink only. For raised colored ink, add $7.00 to the total price of each printed item.

(1) SOLD and SHIP TO:

Name

Street Address
It is important to include your street address (not a Post Office Box). Many shipping carriers cannot deliver to a P.O. Box.   Apt. #

City   State   Zip Code

Work Phone ( )   Home Phone ( )

Bride's Full Name   Date of Order

Groom's Full Name   Wedding Date

(2) INVITATIONS or ANNOUNCEMENTS

Qty.	Item No	Lettering Style	Verse No.	Ink Color	Price*	Proof (add $25.00) Yes ☐ No ☐

(3) Special Instructions:

(4) Front Copy: (only available if catalog shows copy on the front. State names, date and/or quotation):

(5) Invitation Copy:
1.
2.
3.
4.
5.
6.
7.
8.
9.
10.
11.
12.
13.
14.

Add $1.50 per line over 14 lines

(6) Left Bottom Corner Copy ($8.00) ☐   Add $1.50 per line over 5 lines   Right Bottom Corner Copy ($8.00) ☐   Add $1.50 per line over 5 lines
1.
2.
3.
4.
5.

(7) INVITATION ENVELOPE FLAPS or PRINTED OUTER ENVELOPES

Qty.	Item No.	Lettering Style	Ink Color	Price*

Return Address on Flaps:
Street:
City/State/Zip:

(8) LINED INNER ENVELOPES

Qty.	Color	Item No.	Price*

(9) RECEPTION CARDS/FOLDERS

Qty.	Item No.	Lettering Style	Verse No.	Ink Color	Price*
1.					
2.					
3.					
4.					
5.					

Add $1.50 for each line over 5 lines   Attach a separate sheet for extra lines

(10) RESPOND CARDS/ ENVELOPES

Qty.	Item No.	Lettering Style	Verse No.	Ink Color	Price*
1.					
2.					
3.					
4.					
5.					

Add $1.50 for each line over 5. If name & address not given, copy will be taken from Ship To Information

(11) Copy for Respond Envelopes (FREE)

Name / Names (required):
Street:
City / State / Zip Code:

(12)INFORMAL NOTES OR MATCHING THANK YOU NOTES/FOLDER

Qty.	Item No.	Lettering Style	Ink Color	Monogram No. (if applicable)	Verse No.	Price*

Names or Initials for Monogram (if applicable)

(13)INFORMAL NOTES & THANK YOU ENVELOPES

Qty.	Item No.	Lettering Style	Ink Color	Price*

Return Address on Flaps:
Street:
City/State/Zip:

(14) SIGNATURE:

(15) Invitation Order Summary

Item	Quantity	Item No.	Lettering Style or Design No.	Catalogue Price	Extra Lines (add $1.50 for each extra line)	Corner Copy (add $8.00 for each or $12.00 for both corners)	Foreign Wording (add $10.00 for each)	Ink Charge (add $7.00 for each)	Proofs ($25.00 for each)	Total
Invitations or Announcements										
Invitation Envelope Flaps/Printed Outer Envelopes										
Lined Inner Envelopes										
Reception Cards/Folders										
Response Cards & Envelopes										
Informal Notes/Thank You Notes Blank Inside										
Informal Notes/Thank You Notes Printed Inside										
Informal Notes/Thank You Notes with Printed Envelopes										

Special Set Up (add $25.00 to order)

SUBTOTAL

Sales Tax: Orders shipped to CA, add 7.75% sales tax

Shipping Charges: See chart below

TOTAL AMOUNT DUE

Prices subject to change without notice. Please allow up to 10 working days for standard delivery.

Your Satisfaction is Guaranteed: Our guarantee is very simple: we stand behind every product we sell 100% and pledge to give you the best service, quality and value possible. When you order from us, there are no hassles and no risks! No matter what! Our friendly customer service staff is here for you. Simply call 1-800-286-2806. Orders may be faxed to 619-287-1019.

METHOD OF PAYMENT

☐ My check or money order is enclosed for total amount.
$ _____

☐ Please charge my order to my:
  ☐ VISA ☐ MasterCard ☐ American Express

Account No. ☐☐☐☐ ☐☐☐☐☐☐☐☐☐

Expiration Date: _____

Cardholder's Name: _____

Cardholder's Address: _____

Signature: _____

Please sign as it appears on credit card.

SHIPPING CHARGES:

PLEASE CHECK SHIPPING METHOD DESIRED:
☐ Standard Ground Rate
☐ Second-Day Delivery
☐ Overnight Delivery

Order Amount	Continental United States		
	Standard Ground	Second Day	Next Day
Under $20	$7.95	$23.95	$30.95
$20 to $29.99	$9.95	$25.95	$32.95
$30 to $49.99	$11.95	$27.95	$34.95
$50 to $99.99	$13.95	$29.95	$36.95
$100 to $150	$15.95	$31.95	$38.95
$150 and up	FREE*	22% of Merchandise Subtotal	27% of Merchandise Subtotal

Continental US: Our normal shipping method is *Standard Ground*. *Second Day* and *Next Day* are available, please refer to shipping table for pricing.

Alaska, Hawaii and Puerto Rico: *Standard Ground* service is not available. For *Second Day or Express*, please add $6.00 to the Continental US *Second Day* Rate. For *Next Day*, please add $7.00 to the Continental US *Next Day* rate.

Canada: For *Standard*, please add $10.00 to the Continental US *Second Day* rate. For *Express* service, please add $20.00 to the Continental US *Second Day* rate. *Next Day* service is not available.

All Other International Areas: *Standard Ground* service is not available. For *Express*, actual shipping cost will be charged. A minimum of $30.00 will be charged at the time of purchase. The difference between $30.00 and the actual shipping cost will be billed separately on your credit card. International orders must be paid with credit card. *Next Day* service is not available. *Available only within Continental US. Actual shipping cost will be charged for returned items.

RETURN INFORMATION:

No Returns on Personalized Items unless they are received damaged or misprinted. If an item is received damaged or misprinted, we will replace it at no charge or refund your money as long as you notify us **within 3 business days** of receiving your items. All returns must be authorized through our customer service department, which can be reached at customerservice@YourBridalSuperstore.com or via the telephone at 1-800-286-2806.

PROMOTIONAL CODE:
EWSGABAB

Accessories Order Form

GET THIS BOOK FOR FREE! The cost of this book will be reimbursed with your first $100 purchase at *YourBridalSuperstore.com*. To take advantage of this offer, you will need to use the PROMOTIONAL CODE printed at the top of this page. During your on-line purchase, you must enter this code in the "Promotional Discount" box when prompted during the Check-out process. You will then receive your discount reimbursing you for the cost of this book. Please note: if you are ordering ONLY Invitations, you will need to call Your Bridal Superstore (1-800-286-2806) to receive your reimbursement.

FREE SHIPPING! Receive FREE SHIPPING on all orders of $150 or more per collection.

LOWEST PRICE GUARANTEE! If you find any of our items advertised at a lower price, we will not only match the lower price but also give you an additional 5% discount off the price. Please call us at 1-800-286-2806 or visit *YourBridalSuperstore.com* for details.

SATISFACTION GUARANTEE! Our guarantee is very simple; we stand behind every product we sell 100%, and pledge to give you the best service, quality, and value possible. When you order from us, there are no hassles and no risks! No matter what! Our friendly customer service staff is here for you.

PRODUCTS GALORE! We offer thousands of wedding accessories, jewelry, invitations, gifts, and much more from the most popular manufacturers of wedding products. Each of our collections is shipped from different distribution centers located throughout the United States. Therefore, we must charge separate shipping charges for each collection. To see thousands of other wedding products available, please visit *YourBridalSuperstore.com*.

Collection: *Hortense B. Hewitt* (p. 105-124)

Page	Item No.	Description	Specify Color, Size	Qty.	Unit Price	Total Cost
236	22724	Iridescent Pompoms	10 burgundy	4	$5.00	$20.00
		Merchandise Subtotal for the Hortense B. Hewitt collection:				$
		Shipping & Handling Subtotal for the Hortense B. Hewitt collection (**see chart next page**):				$

Collection: *Kerenza* (p. 125-144)

Page	Item No.	Description	Specify Color, Size	Qty.	Unit Price	Total Cost
		Merchandise Subtotal for the Kerenza collection:				$
		Shipping & Handling Subtotal for the Kerenza collection (**see chart next page**):				$

Collection: *Lillian Rose* (p. 145-208)

Page	Item No.	Description	Specify Color, Size	Qty.	Unit Price	Total Cost
		Merchandise Subtotal for the Lillian Rose collection:				$
		Shipping & Handling Subtotal for the Lillian Rose collection (**see chart next page**):				$

Collection: *Cathy's Concepts* (p. 209-234)

Page	Item No.	Description	Specify Color, Size	Qty.	Unit Price	Total Cost
		Merchandise Subtotal for the Cathy's Concepts collection:				$
		Shipping & Handling Subtotal for the Cathy's Concepts collection (**see chart next page**):				$

ORDER FORM CONTINUED ON NEXT PAGE

Collection: *Special Day* (p. 260-288) and *Special Day Personalized Stationery Items* (p. 252-259)
NOTE: Programs and Thank You cards should be ordered using the INVITATION ORDER FORM provided.

Page	Item No.	Description	Specify Color, Size	Qty.	Unit Price	Total Cost

NAPKINS

Item No.:	Design No.:	Ink Color:	Foil Color:
Names:			Wedding Date:

MATCHES

Item No.:	Design No.:	Foil Color:
Names:		Wedding Date:

FAVOR NOTEPADS

Item No.:	Design No.:	Foil Color:
Names:		Wedding Date:

BOOKMARKS

Item No.:	Design No.:	Ink Color:	Tassel Color:
Verse No.:	Names:		Wedding Date:

SCROLLS

Item No.:	Design No.:	Ink Color:	Lettering Style:
Verse No.:	Names:		Wedding Date:

Gold & Silver Rings, Item No.:

PLACE CARDS

Item No.:	Design No.:	Ink Color:	Lettering Style:
Names:			Wedding Date:

Merchandise Subtotal for the Special Day collection: $

Shipping & Handling Subtotal for the Special Day collection (**see chart below**): $

THIS FORM MAY BE COPIED IF ADDITIONAL SPACE IS NEEDED

SHIPPING & HANDLING: Use the following table to calculate the shipping cost for each of the collections you are ordering from. We ship by *STANDARD GROUND*, *SECOND DAY* or *EXPRESS*, and *NEXT DAY*. Please see below for the shipping services that are available in your area.

Continental US: Our normal shipping method is *STANDARD GROUND*. *SECOND DAY* and *NEXT DAY* are available, please refer to shipping table for pricing.

Alaska, Hawaii and Puerto Rico: *STANDARD GROUND* service is not available. For *SECOND DAY/EXPRESS* service, please add $6.00 to the Continental US *SECOND DAY/EXPRESS* rate. For *NEXT DAY* service, please add $7.00 to the Continental US *NEXT DAY* rate.

Canada: For *STANDARD* service, please add $10.00 to the Continental US *SECOND DAY* rate. For *EXPRESS* service, please add $20.00 to the Continental US *SECOND DAY* rate. *NEXT DAY* service is not available.

All other International areas: *STANDARD* service is not available. For *EXPRESS* service, actual shipping cost will be charged. A minimum of $30.00 will be charged at the time of purchase. The difference between $30.00 and the actual shipping cost will be billed separately on your credit card. International orders must be paid with Credit Card. *NEXT DAY* service is not available.

ORDER AMOUNT	Continental United States		
	Standard Ground	Second Day/ Express	Next Day
Under $20	$7.95	$23.95	$30.95
$20 to $29.99	$9.95	$25.95	$32.95
$30 to $49.99	$11.95	$27.95	$34.95
$50 to $99.99	$13.95	$29.95	$36.95
$100 to $150	$15.95	$31.95	$38.95
$150 and up	FREE*	22% of merchandise subtotal	27% of merchandise subtotal

* Available only on shipments within the Continental US.
Actual shipping cost will be charged for returned items.

ENGRAVING / PERSONALIZATION INSTRUCTIONS: For an additional charge of $5.00 per item, most Knives, Servers, Glasses and Gift items can be personalized. To order, simply fill-in the form below. Please print clearly.

Knives & Servers can be personalized with the Bride and Groom's first names on the top line and the Wedding Date on the second line. Date must be indicated numerically: *month ~ day of month ~ year.*

Glasses can be personalized with the Bride's first name and Wedding Date on one glass and the Groom's first name and Wedding Date on the other glass. Name appears on the front of the glass and date appears on the back. Date must be indicated numerically: *month ~ day of month ~ year.*

Gift Items can be personalized with the first name or initials of the person for whom the gift is intended.

Item No.	Bride's First Name	Groom's First Name	Wedding Date	Gift Recipient's First Name or Initials
32825	SARA	BEN	12-04-04	

THIS FORM MAY BE COPIED IF ADDITIONAL SPACE IS NEEDED

ORDER SUMMARY:

Merchandise Total (sum of all "Merchandise Subtotals" from previous two pages):	
Engraving: Number of Items (from all collections) _____ x $5.00 each:	
SUBTOTAL:	$
Orders shipped to California, add 7.75% **Sales Tax** on Subtotal Amount:	
Shipping & Handling Total (sum of all "Shipping & Handling Subtotals" from previous two pages):	
GRAND TOTAL OF ORDER (SUBTOTAL + Sales Tax + Shipping & Handling Total):	$

HOW TO PLACE YOUR ORDER: (1) Order on-line at *YourBridalSuperstore.com.* (2) Fax in your completed three-page Order Form order to 619-287-1019. (3) Phone in your order to 1-800-286-2806. (4) Mail in your order to Your Bridal Superstore, 6347 Caminito Tenedor; San Diego, CA 92120. Orders will ship in two to four days. Please allow one to two weeks for delivery.

RETURN POLICY FOR ACCESSORY ITEMS: Correctly printed personalized items are not returnable or refundable. All items, except items from Cathy's Concepts, may be returned or exchanged for store credit within 15 days of purchase. Contact Your Bridal Superstore at 1-800-286-2806 for a Return Authorization and return shipping instructions. No returns will be accepted without authorization and returns may be subject to a 25% restocking fee. You will be responsible to pay all shipping fees on items returned through no fault of Your Bridal Superstore. If any items returned are received damaged or broken, no credit will be given.

Although every effort is made to ensure that the product you order is as it appears in the catalog, due to the availability of raw materials and the hand-made nature of some items, variations and substitutions may occur.

Prices are subject to change without notice.

SHIP TO:
(Note: Items cannot be shipped to a PO Box)

Name: _____

Street Address: _____

_____

City: _____ State: _____ Zip: _____

Telephone: _____

Wedding Date: _____

E-mail address: _____

METHOD OF PAYMENT:
Please check one of the following payment options:

☐ MasterCard ☐ American Express

☐ VISA ☐ Check or Money Order

Credit Card Number:

__ __ __ __ __ __ __ __ __ __ __ __ __ __ __ __

Expiration Date: __ __ / __ __

Cardholder's Name: _____

Cardholder's Signature: _____

FOR OFFICE USE ONLY:	Approval Code:	PO#:	Date:	Amount:

EWSG0101

FREE*

THE MOST POPULAR AND WIDELY USED WEDDING PLANNING SOFTWARE

A $29.95 VALUE

WHEN YOU VISIT

WWW.YOURBRIDALSUPERSTORE.COM

❧ *Easy Wedding Planning Software* ❧

The wedding planning software preferred by brides nationwide. *Easy Wedding Planning Software* can make planning the wedding of your dreams faster and simpler. This software is based on information found in the best selling *Easy Wedding Planner, Organizer & Keepsake* and is the best wedding planning tool available today. This practical software was designed with two things in mind: first, to simplify the wedding planning process; and second, to be as intuitive and easy to use as possible.

This unique software allows you to create and keep track of:

- ❧ Comprehensive Guest List
- ❧ Interactive Budget Analysis
- ❧ Service Provider Information and Prices

- ❧ Gifts Received, Thank You Notes Sent
- ❧ Things-To-Do Checklist
- ❧ And Much More!

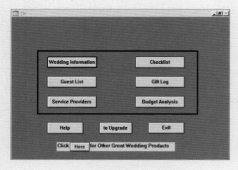

Main Screen

This software contains a world of resources that is unsurpassed by any other wedding planning software on the market today! Clicking on any of the general categories offers an easy way to keep track of your guest list, budget analysis, gift log, service providers, and much more! You'll be amazed at how simple it is to plan a memorable wedding using this invaluable, user-friendly software. No other software offers more!

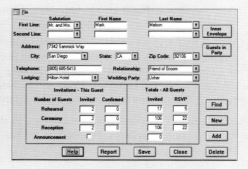

Guest List

The Guest List feature is a handy resource for building a list of detailed information about your guests and wedding party members. It not only keeps a running total of all of guests invited to your rehearsal, ceremony and reception, but also keeps track of how many people have responded. This information then works interactively with other sections of the software. No other program is as versatile or provides you with as much help and information.

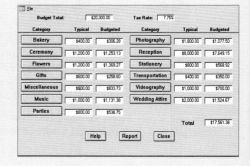

Budget Analysis

The comprehensive Budget Analysis screen will provide you with a record of all expenses that can be incurred in any size wedding, including such hidden costs as taxes, gratuities, and other "items" that can add up to thousands of dollars in a wedding. It also allows you to perform unique "What If" scenarios, allowing you to calculate your wedding budget for any number of guests and quickly see the difference in the total cost of your wedding!

* Visit YourBridalSuperstore.com for details.
Limited Time Only!